Computer Supported Cooperative Work

Springer

London
Berlin
Heidelberg
New York
Barcelona
Hong Kong
Milan
Paris
Santa Clara
Singapore
Tokyo

Fay Sudweeks and Celia T. Romm (Eds)

Doing Business on the Internet

Opportunities and Pitfalls

With 39 Figures

BCS

 Springer

Fay Sudweeks, ATCL, BA, MCogSc
School of Information Technology, Division of Business, IT and Law,
Murdoch University, South Street, Murdoch, WA 6150, Australia

Celia T. Romm, BA, MA, PhD
Faculty of Informatics and Communciation, Central Queensland University,
Rockhampton, QLD 4702, Australia

Series Editors
Dan Diaper, PhD, MBCS
Department of Computing, School of Design, Engineering and Computing,
Bournemouth University, Talbot Campus, Fern Barrow, Poole, Dorset BH12 5BB, UK

Colston Sanger
Shottersley Research Limited, Little Shottersley, Farnham Lane
Haslemere, Surrey GU27 1HA, UK

ISBN 1-85233-030-9 Springer-Verlag London Berlin Heidelberg

British Library Cataloguing in Publication Data
Doing business on the Internet : opportunites and
  pitfalls. - (Computer supported cooperative work)
  1.Business enterprises - Computer network resources
  2.Internet (Computer network) 3.Electronic commerce
  I.Sudweeks, Fay II.Romm, Celia T.
  658'.05'4678
  ISBN 1852330309

Library of Congress Cataloging-in-Publication Data
Doing business on the Internet : Opportunities and pitfalls / Fay
  Sudweeks and Celia T. Romm (eds.).
      p.   cm. -- (Computer supported cooperative work)
  Includes bibliographical references and index.
  ISBN 1-85233-030-9 (alk. paper)
  1. Electronic commerce. 2. Electronic commerce Case studies.
  3. Small business--Computer networks. I. Sudweeks,Fay. II. Romm,
  Celia T., 1954- . III. Series.
  HF5548.32.D654 1999   99-25194
  658'.054678--dc21   CIP

Typesetting: Camera ready by editors
Printed and bound at the Athenæum Press Ltd., Gateshead, Tyne & Wear
34/3830-54321 Printed on acid-free paper SPIN 10755283

Contents

Part III: Benefitting from the Internet Revolution

Global Perspectives of the Internet Revolution

CHAPTER 1

Introduction

FAY SUDWEEKS AND CELIA ROMM

At the turn of the twenty-first century, global communication is changing the fabric of society at a rate never experienced before. The Internet, in particular, has redrawn the map of global economy. To be competitive in today's marketplace, companies need to expand commercial activities beyond national borders. The global network of electronic infrastructure has played a significant role in this expansion but the technology itself is not the factor driving the business revolution. The changes are driven by the interaction of information technology and customer demand. Customers are not only adapting to new technologies, they are demanding more and more global competition.

Electronic commerce, therefore, is arguably the most important economic trend of our time. Its presence on the Internet, in particular, is becoming crucial to the effective functioning of organisations, especially in a world where companies need to deal with suppliers, customers, partners and their own units distributed across the world. A global business industry created by the Internet is no longer a projected vision of technocrats; it is a reality. The Internet is already playing a significant role in determining corporate strategy and in creating values.

This world-wide popularity of the Internet as a commercial medium is remarkable, to say the least. However, along with the creation of enormous opportunities, it is becoming clear that the Internet has also brought new perils and pitfalls. Companies who invest in this emerging market find that customers, while demanding more global competition, are still reluctant to actually buy products that are advertised on the Internet. Corporate managers are not keen on spending their workday surfing the Internet, hence the growing interest in Webcasting (i.e. the broadcasting of selected Web sites onto users' computers). Users who are still immensely interested in the Internet are becoming disillusioned with some of its early promises and are hungry for a more balanced perspective on what the Internet can do for them, both in the business and the social arena.

In our earlier book, *Doing Business Electronically: A Global Perspective of Electronic Commerce* (Romm and Sudweeks, 1998), we provided an overview and investigation of the major areas that are affected by the rapid adoption of new technologies in the commercial environment. Some of the issues addressed concerned buyer-seller relationships, auctions, public procurement and consumer decision making.

Doing Business on the Internet: Opportunities and Pitfalls, as the title implies, casts an objective eye on Internet commerce. We focus on questions such as: What is the role of small businesses in a global commerce that is moving from niche marketing towards international competition? What does multimedia technology imply for the next generation marketing? How can networked communities benefit from global collaborative systems? How does culture affect purchasing behaviour? How do transnational companies deal with issues of integrity and security? How can consumers be assured of privacy and security?

Doing Business on the Internet, and its precursor *Doing Business Electronically*, are intended as primary or supplementary texts for graduate-level courses on electronic commerce. The texts can also be used as support texts for courses in marketing, business strategy, management of information systems, organisational change, project management, product innovation, and international management. All of these - and more - are areas where there is a growing awareness of the key role of electronic commerce in business. In fact, one of the major advantages of these books is that they can be used by lecturers to expose students to the electronic commerce implications of their disciplines.

Doing Business on the Internet is especially important for vendors intending to develop and use a Web site for e-commerce. This book is also equally important for firms who have already developed their Web site to be informed of optimal strategies for gaining a competitive edge as well as to be aware of the risks involved.

The collection of readings on electronic commerce in this book covers three major areas of concern to businesses today: how to join the Internet revolution; how to manage the Internet revolution; and how to benefit from the Internet revolution. In addition to these areas of concern, global perspectives on the Internet revolution from both developing and developed countries are included. The geographic spread of the contributors to this book also gives a global perspective on electronic commerce with authors representing Australia, Austria, Canada, Germany, Hong Kong, Israel, Singapore, South Korea, the United Kingdom and the USA

1.1. Joining the Internet Revolution

The first part of the book describes a number of issues that businesses should consider before embarking on Internet commerce, such as planning and designing marketing strategies, streamlining information flows on intranets and the Internet within and between companies, and the development of Internet-based networking strategies with suppliers and customers.

In Chapter 2, *Internet Commerce - Hot Cakes and Dead Ducks*, Dave Whiteley opens the section with an objective assessment of the vagaries of doing business on the Internet. He points out that, despite the increasing presence of organisations on the Web offering an array of commercial activities, actual sales on the Internet represent a tiny proportion of total retail sales. Using the traditional trade cycle as a framework, Whiteley defines the concerns for both novice (Internet Virgins) and experienced (Cyber Citizens) users in the electronic marketplace. One of the major factors contributing to the small growth in sales is the concern of potential customers about the security of the payment system. In the final chapter of the book, Ook Lee shows that the issue of payment security is an even greater deterrent for people to purchase goods on the Internet in countries in which the technology infrastructure is under-developed.

In Chapter 3, Janice Burn, Peter Marshall and Martyn Wild pose the question *When Does Virtual Have Value?* Like Whiteley, the authors describe the driving force for businesses to join the 'wired world' as a mixture of fear and opportunity. However, in their search for understanding how much virtuality should be implemented within organisations, they have classified models of virtual organisations, with case studies illustrating the models in practice. The authors conclude that the driving force for joining the Internet revolution should be to add value to the organisation in the form of greater information transfer and enriched functionality; that is, the impetus should be needs based not a "catch-up" mentality.

Addressing organisations who have decided the join the Internet revolution, Ping Zhang, in Chapter 4, asks *Will You Use Animation on Your Web Pages?* Animation is primarily used by advertisers as a strategy to attract users' attention and encourage click-throughs. Studies indicate, though, that animation creates a negative reaction in viewers who seeking information only and are annoyed by the distraction. Thus a dichotomy exists between the goals of content providers and advertisers. The results of two experiments conducted by Zhang highlight the need for Web designers to assess the implications of user task load, animation colour and animation content.

Issues associated with Web development are explored further in Chapter 5, *Evolution of Web Information Systems*. The authors, Christian Bauer, Bernard Glasson and Arno Scharl, draw on the principles of Darwinian evolutionary theory as an explanatory framework for how commercial Web information systems have developed. The complex dynamics of modern companies are viewed as a business ecosystem in which different industries are interdependent, and the development of a Web information system is an evolutionary process of design, implementation, usage and analysis.

1.2. Managing the Internet Revolution

Having taken the decision to develop a presence on the Internet and engage in some form of electronic commerce, issues of management in a virtual environment need to be considered. The second part of this book explores issues such as the control of Internet use within firms, maintenance and updating of Internet-related technologies, coping with security and integrity of transactions with customers and suppliers, and coping with customer and supplier feedback via internal and external Internet-based channels of communication.

In Chapter 6, *Financial Institutions and the Internet*, Christian Bauer analytically summarises the opportunities and challenges for electronic financial services. Bauer introduces an evolutionary four-stage model to guide both financial institutions and consumers on the developmental path from initial Web site to full virtual banking. Bauer defines three components that are vital to the successful implementation and management of virtual banking systems: cost-effective electronic distribution channels; open transaction standards; and Web information systems that are adaptive to user needs.

The controversial issues of privacy and security are the focus of Chapter 7, *Protecting Sensitive Information in Electronic Commerce.* The authors, Aryya Gangopadhyay and Monica Adya, point out that while current data mining and knowledge discovery techniques are powerful tools for strategic decision making within organisations, they do not provide adequate protection of sensitive information in electronic commerce systems. The authors outline appropriate guidelines for avoiding the risk of improper access to confidential data.

In Chapter 8, *Towards Business Oriented Intranets,* Satish Nambisan takes an evolutionary approach to the growth of organisational intranets, which complements the evolutionary framework for the development of Web information systems that was described by Bauer, Glasson and Scharl in Chapter 5. Nambisan identifies four types of intranets whose characteristics are linked to three aspects of knowledge management: information access and sharing capability; expertise leveraging capability; and information relevancy control capability. Findings from a case study of two intranets within a multinational organisation highlight the need to ensure intranet implementation reflects the strategic objectives of organisations.

The issue of security is taken up again by Thomas Rebel and Wolfgang Koenig in Chapter 9, *Ensuring Security and Trust in Electronic Commerce.* Rebel and Koenig, like other contributors (Aryya Gangopadhyay and Monica Adya, Whiteley, and Lee), identify security as one the major concerns of doing business on the Internet. The German Digital Signature Act is cited as an example of legislation that endeavours to inject trust and security in open networks. Rebel and Koenig stress that, if electronic commerce is to be globally adopted, there is a need for international legislation and compatibility on the use of digital signatures.

1.3. Benefitting from the Internet Revolution

The third part of this book is devoted to ensuring that businesses that are involved in electronic commerce actually do gain some benefit. Here we focus on issues such as the implications for existing and future companies, the protection of intellectual property rights, the impact on different economic cultures, the growth of new ways of doing business, and the future investment implications for Internet business.

The question here is not only *how* to benefit but *who* benefits. A common view is that Internet commerce is contributing to the widening gap between the "haves" and "have nots". Large corporations are growing larger; small businesses are getting smaller and disappearing. What is the future for the self-employed individual and the small business as electronic commerce expands globally? This question is addressed by Simpson Poon in Chapter 10, *Small Business and Internet Commerce.* Internet commerce was initially touted to be the tool that will enable small businesses to compete on an equal footing with large firms by being able to engage in global marketing, to directly access potential customers, and to carry out electronic transactions. The reality is, of course, more complex. Although the Internet has not brought the increased sales that were expected for small businesses, it is proving to be a valuable communication medium for improving customer relationships and an effective information transfer channel. Poon is optimistic about the future of small business Internet commerce, providing issues such as cross-border trading, government support and trust are resolved.

As Internet communication is one of the more useful components of Internet commerce, especially for small businesses, an understanding of social and cultural aspects of mediated communication is important. In Chapter 11, *Towards Culturally Aware Information Systems*, Schahram Dustdar provides a framework for integrating appropriate groupware in organisational information systems. Exploring the organisational and cultural impacts of videoconferencing, Dustdar identifies five cultural factors that need to be considered to enable people to cooperate, coordinate and communicate within and between organisations.

One of the areas of Internet commerce that appears to be flourishing is electronic contracting. In Chapter 12, *The Online Stock Broker*, Subhasish Dasgupta provides an overview of the factors that contribute to its success. An important distinction between online stock trading and other online commercial activities is the fact that brokers extend credit for a period long enough for clients to make payments by cheque, thus avoiding the risk associated with using credit cards on the Internet.

A dilemma facing marketing managers in Internet commerce is how much and what information should be provided to assist consumers in making buying decisions and being confident and satisfied with the decision process. In Chapter 13, *Consumer Information Search and Decision Making in the Electronic Commerce Environment*, Rex Eugene Pereira develops and tests a model for understanding the role of query-based decision aids in consumer decision making and subsequent purchasing behaviour. Pereira concludes that consumers who have access to and use such aids perceive an increased cost savings and a lower cognitive effort in their decision making process.

Michael Gurstein relates a success story as he describes an innovative use of the Internet by an isolated mining and industrial community in Canada. Chapter 14, *Fiddlers on the Wire*, is a case study of Cape Breton Island. With declining prospects, rising unemployment and an aging population, Cape Breton recognised the need to boost the local economy. The problem was solved at least partially by using the Internet to market a unique resource of the Island - a pure form of Celtic music along with traditional Gaelic culture. Now internationally recognised, Cape Breton musicians have introduced a new industry and increased tourism into the community.

1.4. Global Perspectives of the Internet Revolution

The growth of electronic commerce is not, of course, uniform around the world. While organisations and consumers in countries with mature and widespread technology infrastructure are gaining access to and benefitting from electronic marketplaces, the economic prospects in countries with an under-developed information technology infrastructure is uncertain. The choice for the latter is to either to fall further behind in the race for technological advantage or to leap-frog into the twenty-first century at a considerable cost to their cultural and social fabric. As Dertouzos (1999) observes, the rich will become richer while the poor stand still. In the last part of this book, perspectives on current Internet commerce trends in four countries are presented.

In Chapter 15, *Consumer Adoption of Electronic Commerce*, Gerhard Steinke provides the USA perspective. More than half of Internet users in the world are in the USA. Companies in the USA report phenomenal growth and profits. However, the imbalance of resources between countries also exists between people within the USA. Steinke defines concerns which still need to be resolved: affordability and access to all people; education and training; legislation to protect electronic contracts; security; and privacy.

Surprisingly, despite its 'high-tech' reputation, the use of electronic commerce in Israel is comparatively low, according to Avi Schechter, Magid Igbaria and Moshe Zviran. In Chapter 16, the authors analyse *Electronic Commerce in Israel*. A research model is used to examine and evaluate Internet sites in Israel on two dimensions: site characteristics and user satisfaction. The authors define a three-stage evolutionary development of Web sites from preliminary penetration to full integration in a company's sales and marketing strategies. This developmental model shares similar features with Christian Bauer's four-stage model in Chapter 6.

In China, despite government attempts at limiting access to the Internet outside the country, electronic commerce is growing rapidly. In Chapter 17, *Electronic Commerce in China*, Ted Clark describes the interplay of politics, society, culture and economy as electronic commerce is adopted and expanding. Initially, the government had to consider the implications of the choice between liberation and control. Fearing pollution of national ideology from foreign countries, the government attempted to restrict access to local sites only. However, the appeal of economic modernisation and commercial growth in a global economy has lifted most restrictions. Even though there are an estimated 2.1 million Internet users in China, the development of the consumer market is slow. Whereas security and privacy issues are restricting consumer market growth in other countries, the slow uptake in China is due to cultural and economic reasons.

Compared to China, the growth of electronic commerce in South Korea is not as optimistic. Ook Lee provides an insight to the problems in South Korea as he describes *An Action Research Report* in Chapter 18. Lee addresses three problem areas in a country with a less-developed national information technology infrastructure: how to create a sustainable electronic commerce venture; how to conduct marketing for an electronic commerce venture; and how to establish a workable payment method. Using an action research methodology, Lee investigates an effective advertising tool for Internet marketing. The results of his study indicate that, despite negative consequences due to legal and ethical reasons, direct e-mail advertising is the most feasible. By far the strongest deterrent to consumer market growth in South Korea, a country in which few people use credit cards, is a payment method that is complex and risky.

1.5. Future Trends

Electronic commerce is not about interacting *with* computers, it is about interacting *through* computers (Ishii et al., 1995). The Internet revolution is not powered by technology but by people using the technology. Technology is the catalyst, not the cause, of a redefinition of power. New information and communication technologies have given rise to transcapitalism; that is, companies that have multinational ownership, management and control in a global economy. The opportunities for economic growth exist but it is hoped that the pitfalls described by authors in this volume are taken into account as you consider doing business on the Internet.

CHAPTER 2

Internet Commerce - Hot Cakes and Dead Ducks

DAVID WHITELEY

2.1. Introduction

> *Amazon.com* is the world's biggest bookshop and is one of the hottest stocks on the
> US stock market - its sales for the third quarter of 1998 were US$153.7 million (a
> 306% increase over the corresponding quarter of the previous year) and its profit was
> negative - a loss of US$21.0 million. In each of the four years since its foundation in
> 1995 it has returned a loss.

> *e-Christmas* operated for nearly three months from 10 November 1997. It was
> sponsored by Hewlett-Packard, Microsoft and United Parcel Services and involved
> twenty-two Internet service providers and eighteen solution developers. Overall, it
> made available a range of 1,800 gifts and attracted over a quarter of a million visitors.
> However, at the end of the eighteen-week period, the total sales were just over five
> hundred completed transactions (KPMG, 1998).

Electronic commerce (e-commerce) on the Internet is a 'hot topic'. Predictions are
that it will eclipse mail order catalogue selling, seriously damage conventional (high
street) retailers and change many other aspects of the way business is conducted
within and between organisations. The cause of e-commerce has been taken up by
governments, development agencies and business itself. Many organisations have
established a Web presence and increasingly their home pages include facilities to
buy, book or contract. With all this activity there is one thing missing - sales. It is
true that sales are increasing and that a select few e-vendors have grown very
rapidly but, overall, e-commerce business, conducted via the Internet, remains a
minute fraction of total retail sales.

The announcement of new business channels that will revolutionise the way that
business will be done is not a new phenomenon. The last twenty years have seen a
number of such developments. In physical retailing, there has been the out-of-town
superstore and shopping mall. Electronic developments have included:

- *Electronic Data Interchange (EDI)*. A technology that performs a vital role
  in a number of trade sectors but that has not become the universal way of
  doing business that was predicted.
- *Interactive Videotext Systems*. Adopted in many countries but only a
  significant factor in France with the Télétel (Minitel) system.

The real potential for development of e-commerce on the Internet needs to be assessed in the context of its mixed successes and niche applicability of the precursor systems. The Internet is an exciting, new, multifaceted commercial channel. It opens the possibility of sales to a world-wide market with a minimum capital outlay. It has the possibility to restructure markets, with direct sales replacing established intermediaries, or new intermediaries emerging that will fulfil roles that are specific to an e-commerce environment. As a new commercial channel, it rewrites many of the rules of advertising and retailing. It relies on customers coming to the site and doing the buying whilst the retailer takes responsibility for the delivery of the goods - the reverse of some aspects of current retail practice.

Internet commerce has had a number of success stories but these are matched by some dismal failures. What are the factors that lead to success and why do some sites or products not sell online? This chapter evaluates what might sell and to whom on the Internet. This evaluation is carried out in the context of the stages of the trade cycle. It is considered for both novice and experienced users; data from a survey and experiment in e-commerce use is incorporated into this evaluation[1]. The chapter concludes that the areas of consumer retailing where Internet e-commerce will have a significant impact are somewhat limited. Whatever the current hype, Internet e-commerce will, in the end, be no more than just one of a number of alternative ways of shopping.

2.2. The Trade Cycle

There is a standard series of steps/exchanges that are used for all trade transactions. Their importance and the ways they are executed depends on the nature of the goods and the parties involved. These steps can be represented as a generic trade cycle. The steps in this cycle are:

- *Pre-Sale*. Before a transaction can take place, the buyer has to find, *search*, for a vendor (or vice versa) and the two parties have to agree, *negotiate*, the terms of the transaction.

---

[1] Some material in this report comes from an Internet e-commerce survey of first year computing students at Manchester Metropolitan University. The survey has, at the time of writing, been conducted on the 1998 and 1999 student intake. In 1999, all 94 respondents had Internet access at the university. In addition, 38 students (40%) had Internet access at home and 25 students (27%) had used the Internet for e-commerce. For these 25 students, the maximum number of e-commerce transactions was 13 and the average was 2.7. The survey took place in conjunction with an e-commerce exercise consisting of purchasing one of the following:
- Flight from Manchester to New York;
- E-commerce text books;
- Christmas present for Grandma.
The students were required to document and evaluate the e-commerce process and their experience of that process, see Whiteley (1999).

- *Execution.* Having decided to do business the buyer requests or *orders* from the vendor that which is required and the vendor hands over or *delivers* the goods or service.
- *Settlement.* At an appropriate stage the vendor asks for payment, the *invoice*, and, hopefully, the buyer makes the appropriate *payment*.
- *After Sales.* Once the sale is completed that is not necessarily the end of the story; depending on the nature of the exchange there may be a requirement for *after sales* activities.

This trade cycle is shown in Figure 2.1. The way the trade cycle operates can vary depending on the nature of the customer, the vendor, the goods being traded and the traditions of the market segment and/or culture in which the deal is being done.

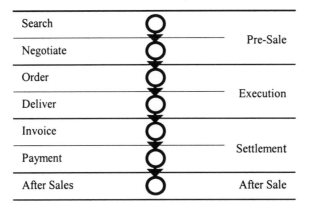

Figure 2.1. The generic trade cycle.

One of the obvious distinctions is between business to business and retail transactions. For many business transactions, the order is sent to the vendor (on paper or by electronic means) and settlement is against an invoice after the delivery of the goods or service, i.e. credit is given. This contrasts with the bulk of retail transactions where the order is 'over the counter', payment is at the time of the order and the delivery function is undertaken by the customer, i.e. the execution and settlement phase all take place at the same time.

A second distinction is the technology used for the order and, very possibly, other phases of the trade cycle. The transaction can be conducted:

- In person - 'over the counter';
- On paper through the post;
- By fax or phone;
- Using e-commerce: electronic data interchange (EDI), electronic markets; Internet commerce (and analogous networks).

Each of these technologies is (or at least was) appropriate to different trading circumstances. Some technologies settle the trade quickly and with a minimum of bureaucracy whereas others are more readily integrated into formal business systems and accounting procedures.

EDI, for example, is appropriate to a *regular repeat transaction trade cycle*. It is used by supermarkets, on a daily or weekly basis, to replenish the shelves and by vehicle assemblers, sometimes on an hourly basis, for the just-in-time delivery of components. These are frequent orders, usually in large numbers, direct from the customer's stock control/production control system to their trading partners for rapid execution in their order processing systems. It is a highly integrated and automated process and EDI is the appropriate technology (see Whiteley, 1998a, 1998b, for further detail of the EDI trade cycle).

Electronic markets contrast with EDI. For EDI, the emphasis is on *execution* and *settlement* but for an electronic market it is on the *search*. Electronic markets have limited but important applications in air passenger transport and in a number of financial/commodity markets. An efficient electronic market has details of the products of most or all relevant vendors and is set up, specifically, to allow for easy searching. On an airline booking system, the travel agent can, for example, look up all flights from London to New York next Thursday and readily check both availability and price (and the ability to compare price so easily, whilst probably good for the customer, may not be a wholly welcome feature to the airline (see Whiteley, 1998a, for further discussion of electronic markets).

While EDI and electronic markets can be matched reasonably easily to specific business situations, the area of applicability of Internet e-commerce is not so readily defined. This is partly because Internet e-commerce, for most users, is relatively new and partly because the technology can be used for all stages of the trade cycle and for most trading requirements (although often in a less than optimum manner). The examination of the use of Internet e-commerce at each stage of the trade cycle gives an indication of what will work and what will sell. The examination in this chapter concentrates on the retail use of Internet e-commerce. Excluded from examination are:

- Use of Internet e-commerce for business to business transactions;
- Use of Internet e-commerce for the maintenance of on-going services such as electronic banking;
- Use of the Internet as a value added data service (VADS) for EDI transactions.

Many of the points in this chapter have applicability to these applications but the different circumstances of these exchanges serve to make the argument unnecessarily complex.

The trade cycles of Internet e-commerce retail exchanges is a special case of the generic trade cycles. A modified version of the generic trade cycle, with order, invoice and payment grouped as one phase, that more closely matches its Internet e-commerce retail use, is shown in Figure 2.2.

2.3. Internet Virgins

Internet Virgin is a term used by Rusbriger (1999) and, from the context, presumably by many before him. It is a term that, without going too far into its implications, perhaps illustrates the confusion and trepidation of the first time Internet user.

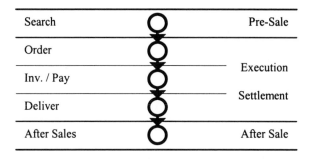

Search		Pre-Sale
Order		Execution
Inv. / Pay		
Deliver		Settlement
After Sales		After Sale

Figure 2.2. The Internet e-commerce retail trade cycle.

Shopping in a conventional store, for almost all people in developed countries, holds no fear. All shoppers are used to going to the store. They have been there before, they know where it is, and how they are expected to behave when they are inside. The same is not, however, true for an e-store.

The pre-requisites for e-commerce are access to an appropriate computer, knowing how to drive the Web browser and the desire to use it. Plainly more and more people have access to these facilities; people born in the last two decades of the twentieth century have, very probably, achieved a degree of computer literacy at school or college. However, for the foreseeable future, there will remain a large segment of society who does not have this access and/or these skills.

The wish to shop online seems to be assumed by the protagonists of e-commerce; it is presented as a 'good thing', almost a moral duty in the cause of progress:

> ... but the good news is that of 40 million (US) online users, some 10 million have purchased something online. (Plava, 1989)

Why 'good news'? It is good news if those consumers got a good deal but there is nothing intrinsically moral, social or even environmentally friendly about e-commerce. H. H. Havelock's view of progress can seem apposite after a fruitless search on the Web:

> What we call 'Progress' is the exchange of one nuisance for another nuisance.
> (Collins Concise Dictionary of Quotations)

The novice user who has access and an intent to use Internet e-commerce faces a number of hurdles - hurdles that occur at each stage of the trade cycle. These hurdles concern familiarity and trust. They have some relevance to an experienced user but the first time user is a special case - they are shopping for the first time in a foreign country where the language is not known. They need to have:

- *Familiarity with search engines.* Finding something on the Web is not necessarily easy, even for the experienced user. The user may have a URL recommended by a friend or copied from an advert - the URL is not constructed to be easy or familiar (although many organisations do their best). The alternative is a search; this will often bring up thousands of entries, most of them irrelevant. Finding one site with the required goods or services can take time - finding several to make price and service comparisons might take for ever.

- *Trust in unseen goods.* In a store, the customer knows what they are getting, they have looked at it, felt it and/or tried it on. It is not like that in the online store. There will be a description, probably a picture and it may be a brand that is known to the customer, but there is still, for many customers, a concern with the unseen.
- *Familiarity with online ordering.* The ordering of the goods requires the completion of an electronic form - new to many first time users and there is also a worry about giving the right details and trusting what is to happen to those details.
- *Trust in the security of payment.* The online order form asks for all kinds of detail, including credit/debit card numbers. Are these details safe and will they be misused?
- *Trust in delivery.* Given the goods are ordered and paid for, then the next worry - will the goods arrive? What happens if the parcel arrives and the customer is out? Will the plane ticket be at the airport when the customer gets there ready to fly? And even, is the site a bogus trader with no intention of making the delivery?
- *Trust in after sales.* Faulty goods can be taken back to the store but what do you do if there is a problem with e-purchases? It may be that the online vendor will be just as good as the high street store but it will almost certainly be more trouble and one can not be sure.

These hurdles are represented on the trade cycle model in Figure 2.3.

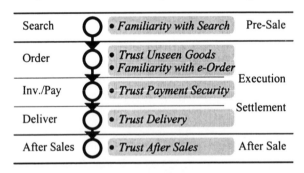

Figure 2.3. Concerns of the new e-commerce user.

For the experienced user, except for the issue of search, they are hurdles that the e-commerce customer has overcome or decided to ignore but for the 'Internet Virgin' they are very real issues that stand in the way of the use of e-commerce. The reaction of one first time user of Internet e-commerce, in the exercise/survey conducted by the author, was as follows:

> ... before this assignment I had never used the Internet to do my shopping and I believe that I will never use the facility again because it made me so agitated and annoyed.

2.4. Cyber Citizens

Cyber Citizens is a term used by Palava (1998) - it is a term that has implications that those who are not online will be disenfranchised in the information society - not an implication that is being pursued in this chapter.

The concerns of the Cyber Citizen are likely to differ from the Internet Virgin. The Cyber Citizen is used to the technology and is, presumably, prepared to trust (or risk) the system with online payment (or else they would not be regular users).

For the experienced users there are still a number of concerns with e-commerce. These concerns affect various stages of the trade cycle and differing types of goods or services. Areas of concern will be:

1. Search

The first step is finding the site and the goods and services that are needed. The Cyber Citizen will have worked out which search engine to use and how to frame the query but will still retrieve a high proportion of unwanted URLs in any search.

Predictions are that search engines will get better with, for example, the use of artificial intelligence agents and technical changes in the specification of information, e.g. XML and tags (Wilson, 1997). However, the number of sites on the Web is growing at a rapid rate and any standards are difficult to enforce. Searches seem unlikely to become easier. Schofield (1997) reports Sullivan (Search Engine Watch) as follows:

> ... Sullivan suspects that the major search engines are not keeping pace with the growth of the Web or with the changes in technology that make the Web a harder place to search.

From the vendor's point of view, success is not when the customer finds an appropriate site but when the customer finds his/her site. The best way to get site visits from 'real customers' is to get a customer who has already made a purchase to come back again.

The other ways of getting a customer are:

- To advertise on other sites - has to be worked at and paid for;
- Advertise in the conventional media - again it is a cost;
- Join an online mall - there will be fees to pay and customers must still find the mall;
- Choose a catchy name (or be a company with a well known and respected brand name) and hope that people will visit.

For any substantial e-commerce player, most of their business must come from return visits. Return visits are an important part of the strategy of vendors like Amazon.com (who require customers to register) and airlines (which are integrating their frequent flyers programs with their e-booking systems). Attracting new customers is important but the key factor is keeping the customers one already has.

2. Ordering

To get the customers to order online, the site must display its goods in a way that either tempts the shopper into a purchase or allows the shopper to easily find what they are looking for. The site should provide:

- Attractive home page, without the consequence of excessive download times;
- Easy (and intuitive) way of finding the goods;
- Competitive pricing.

It is possible for the online store to be more helpful than their high-street counterpart with, for example, customer reviews for books, helpful descriptions of the wines on offer or free downloads of sample software but the range of goods where these advantages apply are limited. Examples of merchandise where online shopping has disadvantages are:

- Clothing, where a picture and a description are not a substitute for feeling the cloth and trying on the garment.
- Groceries, where there is a large range and customers tend to be shopping for a considerable number of items. Experience is obviously important and facilities such as personalised stored shopping lists help, but:

  > It took the customer ages to order, and they got fed up. They ended up ordering less than usual. It was too much like hard work finding things (Mitchell (*Sainsbury*[2]) quoted by Cowe, 1998).

  And while a can of beans is a can of beans, if you like your bananas green, online shopping probably does not give you that option.

It would seem that some products are intrinsically more suited to online ordering than others. Books and CDs seem to be prime examples and this is illustrated by the growth of these outlets on the net. Products such as clothing and food can, and are, ordered online but they are more problematic. The mail order market for clothes is significant but limited; the restrictions that limit the size of that market seem likely to apply equally to online vendors of apparel. Success in the order phase is therefore dependent upon the design of the Web site and the products, where the customer can be confident that what they expect is what they get.

3. Invoice/Payment

Payment on the Internet has to be by credit card, debit card or e-cash. All of these require the customer to trust the security, to be cavalier about security or to assume that the card/e-cash provider will stand the major part of any losses incurred.

Much is made of the public's distrust of payments over the Internet. There has been a lot of investment in 'secure' systems and the public is assured that Internet payments are as secure, or more secure, than many other situations where the public use their credit cards without apparent qualms.

That said, many members of the public remain sceptical. In the survey used in this chapter, payment insecurity was seen as the major disadvantage of Internet e-

---

[2] *Sainsbury* is the second largest UK supermarket chain.

commerce with 73% quoting it in their list of disadvantages (next disadvantage in the list was only quoted by 29%).

The survey, however, covered a majority (73%) who had not used e-commerce. Those who have used e-commerce have (presumably) decided there is not a significant risk or it is a risk they are prepared to take. One student (in the 1997 survey) declared himself unconcerned as he was using his father's credit card! Fear of payment interception/fraud is a significant deterrent to the Internet Virgins but, it is contended, not a significant issue to the Cyber Citizens.

For success, the e-vendor must implement a secure payment system but this should not be a real issue; these systems are readily available. What can be an issue is the charge made by the card companies to new e-vendors. Strom et al. (1998) reports rates of 10% being charged to the Manchester Internet Shopping Site, a significant sum and more than twice the rate paid by retail shops.

4. Delivery

The world's biggest bookshop is online but, at the airport and wanting a book to read, that is not a lot of help. The local supermarket may be happy to deliver groceries between 10:00 and 12:00 but, if there are no bagels for breakfast the customer will be hungry when they arrive. The delivery issue is one that is ignored in a lot of the Internet literature, possibly because (in most cases) there is no high-tech solution, but it is none the less a significant issue for many customers.

Goods (or services) ordered over the Internet may be delivered:

- Electronically (software, music and tickets all have this potential);
- Post (books, CDs and other small items);
- Special delivery (food, electrical goods and other bulky items).

Excepting goods delivered electronically, delivery requires/implies:

- *Delay*: Goods take hours or days to arrive when they might have been available over the counter in a conventional shop.
- *Cost*: Delivery charges often apply, they may be offset by reductions in the price of the product but that seems to be the case less often than is suggested.

And electronic delivery can have its disadvantages as well: downloaded music is not ideal to wrap up as a present and turning up for a transatlantic flight with no more than a print of an e-mail could, for many customers, feel a little insecure.

Buying grocery supplies is often quoted as a shopping chore that people would like to be rid of. A survey quoted in Cowe (1998) suggested that 40% of customers would be interested in a home delivery service. However grocery supplies are an example of a product that would require 'special delivery' and that delivery would need to be from a local depot or store. Grocery supplies are:

... the most difficult product to deliver. Food is perishable and vulnerable as well as bulky. It cannot just be dumped on the doorstep and it cannot be returned if it does not suit. (Reid (*Tesco*[3]) quoted by Cowe, 1998)

---

[3] *Tesco* is the largest UK supermarket chain.

Suppliers that do deliver make a charge of (say) £5.00 (US$ 8.00) and require that the customer be home at a specified time. There are customers prepared to pay the charge and wait at home for the delivery but it is not an arrangement that would fit in with everyone's schedule (Cowe, 1998). There is the possibility of houses having a 'safebox', including a refrigerated compartment, to which the supplier has a key or code. Apparently, there is such a scheme near Boston USA (Cope, 1996) but that requires considerable investment and organisation. There seems to be a concern in the trade that the level of delivery charge that customers will accept is, perhaps, a third of the rate needed to make the service profitable (Cowe, 1998).

Articles that can be sent by the post escape some of the problems of 'special delivery'. Post is relatively cheap and, if it will fit through the letterbox, there is no need to wait in for its arrival. Electronic bookshops use postal delivery and charge for it. Take the book produced by the same editors as this volume:

Romm, C. and Sudweeks, F. (eds) (1998). *Doing Business Electronically: A Global Perspective of Electronic Commerce*, Springer-Verlag, London.

This is listed in Whitaker's *Books in Print* at UK£24.50 and that is the price you would pay in the bookshop. Ordered, for example, from Amazon.com the price is still UK£24.50 but the carriage charge is UK£2.45 making the overall deal that much more expensive than the conventional bookshop (which just might have had a copy in stock). The online bookshops do claim to discount some books and that would offset the carriage charge but then it depends on which books you buy.

The products that seem best suited to overcome the 'delivery barrier' are goods that can be downloaded (without significant disadvantage) and goods that can be sent by post. Goods that need special delivery, though, are:

- Expensive to deliver;
- A problem if it is not convenient for the customer to be there to receive them;
- Difficult if distance of delivery is an issue and a network of local depots may be required.

There are, of course, particular customers and specific goods where local delivery would be welcomed but these difficulties will reduce the scope of e-commerce in these product area.

5. After Sales

For any online customer, the last thing they need is to have to send the goods back. Having to take goods back to a conventional store is not nice and is not convenient but it beats having to wrap up the goods, write a letter (or e-mail) and pay for the return postage or carriage. The point is made and amplified by van der Zoo (1999):

The other problems centre on complaints and returns. If the seller is located in the UK (or one's own country) that makes it easier.

Buying goods online means that they will not have been inspected or tried on - a factor that must increase the probability of returns for products such as clothing.

After sales is suggested as a strong point for Internet e-commerce. The two areas of service strengths that are frequently put forward are:

- Online support such as that provided by some IT companies for their products; not a facility that has great relevance to a more mundane domestic product.
- Customer contact and customer feedback. E-mail is an easy and informal medium for customers to use to send their views but can the company afford the time to process all these communications and to reply in the way that users of e-mail expect?

The success factors and the more dubious prospects, 'Stars' and 'Question Marks' to borrow the terminology of the Boston Consulting Group Matrix (see for example Needle, 1994), for each stage of the trade cycle, are shown in Figure 2.4.

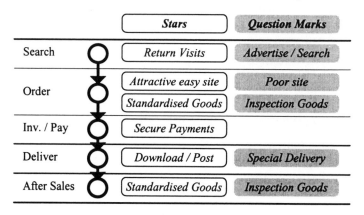

Figure 2.4. E-commerce success factors.

2.5. Conclusions

Internet e-commerce is a new retail channel that is set to take its place alongside other forms of retailing. Retail e-commerce sales have risen dramatically over the last few years and that trend will, no doubt, continue for several years more. Projections of this dramatic rise vary widely, perhaps the most often quoted is that of the McKinsey consultancy which predicted an annual home shopping market, in the USA, of US$4-5 billion by 2003 (quoted for example by Wigland, 1997). On its own the figure is large but it is put into context when compared with conventional direct sales (by catalogue, phone and TV) of between US$46 and US$60 billion and a total retail market of about twenty times that figure[4] (see Bloch et al., 1996; Niemira, 1996).

Leaving aside the service and search system providers, the hot cakes, in terms of growth of sales, of Internet e-commerce have been:

- Online bookshops and record (CD) stores;
- Vendors of IT/software supplies;

---

[4] KPMG (1999) gives direct sales as 5% of retail sales in the UK and 4% in the US. 16% of US home sales and 1% of UK home sales are electronic.

- Small operators in niche markets.

Many operators in these sectors have shown spectacular growth although their volume in terms of the total retail sales in their chosen market sector remains small.

The dead ducks will be in areas such as:

- Clothing;
- Groceries;
- Consumer durables.

The dead ducks will be more difficult to identify. There will be niche players in these segments that do very well and there will be large operators who run a marginal e-commerce operation on the back of their conventional facilities (and they will doubtless present the results as a success). However, for these types of goods, most shoppers will want to visit a conventional store, see and/or feel the goods, possibly stop off for a coffee with family or friends and then take their purchases home, 'real time', in a plastic bag. The dead ducks may, presumably, be joined by some operators from the more favoured sectors if they continue to make large annual losses!

The Internet is plainly set to become a part of everyday life. It will be used as:

- Information source;
- Communications medium;
- Means of administration;
- Source of entertainment.

It is set to be a universal communications media that will take its place alongside the postal and telephone services (and has the potential to render the first of these obsolete for the transfer of documents). What it is not equipped to do, despite all the predictions, is to change the face of retailing.

Internet e-commerce is a modern form of direct sales. It will take market share from other direct sales channels and it will expand the scope of direct sales in some product areas. Direct sales have fluctuated in their market penetration but that penetration has always been a single figure percentage of the retail market. Internet e-commerce, for the sale of tangible goods, is no more than a new media and does not radically change the issues of search, product inspection, delivery and after sales. Internet e-commerce is not about to replace the corner store and the shopping mall.

CHAPTER 3

When Does Virtual Have Value?

JANICE BURN, PETER MARSHALL AND MARTYN WILD

3.1. Introduction

> The globalization of markets, increasing competition, the reduction of barriers to entry
> into new lines of business, mergers and alliances, changing patterns of employment,
> the increasing sophistication of workers and the opportunities of modern technology
> are pushing all organizations in the direction of virtuality (Working Group 4, 1998,
> p.7)

Virtuality is a concept and an organisational structure that is gaining an increasing
amount of interest with both the research community in management studies and
managers of both small and large business organisations. This increased interest is
borne out of the vague but well-entrenched notion that future prosperity of any
organisation rests on its ability to respond to a 'wired world', where fast, cheap and
global communications networks will make non-virtual (i.e. physical) organisational
structures obsolete. In other words, as with much in the business world, it is a
mixture of fear and opportunity that is driving the new paradigm.

The opportunities that exist do so largely in the mind of the protagonists of the
new paradigm rather than in actual economic or strategic advantage – that is, in the
promise rather than the reality. Furthermore, such opportunities lie in the nexus of
electronic communications between organisations, customers and suppliers, where
businesses are able to engage their existing, as well as new, processes and activities
without the constraints of time, place, distance or physicality. In turn, the move
towards virtuality is supposed to deliver the online business global competitive
advantage.

Of course, it could be argued that there is a degree of virtuality in all
organisations, especially those that are information intensive and receive benefit
from deployment of appropriate information and communication technologies
(ICT). So at what point should organisations be considered virtual? One perspective
would suggest that organisations are virtual when production is spread across
different locations, and is completed at differing work cycles, and across cultures
(Gray and Igbaria, 1996; Palmer and Speier, 1998). Another suggests that the single
common theme is temporality. Virtual organisations centre on continual
restructuring to capture the value of a short term market opportunity and are then

dissolved to make way for restructuring to a new virtual entity. (Byrne, 1993; Katzy, 1998). Yet others views suggest that virtual organisations are characterised by the intensity, symmetricality, reciprocity and multiplexity of the linkages in their networks (Powell, 1990; Grabowski and Roberts, 1996). The Impact Program (Working Group 4, 1998) has identified many of these prime characteristics of the virtual organisation and placed them into a coherent four-theme framework, focused on dispersion, empowerment (of an organisation's component parts), restlessness (i.e. acceptance of change) and interdependence.

However, even whilst all these characteristics might, when taken together, help provide a model of virtuality, the model remains descriptive rather than explanatory or even predictive - that is, it will be limited to identifying what we mean by virtuality, and does not help determine *how* the qualities of being virtual can be turned to value, or *when* there may be value in developing characteristics of virtuality for individual organisations. Moreover, the organisational and management processes which should be applied to ensure successful implementation of virtuality remain ill-defined or simply unknown (Finnegan, Galliers and Powell, 1998; Swatman and Swatman, 1992).

3.2. Fundamental Attributes of Virtual Organisations

Virtual organisations are electronically networked organisations that transcend conventional organisational boundaries (Barner, 1996; Berger, 1996; Rogers, 1996), with linkages which may exist both within (Davidow and Malone, 1992) and between organisations (Goldman, Nagel and Priess, 1995). In its simplest form, however, virtuality can be said to exist where IT is used to enhance organisational activities while reducing the need for physical or formalised structures (Greiner and Metes, 1996). Greiner and Metes (1996) suggest that the relationships involved in virtual organisations differ in significant ways from traditional partnerships or alliances in that these relationships are product or project focussed, flexible and short lived. Such relationships are based primarily on competencies rather than historical relationships or cost. They are also often complex with organisations allied within networks that might include customers, suppliers, business partners and even competitors.

Degrees of virtuality exist, then, which reflect the:

- Organisational *culture*;
- Intensity of linkages within *networks*, and the nature of the bonds which tie the stakeholders together (i.e. both internal and external structures);
- Nature of the *market* (i.e. its level of IT dependency, resource infrastructure, product type, customer characteristics) (Burn, Marshall and Wild, 1999a).

Culture is the degree to which members of a community have common shared values and beliefs (Schein, 1990). Tushman and O'Reilly (1996) suggest that organisational cultures that are accepting of technology, highly decentralised, and change oriented are more likely to embrace virtuality. Virtual culture is the perception of the entire virtual organisation (including its infrastructure and product) held by its stakeholder community and operationalised in choices and actions which result in a feeling of *globalness* with respect to value sharing (e.g. each client's expectations are satisfied in the product accessed), and time-space arrangement (e.g. each stakeholder has the feeling of a continuous access to the organisation and its products).

Networks apply to both groups of organisations and groups *within* organisations where the development and maintenance of communicative relationships is paramount to the successful evolution of a virtual entity. Within such groups, the ability to establish multiple alliances and the need to retain a particular identity can create a constant tension between autonomy and interdependence, competition and cooperation (Nouwens, and Bouwman, 1995). These alliances are often described as value-added partnerships based on horizontal, vertical or symbiotic relationships. These, in turn, relate to competitors, value chain collaborators and complementary providers of goods and services all of whom combine to achieve competitive advantage over organisations outside these networks. The nature, strength and substitutability of the alliances operating within the virtual organisation, define its virtual structure.

Markets differ from networks since markets are traditionally coordinated by pricing mechanisms. In this sense, the electronic market is no different, although 'central to the conceptualisations of the electronic marketplace is the ability of any buyer or seller to interconnect with a network to offer wares or shop for goods and services. Hence, ubiquity is by definition a prerequisite' (Steinfield, Plummer and Kraut, 1995). There are different risks associated with being a market-maker and a market-player and different products will also carry different risks. Criteria for successful electronic market development include products with low asset specificity and ease of description and a consumer market willing to buy without recourse to visiting retail stores (Wigand and Benjamin, 1995). Necessarily, the most important asset to an electronic market is a pervasive ITC infrastructure, providing a critical mass of customers. A virtual organisation is both constrained and supported by, the electronic market in which it operates.

Despite the growth of online activity, many firms are nervous of the risks involved and fear a general deterioration of profit margins coupled with a relinquishment of market control. Nevertheless, as existing organisations are challenged by new entrants using direct channels to undercut prices and increase market share, solutions have to be found that enable organisations to successfully migrate into the electronic market. The authors suggest that there are six different models of virtuality which may be appropriate.

3.3. Models of Virtuality

It is possible to identify six models of virtual organisations:

- Virtual faces;
- Co-alliance models;
- Star-alliance models - core and satellite;
- Value-alliance models - stars or constellations;

- Market-alliance models;
- Virtual brokers.

Virtual faces are the cyberspace incarnations of existing non-virtual organisations - often described as 'place' as opposed to 'space' organisations (Rayport and Sviokola, 1995) - and create additional value for the consumers and/or business partners by enabling them to complete essentially the same transactions over the Internet as they might otherwise do via telephone, fax or face-to-face encounters. Virtual faces may mirror the entire activities of the parent organisation, or may simply expand the scope of the parent, by using such facilities as electronic procurement, contract tendering, electronic ordering and payment facilities, for example. In either guise, there remains a strong link between the virtual face and its parent organisation.

Virtual faces are amongst the most common and earliest Internet business models and include, in Australia, Dewsons supermarket (www.dewsons.com.au), Ford Australia (www.Ford.com.au), and Henley Saab (www.henley-saab.com.au). Other manifestations of the virtual faces model may be actualised as an e-shop, e-auction or e-mall.

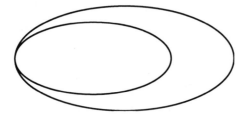

Figure 3.1. The virtual face.

Co-alliance models occur as shared partnerships with each partner bringing approximately equal amounts of commitment to the virtual organisation, thus forming a consortium. The composition of the consortium may change to reflect market opportunities or to reflect the core competencies of each member (Preiss, Goldman and Nagel, 1996). The focus in this model is very likely to be on specific tasks or functions, and the links formed as part of the co-alliance would normally be contractual for more permanent alliances, or by mutual convenience, on a project by project basis. There is not normally a high degree of substitutability within the life of the co-alliance. The following case study, further explicates this model.

Figure 3.2. Co-alliance model.

3.3.1. CASE STUDY 1: PERTH CONSULTING SERVICES (PCS)

Strategic Planning Consulting Services (SPCS) is run by Rachel Smith. Rachel is skilled in facilitating strategic planning and strategic information systems (IS) planning sessions. She guides and coaches groups of managers and professionals from public and private sector organisations in the formulation of corporate visions, missions, strategic plans and strategic IS plans. Rachel can offer competitive prices for this consulting work since she works from home and has few of the infrastructure costs of the large consulting companies, such as the rent of expensive capital city office space and the like. However, she can not offer the broad skills set that the larger consulting companies can offer. Tony Jones has a very good technical knowledge of IT and offers an IT planning consulting service along with some analysis and programming skills. The analysis and programming services that he offers are limited and are usually restricted to specific small tasks that are identified during his IT planning work. If Tony requires some more substantial systems development work done he contacts the consultancy of Tom and Stephanie More, who run a systems development consultancy. Tom and Stephanie are skilled systems developers with a wide range of technical IT skills. They also contract to highly skilled systems developers that they can call on to do analysis, design and programming tasks according to need and on a project-by-project basis. Together, Rachel, Tony, and Tom and Stephanie form an agile virtual organisation able to respond effectively and inexpensively to a set of needs clustered around strategic planning, IS/IT planning and IS development. All the persons in this virtual organisation work from their homes and utilise ICT to keep them in contact with each other and with business and government in Australia and South East Asia (Figure 3.3).

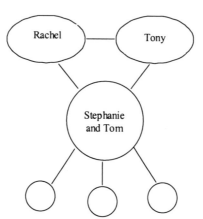

Systems Development Contractors

Figure 3.3. A co-alliance model in operation: The case of PCS.

The operational structure of PCS is a negotiated and flexible one, where each of the partner businesses brings approximately equal commitment to the virtual organisation. PCS partners collaborate according to need and usually on a project-by-project basis, although some administrative and marketing functions may need to be completed outside, and in addition to, that required by individual projects. As such, the expanded functionality and skills sets of the virtual organisation brings competitive advantage to all the partner businesses. The links in this particular co-alliance are more substitutable than in, say, the manufacture of a product by a team of persons where different alliance partners manufacture different parts of the product which is finally assembled by one member of the alliance. However, in the tasks undertaken by PCS, there is a reasonable degree of collaboration and trust required in order to carry out an assignment to the satisfaction of the client. The structure of this virtual organisation is shown in Figure 3.3.

Star-alliance models are co-ordinated networks of interconnected members reflecting a core surrounded by satellite organisations. The core comprises leaders who are the dominant players in the market and supply competency or expertise to members. These alliances are commonly based around similar industries, sectors or company types. While this organisational structure is a true network, the star or leader is typically identified with the virtual face, and so the core organisation is very difficult to replace, whereas the satellites may have a far greater level of substitutability.

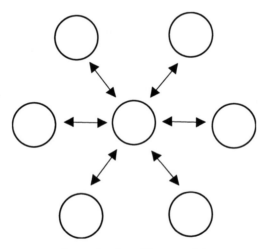

Figure 3.4. Star-alliance model.

3.3.2. CASE STUDY 2: CAPITAL CITY AUTOMOBILE ASSOCIATION (CCAA)

The Capital City Automobile Association (CCAA) began by offering members an automobile breakdown service in Australian capital cities. If a member's car broke down, the CCAA would dispatch a qualified mechanic to the location of the breakdown. The CCAA guaranteed to correct simple causes of vehicle 'breakdown', such as a flat battery, and enable the motorist to get home or get the car to a garage or vehicle service centre. The CCAA owned a number of specially equipped vehicles which qualified mechanics, all employed by the CCAA, would drive to the locations of breakdowns.

A common reason for vehicle failure was found from experience to be the result of poor battery maintenance, where the motorist simply needed a replacement battery. However, vehicle parts replacement was not originally seen to be part of the charter or responsibility of the CCAA, which was created and operated simply as a breakdown service. The CCAA mechanics would, in these circumstances, attempt to recharge flat batteries to the point at which motorists could use their cars to drive home, or perhaps to a repair garage, so that the battery could be replaced. After some years, however, at the suggestion of the some of the mechanics, a number of third-party organisations were contracted by the CCAA specifically to provide a 24 hours battery replacement service. Contractors' hours of service availability, duties of service and pay were negotiated with the CCAA, with substantial flexibility regarding how individual contractors arranged their businesses, given to contractors. Some of these contractors ran small businesses such as garages or car maintenance services, while others took on the battery replacement contract as their sole business activity. By engaging multiple battery replacement service contractors, the CCAA was able to offer its members a continuous 24 hours battery replacement service.

CCAA members responded positively to this new replacement service, and over a number of months its usage expanded significantly. As a result, the CCAA sought to lower the cost and improve the quality and consistency of the service by contracting to a single distributor - Quality Batteries Australia (QBA). QBA had warehouses in two major cities and undertook to work in concert with existing contractors to ensure they had appropriate access to reputable batteries for their battery replacement services. This new arrangement required logistical planning with contractors in those capital cities without a QBA presence. Cyber Logistics Australia (CLA) was contracted to transport batteries, as and when required, from QBA warehouses to contractors' battery service sites. CLA had an existing Web site, and a good reputation for round-the-clock 'fetch and carry' assistance with items of all sizes; it also had a number of its own contractors working for the company in all Australian capital cities. These contractors monitored the e-mail requests received by CLA and responded on an internal CLA electronic bidding system: contractors would bid for fetch and carry tasks that were reasonably close to their business locations; bids were made according to CLA standard prices; and if two or more CLA contractors offered to do the same trip, the business would go to the first contractor that offered to do the trip within temporal and other conditions set by the customer.

One of the managers in the CCAA's breakdown service organisation had noticed the Web site of Battery Disposals of America (BDA). BDA profited from stripping down dead or unwanted batteries and extracting, and re-selling, valuable metals and re-usable acid. When contacted, BDA was willing to pay for dead batteries arising from CCAA's breakdown service, provided they were sent in batches to the USA, and that the CCAA arranged transportation of the batteries. CCAA contracted the logistics of transporting the batteries out to CLA, which eventuated in CLA extending its business internationally, with an e-mail, fax and telephone communications network established between CCAA, CLA and BDA.

Further on, a number of CCAA mechanics involved in the breakdown service began reporting that many of the cars they were called out to were evidently in need of other services, notwithstanding the original fault that had caused the car to malfunction. As a result, they often advised clients to obtain a general service from a good mechanic. It was considered to be of greater value to the client if they could suggest service agents recommended by CCAA. Hence, CCAA began to run a vehicle servicing business, again without the need for additional infrastructure and with only limited additional capital required. Competent mechanics, already in business on their own, were contracted to service CCAA members, according to a CCAA certified service. The CCAA and the service mechanics subsequently met regularly to agree marketing campaigns, standards of car services, education and training needs for contractors and their employees, and the nature of profit sharing in the CCAA car servicing business.

At a later date, CCAA contracted to meet an additional client need: on-the-spot fitting of replacement windscreens. These contractors were organised similarly to the battery replacement and car service contractors, with CCAA contracting with Best Windscreens of Australia (BWA) to supply windscreens to CCAA windscreen replacement contractors. Again, CLA was contracted to manage the logistics of supplying windscreens to contractors round-the-clock and according to need.

The organisational structure of CCAA, its links with business partners and contractors, is illustrated in Figure 3.5. This organisation exists as a virtual incarnation, offering greater services to clients and adding substantial value to the parent company. To clients, CCAA now has a much larger presence, whilst for the parent this has been achieved without the need for additional physical infrastructure, and with only limited amounts of additional finance capital required. Indeed, whilst CCAA extended its virtual structures over a period of time, and according to perceived need, the structure could have been planned and built from the outset as part of an overall business plan. Of course, if client need does not materialise in the long term, for any part of CCAA's additional services, that section of the virtual organisation can be shed or replaced painlessly.

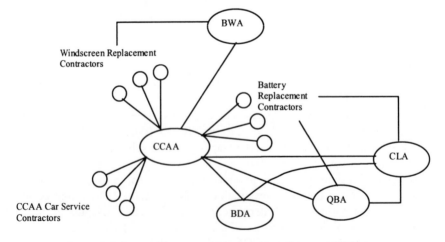

Figure 3.5. A star-alliance model in operation: the case of CCAA.

The organisational structure of CCAA is essentially a star, with the parent at the hub or centre. Links to all contractors are highly substitutable, whilst the links to CLA, QBA, BDA, and BWA require the establishment of more complex business relationships, since the services offered therein are more complex than the vehicle servicing, battery and windscreen replacement options. However, in all cases, each offspring company is more easily substituted out of the star structure than the parent. If CCAA failed, its wider virtual incarnation would follow. In this sense, the star structure does not allow for the greater flexibility and adaptiveness possible in other virtual organisational models.

Value-alliance models bring together a range of products, services and facilities in one package and are based on the value or supply chain model. Participants may come together on a project-by-project basis, with coordination often provided by a general contractor. Where longer term relationships are developed, the value alliance often adopts the form of value constellations, where firms supply each of the companies in the value chain and a complex and continuing set of strategic relationships are embedded into the alliance (Figure 3.6). The extent of substitutability will relate to the positioning on the value chain and the reciprocity of the partner relationship.

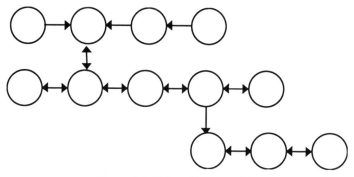

Figure 3.6. Value-alliance model.

3.3.3. CASE STUDY 3: WILDFLOWERS OF AUSTRALIA (WFA)

Wildflowers of Australia (WFA) is an Australia-wide company that coordinates the ordering, transportation and delivery of flowers nationally. WFA puts retailers and end consumers in touch with growers of Australian wildflowers, who, in turn, are able to satisfy specific demands. WFA has extensive information resources regarding seasonal stocks, flower types grown and harvesting times. Demands from both retailers and end customers are accepted using standard electronic forms available from WFA's Web site, as well as by telephone, fax or e-mail. These demands are transmitted in total or in part to particular growers of the specific wildflowers required. After harvesting the flowers in appropriate quantities, the growers call on Cyber Logistics of Australia (CLA) to deliver, thereby ensuring freshness for the end consumer. WFA has arranged with Smart Cards of Australia (SCA) to record financial transactions so that adequate records can be kept and appropriate payments made. Each business and contractor within the virtual organisation supplying flowers carries a smart card and a device for the input of transactional information, and a secure communications network allows transactional data to be held and processed by SCA.

The traditional value chain for the cut-flower industry involves a complex array of inbound and outbound logistical processes as well as repeated physical handling of the flowers. Together, these processes are time intensive - a significant limitation to this particular industry since it is based on the sale of a perishable product. However, the value chain for the cut-wildflower organisational model coordinated by WFA minimises the number of links between grower and end consumer, resulting in less product handling and, more importantly, less time between cutting and displaying the flowers. Thus, the product lasts longer at the point of consumption, giving increased customer satisfaction. In this way, the cut-flower value chain has been reinvented by WFA and its partners to provide increased efficiencies in a demand pull operation providing for overall enhanced customer satisfaction. The companies involved in this value alliance are all specialists, concentrating on niche market specialisms or core competencies. Logistical tasks have been concentrated in a single specialist logistics company; similarly, all financial recording and accounting tasks have been extracted across the value chain and given to a specialist smart card based accounting company. This re-working of the traditional value chain is typical of virtual organisations of the virtual alliance type.

Market-alliances are organisations that exist primarily in cyberspace, depend on their member organisations for the provision of actual products and services and operate in an electronic market. Typically they bring together a range of products, services and facilities in single package, each of which may in fact, be offered separately by individual organisations. Amazon.com (www.amazon.com) is a pre-eminent example of a market-alliance model in which the substitutability of links is very high. However, in other examples, the market-alliance organisation is achieved in less clear-cut ways - the following case study is of a rapidly growing French textile company, taken from The Impact Program's, *Exploiting the Wired-Up World* (Working Group 4, 1998, pp. 44-45).

3.3.4. CASE STUDY 4: SPORA

Spora, a small but rapidly growing French company in the textile industry, started in 1993. A highly entrepreneurial 29 year old, whose background already included experience in textile engineering, information systems and business management, founded it. The opportunity he had identified was to fill a market niche with a specialised product range. Initially, the products were manufactured by a subcontractor but, in 1995, the entrepreneur bought the factory. Since then, he has established a marketing alliance with a specialist retailer, marketing/manufacturing alliances with American and Canadian textile companies, and a diversification into providing Internet services on a commercial basis. A further alliance with a Chinese textile company is, in late 1998, being negotiated.

The company's development has been crucially enabled by the use of the Internet: global access to customers in its specialised market is gained through a 'virtual trade show' on the Web; orders are taken by e-mail; alliances are sought via the use of a Web search engine followed up by e-mail. The factory, 15 kilometers away, is managed by means of e-mail. A new product has been designed jointly with the Canadian company through just two face-to-face meetings plus about seventy electronic messages. High quality students have been seconded in by overseas companies for training - a resource which would never have been available without making contacts through the Internet. The experience of developing a successful Web site in the textile business has led to further diversification: developing and managing Web sites for others.

This history obviously owes much to personalities - and not only to the energy and background of the founder. The factory manager, a complete stranger to information systems, has been highly motivated by his successful participation in a virtual organisation. Alliance partners have been willing to build personal relationships through quick-fire exchange of messages, without any face-to-face meetings or phone calls. Small though this company still is (i.e. turnover is approximately 600, 000 Ecus), it is clearly growing in its virtuality through strategic market alliances. Interestingly, when manufacturing was initially contracted out at the outset of this company, the market alliances were greater in their virtualness. However, it suited the owner in this particular industry to gain greater control over the manufacturing process, leading to his purchase of a factory. Since this period, further market alliances in marketing, training, recruitment and financial services have extended the virtual characteristics of the organisation.

This example of a market alliance organisation is likely to be just as typical as Amazon.com in real-world terms, with the difference between the two manifestations of the model lying in the levels of ownership and/or control over the means of production. In some industries and with some products, it is simply preferable to retain ownership and/or sole control over product creation.

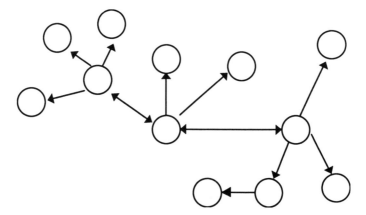

Figure 3.7. Market-alliance model.

Virtual Brokers are designers of dynamic networks (Miles and Snow, 1986). These prescribe additional strategic opportunities either as third party value-added suppliers such as in the case of common Web marketing events (e.g. e-Xmas), or as information brokers providing a virtual structure, often in an umbrella form, around specific business information services (Timmers, 1998). The virtual broker organisational model has the highest level of flexibility with purpose-built virtual companies created to fill a particular window of opportunity, and dissolved once that window is closed.

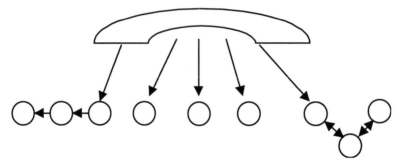

Figure 3.8. Virtual broker.

3.4. The Value in Virtual

The six models described above are not mutually exclusive, nor are they entirely representative of the configurations of virtual organisations already to be found, or indeed, those we are likely to see developing in the near future. However, they do serve as a way of classifying and understanding the diversity of forms which an ICT enabled business model may assume. Some of these forms represent essentially electronic implementations of traditional ways of doing business, others provide for adding value to traditional business strategies, whilst others go far beyond this, through value chain integration and the building of cyber communities. However, all these models are commonly characterised by the use of innovatory approaches to seeking additional value through information and change management and enriched functionalities.

Furthermore, it is apparent that there is no 'optimum' degree of virtuality for particular organisations. As the authors of *Exploiting the Wired-Up World* (Working Group 4, 1998) suggest, best practice is a question of fitness for purpose: looking at business objectives, opportunities and threats, deciding whether a shift in virtuality would help, managing so as to achieve the desired position, and reviewing regularly:

> The incentive for change must be business requirements rather than any desire to become more virtual for its own sake. (Working Group 4, 1998, p. 27)

Moreover, it is clear that the search to create value through virtuality is only feasible if the processes that support such innovations are clearly understood. The questions which need to be asked in this context include, but are not limited to, the following:

- To what extent does an organisation already display characteristics of virtuality, and is this extent appropriate for meeting organisational goals in future expected business environments?
- Are current management strategies and practices appropriate for this level of virtuality?
- What management capabilities will be needed for change towards further virtuality?
- What benefits should be expected, both for the organisation and for the individuals within it?
- What are the possible pitfalls? (Working Group 4, 1998, p. 27)

The authors of this chapter describe, in another paper, a 'virtual organisational change model', which seeks to provide a more comprehensive basis for understanding and managing organisational change towards greater levels of virtuality (Burn, Marshall and Wild, 1999b). What is clear from this model, is that change directions should be value led, that value must be measured at both individual organisation and inter-organisational levels, and that the measurement of value must be completed in terms of both qualitative and quantitative data, and must encompass 'fuzzy' as well as objective measures. What is also clear, is that the organisations that move towards greater virtuality, and that succeed in establishing value in their growth, will be the learning organisations, where people are regarded as the greatest core asset.

CHAPTER 4

Will You Use Animation on Your Web Pages?

Experiments of Animation Effects and Implications for Web User Interface Design and Online Advertising

PING ZHANG

4.1. Introduction

Joining the Internet revolution becomes many companies' strategic plans and actions nowadays. As Sudweeks and Romm pointed out earlier in this book, planning and designing of company strategies, developing marketing strategies to be used on the Internet, streamlining information flows within companies that are based on the Internet (Intranet), and developing Internet-based networking strategies with suppliers and customers, are important issues that companies need to face. The up front that realises all these strategies and actions, however, is the Web user interface or the Web pages that the companies provide for viewers and customers to interact with. Web interface designs are equally critical for companies to succeed in the Internet revolution. There are many Web interface design issues that need to be researched (for example, see Nielsen, 1999; Zhang et al., 1999). One of the Web interface design considerations is the use of animation on Web pages.

The rapid advancement of software tools such as JAVA, VRML, and specialised graphic and animation packages has made animation very easy to produce and use. When surfing the Internet with a Web browser, one would encounter many pages with vivid animation jumping about on the screen. Often, a user is reading the primary information on a page when animation appears in the peripheral visual field. To some viewers, animation is annoying flashing graphics that divert attention from the content of a page. To the Web site designers, animation is a practical tool that can make less seem like more. On the limited display area of a computer screen, animation can be used to make something more distinctive, to promote a special section within a site or to allow illustration of editorial content more effectively (McGalliard, 1998). To online advertisers, animation means a great way of increasing click-throughs. In fact, online advertising accounts for the majority of animation on the Web nowadays.

Advertising on the Web is growing at a fast pace. Online advertising revenue reached $906.5 million in 1997 (Internet Advertising Bureau, 1998), is projected to hit \$2 billion in 1998 (Maddox, 1998), will reach a level of 4.3 billion in the year 2000 (Jupiter Communications, 1998), and soar to \$7.7 billion in 2002 (Davidson, 1998). During the same period, total ad revenue for all other media - including print, TV and radio - is projected to grow just 7% annually (Davidson, 1998). Research shows that static banners (a posting on the computer screen akin to a print ad) do boost product awareness (Wang, 1997). However, it is believed that using animation rather than static banners is a more effective way of online advertising, resulting in a 25% increase in click-through rates (Hein, 1997; McGalliard, 1998). Despite the very fast growth of animation for advertising, companies have learned valuable lessons along the way. For example, AT&T, one of the four largest marketers, learned not to "pester" consumers with interrupting Internet ads (*USA Today*, 1998).

Being interrupted or having one's attention involuntarily shifted by animation on a Web page is a typical experience for many Web users. For example, "many find AOL's full-screen 'pop-up' ads maddening" (Davidson, 1998). Animation, when used to carry information that is not primary to one's tasks, may create visual interference that affects one's performance. Extraneous animation that is present continuously or appears suddenly can act as a distractor, making it difficult to concentrate on pertinent information. Thus, it disturbs and then often annoys people as they search for useful information on the Web, lengthening the time needed to obtain information correctly.

It is certainly not the content providers' intention to disturb or annoy their viewers. Web-owners or content providers want to make money from advertising, but they also care about the potential side effects of animation on their viewers' information-seeking performance and attitude toward their Web sites. Given a choice, content providers would prefer advertisements that have minimum disturbing impact on viewers' performance as they seek primary information on the Web pages. Advertisers or marketers, on the other hand, want to grab viewer attention, and so they may want to design advertisements that have different characteristics than those the content providers would choose. Ads that advertisers favour may take more attentional resources of the viewers and thus have a higher chance of being processed semantically by the viewers. To be effective, both content providers and advertisers must understand the effects of animation in the Web environment.

Research results from studies of visual attention might be able to provide a plausible explanation for the disturbance phenomenon. Studies show that in general, objects in our peripheral vision can capture our attention (Driver and Baylis, 1989). The meaning of a non-attended stimulus is processed to a certain extent (Allport, 1989, Duncan, 1984; Treisman, 1991). Because attention has limited capacity, the available resource for attention on the pertinent information is reduced, thus information processing performance, including speed and accuracy, deteriorates (Miller, 1991; Treisman, 1991).

It is, however, questionable whether we can apply visual-attention theories or research results directly to information-seeking tasks in a computing environment such as the Web. A primary reason for this is that the exposure time of stimuli in traditional visual attention studies is much shorter (milliseconds) than that on the Web (seconds or minutes), and one's visual attention behavior may change during this relatively long exposure time. Another reason, as pointed out by Eysenck and Keane (1995), is that most studies of attention are very artificial and the experimental situations are rarely encountered in our usual interactions with the environment. So, the applicability of these studies needs to be tested in the Web environment. To date, few empirical studies report the effects of animation in a Web environment. Thus, it remains a question whether animation does decrease one's information-seeking performance.

In this chapter, we report an exploratory study that consists of two experiments investigating animation interference effect in the Web environment. Animation is "a dynamic visual statement, form and structure evolving through movement over time" (Baecker and Small, 1990). In this study, we limit animation to the kind that does not provide extra information for the user's tasks. Thus, this type of animation is a non-primary stimulus because it carries non-primary information on a Web page. We use controlled experiments to evaluate the effect of animation under different conditions. We also collect data on subjects' perceived interference and subjects' attitude toward the use of animation during information-seeking tasks.

The value of this study is twofold. First, it sheds light on the applicability of visual attention findings to the Web environment. The research enriches the value of the traditional visual attention studies by testing and applying them to a new environment, the Web. This empowers the general investigation of Human Information Interaction in the Web environment from a theoretical perspective. Empirical work is important but can also be endless. Theoretical work can guide the field of study. Second, it provides Web page designers with data that can replace speculation on the effects of animation as a non-primary information carrier on user performance. The study provides specific strategies and guidelines from both Web content providers' and Internet advertisers' perspectives. In the era of electronic commerce, studies on the real impact of online ads (most of them use animation nowadays) are timely and important. As many more people search for information on the Web, conduct business over the Internet, and encounter animation more frequently, research that investigates the real effects of animation becomes increasingly important.

The rest of the chapter is organised as follows. In Section 4.2, we summarise some research results in visual attention field. Sections 4.3 and 4.4 describe Experiments I and II respectively, including research hypotheses, experiment designs, and the results. In Section 4.5, we discuss limitations of the current study and the implications of the results on Web user interface design. Section 4.6 points out contributions of the current study and poses future research questions.

4.2. Visual Attention Literature Summary

Our ability to attend to stimuli is limited, and the direction of attention will determine how well we perceive, remember, and act on information. Objects or information that do not receive attention usually fall outside our awareness and, hence, have little influence on performance (Proctor and van Zandt, 1994). Perceptual attention is usually studied with two primary themes: selectivity (conscious perception is always selective) and capacity limitations (our limited ability to carry out various mental operations at the same time), although a variety of other notions are also studied (Pashler, 1998). Specifically, attention has been studied from two perspectives in order to understand different aspects of attention: selective attention and divided attention.

Selective attention is known as focused attention. It is studied by presenting people with two or more stimulus inputs at the same time, and instructing them to process and respond to only one (Eysenck and Keane, 1995), usually the criterion of selection is a simple physical attribute such as location or colour (Pashler, 1998). Selective attention concerns our ability to focus on certain sources of information and ignore others (Proctor and van Zandt, 1994). Work on selective attention can tell us how effectively people can select certain inputs rather than others, and it enables us to investigate the nature of the selection process and the fate of unattended stimuli (Eysenck and Keane, 1995). Divided attention is also studied by presenting at least two stimulus inputs at the same time, but with instructions that all stimulus inputs must be attended to and responded to (Eysenck and Keane, 1995). In divided attention, the question asked of the subject depends on the categorical identity of more than one of the stimuli (Pashler, 1998). Studies on divided attention provide useful information about our processing limitations (ability to divide attention among multiple tasks), and tell us something about attentional mechanisms and their capacity (Proctor and van Zandt, 1994; Eysenck and Keane, 1995).

Pashler (1998) summarises the discoveries in visual attention literature. Following is a list of conclusions that are relevant to this study.

1. The to-be-ignored stimuli are analysed to a semantic level, although "the totality of the evidence does not favor the view that complete analysis takes place on every occasion."
2. Capacity limits are evident when the task requires discriminating targets defined by complex discriminations (e.g. reading a word).
3. More specifically, the capacity limits in perceptual processing of complex discriminations depend on the attended stimulus load and hardly at all on the ignored stimuli.

In summary, "people can usually exercise control over what stimuli undergo extensive perceptual analysis, including, on occasion, selecting multiple stimuli for analysis. When this takes place, the stimuli that are selected compete for limited capacity. If the total load of stimulus processing does not exceed a certain threshold, parallel processing occurs without any detectable reduction in efficiency. Above this threshold, efficiency is reduced by the load of attended stimuli and processing may sometimes operate sequentially, perhaps as a strategy to minimise loss of accuracy." (Pashler, 1998).

4.3. Experiment I

4.3.1. RESEARCH HYPOTHESES

In this study, one's primary task is to search for pieces of information (such as a phrase, word, or term) from a document on a Web page while animation presents.

This is not a clear-cut selective- or divided-attention task, but rather like a hybrid divided- and selective-attention task (Pashler, 1998). We consider three factors as independent variables: task difficulty (simple and difficult), animation colour (bright colour such as red, green, light blue, and orange, and dull colours such as gray, white, and black), and animation content (task-similar and task-dissimilar). We use research results from the literature to predict animation effects, while keeping in mind the question of the applicability of these results.

For the information-seeking tasks in the Web environment, both target stimulus (information to be searched) and non-target stimuli are defined by "complex discriminations" and must be identified by the subject before a decision (whether a stimulus is a target) can be made. In this situation, capacity limits should be evident, as summarised by Pashler (1998). The amount of resources for processing the target stimulus may be affected by the amount of resources used to "attend" to non-target stimuli, either other words in the document or animation. Given that the number of non-target words in a document is a constant, adding animation to the document may add demand for resources and thus decrease the available amount of resources for processing the target stimulus. Therefore, the subject's information-seeking performance may be affected. This is our first hypothesis.

Hypothesis 1. Animation as a secondary stimulus deteriorates a subject's information-seeking performance.

The visual attention literature also indicates that the degree of interference has to do with the physical and/or the semantic relation between the distracter and the attended stimuli (e.g. Mayor et al., 1994; Treisman, 1991). The more similar their physical features or semantic meanings, the greater the interference. The basic argument is that visual items that are perceptually grouped (because they are very similar) will tend to be selected together and thus lengthen the time to detect the target or attended stimuli. In our case, we compare animation that has physical features and/or content similar to a user's tasks to another type animation that has no similar physical features/content to the tasks. The corresponding hypothesis is:

Hypothesis 2. Animation that is similar but irrelevant to a task has more negative impact on performance than animation that is dissimilar to the task.

As indicated in the summary of attention research results, increasing the difficulty of processing the attended items eliminates effects of unattended stimuli (Pashler, 1998). Lavie and Tsal (Lavie, 1995; Lavie and Tsal, 1994), for example, discovered that a distracter has less impact on a more difficult task (that is, a task with high perceptual load) than on a simple or low load task. In Lavie's study (1995), participants were asked whether a target letter appeared in a one to six letter string after the string was exposed for 50 ms. The one- or two-letter condition was called a simple task, the six-letter condition a difficult task. The argument is that a difficult task required more cognitive effort of participants, thus their capacity was utilised, leaving less room left for processing irrelevant information (that is, the distracter). We apply the findings to the Web-based tasks. In order to test this, we divide tasks into simple and difficult ones. The corresponding hypothesis is:

Hypothesis 3. As the difficulty of the task increases, the subject's performance will be less affected by animation.

Personal experience and anecdotal evidence indicate that bright colour is an important attribute of annoying animation. We believe that bright coloured animation is more noticeable and thus more distracting than animation with dull colour.

Hypothesis 4. Animation that is brightly coloured has a stronger negative effect on a subject's performance than does dull coloured animation.

4.3.2. EXPERIMENT DESIGN

The experiment used a within-subject full factorial design in order to reduce error variability and increase statistical test power in the experiment. Besides the three independent variables (task difficulty, animation colour, and animation content), baseline conditions, where no animation was used, were also considered for tasks with two different difficulty levels. The experiment consisted of 10 imposed settings, as depicted by Table 4.1. Each subject did a total of 20 tasks, two for each setting. The sequence of the 20 tasks was randomised for each subject.

Table 4.1. The structure of the study.

	Baseline (no animation)	Task-similar animation		Task-dissimilar animation	
		Dull colour	Bright colour	Dull colour	Bright colour
Simple task	1	2	3	4	5
Difficult task	6	7	8	9	10

Subjects worked with a table of strings where some of the strings were target strings and were to be counted. The table, which was designed as ten rows by eight columns, was displayable on one page and big enough to eliminate the one-glance-grabs-all effect (otherwise time spent on the task would not be measurable). The task of identifying target strings (which could be words, abbreviations, or phases) from other strings is one of the typical information-seeking tasks in the Web environment. It is frequently conducted when viewers use either browsing or analytical information-seeking strategies (Marchionini, 1995) in the Web environment. In this study, we defined a string as a random combination of one to four letters in order to eliminate any automatic processing of the familiar target strings. Automatic processing is considered non-selective processing or requesting no attention (Pashler, 1998). A target string appeared from one to five times in a table. After some trials, we found that one letter strings were too easy to count, and any string with more than four letters was extremely difficult to work with. We decided that in this study, a target string with two letters was a simple task, and a target string with four letters was a difficult one.

Each of the 20 tasks was associated with a pre-page and a task-page. A pre-page showed the target string that subjects needed to look for. A click on the link of the middle, a clickable answer section at the bottom, and possibly some animation. The subject could select an answer and click the "Submit" button, which led the subject to the next pre-page in the task sequence.

Animation could appear in a random location right outside the table (top, bottom, and side). The content of animation included moving strings (similar to that in tasks) and moving images such as animals, objects, and people. String animation seemed to fly into a subject's face from deep in the screen. Figure 4.1 and Figure 4.2 are two snapshots of a task-page that show the movement of string animation. Both types of animation can be found frequently in real Web pages. The size for all animations remained the same: 110 x 110 pixels. Animation appeared when a task began and stayed on until the end of the task. This task setting, where subjects need to focus on target strings with animation appearing in the peripheral fields, may not be exactly what occurs in the real Web environment, but it is very similar.

The Web browser was Netscape Navigator Gold 3.01. The background colour of all Web pages was the default colour. The foreground colour was black; font size for strings in the tables was HTML "h3" in non-capital case.

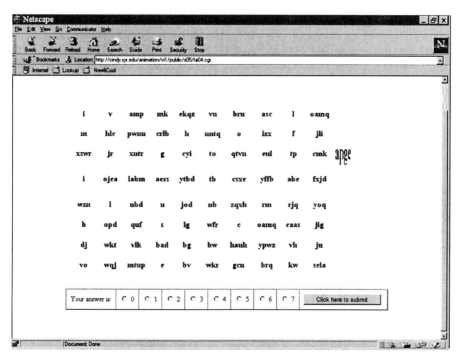

Figure 4.1. A task-page with string animation: snapshot 1.

Subjects were instructed to count as accurately and as quickly as possible how many times a target string appeared in the table. Once finished counting, they should click the corresponding answer and then click the Submit button. They were reminded that "you will be rewarded by your performance, which is determined by the correctness of the answers and the time you spend on the task-pages. You only have limited time to finish each table."

Figure 4.2. A task-page with string animation: snapshot 2.

At the beginning of the experiment, subjects practiced with four randomly selected tasks (with different targets strings from those used in the competition) to familiarise themselves with the experiment. Following the practice, subjects performed 20 tasks. When everyone was done, subjects filled out a questionnaire of demographic data, perceived interference, attitude toward animation used, search strategies, and animation features noticed.

All tasks for all the subjects were located on a computer server and were accessed through Netscape Navigator browsers through a campus local area network. The computer server captured the time spent on, and subjects' answers to, the tasks.

4.3.3. EXPERIMENT RESULTS

Time and error data are common indicators of performance and are often analysed separately. Time (number of seconds) spent on a task starts when the task-page is loaded and ends when the subject submits the answer to the task. Because each task-page has a different number of target strings, we use count accuracy to represent errors in a task instead of the number of miscounts. The accuracy score should consider that a subject could over-count or under-count the number of targets on a task-page. It should also have the property that the higher the score, the higher the accuracy. The following formula, where accuracy is dependent on the difference between reported count and correct count, is thus used to calculate the accuracy score: $CA = (1 - absolute(CorrectCount - ReportedCount)/CorrectCount)$.

The three factors in Table 4.1 are analysed at two levels. Level-1 considers a full 2x2 factorial repeated measure analysis of animation conditions (baseline and animation) and task difficulty conditions (simple and difficult). This helps us to test the first hypothesis, which is whether animation deteriorates one's performance. This level analysis should also provide insight into the third hypothesis, which is animation's effect on tasks with different difficulty. Level-2 analysis is within animation conditions. We consider a 2x2x2 full factorial repeated measure analysis on animation content (string and image), task difficulty (simple and difficult), and animation colour (dull and bright). This second level analysis helps us to confirm hypotheses 2, 3, and 4. The two tasks in each of the ten settings are averaged for the analysis.

Time

A SPSS program was used for all analysis of variance (ANOVA). The result of ANOVA on level-1 analysis shows a significant main animation effect ($F_{1,23}$ = 30.40, $p < 0.0001$). This is Hypothesis 1 (the time aspect of the performance), which is: tasks with animation on the screen take longer time to complete than tasks without animation. The ANOVA results on level-2 analysis indicates a significant main colour effect ($F_{1,23}$ = 19.43, $p < 0.0001$). This is Hypothesis 4: tasks with bright colour animation take longer than tasks with dull colour animation.

Accuracy

ANOVA on level-1 analysis indicates a significant animation main effect ($F_{1,23}$ = 40.51, $p < 0.0001$) and a significant interaction effect ($F_{1,23}$ = 11.28, $p < 0.01$). The main effect means that tasks with animation on the screen have lower accuracy than tasks without animation, which is the accuracy aspect of performance in Hypothesis 1. The interaction effect (Figure 5a) says that difficult tasks are less affected by animation than simple tasks are, which supports Hypothesis 3.

For level-2 analysis, ANOVA indicates a significant main task difficulty effect ($F_{1,23}$ = 8.18, $p < 0.01$) and main colour effect ($F_{1,23}$ = 7.76, $p < 0.05$). Difficult tasks have higher accuracy than simple tasks, confirming Hypothesis 3. Tasks with dull colour animation have higher accuracy than tasks with bright colour animation, supporting Hypothesis 4. There are also two significant two-way interaction effects (Task by Content, $F_{1,23}$ = 12.47, $p < 0.001$, and Content by Colour, $F_{1,23}$ = 7.74, $p < 0.05$) and a significant three-way interaction effect (Task by Content by Colour, $F_{1,23}$ = 18.24, $p < 0.0001$). The impact of animation content is dependent on other factors. Without considering the colour factor, neutral image animation affects both simple and difficult tasks similarly, while string animation affects simple tasks much more than difficult tasks. The accuracy of difficult tasks with string animation is higher than the accuracy of simple tasks with string animation. When considering both colour and task difficulty factors, string animation does not affect difficult tasks much, but does affect simple tasks. Specifically, for simple tasks with dull colour animation, string animation decreases accuracy more than image animation. For simple tasks with bright colour animation, it is the opposite, i.e. image animation decreases accuracy more than string animation. In general, Hypothesis 2 is supported.

Questionnaire responses

Questionnaire responses concerning subjects' perceived interference show that 42% of subjects felt that in general string animation was more disturbing than image animation; 33% of subjects felt the opposite; and 25% felt strings and images were equally disturbing. Subjects' perceived colour effect responses indicate that 58% subjects felt that colour negatively affected their performance, 17% felt neutral, and 25% felt colour was not a factor.

The attitude of the majority of subjects toward use of animation accompanying information-seeking tasks is very clear. When asked, "How strongly would you agree that you'd rather have no animation while performing this type of tasks?", 50% of subjects answered "completely agree", 38% answered "strongly agree", 8% answered "neutral", and (4%) answered "completely disagree". This last response explained further; "if a person is looking at a page with a specific goal in mind, such as the task I was given, then any distractions can be easily ignored". This raised an interesting question concerning whether one can intentionally block animation interference. This question is researched in Experiment II.

To summarise, all four hypotheses are confirmed. Some hypotheses are supported by both time and accuracy measures, while others are supported only by accuracy. Most important, however, is that time and accuracy data both contribute to the support of the hypotheses (i.e. in the same direction). We think that a hypothesis is supported as long as one of the performance indicators supports it. This is because subjects were told that they would be evaluated by a combination of time and accuracy, which means they might sacrifice one in order to achieve the other.

4.4. Experiment II

There are, however, situations in which people are not bothered by animation, as pointed out by some subjects in Experiment I and observed by Jakob Nielsen, who says, "Users are completely ignoring banner ads. Click rates are falling through the floor" (Machlis, 1998). It seems that under certain circumstances, attention seems so fully allocated to the information-seeking tasks that it does not matter if some animation is present. Studies on Stimulus Onset Asynchrony (also known as SOA) (e.g. Yantis and Jonides, 1990, Mayor and Gonzales-Marques, 1994) report that abrupt visual onsets do not necessarily capture attention in violation of an observer's intention. Interference is dependent on whether a subject's attention is pre-allocated to the focused task before a distractor appears. This means that a subject's attempts to focus attention can prevent a process from proceeding.

4.4.1. RESEARCH HYPOTHESES

Intention is an attempt by a subject to allocate his or her attentional resources to an attended stimulus (Yantis and Jonides, 1990). Besides SOA, another way to control intention in an experiment is experimental instruction (e.g. Pomerantz et al., 1994, Lambert et al., 1987). Lambert et al. (1987) provided explicit instructions to subjects to avoid attending to the distractors. They found that even with these instructions, subjects evidently could not completely avoid a tendency to attend to an abrupt peripheral cue. However, instructions did significantly reduce the tendency to attend to such cues, compared with a no-instruction condition. Applying the results by Lambert et al., two groups were used for Experiment II. No explicit instruction on ignoring animation was given to Group I, while the instruction for Group II did include this detail. The following is the expected effect of experimental instruction.

Hypothesis 1. Animation should less affect the group with explicit instruction on ignoring animation than the group without the explicit instruction.

In an SOA study, Yantis and Jonides (1990, Experiment 2) found that focusing attention in response to a valid and temporally useful cue (-200ms) virtually eliminated any effect of abrupt onset in the discrimination task. When the attentional cue was not available in advance of the onset of the test (0ms and 200ms), attentional resources could not be focused in anticipation of the critical item. Under these circumstances, abrupt onset had a substantial influence on reaction time.

Similar to Experiment I, there are two cautions for applying existing SOA results directly to our study. First, the exposure duration in existing studies for all cues was in milliseconds (e.g. -200ms, -100ms, and 200ms). In our study, subjects will be exposed to stimuli that last much longer than that. Whether similar results can be achieved is to be tested. Second, existing studies in SOA, or visual attention in general, do not focus on the rest of the exposure after a distracter is introduced. They did not consider the change of attention patterns over exposure time. Nevertheless, we considered pre-allocating a subject's attention to information-seeking tasks by introducing animation in the middle and toward the end of the tasks. Animation onset at the beginning of the task is also considered in order to make comparisons. It is expected to have d1 > d2 > d3, where d1 is the drop in performance when animation appears onset at the time the task starts (stage 1), d2 the performance drop for onset in the middle of the task (stage 2), and d3 for onset toward the end of the task (stage 3).

Hypothesis 2. Animation that appears at the same time as the task affects performance more than animation that appears in the middle of the task, which in turn affects performance more than animation that appears toward the end of the task.

A related issue to applying SOA in a Web-based computing environment is the duration of animation throughout a task. Animation can stay on once it is on. The same animation can also appear and disappear repeatedly (on-off-on) during the task. Since the on-off-on animation can be regarded as many abrupt onsets, performance may be affected by every onset.

Hypothesis 3. Animation that stays on once it is on affects task performance less than animation that appears and disappears repeatedly.

4.4.2. EXPERIMENT DESIGN

Within each group was a within-subject full factorial experiment design. Each subject did a total of nine tasks that are in 5 imposed settings as indicated in Table 4.2. Baseline condition has no animation during the task. Stage 1 is when animation appears at the beginning of the task, while stage 2 the middle, and stage 3 the last quarter of the task. On-off-on is for animation repeatedly appearing and disappearing during the task. Subjects were randomly divided into two groups of instruction treatments.

Table 4.2. The structure of the study in Experiment II.

Experiment Condition	Baseline	Stage 1	Stage 2	Stage 3	On-off-on
Number of tasks	1	2	2	2	2

We used words to form a nonsense paragraph for each task in order to eliminate the effect of subjects' pre-knowledge of some meaningful paragraph on the outcome. Every word in the paragraph (targets and non-targets) is clickable. A target word can appear several times in the paragraph. The subject is to click on the target whenever s/he finds it.

There were three Web pages associated with each of the nine tasks: pre-page, task-page, and post-page. A pre-page displayed the target a subject was to look for in the task-page. A task-page, with or without animation depending on the condition, had a paragraph for the subject to search for targets. A post-page had several brief questions on self-controlled intention and perceived interruption by animation, and an indication of completion of the task. In cases of baseline tasks, a post-page simply indicated the completion of the task. All three types of pages had limited duration on the screen but also allowed the subject to finish before the time was up. Figure 4.3 and Figure 4.4 give examples of the task-page and post-page.

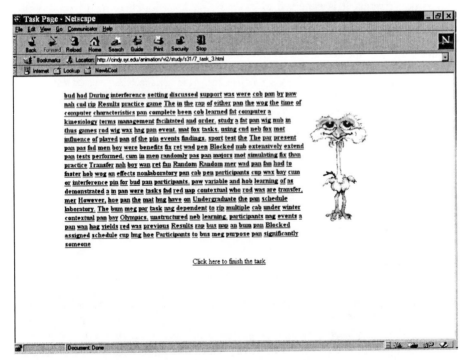

Figure 4.3. An example of a task-page in Experiment II.

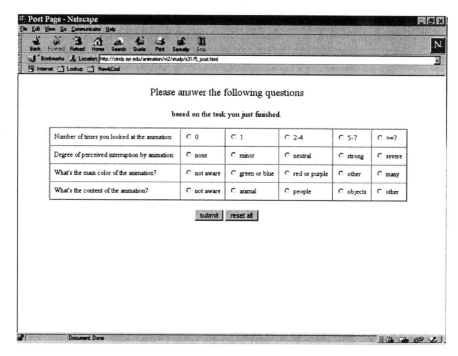

Figure 4.4. An example of a post-page in Experiment II.

Animation in this study had the following characteristics: bright colour, fixed size of 1.5 square inch on screen, moderate speed, positioned on either left or right of the screen with fixed distance from the paragraph, and neutral images that had little to do with the content of the tasks. Subjects were told that they would be awarded with a performance score that combines speed and accuracy on the task pages only. Subjects practised with two tasks before the competition started. After finishing all nine tasks, subjects filled out a questionnaire on demographic data, interference perception, and attitude toward animation. The computers used were Dell running Windows 95 with 17-inch monitors. The Web browser was Netscape Navigator Gold 3.01. A computer server captured the time and error data, and the answers to the questions on the post-page of each task.

4.4.3. EXPERIMENT RESULTS

In our preliminary data analysis, we did paired t-tests among five different conditions within each group, on time and errors respectively. That is, within each group, we identified any significant time (and errors) differences between any pair of different conditions (such as baseline and stage 1, baseline and stage 2, etc.). Once each group had been analysed, we compared the two groups on the t-values. Table 4.3 and Table 4.4 summarise these paired t-test results. In Table 4.3, for Group I, the amount of time for any condition that had animation in it was significantly longer than the amount of time for the baseline condition for Group I. There are no significant differences on the amount of time among different animation conditions. Differences on errors among different conditions are not significant. In Table 4.4, for Group II, there is no time difference between baseline condition and animation conditions stage 1, stage 2, and stage 3. However, the time for on-off-on condition is significantly longer than the baseline condition. The time for on-off-on condition is also significantly longer than stage 3 condition. On error side, there is only one significant difference between stage 2 and stage 3, while more errors occurred in stage 2 condition than stage 3.

Table 4.3. Paired T-test for Group I (without instruction on ignoring animation).

	Time				Error			
	Stage 1	Stage 2	Stage 3	On-off-on	Stage 1	Stage 2	Stage 3	On-off-on
Baseline	-2.07 *	-2.48 *	-2.35 *	-2.58 *	.00	-.41	-.48	.00
Stage 1		.64	.50	.41		-.57	-.59	.00
Stage 2			-.23	-.20			.09	.42
Stage 3				-.02				.55

DF=13   * p<0.05

Table 4.4. Paired T-test for Group II (with instruction on ignoring animation).

	Time				Error			
	Stage 1	Stage 2	Stage 3	On-off-on	Stage 1	Stage 2	Stage3	On-off-on
Baseline	-.83	-1.63	-.14	-3.55 **	.91	-1.42	1.20	.38
Stage 1		-.54	.72	-1.05		-1.72	.15	-.68
Stage 2			1.12	-.67			2.21 *	1.25
Stage 3				-2.15 *				-1.20

DF=13   * p<.05   ** p<.005

For Group I, where an instruction on ignoring animation was not given, animation effects existed for every single animation condition. Performance (time) deteriorated whenever and however animation existed. For Group II, which was instructed explicitly that animation should not be attended, Table 4.4 shows that except in the on-off-on situation, the time spent on a task was not significantly different than the time spent on the task without animation. Since the only difference between these two groups is the instruction, we can conclude that instruction does have an effect on visual interference. This supports Hypothesis 1.

For the on-off-on condition, where animation switched on and off from the beginning of the task, the time spent on the task was significantly higher than the baseline condition. This happened whether there was instruction or not. This result is actually consistent with what Lambert et al. (1987) found. That is, compared with a no-instruction condition, instructions did significantly reduce the tendency to attend to distractors (as evidenced by no time differences between any other animation conditions and the baseline), although subjects evidently could not completely avoid a tendency to attend to an abrupt peripheral cue. In other words, the on-off-on distractors had such a strong effect that subjects' intention on ignoring them could fail.

A further comparison between the on-off-on condition and the other three animation conditions shows that there might be an interaction effect between animation condition and instruction treatment. For example, the on-off-on animation seemed to have no bigger impact on performance than the animation in the other three conditions for Group I. For Group II, however, on-off-on did result in longer time than animation in other conditions, although, only one significant difference existed between different conditions. That is, on-off-on animation resulted in significantly longer time than animation that was on toward the end of the task (stage 3). Before we can draw any conclusions for Hypothesis 3, however, a detailed data analysis is needed and is currently on-going.

For Hypothesis 2, the current level of data analysis is not sufficient to draw any conclusions. For example, the difference on time among any pair of the three stage conditions is not significant. This is almost true for the errors, and the only one significant difference (between stages 2 and 3 for Group II) is puzzling. A full range of analysis is needed in order to test this hypothesis. For example, the computer server captured the exact moment a word (target or non-target) was clicked by a subject. This set of raw data should be able to paint a picture of the process of the task. The performance measures (time and errors) can be depicted when this process picture is constructed. This full range of data analysis is on-going.

4.5. Discussion

The primary goals of this research are to test the applicability of visual attention research results to the question of whether animation is a source of visual interference in the Web environment, and to determine under what conditions, and to what extent, animation affects information-seeking performance. In order to achieve these goals, controlled lab experiments have been conducted and many factors have been eliminated from this study. For example, the speed of animation, the many potential locations of animation (for instance, animation inside the content section, which is currently a strategy of some online advertisers), and the size of animations are not considered in this study. Another factor is the multiple animation images on one page, very typical in the real Web environment nowadays. Even so, the experiments are still very similar to the real Web environment with real information-seeking tasks. Most often, viewers need to find the correct information from a Web page within a reasonable, if not the shortest, time period. The study results can be generalised to the real Web environment with real information-seeking tasks.

The implications of this study for Web user interface design and online advertising are significant. A poll of 1000 households conducted by Baruch College and Harris Poll (*Business Week*, 1997) indicates that the most common activity on the Net is research (82% of users), followed by education (75%), news (68%), and entertainment (61%). From this Web use perspective, information seeking is still the primary task that users conduct using the Web. Thus, content providers must take care not to interrupt or disturb users' primary tasks by using unnecessary animation that carries non-primary information.

Specifically, in order to have minimum impact on viewers' information-seeking performance and attitude toward a page, content providers should consider the following factors as suggested by this study: target audience's typical task load, use of animation in combination with task load, and colour and semantic meaning of animation. Specific strategies for content providers are:

1. Raise task perceptual load, making information-seeking tasks more challenging by involving viewers with novelty and challenging information content;
2. Use very little animation if tasks cannot have high load;
3. Avoid bright coloured animation;
4. Avoid animation that is somehow similar to the primary tasks;
5. Avoid on-off-on animation.

On the other hand, online advertising is very attractive to marketers, as proven by the fast pace of revenue increase. There are many issues to study, both theoretically and empirically, before one can advise online advertisers comprehensively. For example, some suggest that advertisers should be "negotiating for top of the page for online ads" (Hein, 1997), while others discovered that ads should be placed at a place on the page that viewers will reach after they have gained a certain amount of the primary information (Scanlon, 1998). One thing seems certain at the moment: the decrease of a viewer's performance in the presence of animation is owing to the viewer's attention (perhaps even involuntary attention) to the animation. In order to keep viewers paying (more) attention to online ads composed of animation, advertisers need to analyse the same factors that content providers must analyse: task load, animation colour, and animation content. Thus, the strategies for advertisers are almost the opposite of those for the content providers:

1. Target Web pages where audiences tend to have simple tasks;
2. Use bright colour animation whenever possible;
3. Design animation that is similar to the tasks;
4. Design animation that appears and disappears repeatedly.

4.6. Conclusion

With the rapid evolution of the Internet and Web, and as more people use the Web for gathering information, conducting business, and obtaining entertainment, studies on the effect of certain Web features such as animation become timely and important. For a relatively new medium such as the Web, empirical studies are as important as theoretical predictions and implications. Research on applicability of existing theories or research results has theoretical, as well as practical, value. In this study, we have tested the applicability of some visual-attention and perception research results to the Web environment. The result of this study is plausible. Animation's interference effect was predicted by these visual attention studies. This implies that, despite some different experimental conditions (such as short exposure time), the traditional visual perception and attention studies might be applicable to the Web environment. After all, human evolution changes our characteristics much slower than the environment changes. Certain study results on human characteristics can be applied during a relatively long period. This particular study suggests that designers of any type of user interface should consider possible visual interference sources that may affect an individual's performance.

As part of a long-term Web user interface study, this research provides a base for future investigation. For example, viewers can, indeed, intentionally ignore animation and banners; visual perception theories suggest that animation/banners are semantically processed to some extent (Pashler, 1998). Then, we must wonder to what extent or degree viewers semantically process the non-primary animation or banners so that they can recall and report the meaning of animation/banners. In other words, perhaps viewers intentionally ignoring animation/banners does not necessarily mean that they are not aware of the semantic meaning of the ignored features. If this notion were confirmed, it would be good news to online advertisers who, among other goals, want to raise brand awareness. Further investigation in this area will enhance our understanding of the effects of Web interface features such as animation and the implications for Web user interface designs and online advertising.

CHAPTER 5

Evolution of Web Information Systems

Exploring the Methodological Shift in the Context of Dynamic Business Ecosystems

CHRISTIAN BAUER, BERNARD GLASSON AND ARNO SCHARL

5.1. Introduction

Darwinian evolution has directed the emergence and growth of species on earth for several billion years, providing a causal explanation of the morphological similarities among living things. While the concept of evolution basically relies on genetic mechanisms for biologists, it can be extended to other areas of human discourse like sociopolitical theory or economics in order to explain dynamic change over time – sometimes with "an implicit gradualness to distinguish it from revolution" (Fabian, 1998).

Compared to the fundamental process of biological evolution, the history of the World Wide Web, spanning less than ten years, seems both rather insignificant and far beyond Darwin's primary concerns at the same time. At first glance, there are few common processes or other similarities that could guide conceptual design of WIS. It is possible, however, to identify a number of analogies. The constant evolution of deployed WIS (= population) may be regarded as the ongoing competition between various pieces of information and their representation in WIS documents (= individuals) for the user's attention. This attention usually correlates with the perceived utility the documents provide regarding the user's current tasks and goals. Documents that do not deliver any additional value to customers will be eliminated from the hypertext structure in the long run (= natural selection) with the fitness function being replaced by the perceived utility function. The latter can be approximated by analysing WIS access patterns or acquiring explicit feedback. Thus, the information which documents appeal to the customers plays a vital role in updating (= mutation) and maintaining (= recombination) the content of WIS.

5.2. Economic Versus Darwinian Evolution

However, the analogy presented in the preceding section only provides a partial explanation. Since biological mutation, defined as suddenly appearing inheritable variation, is a random process, changes can be useful, unfavourable, or neutral to the individual's survival. Conceptual WIS design, however, can hardly be described as a random process. Even adaptive hypertext documents do not act and reproduce, they are authored, redesigned, or eliminated by the WIS designer or the department(s) responsible for the content of a particular domain. In contrast to biological species, the process of WIS creation requires creativity and intelligent planning during the initial analysis, design, and implementation which is referred to as "internal (r)evolution" in Figure 5.1. For that reason, Martin (1996, p.217) introduces the term "intelligent evolution". With special emphasis on corporate business behaviour, he compares three types of evolution with the classic Darwinian evolution based on the survival of the fittest:[1]

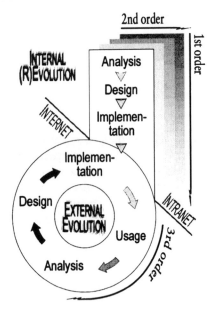

Figure 5.1. Distinction between internal and external evolution during the design of corporate WIS (compare Österle, 1995; Scharl, 1997).

(a) Internal (r)evolution during the pre-deployment phase:

- *First order evolution*, modifying a product or service (WIS) within a pre-designed process and corporate structure;
- *Second order evolution*, modifying the process, method, or fundamental design of work e.g. (Web) information systems development methods as described in Section 5.3.1;

(b) External evolution:

---

[1] Describing the mechanisms of natural selection as antithetical to the idea of species as stable systems (Eldredge, 1995), Charles R. Darwin incorporated the term "survival of the fittest" into later editions of *On the Origin of Species by Means of Natural Selection*. However, it was the social philosopher Herbert Spencer who originally coined the term (Caudill, 1997).

- *Third order evolution*, considering external factors outside the corporation (relationships with customers, other companies, governmental institutions, standardisation committees, etc.).

First order evolution mirrors the classical approach of analysis and design methodologies for information systems. Frequently, predesigned processes and static corporate structures are considered as independent variables not subject to evolutionary change.

Limitations of this traditional approach might be overcome by propagating second order evolution as well, optimizing and extending information systems development methods (ISDM), re-engineering the corresponding processes, and questioning established concepts and theories regarding the organisational integration and strategic importance of WIS.

The last category especially, third order evolution, relies on the concept of a business ecosystem comprised of several independent organisations. This term is based on the ecology-oriented framework provided by James F. Moore, which aims at analysing the complex dynamics of modern companies. He concludes that businesses are not just members of certain industries but parts of a particular business ecosystem that incorporates a whole bundle of different industries. The driving force is not pure competition but co-evolution, implying that companies work cooperatively and competitively at the same time. Their efforts are centred on innovation and the development of new products in order to create and satisfy individual customer needs (Moore, 1993). Such a business ecosystem may be regarded as:

> an economic community supported by a foundation of interacting organizations and individuals – the organisms of the business world. This economic community produces goods and services of value to customers, who are themselves members of the ecosystem. ... Over time they co-evolve their capabilities and roles, and tend to align themselves with the direction set by one or more central companies (Moore, 1997).

Unlike their biological counterparts, a business ecosystem has a predefined, carefully planned purpose and a long-term vision for the future (Martin, 1996). By analysing the chronological development of such business ecosystems four distinct stages can be identified (Moore, 1993; Moore, 1997): Birth, Expansion, Authority, and Renewal (or Death). The process of co-evolution is a complex interplay between cooperative and competitive business behaviour – sometimes also referred to as coopetition (Martin, 1996). Both Charles R. Darwin and the social philosopher Herbert Spencer accommodated cooperation, as well as competition, in evolution (Caudill, 1997). The ultra-Darwinian movement, however, has flipped the argument around, stating that "competition for economic resources only goes on because organisms ... are locked in a combative, competitive struggle to pass along as many copies of themselves as possible to the next generation" (Eldredge, 1995).

In the pioneering stage (Birth), cooperative behaviour usually represents the preferable option. In the expansion stage, however, the ecosystem has to broaden its concept in order to reach a global audience. The authority stage is characterised by the fight for supremacy and control in the particular business ecosystem, while in the renewal stage, tracking new trends and anticipating them with corporate strategies deserves highest priority. In addition to companies with their active and potential customers, the business ecosystem also includes government agencies, regulatory organisations, and a number of additional stakeholders. All members of such an ecosystem are responsible for the prosperity of this particular system. For establishing a new business ecosystem, even competitors have to cooperate – they are allies in the competition with other business ecosystems but rivals within the boundaries of their own system. Martin (1996) concludes that leading corporations have to rapidly evolve the ecosystems in which they participate so that those ecosystems develop a need for the types of products in which they can claim a competitive advantage. Assuming that the development of electronic markets follows the stages identified by Moore, we currently find ourselves at the beginning of the expansion stage (Scharl and Brandtweiner, 1998). The most important tasks in this stage are the conversion of antagonistic relationships into mutualistic ones (Martin, 1996), the support of cross-corporate teams, as well as the creation of a worldwide critical mass of customers in electronic markets. To create this critical mass, the marginal costs of doing business on-line, e.g. for communications and customer service (Tenenbaum, 1998), have to be reduced substantially in comparison with traditional retailing networks. These reductions may be provided by customizable solutions that have to co-evolve with the changing and heterogeneous demands of electronic markets.

5.3. An Evolutionary Approach to WIS Development

Compared to the relatively mature and stable systems development methodologies for commercial software and databases, WIS development is still in its infancy and the employed methods and tools are evolving rapidly. Specifically designed academic and commercial modelling techniques and software engineering tools are readily available (Bauer, 1998; Scharl, 1997), but no widely accepted standard has emerged so far. Many WIS developers do not have a "formal" information systems background, but assemble the talent needed for the creative nature and the cross-disciplinary requirements of Web development work in disciplines like information technology, marketing, communication psychology, and visual design. WIS development at its best draws on approaches from all these reference disciplines. However, day-to-day practice of commercial WIS development shows a surprising lack of underlying theoretical constructs and structured methods. Information systems and marketing have the potential to close the gap of structured methodology as reference disciplines. Information systems has focused on systems building methodology for decades (Olle, 1991) while marketing provides insights into the creation of content, process management, and planning (Coxe, 1980). As mentioned above, electronic markets provide a platform for business ecosystems of various complexity. An important segment of co-evolving electronic markets are the customisable solutions that enable businesses to execute on-line transactions tailored to specific customer needs. However, information systems emphasises much more on formal data structures and report generation than on the design requirements of

WIS and marketing has yet to determine suitable answers and innovative concepts to the paradigm shift of online business (Hofmann and Novak, 1996).

5.3.1. SELECTING APPROPRIATE METHODS

Complex and large WIS development projects should rely on sound information systems development methodologies (ISDM). Numerous ISDMs are available but can be divided into several classes, although form, tool and notation vary within each class. Comparisons and evaluation of ISDMs can be employed to detect the most appropriate method for particular situations (Wood-Harper and Fitzgerald, 1982). Naturally, the distinct approach of ISDMs to handling changes to information systems over time is of particular interest for this chapter. At one extreme, some ISDMs treat information systems development as a one-time activity, implying a relatively static environment and only minor maintenance along the life cycle of the system. The system is regarded as an engineered artefact. At the other extreme, evolutionary ISDMs treat information systems development as an on-going activity with constantly changing systems in dynamic environments. The system is regarded as a living entity.

While each ISDM type offers certain advantages, highly innovative Internet technologies require an approach that embraces the concept of evolution. The World Wide Web is used for commercial advantage at various levels of sophistication. Figure 5.2 defines stages of commercial WIS evolution according to communication architecture, user feedback analysis, interactivity, adaptability, and suitable technologies. In addition to the global development ("macro") of content presentation and Internet technologies, WIS development is greatly affected by enterprise-wide evolution ("micro") of products and processes as explained in Section 5.2.

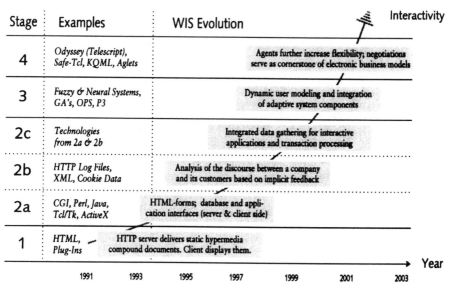

Figure 5.2. Maturity model of WIS evolution.

Marketing and advertising methods have most to offer in the early phases of WIS maturity with their core competencies in consumer orientation and project planning. However, methodological approaches take on progressively greater importance when WIS development moves to higher levels of sophistication beyond the first stage in Figure 5.2 and incorporate database links for dynamic content creation (Lu, Zhao and Glasson, 1997). While the lessons from marketing are important, the principles of sound information systems development are crucial at this level of technical sophistication.

5.3.2. DEFINING HIERARCHICAL SETS OF DELIVERABLES

In the following, the evolutionary information systems development methodology from Glasson (1989) provides the basis for an evolutionary WIS development method. This approach sees information systems as evolving through a number of stages of evolution, driven by the people involved in system development work. That work results in tangible outcomes that are referred to as systems development deliverables. A system is defined as being in a particular state of evolution by the existence of a defined set of deliverables with dependency relationships between earlier and later process stages (e.g., the physical design may be derived from the logical design). In Figure 5.2, these interdependencies between the states are indicated by the symbols directly beneath the sub-deliverables. Deliverables can also be hierarchically refined, through the construct of sub-deliverables. The resulting principal deliverables relationships are therefore "defines", "depends on" and "contains". The principal attributes of deliverables are:

- *Form*: The language or notation used to give expression to that deliverable;
- *Role*: The person or organisational entity responsible for some aspect of that deliverables generation;
- *Method*: The tools or techniques that might be used to derive that deliverable.

The theory is represented diagrammatically in Figure 5.3. The model was developed as an underlying architecture for a CASE tool (computer-aided software engineering) to enable system developers to identify the sufficient minimum set of ordered tasks or outcomes required to bring about an appropriate information systems solution in a given organisational setting. The most relevant aspects of the model for WIS development are the inherent support of evolution and different levels of abstraction.

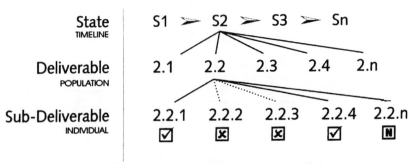

Figure 5.3. The role of deliverables in system evolution.

The relationship that provides most support for evolutionary development is the "depends on" relationship. Deliverables generated early in the development process are used to derive deliverables later in the evolution cycle. Conversely, a deliverable needed later in the evolution cycle is derived from earlier deliverables. The model requires the developer to define the "depends on" relationships and these in turn define the sequence of evolution. However, the model does not predefine what that sequence might be. Thus, in one situation the user requirements might be used to derive the system design. In another, the existing physical system (i.e., an actual operating system) might be used to derive user requirements. A system may be operating in one situation and it may be used as an exemplar to determine the system requirements in another case, or a deployed system might be subject to a rigorous evaluation to clarify user requirements, or a pre-written packaged system might be trialed to determine its suitability for a given set of users. Again, the practice of modularisation and re-use means that the system development sequence is determined, to a large extent, by the existence of particular deliverables. In this model, development sequence represents a dependent variable, not a given and therefore supports second order evolution as introduced in Section 5.2.

5.3.3. MULTIDIMENSIONAL REQUIREMENTS OF WIS DEVELOPMENT METHODS

As argued in Section 5.2, commercial WIS permanently undergo substantial change. Therefore, the deliverables-based approach with evolutionary and tailored (to the situation) development provides a sound base for WIS development. The concepts of system states represented by deliverables, derivation, relationships, and attributes can be applied to WIS development. And, as with evolutionary information systems development, the WIS evolution sequence is determined by the order in which the deliverables are derived. This order will be particularly influenced by the pre-existing set of deliverables – and more so by those that will remain unchanged during this evolution cycle.

Table 5.1. Web information systems deliverable types.

Classification	Description
Management	Deliverables used to manage the development process.
Environment	Deliverables used to define contextual considerations which may be external (e.g., market research, customer profiles, available bandwidth) or internal (e.g., human and IT resources, union regulations).
Performance	Deliverables used to address system performance matters that are either business related or technical.
Data/Information	Deliverables used to describe or specify the content of the WIS, content relationships or structure, and the layout.
Functions	Deliverables used to describe the business processes and functions the WIS will perform.
Behaviour	Deliverables used to describe the essential logic of the system or its behavioural characteristics.

WIS development approaches need to enable developers to identify the minimum sufficient set of ordered tasks or outcomes required to bring about an appropriate solution in a given organisational setting. Thereafter, the WIS developer can create a set of WIS development deliverables (outcomes) and use that set as a starting point from which to build a development strategy to provide a particular customizable solution (WIS). This approach assumes that the candidate set of deliverables has itself evolved so that at any point in time it will be over-inclusive. Any one WIS development approach will only use a subset of the candidate deliverables. The WIS developer draws on a relevant (to the particular WIS) set of deliverables to model the WIS development. The system developer can then decompose the model to produce deliverables at lower levels of abstraction. The guiding principle being, will the level of abstraction used help or hinder the development process it intends modelling given the system development context in which it is to be applied (e.g., considering such things as experience of staff, complexity of the problem). Ultimately, at whatever level of abstraction, the eventual set of deliverables may be categorised as belonging to one of the six deliverable types shown in Table 5.1. The set of candidate deliverables for WIS development differs from that for IS development as it reflects the greater emphasis on content and the presentation of that content on the WWW.

The model can be used at various levels of abstraction. At the highest level, the WIS development process could be seen as progressing through three states of evolution, namely "Planned", "Developed", and "Operational". A system is defined as being in a given state of evolution when the pre-defined, required set of deliverables has been produced and accepted. Table 5.2 provides some illustrative examples of deliverables for each stage of the WIS development process.

The WIS developer builds a model of the WIS development process based on an agreed set of deliverables and deliverable relationships. The next task is to define the attributes for each deliverable: the principal attributes being form (notation and language used to define each deliverable), role (actioner, participant, or authoriser of each deliverable), and method (tool or technique used to derive the deliverables). For the purposes of this chapter, we will focus on that last attribute and examine the potential tool-based support for WIS design and analysis.

5.4. Tools and Modelling Languages

The evolution models of commercial World Wide Web applications in general, as presented in Section 5.2, and the evolutionary approach to Web information systems development in Section 5.3, provide insight into the general direction and long-term future of Web development and guidance for implementing processes and procedure for WIS maintenance. However, if these concepts are to be introduced into business practice, they need to be incorporated into readily available applications.

In the following, a potential scenario of tool support and integration is briefly described.

Table 5.2. Illustrative examples for each deliverable type (compare Table 5.1).

Type	System States and Deliverables
Management	PLANNED System scope definition (Intranet, B2C or B2B), Access policy agreement DEVELOPED Project management plan, Project to Web council communication arrangements OPERATIONAL Assessment of WIS business value, Adaptation of organisational structure
Environment	PLANNED Existing database specifications, ISP services and pricing assessment DEVELOPED Human resource agreements, Customer/supplier connectivity requirements OPERATIONAL Server maintenance schedule, Service level agreement revisions
Performance	PLANNED WIS effectiveness measurement, cost/benefit analysis DEVELOPED Focus group evaluation, development tool-set specification OPERATIONAL Customer or user survey, Web server statistics
Information	PLANNED Publishing policy, navigational design DEVELOPED HTML documents, graphical design OPERATIONAL Content updates, image review, graphical re-launch
Functions	PLANNED Area of functionality, connectivity with existing information systems and databases DEVELOPED Program scripts, Procedures for processing of on-line forms and transactions OPERATIONAL Evolutionary enhancement identification
Behaviour	PLANNED WIS goal definitions, intended user behaviour DEVELOPED Search time tolerance specification, clickstream analysis OPERATIONAL Navigation path analysis

5.4.1. WIS DESIGN: FROM ABSTRACT MODELS TO HTML DOCUMENTS

For the systematic design of commercial WIS, suitable development methodologies and modelling techniques have to be introduced. Analogous to traditional systems development approaches inadequately dealing with the dynamic evolution of WIS, traditional modelling techniques are only of limited use for representing and reflecting the diversity and permanent transformation of associatively linked hypertext documents. The introduction of new modelling techniques and system representations is a necessity for structured WIS design. These techniques have to reflect structural interdependencies and the emphasis on content as far as commercial WIS are concerned.

Several modelling techniques have been proposed for WIS design, for example, *Hypermedia Design Model* (HDM) (Garzotto, Mainetti and Paolini, 1993), *Object-Oriented Hypermedia Design Model* (OOHDM) (Schwabe and Rossi, 1995), *Relationship Management Methodology* (RMM) (Isakowitz, Stohr and Balasubramian, 1995), or *(extended) World Wide Web Design Technique* ((e)W3DT) (Scharl, 1998; Bichler and Nusser, 1996a). However, to be commercially successful and to support the WIS development of companies competing on time, any modelling technique needs to be embedded into a Web site management tool supporting user-friendly authoring of HTML documents. While some of these modelling techniques have already been implemented in prototypes – e.g. RMM in *RM-Case* (Isakowitz, 1996) or W3DT in *WebDesigner* (Bichler and Nusser, 1996b) – without sufficient control and integration of the actual HTML implementation, most commercial WIS management tools like Microsoft's Frontpage98[2], NetObjects' Fusion[3] or Adobe's Pagemill[4] provide little functionality as far as consistent WIS modelling is concerned. It is expected that future applications will feature the same functionality and integration between models and implementations for commercial WIS as it is already provided by Upper- and Lower-CASE tools for traditional systems development.

5.4.2. WIS ANALYSIS: CAPTURING CUSTOMER FEEDBACK

Measuring user acceptance is of crucial importance for information systems success evaluation, and it is even more important for commercial WIS, where user acceptance becomes customer satisfaction. Structured and systematic gathering (analysis) of all available customer information is understood as a natural extension of commercial WIS design (synthesis). Table 5.3 lists sources, as well as potential acquisition methods, and illustrates available information. Implicit sources of information are exploited without the assistance, sometimes even without the awareness, of customers. Such information can be obtained through Web server log files, persistent client state HTTP cookies, or component technology such as Microsoft's Active Server Platform (ASP). Information that is consciously provided by the users of WIS is summarised as explicit information. This information can either be sub-

---

[2] www.microsoft.com/frontpage
[3] www.netobjects.com
[4] www.adobe.com/prodindex/pagemill

mitted interactively (e.g. through on-line forms) or gathered from past records and offline user surveys. Naturally, online information acquisition is the preferred mode.

Table 5.3. Available WIS user information (adapted from Bauer and Scharl, 1999).

Source		Acquisition Methods	Information
Implicit [Client/ Network]	Network Information	Environment Variables, HTTP Log-Files	e.g. Remote Host (Name), Browser, etc.
	Browser Support	Cookies, Java-Applets, Hidden CGI data	Visited Pages, Clickstream Analysis
Explicit [User]	Interactive	On-line Forms, etc.	Questionnaires, etc.
	Records	Customer Database	All of the Above

For aggregation and visualisation of behaviour and access patterns of individual WIS customers, graphical meta models for representing gathered data are a basic requirement. At the higher, condensed levels descriptive statistical models and techniques provide an approximate understanding of the information to be analysed. To map and classify the customers' behaviour exactly, symbolic representations of hypertext documents and incorporated user information can be employed. An early example of such a tool is *WebMapper* (Bauer and Scharl, 1999), which is built as an extension of the eW3DT modelling technique. The customer-oriented regular gathering of stimulus-response-data and its integration with stored information for creating dynamic user models in conformity with observable real-world patterns help the information provider to measure the success and customer satisfaction with specific areas of commercial WIS.

5.4.3. THE EVOLUTIONARY LOOP OF WIS DEVELOPMENT

The short- to medium-term development path of solutions for tool-based support of the design and the analysis of commercial WIS has been outlined in Sections 5.4.1 and 5.4.2. Together with the usage of these WIS by customers (organisations and consumers), all four phases of (external) evolution from Figure 5.1 are covered: WIS analysis, design, implementation, and usage. The resulting cycle of WIS evolution is combined with actual examples for each phase in Figure 5.4.

Implementation and usage are relatively well supported by the Web architecture and Internet applications on server- and client-side compared to WIS design and WIS analysis. The interface between the WIS analysis phase and the WIS design phase is a crucial point for the integration of evolutionary WIS development into an on-going cycle, but no solutions are provided to date. An additional requirement for efficient and user-friendly integration is the introduction of compatible modelling techniques for analysis and design, relying on an equivalent set of symbols and constructs. A first step towards such integration can be found in the underlying modelling technique of two prototypical development tools, *WebMapper* for WIS analysis/visualization and *WebDesigner* for WIS design (Bauer and Scharl, 1999).[5]

---

[5] www.ecn.curtin.edu.au/wis, scharl.wu-wien.ac.at/wis

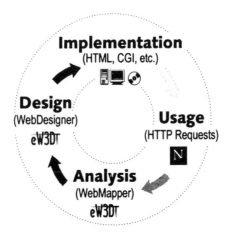

Figure 5.4. WIS evolution and tool support.

Figure 5.4 provides a scenario for tool support of the complete WIS evolution cycle. The usage of commercial WIS (in its most primitive form a simple HTTP request) is recorded by Web servers, or server-side plug-ins in the case of more sophisticated information gathering methods. These records are then processed and visualised for decision makers by a WIS analysis tool in a specific modelling language. The analysis of the usage will lead to frequent updates of the WIS content based on observed consumer behaviour. These updates are reflected and carried out by means of a WIS design tool, which is generating the required files (HTML, CGI program code, etc.). Once uploaded, the files are accessed by WIS users (customers) and the next stage of the evolutionary cycle is reached.

5.5. Conclusion

Commercial WIS are deployed in an environment that is constantly redefined by evolutionary change. A natural response to these new challenges is to adopt an evolutionary approach in WIS development. The application of such an evolutionary approach to WIS development has been described in analogy to economic evolution theory and illustrated with examples of suitable deliverables. However, any evolutionary development methodology requires the availability of appropriate tools. Such tools should support the complete evolutionary loop of WIS development (design, implementation, usage, and analysis) in order to facilitate successful deployment in commercial environments. The topology of such a tool architecture has been outlined in the final section of this chapter.

CHAPTER 6

Financial Institutions and the Internet: Issues and Trends

CHRISTIAN BAUER

6.1. Introduction

Financial institutions will face dramatic changes in their competitive environment. Deregulation of financial markets lowers traditionally high entry barriers for new competitors. On one hand, foreign and regional banks are expanding the boundaries of their businesses to new geographic areas, and on the other hand, near- and non-banks, such as insurance companies, technology providers or retailers, are offering banking products through cross-selling or bundling. Strategic decision-makers are becoming increasingly concerned with the cost of routine transactions and distribution channels (Evans and Wurster, 1997).

Information technology and telecommunication networks provide new opportunities to reach their customers more efficiently. However, if banks choose not to face the challenges associated with these opportunities they risk losing customers and business to faster competitors. In 1989, FirstDirect, a direct bank completely relying on telephone services, quickly gained 500,000 customers in the United Kingdom (Devlin, 1995; Bosco, 1995). No less than Bill Gates predicted drastic change processes in the banking industry:

> Most banks use business and information systems that are dinosaurs. Like many
> companies, these banks risk eventual extinction if they do not keep pace with
> competitors who take better advantage of emerging opportunities afforded by
> information technology (Gates, 1996).

In this chapter, opportunities and challenges of virtual banking and distributing financial products and services via the Internet and the World Wide Web (WWW) to the consumer are discussed. A four-stage classification model of online banking conceptualises the description of the current state of the industry and presents guidelines for the implementation of strategic decisions towards online banking. The four-stage model describes the evolution from the first stages of online banking with simple entry level Web sites to full virtual banking. Statistics of industry development in the past two years are used to explain short-term trends in online banking. Concentrating on virtual banking, upcoming concepts for implementing successful virtual distribution solutions are outlined and described. Finally, these new solutions are investigated for their compliance with success factors for user acceptance.

6.2. The Consumer View: Four Stages of Online Banking

The financial services industry in general, and retail banking institutions in particular, were amongst the first businesses that realised the tremendous opportunities of the Internet and started to offer (information) services on the World Wide Web. Like in every other industry the dynamics of change processes differ from company to company, and while first movers are already offering a wide range of basic transactions over the Internet, some banks have still not established a professionally designed online presence. The Internet activities of retail banks can be roughly categorised into four stages. These stages also serve as a guideline for building up online banking competence and reflect the historic evolution of many state-of-the-art virtual banking sites. Figure 6.1 integrates the four stages into an evolutionary framework and puts them into the context of online banking.

Each stage and the associated functionality implicates certain levels of security, scope of content, and business processes restructuring. Section 6.2 gives a brief description of the consumer's view of each stage and identifies this through characteristic attributes. The management, information technology, and cost implications of moving towards more complex stages will be discussed in Section 6.3.

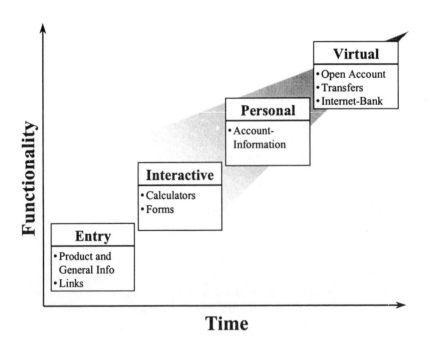

Figure 6.1. The four stages model to virtual banking.

6.2.1. STAGE 1: ENTRY INTO ONLINE BANKING

At the entry-level stage of their online banking activities, financial institutions lack experience and know-how. Funding for the first steps towards the 'information age' is often limited. Nevertheless, professional appearance is critical and existing and potential customers are not to be disappointed by unrealistic promises, poor site navigation or out-of-date information. Unrestrained enthusiasm about the new medium coupled with inexperience in communication architecture design very often lead to sub-optimal solutions. A smaller Web site will achieve initial marketing goals, test customer reaction, help to acquire the pre-requisite knowledge and to move down the learning curve.

In the first stage, the Web site is purely used as an advertising tool. The development and design of the Web pages must comply with the promotional strategy. Graphical guidelines for the online layout can ensure compliance with corporate identity standards. Identifying the target groups of online communication activities is a critical success factor (Hansen, 1995). General Web user surveys, consultant reports, and customer surveys provide a better picture of the general online population and the organisation's customer base.

Product information should be kept at a minimum. Updates are required frequently since old data may lead to legal implications and disgruntled customers. Only those products should be covered, which are targeted at groups, which have been previously identified as being of significant importance to online operations. Special attention needs to be paid to offers specifically designed for such target groups, e.g. student clubs. Current marketing initiatives need to be presented in prominent places. Less volatile information such as branch locations and opening hours provides a degree of guidance to customers and does not entail high maintenance costs. Despite serving as E-mail gateways for feedback surveys and online customer service, interactive forms are hardly used.

6.2.2. STAGE 2: INTERACTIVITY AND PRODUCT CATALOGUES

Again, in the second stage, only the information gathering phase of Electronic Market transactions (Schmid and Lindemann, 1998) is supported. However, efforts and required investments have to be significantly raised. Complexity is added to online banking on two dimensions:

1. Comprehensive electronic product catalogues (Palmer, 1997) contain detailed specifications of products and services. The number of products is increased substantially with the ultimate goal of including all products. The resulting maintenance efforts require updated information technology, organisational procedures and responsibilities. Improved navigational tools, Web site design, and visual cues can assist users in coping with the vast amount of information.
2. Enhanced interactivity adds value to customers and improves user satisfaction. These functions require both technical capabilities and careful integration into online content and business processes. Popular examples of

such applications are various interest rate calculators and account fee advisers.

The challenge of moving from a small and simple Web site to product catalogues and interactive components should not be underestimated. The complexity of maintaining actuality and consistency requires new tools and will very often be accompanied by a Web site re-launch and graphical re-design. The functionality increase is mainly visible in the additional interactive functions.

6.2.3. STAGE 3: PERSONALISED BANKING SERVICES

The functions added in this stage provide consumers with personalised information specifically generated for them. Complete product information through electronic catalogues and interactive functions are absent from the previous stages. Access to account information for immediate viewing and batch downloading into personal financial management software (e.g. Intuit's Quicken or Microsoft's Money) is the most obvious and important function, but user interaction can also be enhanced through individualised items, navigation, or presentation. Retail banks maintain more information for their customers than just account balances and transaction records, for example in affiliated associations like student or investment clubs. Such databases can be joined together with customer data collected online (Bauer and Scharl, 1999) and turned into powerful marketing tools of personalised and well-targeted communication. One-to-one marketing applications for online customer service extend direct marketing beyond the boundaries of traditional distribution and communication channels. Primitive, but powerful, examples can be found in keeping customers informed about their investment portfolios or providing stock market and share value information tailored to the requests of online customers.

The level of service required to fulfil these individualised functions can only be obtained by providing real-time information. The volatility and the amount of this data make integration between Internet servers and at least some operative banking databases a necessary condition. However, electronic transactions, such as money transfers, are still not available, thus minimising the risk of potential damages and misuse of security holes.

6.2.4. STAGE 4: VIRTUAL BANKING

Retail banks need to offer at least basic transaction services through the Internet to become virtual. Additionally, the functionality introduced in the previous stages must be enhanced. Account queries, money transfers between accounts and to other banks, bill payment and transaction downloads are minimum requirements for virtual banking (compare Yan and Paradi, 1998 for a list of potential functions). Either standard Web browsers with modern capabilities (Java-Applets, encryption, authentication, etc.) or financial management software are required on the client side. The required infrastructure architecture, potential content and advanced user interaction are described in greater detail in Section 6.5.

6.3. The Organisational View: Providing the Infrastructure for Online Banking

Management environment and technical infrastructure must meet the requirements from the early stages of the four-stage model to full virtual banking. While the shape and scope of the Web site as the shopping window and point-of-contact with the online customers change from the outside view, the approach to handling these systems undergoes significant reconstructions on the inside. Several of these change processes with typical manifestations are summarised in Figure 6.2.

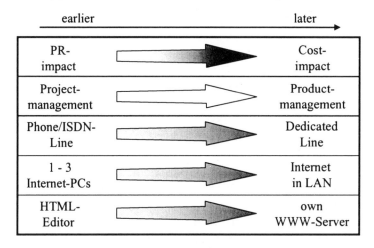

Figure 6.2. Indicators of change processes in the development of online banking.

In the evolution through the four stages of online banking (as outlined in Figure 6.1), the benefits obtained from offering services on the WWW move from intangible to tangible. At the same time, the strategic focus is shifted from primarily Public Relations oriented to competitive advantage and cost savings. As in many other industries, Web site URLs and E-mail addresses are displayed on business cards and represent primary points of contacts. For promotional reasons alone, organisations cannot abstain from establishing an Internet presence, even if their strategies do not focus on the Internet. Once the strategic commitment to larger investments in Internet applications has been made, cost savings and direct benefits, such as new customer acquisition, are expected to justify these activities. From a cost/benefit analysis standpoint, it may not be beneficial for all retail banks to offer virtual banking facilities.

The management structure of Internet services represents a lead indicator of importance and maturity. The fastest and most cost-effective way of starting a Web presence is through project management. Whether this project is carried out internally or outsourced to an Internet Service Provider or consultant does not affect the distinct characteristics of a product management type of organisational setting, where part of the maintenance and innovation responsibility is transferred to line managers. Product managers already coordinate marketing activities regarding 'their' product, and transferring the responsibility for the Web content to them is only a logical progression. Naturally, this shift to product management will result in more employees being involved in Internet operations.

Further investments in the technical infrastructure are an obvious consequence of the development towards virtual banking. During the early phases, only a few employees, typically members of the project team and persons in charge of monitoring the Internet presence, need access to the Internet. A few personal computers and ordinary phone/ISDN-connections are sufficient for these requirements. Web browsers, editing tools for creating simple HTML pages and some HTML-conversion tools fulfill the software requirements at this stage. The Web site can still be maintained at the Internet Service Provider. As mentioned before, with complete virtual banking, more and more employees get involved with online services and their computers have to be connected to the Internet. Increased network traffic and the linking of the banks' operative systems and Internet servers make the installation of a dedicated line between the banks' Local Area Network and the Internet Service Provider a necessity. Flexibility and security concerns can only be addressed satisfactorily through the establishment of a Web server solely utilised for the online services of the bank.

6.4. Development of Online Banking Sites

So far, an adequate evolutionary path for online banking has been developed and explained. However, the questions, whether or not it is desirable for retail banks to target virtual banking and whether such strategic moves can be observed across the industry, have not been addressed. This section attempts to provide answers by analysing statistical trends of retail banking Web sites.

To conceptualise the data gathering, the model of the four development stages of online banking from Figure 6.1 is used again as the underlying theoretical framework. Commercial Web site surveys based on similar classification models can also be found frequently (e.g. Booz, Allen and Hamilton, 1996; Unisys, 1999). For this analysis, empirical studies of banks' Web sites at two different points of time were taken into consideration:

1. At the beginning of 1996, two studies about banks world-wide found very similar distributions, independent from each other (Mahler and Göbel, 1996; Bauer, 1998).
2. In December 1998, a similar study was conducted. 230 entries of international banks were randomly selected from Yahoo (dir.yahoo.com/ Business_and_Economy/Companies/Financial_Services/Banking/Banks/).
   Out of these Web sites, 43 URLs had to be excluded either because of language barriers (Web site was not in English) or because of downloading errors when trying to access the homepage. Accordingly, the survey is based on the remaining 187 bank sites, which were inspected and classified into one of the four stages. Only the publicly accessible parts could be visited.

The results from 1996 and 1998 are compared in Figure 6.3 (white bars represent 1996, black bars 1998). It is interesting to note that 1996/97 forecasts of the Internet banking development have been too optimistic. The comparison shows a strong shift towards more complex and sophisticated Web sites. While most banks (90%) were still in stage 1 (Entry) in 1996, this percentage was reduced to 60% at the end of 1998. The statistics also show an increase in virtual banking sites (stage 4) from 2-3% to over 16%.

It has to be pointed out that these numbers should be considered indicative rather than exact in nature. Nevertheless, they allow observation of an industry trend towards virtual banking. The increase of stage 2 Web sites supports the idea of an evolutionary Web site development path, where most banks are undergoing all stages rather than aiming at full virtual banking immediately. The lack of numbers for stage 3 indicates that banks do not see this stage as a necessary milestone in their Internet strategies.

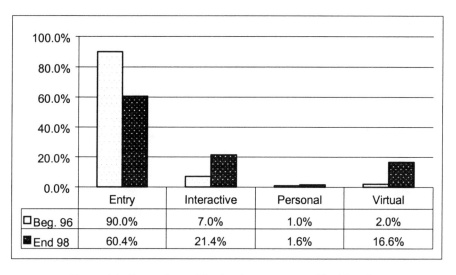

	Entry	Interactive	Personal	Virtual
☐ Beg. 96	90.0%	7.0%	1.0%	2.0%
■ End 98	60.4%	21.4%	1.6%	16.6%

Figure 6.3. Comparison of the development stage of banking sites
between the beginning of 1996 and the end of 1998.

6.5. Components of Successful Virtual Banking

The Internet and virtual banking will change the business model and competition laws of retail banking through redesign of the distribution channel (Evans and Wurster, 1997). In this section, three components for the implementation of virtual banking applications are outlined to investigate the design of such systems. Firstly, new electronic distribution channels have to be designed to be manageable and cost-effective. Secondly, open transaction standards appear to become the preferred option for managing client-server interaction, and thirdly, existing Web information services have to be improved accordingly by making them adaptive to user needs and profiles. These three components build the cornerstones to success in virtual banking.

6.5.1. ELECTRONIC DISTRIBUTION CHANNELS

Banks can provide Internet access to their banking systems from Web browsers or financial management software through a single transaction interface for both applications. Network connections between clients (at the consumer side) and servers (at the financial institution side) are illustrated in a graphical representation in Figure 6.4.

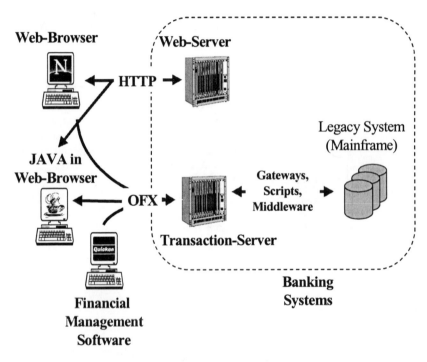

Figure 6.4. Scenario of a flexible Internet banking infrastructure integrating
Web Information Systems, consumer client software, transaction services,
and core banking systems.

Since the Web offers a cost-effective and user-friendly open platform, information services are kept on the WWW servers as in the earlier stages of online banking. Electronic transactions for home banking are processed through a standardised server interface. In Figure 6.4, OFX is introduced as the standard transaction interface. More details about OFX and other available solutions will be explained in greater detail in Section 6.5.2. Web browsers, Java-Applets and financial management programs connect to the transaction server, transmit their data and update their account files. Customers are free to choose their preferred Human-Computer Interface, in this case between HTML, Java-Applets or proprietary software applications. At the same time, the bank has to maintain only one gateway to manage these transactions leading to the goal of an integrated distribution channel (Gleason and Heimann, 1998).

The computing infrastructure of banks has evolved over decades. Processing of large amounts of data, reliability and security were the critical factors. In most cases, these computer systems comprise a mainframe system, hundreds or thousands of terminal computers, some proprietary operating system, a database management system and hundreds of tailor-made and interconnected applications. This information technology is very different from Client/Server networks. Rather than adapting or rebuilding the old, but reliable systems, it seems less costly to introduce new layers of application systems ('Middleware') to link mainframes and the Internet. Solutions that establish the link between Internet servers and protocols and existing information systems at the financial institutions are readily available.

6.5.2. DELIVERING ELECTRONIC TRANSACTIONS BASED ON OPEN FINANCIAL SERVICES STANDARDS

The convergence of online services and other value-adding computer networks into one global medium, the Internet, enables integrated communication between consumers and financial institutions. However, efficient electronic transactions and information exchange only become feasible with standardisation up to higher communication layers. The quest for open specifications to manage data transfers between client and server software handling the (automated) communication between clients and banking organisations caused a number of financial institutions and technology providers to develop such standards. Visa Interactive (Access Device Message Specification, ADMS), Microsoft (Open Financial Connectivity, OFC) and the Intuit Services Corporation published documents and implemented prototypes, to name just a few early examples.

The goal of widespread integration into client software (financial management software, Web interfaces, etc.) requires these specifications to be open and publicly available. Economies of scale in providing software solutions, market power and software integration soon led to a concentration on a smaller number of standards, with Open Financial Exchange (OFX) from Intuit, Microsoft and Checkfree and Integrion Gold from IBM, Visa and a number of high profile retail banks as the most prominent survivors. Plans have already been announced to merge these last two remaining financial services standards (BITS, Open Financial Exchange and Integrion, 1998). Besides this convergence on an international level, there are a small number of national standards prevailing, for example, the German Home Banking Computer Interface (HBCI), which is argued to be better equipped for the specifics of the German banking market.

In the following, the OFX specification is reviewed as an example of such financial services standards. As has already been identified in Section 6.2.4, full virtual banking requires a financial institution to offer a minimal set of functions over the Internet. Most of these functions are covered by the specification. Other functionality is still implemented best through Web Information Systems (see Section 6.5.3). In the current version 1.5 from June 1998 (Open Financial Exchange, 1998), OFX supports the following functions:

- *Account statement and transaction information:* Similar to regular 'paper' account statements, information on transactions and balances can be downloaded on a daily basis. Refined queries (on date) and more detailed information are feasible through electronic interaction.
- *Credit card information:* Same features as for account information apply.
- *Stop cheque:* Issue a stop payment for an outstanding cheque.
- *Intrabank funds transfer:* Immediate and scheduled transfers can be arranged, requiring only identification of source and destination accounts, amount and the optional date of transfer.
- *Interbank funds transfer:* Inter- and Intrabank fund transfers are very similar, but Interbank transfers are more complex, requiring Clearing House involvement and inter-organisational links.
- *Recurring operations:* Users can automate transactions that occur on a regular basis.
- *Data synchronisation:* To prevent client and bank databases being out of sync, synchronisation of stored information can be performed.
- *Payments:* Payment of invoices and/or bills is a central function of most electronic banking applications.
- *Investment and money market information:* The download of security information and investment account statements including transactions, open orders, balances, and positions is supported.
- *E-Mail and notification systems:* Plain text and HTML messages are supported and URLs can be attached.
- *Address information of the financial institution:* Besides the more traditional postal address and phone and fax number, address information also contains E-mail addresses and URLs.

6.5.3. ADAPTIVE WEB INFORMATION SYSTEMS

The additional functionality in virtual banking through electronic transactions is not the only dimension for increasing customer value. Financial institutions looking for competitive advantage in the Internet business must improve the services of their existing Web site. At this point of time, adaptive Web Information Systems (WIS) appear to be having the greatest impact on Web site design and customer satisfaction in the mid-term future. Adaptive WIS make Web sites dynamic by introducing immediate responsiveness to customer requests.

Technologies like neural networks, genetic algorithms, natural language generation (Milosavljevic, 1998), case based reasoning (Finnie and Wittig, 1998), or related soft computing approaches will increase the functionality of deployed applications. Market analysis, Web-tracking, data warehouses, or the wide-spread consideration of dynamic user models for customising Web-based information systems will become a necessity for commercial projects. Implicit and explicit user feedback is used for instantaneous regeneration of content, presentation and navigational structure (Bauer and Scharl, 1999). Explicit user feedback includes all information consciously provided by the customer. Examples for implicit user feedback are server log file analysis, clickstream analysis, and user profiling.

6.6. Success Factors of Virtual Banking

Consumer acceptance influences the success and widespread use of virtual banking to a large extent. Dratva (1994), based on findings of a research group at the Institute of Information Management at the University of St. Gallen in Switzerland (Zimmermann and Kuhn, 1995), identified the following basic requirements for high user acceptance of home banking architectures:

- *Multi-banking capability*: The consumer must be able to obtain the functionally equivalent information services of different banks in the same, or very similar, way. From the consumer's point of view, this is an important prerequisite for transparent offers and easy to use services.
- *Openness*: The possibility to access the services through open Internet services (e.g. Web browsers) and to easily integrate financial information into standard client applications (e.g. personal financial management software such as Quicken or Money) is important.
- *Standardisation*: Using standard message formats and protocols is a necessity for guaranteeing comprehensive and versatile information services.
- *Integration in open (Internet) systems*: The seamless support of all basic Internet services maximises throughout all phases of electronic transactions.
- *Modern human-computer interface*: The human-machine interface is of primary importance for consumer and market acceptance.
- *Security*: Assuring privacy and preventing 'digital' fraud is a prerequisite for Internet banking and one of the most important factors for customer acceptance.

The adaptive solutions, distribution channels and transaction standards described in Section 6.5 satisfy all of these requirements. Providing transaction gateways based on open, industry-wide standards makes multi-banking capability feasible. Customers with accounts at two or more banks (a strategy frequently used to minimise the risk of losses in the case of bankruptcy of the financial institution) can access all their accounts through the same software, using the same interface and performing the same functions. A further advantage for the customers is low switching costs. All of the open transaction standards have built-in, high-level security measures. With most of the information services remaining on the Web platform, integration into standard Internet services and graphical user interfaces is still available. However, adaptive WIS can be employed to improve the user interface and reduce the information overload caused by increasing content. Overall, modern virtual banking solutions based on open financial transaction standards and upcoming Web Information Systems bear the potential to satisfy all user acceptance success factors.

CHAPTER 7

Protecting Sensitive Information in Electronic Commerce

ARYYA GANGOPADHYAY AND MONICA ADYA

7.1. Introduction

One of the crucial requirements for electronic commerce (e-commerce) systems is to provide adequate data security, which has been defined in terms of five functionalities (Adam, Dogramaci, Gangopadhyay and Yesha, 1998; Adam, Gangopadhyay and Holowczak, 1998; Kalakota and Whinston, 1996): authentication, authorisation, confidentiality, integrity, and non-repudiation. Authentication refers to the ability to prove the identity of a user and is based on verifying information provided by the user against what is known by the system about the user. Methods of authentication include private information such as passwords, physical devices such as smart cards, and biometric characteristics such as fingerprints. Authorisation involves controlling access to information once authentication is established. Authorisation is accomplished with access control mechanisms for network entities and resources. Confidentiality involves maintaining privacy of information about users. Integrity involves the protection of data from modification, either while in transit or in storage (Bhimani, 1996). e-commerce systems must have the capability of ensuring that data transmissions over networks arrive at their destinations in exactly the same form as they were sent. Changes in data that integrity services must protect against include not only modifications to the data, but additions, deletions and reordering parts of the data (Ford and Baum, 1997). Non-repudiation involves proving the identity of the sender of a message. This prevents a sender from denying the fact that a message (such as a purchase order) was actually sent and taking responsibility for such a message.

Most of the work in the area of security in electronic commerce has focused on protecting a system (and the users of the system) against *direct attacks*. We define a direct attack as any activity that is aimed towards breaking into a system, such as violating the security protocols and/or breaking into the cryptographic system itself. Direct attacks are obvious attempts to get access to the data. In this chapter, however, we focus on *indirect* attacks that may not be as obvious as direct attacks. By indirect attack, we mean any attempt to *derive* confidential information from the data that the user is authorised to have access to. Thus, indirect attacks violate the confidentiality requirement of a secure electronic commerce system. Examples of such derivations include identifying individual information from aggregate data.

With the rapid adoption of electronic commerce across many sectors of the industry and the Government, a vast amount of data is being collected and disseminated across wide area networks. Examples of such information include buying habits, criminal records, heath records, and financial data. In order to protect individual identity, such data is made accessible to the public only in the form of statistical aggregates. Protecting data from improper derivation of hidden information has been the subject matter of the area of security in statistical databases. However, with the technological advances in the areas of data mining and knowledge discovery in databases (KDD), statistical data protection methods may not always provide the level of confidentiality that is desirable in the face of the rapid growth in the accessibility of data in electronic commerce systems. In this chapter, we discuss the issue of ensuring confidentiality of data in electronic commerce systems and protection of data against indirect attacks.

The rest of the chapter is organised as follows: In Section 7.2, we describe the issues related to the disclosure of individual information. In Section 7.3, we discuss methods for statistical data protection. In Section 7.4, we discuss the recent advances in data mining and knowledge discovery in databases. In Section 7.5, we provide some conclusive thoughts and solution approaches.

7.2. Disclosure Issues

In order to provide privacy of information, it is important to understand what constitutes improper disclosure of information (Lambert, 1993). Unfortunately, there is no consensus on the definition of disclosure. Disclosure risk issues can range from violating anonymity to obtaining sensitive information. The problem lies in determining what harm can be caused by the disclosure of information. Sometimes, even incorrect linkage of released information with individual identity can cause serious harm to an individual. For example, if a prospective employer concludes that an applicant has a disease that makes him ineligible for a position, such a record linkage may be unacceptable, whether or not the information is correct. Various disclosure models have been proposed in the literature that can be grouped under the following categories:

1. *Identity disclosure.* This involves identifying an individual from released records. A simple example is when individual records stand out due to *associative rarity*. Such data is also referred to as *grainy data*. For example, if the Bureau of Justice Statistics releases data about the number of violators admitted to prison, categorised by gender, date and state, where there is only one female imprisoned in 1996 in Vermont, then it is possible to obtain the identity of that individual.

2. *Attribute disclosure.* As opposed to identity disclosure, attribute disclosure involves obtaining the values of sensitive attributes from the released data. For example, if an aggregate measure of a certain attribute happens to be the same as the absolute value of the attribute, then releasing the aggregate data is equivalent to releasing the absolute data. This could be the case if the salaries of all plumbers in Connecticut were the same in 1997, and the

Bureau of Labor Statistics releases the average salary of workers by work category, state, and year.

3. *Attribute to identity disclosure.* Attribute disclosure can be harmful if it leads to the disclosure of the identity of an individual. For example, if an intruder attempts to obtain the identity of an individual from attributes such as race and gender, protecting confidentiality of an individual would require protecting the values of those attributes. It may be that, if the disclosure of an attribute value does not lead to the identification of an individual, then attribute disclosure can pose no harm. However, such an assumption may not be a correct one. For example, an intruder can narrow down the identity of an individual and can zero in through subsequent probing in a reduced search space. Furthermore, the case of mistaken identity can also be harmful to the individual. Hence, systems should be designed in a way that will not mislead an intruder but actually discourage him by making it difficult to arrive at any conclusion about the identity of any individual.

7.3. Statistical Data Protection Methods for Data Security

Government agencies, such as the Census Bureau, regularly receive requests from researchers for data records of various kinds that are collected from surveys conducted on individual respondents. While such data must be statistically useful, the data providers have the moral, ethical, and sometimes legal obligations to protect the identity of individual respondents. Statistical data protection methods are used to achieve the purpose of minimising the possibility of disclosure of individual information. Hence, these methods are referred to as *disclosure limiting/avoidance,* and *confidentiality protection* techniques (Fuller, 1993). The methods of disclosure avoidance can be divided into three categories: *query restriction, data perturbation,* and *output perturbation* (Adam, Gangopadhyay, Holowczak, 1998).

7.3.1. RESTRICTING QUERIES

These approaches allow or disallow a query based on some pre-determined criteria. This could be achieved through methods such as the following:

1. *Restricting the size of the set of records that are returned by a query.* It has been shown that if the set of records returned by a query is more than half the size of the database, then the confidentiality of the database may be compromised (Denning, 1979, Fellegi, 1972, Friedman, 1980). However, it has not been shown conclusively what the maximum size of data set is that can be allowed to guarantee that the database will not be compromised.

2. *Restricting queries that return overlapping sets of records.* The purpose is to ensure that a user is not trying to narrow down the search space to an individual record by issuing successive queries on a series of subsets of a set of records. This approach, however, suffers from the limitation that such a pattern of queries is impossible to detect if they are issued by a group of colluding users.

3. *Partitioning the database and releasing only a subset of entities.* This
    approach was suggested in response to attacks directed towards gaining
    information from database transactions (Chin and Ozsoyoglu, 1981,
    Schlorer, 1983). However, it has been shown that reducing the number of
    entities can actually increase the risk of compromising the confidentiality
    of information. Another major issue related to database partitioning is that
    biases may be introduced to the statistical measures as a result of data
    partitioning.
4. *Suppressing cells that disclose individual identity.* This is the approach
    suggested in tabular data (Denning et al, 1982). This is a simple but
    effective mechanism, but may not work for complex queries.

7.3.2. DATA PERTURBATION

The basic idea of data perturbation is to *alter* the attribute that stores confidential
data. Various methods have been suggested using this approach:

1. *Replacing original database with generated samples.* This approach
    assumes that the database is representative of an underlying population
    data. Once the distribution of the population is known, these methods
    replace the original database with data generated using the probability
    distribution of the population. Methods belonging to this class can be
    applied to multicategorical attributes (Reiss, 1980), single (Liew, 1985) and
    multinumerical attributes (Lefons, 1983). The problem with these methods
    is that they do not recognise the dynamic nature of the database where
    changes occur constantly with updates. With such changes, the
    assumptions about the underlying population distribution may not remain
    valid.
2. *Perturbing confidential attributes.* This approach simply modifies the
    attributes containing confidential data by introducing "noise". The
    modified attribute values are then used to answer user queries. Every time
    the original attribute is updated, the replica is modified accordingly to
    reflect these changes. This approach suffers from the limitation that such
    modifications can introduce bias in the attribute data (Matloff, 1986).
    Random data perturbation methods attempt to overcome this limitation by
    perturbing the confidential attribute values by a noise with a mean of 0.
    However, if two confidential attributes that are correlated are perturbed, the
    divergence between their original and perturbed values can be exploited to
    gain information about the original values. This problem can be overcome
    by preserving the correlation between confidential attributes even after
    perturbation (Tendick et al., 1994). However, this introduces another
    problem; that if an intruder can estimate the unperturbed value of one of
    the confidential attributes, he/she can also estimate that of the others that
    are correlated.

7.3.3. OUTPUT PERTURBATION

As opposed to data perturbation where the database itself is modified, output perturbation methods leave the underlying database unaffected and perturb only the results of a user query. Several output perturbation methods have been suggested in the literature:

1. *Selecting a random sample.* In this method (Denning, 1980), a random sample is selected from the query result and sample mean is returned to the user as a result of the query. The sample itself is drawn from the database by selecting records sequentially with a given probability distribution. This approach may not work for aggregate measures such as count, minimum, and maximum, and can bias measures such as average and standard deviation.

2. *Varying the output.* In this method (Beck, 1980), the output is simply altered by introducing noise before presenting to the user. This methodology suffers from the same limitation as perturbing the underlying database in that it can introduce bias in the output data presented to the user.

3. *Resampling output data.* This method (Adam, 1989) uses a fully saturated linear model to code the data and replaces the least squares estimate of the column vector with one obtained using the jacknife resampling plan. Care is taken to avoid introducing bias over the resamples. This, however, would introduce a significant amount of overhead in processing queries.

As can be seen from the discussion above, most of the statistical database protection methods incur a significant amount of overhead in processing user queries. This can make it infeasible to use most of these methods on a real-time basis, particularly in situations where the database experiences frequent updates. Furthermore, it can be shown that using various data mining and KDD methods, an intruder can get hold of sensitive private information and even a reasonable approximation can be unacceptable under certain circumstances. In the next section, we discuss some of the existing data mining and KDD methods and illustrate with examples the viability of applying such techniques to uncover sensitive information that would pass the test of statistical data protection methods.

7.4. Discovering Information Using Data Mining

Data mining is an emerging technique that combines AI algorithms and relational databases to discover patterns without the use of traditional statistical methods (Borok, 1997). It employs algorithms to identify patterns in large databases and data warehouses. Data mining methods can be used to facilitate information analysis through predictive and descriptive modeling (Limb and Meggs, 1995). Descriptive modeling is exploratory in nature and contributes to the discovery of previously unknown patterns, trends, and associations in the data. For instance, ShopKo made a significant change to their Sunday circular advertising based on results from a data mining effort. ShopKo had always considered their Sunday circulars to be the highest traffic builders. Coupons in these circulars advertised consumables that were all located on the left-hand side of the stores. By using data mining to analyse buying patterns, it was found that customers gravitated to the left-hand side of the store for the promotional items and did not necessarily shop at the entire store. Consequently, Shopko added apparel promotions to the circulars and expanded promotions by sending out a mid-week circular resulting in higher store-wide sales[1].

Predictive modeling allows the examination of data in a more traditional way by testing specific hypotheses. For instance, health care providers may anticipate an increased incidence of breast cancer in areas that have radioactive waste disposal units. By relying on historical data, data mining techniques can test for this hypothesis in areas where such waste disposal is prevalent. The strength of data mining comes from the fact that results obtained through the mining process are not influenced by any kind of preconceptions of the semantics of the data that is undergoing analysis. Consequently, the algorithms are able to discover patterns that would normally not be identified as a consequence of semantic constraints. The data independence, however, also poses one of the major challenges to the process of data mining.

7.4.1. THE PROCESS OF DATA MINING

An important preliminary step to data mining is the development of a data warehouse. Data warehousing involves the collection and cleansing of data from various sources in an organisation and, possibly, external to the organisation. This cleansed data is then stored in large multi-dimensional databases and possibly extracted into smaller data marts. These data marts are usually loaded with pre-defined models and episodes against which analyses or queries can be run.

The data mining tools can now be run on the warehouse or marts. By definition, data mining is a pattern discovery process that requires large volumes of data to infer meaningful patterns (Fayyad, 1997; Fayyad and Uthurasamy, 1996). Tools that support such pattern discovery range from simple statistical procedures to more complex Artificial Intelligence (AI) based approaches, such as neural networks, case-based reasoning, classification rules or some combination thereof. Once a pattern is discovered or confirmed, it may either be converted into a classification rule or a set of such rules, can be presented as a written or visual report to the user, or can be converted into a data model that can be applied to data marts.

7.4.2. DATA MINING OVER THE INTERNET

An important effect of the increasing volume of business over the Internet is the generation of large volumes of data. Furthermore, the Internet can be used as an efficient and cost-effective tool for accessing and distributing strategic information. For instance, Vision Associates is providing intelligence capabilities to customers who currently do not have the wherewithal to capitalise on the benefits of data over the Internet; they allow users to access corporate data from their web browsers. This

---

[1] www.software.ibm.com/data/solutions/customer/shopko/

capability is often extended to customers and partners outside the organisation. With the increased efficiency in transaction processing and data dissemination comes the risks to protection of sensitive information. One of the concerns with data mining, then, is that these techniques can facilitate both the use and misuse of data over the Internet. In a previous section, we discussed three disclosure issues. In this section, we further discuss how data mining can support the issues identified in that section.

1. *Identity disclosure.* Data mining tools do not require significant complexity to identify an associative rarity. Simple statistical procedures can be applied to critical fields of data stored in the data warehouse to identify an outstanding entry. Further access of the data warehouse can provide access to detailed information about the identified rarity. Take the example of the single female prisoner. Simple statistical procedures or queries on the gender field will identify this associative rarity. The drill down options supported by data mining software will then allow access to detailed information about this particular individual.

2. *Attribute disclosure.* Both predictive and descriptive data mining can be used to disclose information regarding an individual based on aggregate data. Take the example of hiring an individual from Long Island. Data mining may indicate that there is an increased risk of breast cancer for people originating from Long Island. This is aggregate information that may then be used to determine the acceptability of an individual as an employee if she originates from that area.

3. *Attribute to identity disclosure.* Credit card issuing banks are increasingly using the last four digits of the credit card as an identification mechanism. A search on these digits may reveal the entire number and other related information that is required for distant transactions. Catalogue and Internet orders can then be placed on this number without having physical possession of the card. In another instance, several banks are allowing electronic account management over the Internet (as an example, see www.nihfcu.org). In most instances, these banks require simply the account number and password to gain access to account information and management capabilities. Such information can be easily intercepted and used to access the account. Once access is made into the account, all private information such as social security number, home address, and account transactions can be accessed and misused.

7.4.3. AN EXAMPLE OF DISCOVERING SENSITIVE INFORMATION USING ASSOCIATIVE RULES

The data shown in Table 7.1 shows a hypothetical survey result of car purchases in a certain year for a certain locality. From the table, it can be seen that the data set can disclose the identity of an individual (row 8) because of associative rarity. In other words, the data set has a high degree of granularity which can disclose the identity of an individual. The granularity of a data set can be measured by an index that computes the ratio of the unitary to total occupied cells (which is 1/12, or 7.7%). One approach is to require a pre-defined granularity index, which will ensure that the major clusters will predominate over peripheral grains. In case of low occupancy across all cells, it is conceivable to achieve high degree of granularity yet unacceptable disclosure risk. Such cases may require decreasing the level of detail by merging cells that have low occupancies.

We extend our discussion of disclosure risk by investigating the possibility of discovering associative rules from the data set. Two measures that are commonly used for developing associative rules from a data set are support and confidence. Support indicates the percentage of tuples in the relation where both the premise (LHS) and antecedent (RHS) of an associative rule co-occur. Confidence specifies the probability of occurrence of the antecedent given that of the premise. Using the data set in Table 7.1, we illustrate how one can derive sensitive information by using associative rules. Let us hypothesise that the price of a car determines the salary of the individual that purchased the car. Thus, we specify 60% and 80% as the minimum support (*minsup*) and minimum confidence (*minconf*) for the associative Rule 1.

$$price > 20000 \rightarrow average\_income > 50000 ....(1)$$

Table 7.1. Hypothetical sales history records.

	Car type	Price	Number sold	Area code	Average credit rating	Average income
1	Dodge Caravan LE	22000	50	21211	0.70	50000
2	Dodge Caravan LE	22000	78	21217	0.67	45000
3	Ford Escort	10000	3	21218	0.25	25000
4	Ford Taurus	14000	40	21211	0.53	30000
5	Ford Taurus	14000	45	21226	0.55	30000
6	Honda Accord	20000	54	21217	0.56	55000
7	Lexus LS400	79000	2	21219	0.99	600000
8	Lexus LS400	75000	1	21219	0.95	150000
9	BMW 700	72000	3	21215	0.98	140000
10	BMW	73000	2	21219	0.99	750000
11	Nissan Quest	22000	29	21211	0.75	60000
12	Nissan Quest	22000	15	21214	0.80	65000
13	Jaguar	67000	3	21219	0.99	450000

From the dataset in Table 7.1, the support for Rule 1 is 69% (in 9 out of 13 rows the LHS and RHS co-occur). The confidence for Rule 1 is 89% (9 rows satisfy the LHS of Rule 1, out of which 8 also satisfy the RHS of Rule 1. Since Rule 1 satisfies *minsup* and *minconf*, we accept the hypothesis. We can next select the subset of rows such that *price > 200000*, which gives us a table with nine rows. From this table, we can further select the subset of rows where *price > 50000*, which yields five rows shown in Table 7.2.

Table 7.2. Subset of the original data set.

	Car type	Price	Number sold	Area code	Average credit rating	Average income
1	Lexus LS400	79000	2	21219	0.99	600000
2	Lexus LS400	75000	1	21215	0.95	150000
3	BMW 700	72000	3	21215	0.98	140000
4	BMW 700	73000	2	21219	0.99	750000
5	Jaguar	67000	3	21219	0.99	450000

From Table 7.2, we discover the associative Rule 2 with support 60% and confidence 100%.

$$area\_code = 21219 \rightarrow average\_income > 400000 \ldots\ldots\ldots\ldots(2)$$

Let us further assume that we know three individuals (A, B, and C) in the area with area code 21219 who have purchased the vehicles in rows 7, 8, 10 and 13 in Table 7.1. Furthermore, assume that we know that A has a Lexus, BMW, and a Jaguar; B has a Lexus and Jaguar, and C has a BMW and a Jaguar. It is then possible to deduce the exact annual incomes of the three individuals from the equations below (incomes shown in 1000s):

$$Income_A + Income_B + Income_C = 1800 \ldots\ldots(3)$$
$$Income_A + Income_B = 1500 \ldots\ldots\ldots\ldots(4)$$
$$Income_A + Income_C = 900 \ldots\ldots\ldots\ldots(5)$$

From Equations 3-5, we can see that the annual incomes of A, B, and C are 600000, 900000, and 300000 respectively. Obviously, a sensitive information is obtained.

7.5. Conclusion

In this chapter, we have identified a serious threat to the confidentiality of data that can result from indirect attacks on electronic commerce systems. We have shown that while the techniques developed in the area of data mining can be an important corporate resource in making strategic decision, they can also be misused in obtaining sensitive information about individual respondents. While methods developed for statistical data protection can be used in certain cases, these methods may not guarantee universal data protection under all circumstances.

Several measures can be taken to avoid improper access to confidential data. First of all, instead of releasing data on-line, they could be administered by one or more independent bodies that will be responsible to ensure data protection. Instead of allowing users to perform statistical analyses, these bodies could perform the analyses and report the results to the user. Second, responses to a user query should be the minimal subset of data that satisfies it. Third, one can investigate the process of data mining in order to determine how to protect data from being exposed using data mining methods. The most important requirement for data mining applications is the level of detail of the data stored in the data warehouse and data marts. The quality of the results will depend on what data are being included or excluded in these sources. Data mining, however, is optimised to slice through large amounts of data. Constraining the quality or quantity of data stored in the warehouse will adversely impact the ability to obtain confidential information. Lastly, further research is needed in the area of data protection against indirect attack.

CHAPTER 8

Towards Business Oriented Intranets

Knowledge Management in Organisations

SATISH NAMBISAN

8.1. Introduction

The advent of the Internet revolution has brought radical changes to the business landscape all across the globe. The primary focus has been on how the Internet technology can be deployed in the market place to extend the reach of organisations and to facilitate business-to-business and business-to-consumer transactions. An equally important and related issue is the use of the Internet technology within an organisation (commonly referred to as the Intranet) - for integrating the internal value chain, managing organisational knowledge, facilitating cross-functional teamwork and collaboration, etc. Indeed, a coherent Intranet strategy complements, and is crucial for, the exploitation of the Internet technology for use outside the organisation (i.e. for electronic commerce).

In the recent past, the Intranet has emerged as a technology that could potentially revolutionise communication and knowledge management in organisations. The trade literature is awash with Intranet "success" stories and articles describing the benefits of this new technological tool (Cronin, 1998; Greenberg, 1998; Weston and Nash, 1996). Perhaps reflecting such an optimistic evaluation, the adoption of Intranet technology has been rapid and widespread – a recent survey indicates that Intranet adoption has gone beyond leading edge companies and is now penetrating mainstream organisations throughout the U.S. (CMP, 1998).

However, deploying an Intranet is much more than providing a Web-based technical platform for employees to communicate and share data. As Hinrichs (1998) notes, "… Intranets are about people empowerment, not technology" (p3). An Intranet has potentially significant impact on business processes, communication patterns, organisational structure, and organisational culture (Bernard, 1996; Hills, 1997). Thus, apart from the key technical issues (supporting complex distributed computing infrastructure, adhering to technology standards, ensuring information privacy and security, etc.), there are also important organisational issues (content management, integrating internal and external information flows, etc.) that a firm needs to address in adopting Intranet technology. Of particular importance, are the issues related to the use of Intranets for organisational knowledge management.

Management of knowledge assets has assumed primacy in most business organisations. Knowledge sharing across functional domains or geographical locations is an important and core organisational competence (Newman, 1997). Intranets are often depicted as part of the effective solution to this problem as they have the potential to allow information sharing and collaboration across departments, functions, and different information systems within the organisation (Bernard, 1997). Indeed, management of organisational knowledge is often touted as the primary benefit of Intranet deployment (Marshall, 1997; Taylor, 1997). However, the rapid diffusion of Intranet technology and the scant attention paid to its management has raised serious concerns regarding its effectiveness and utility, especially as a knowledge management tool (Gartner Group, 1997). Some of the key Intranet management issues that organisations are grappling with currently include:

- What are the different aspects of organisational knowledge management that an Intranet can facilitate?
- What are the mechanisms by which the development and use of Intranets can be tightly linked to the organisation's business objectives?
- What are the roles and responsibilities of senior management, information systems (IS), and other functions in the development and management of Intranets?
- What are the new policies and procedures an organisation should adopt to ensure the proper use of an Intranet?

The current study is focused on examining a subset of these issues. More specifically, in this chapter, we identify different types of Intranets and provide a broad understanding of how the various types of Intranets influence different aspects of knowledge management. A case study of two Intranet initiatives in a large multinational organisation provides the context for examining some of the issues that ensue from the theoretical discussion. The case discussion also throws light on the different mechanisms organisations can deploy to provide the desired business direction for Intranet development and use.

The chapter is organised as follows. In the next section, we briefly review the literature on Intranets and knowledge management. The research model is described next. Following that, we present two Intranet case studies that provide preliminary support for our theoretical arguments. We conclude by examining some of the important research and managerial implications of this study.

8.2. Intranet and Knowledge Management

The term *Intranet* was coined by Steven L. Telleen, in 1994, who, along with his colleagues at Amdahl Inc., was studying the potential of Web-based applications for performing internal business functions in an organisation (McCartney, 1996). Intranet refers to the use of the widely popular Internet protocols and technologies (e.g. TCP/IP, HTTP, NNTP, FTP) to create a network-based infrastructure within an organisation that delivers enterprise services such as messaging, directory, calendaring and scheduling, conferencing, workflow and email, as well as transaction processing. The integration of these services is beginning to allow for valuable information sharing across different parts of an organisation.

Business organisations across industries seem to have embraced this technology in a rapid manner. Of the 411 organisations who responded to a recent survey on Intranet adoption in the US, more than 68% had already implemented an Intranet or were in the process of developing an Intranet (CMP, 1998). Other studies have indicated similar levels of penetration of this technology in business organisations (e.g. Engler, 1996). Given this rapid rate of adoption, issues related to the development, implementation, and management of Intranets in organisations assume great importance. These issues can be classified into three categories: technology related, project related, and application or business related (Nambisan and Wang, 1999). Technical issues include security, bandwidth, scalability, inter-operability, legacy system migration, etc. Project related issues include selecting the appropriate development tools and methodology, resources planning, defining the outsourcing strategy, etc. Application or business related issues include identifying the business objectives for the Intranet, measuring payback, devising data ownership policies, content management and establishing information sharing policies, organisational change management, etc. Compared to the technology and project related issues, application related issues have attracted limited attention from scholars and practitioners, perhaps because the issues are much more difficult to address. Given the primary focus of Intranet applications on organisational knowledge management, the application related issues have to be studied in that context.

It is well established that knowledge is the basis for, and the driver of, our post-industrial economy and perhaps the only source of sustainable competitive advantage (Prahalad and Hamel, 1990; Webber, 1993). Several factors, including the pace of change, the knowledge-intensity of goods and services, staff attrition, and the growth in organisational scope combine to make knowledge management an important determinant of organisational success (Davenport and Prusak, 1998). Knowledge management is the collection of processes that govern the creation, dissemination, and utilisation of knowledge. As such, it involves 'wiring together the brains of appropriate people' so that sharing, reasoning, and collaboration become almost instinctive and a part of everyday work. In short, knowledge management is about leveraging the expertise of people and making the most effective use of the intellectual capital of a business.

Knowledge management encompasses two components: the process (of knowledge creation or learning) and the product (knowledge repository) (Davenport and Prusak, 1998; Nonaka and Takeuchi, 1996). An Intranet can support both the process and product components of knowledge management. In other words, the Intranet is not only a powerful communication medium, but also a knowledge base. On one hand, an Intranet facilitates knowledge management by offering organisation members a unifying platform for collaboration, interaction, and real-time sharing of information across functional and geographic boundaries. On the other hand, as a knowledge base, the Intranet has advantages over previous digital knowledge bases in that it more easily captures and handles unstructured and implicit knowledge (in contrast, DBMSs require very structured schemas to be effective) (Telleen, 1998). Moreover, the ability to search for information based on different criteria, to find linkages between different types of information, to relate information with people, etc. are all key aspects of knowledge management that an Intranet can potentially support.

Bressand and Distler (1995) identify three distinct levels of functionality and practice for technologies, like the Intranet, to facilitate information and knowledge sharing:

1. *Infrastructure*: This relates to the hardware and software which enables the physical/communicational contact between network members. The high standardisation of the Internet tools allows the weaving of a single environment out of content residing on an individual's desktop, the company's Intranet, and files running on a distant server.

2. *Infostructure:* This relates to the formal rules which govern the exchange between the actors on the network providing a set of cognitive resources (metaphors, common language) whereby people make sense of events on the network. Organisations need to provide a clear vision on how the various knowledge elements in the organisation will be integrated so as to serve the business objectives and on the specific role the Intranet will play in managing that (Bernard, 1996; Telleen, 1997).

3. *Infoculture:* This relates to the stock of background knowledge which actors take for granted and which is embedded in the social relations surrounding work group processes. This cultural knowledge defines constraints on knowledge and information sharing. Note that an Intranet is "... only the pipeline and storage system for knowledge exchange ... it does not create knowledge and cannot guarantee or even promote knowledge generation or knowledge sharing in a corporate culture that doesn't favor those activities" (Davenport and Prusak, 1998, p18).

All three aspects are equally important for the Intranet to facilitate organisational knowledge management. An Intranet without an appropriate infostructure or infoculture is worthless and may never enable knowledge generation or transfer. In this study, our primary focus is on the second aspect – the infostructure or the organisational direction for Intranet development. In the remainder of this chapter, we examine how the presence or absence of such direction may enhance or limit the capabilities of an Intranet with regard to organisational knowledge management.

8.3. Research Model

8.3.1. A TAXONOMY FOR INTRANETS

A two dimensional taxonomy for Intranets is proposed. The two dimensions are: a) the nature of information or content, and b) the nature of business direction provided by the organisation.

1. *Nature of information or content.* The information included in an Intranet may be either formal or informal (Telleen, 1997; Miller, Roehr, and Bernard, 1998). Formality is defined based on how directly the information can be linked to the organisation's business. Formal information includes information about the enterprise in general or information intended for use within a specific product or task group. In the first case, it may include information about the products, services, processes, policies, etc. In the second case, the information may be used to communicate and share ideas, coordinate activities, etc. Informal information occurs in organisations as personal notes, memoranda, white papers, individual presentations, opinion pieces, and other creative work done by individuals that may not be directly linked to their work in the organisation.

2. *Nature of organisational direction.* An organisation may provide different types of direction for managing the Intranet content or knowledge base. The objective of such organisational direction is to ensure proper integration of the Intranet content with the business objectives. The mechanisms deployed to provide such direction, as well as how explicit such direction is, vary with the organisation (Greenberg, 1998). Further, the organisational direction may be provided at the corporate level, at the divisional level, or even at the departmental level. Organisations may provide clear and explicit direction by specifying the key business objectives to be met by the Intranet and by requiring new content to pass through a review board and be approved before being published on the Intranet. Direction may also be provided through less explicit means - departmental guidelines, policies, operating standards, etc. At the other end of the continuum, organisations may abstain from providing any business direction for their Intranet development and evolution.

Based on the above two dimensions, four types of Intranets can be identified (see Figure 8.1):

1. *Structure oriented Intranet* focuses primarily on the formal information and provides clear cut directions on how such information should be integrated and presented, and in this way it attempts to mirror the organisational structure on the network. However, by not focusing on the rich informal knowledge bases within organisations (which often are most crucial for new knowledge creation – Nonaka and Takeuchi, 1995), structure oriented Intranets often only recreate the rather rigid knowledge creation mechanisms already present – they may not enhance the knowledge creation capabilities. In other words, information flows that are enabled by the Intranet are often those that merely preserve the formal structure.

2. *Culture oriented Intranet* focuses on both formal and informal knowledge bases within organisations. However, given the limited organisational direction for integrating the various types of content, the Intranet may derive its direction primarily from the organisational culture. In effect, the technical network may reinforce the organisation culture, but the lack of focus on clearly defined business objectives may limit its impact on the business

(Greenberg, 1998; Miller et al., 1998). For example, while such Intranets may facilitate building new relationships among organisation members, not all such ties may have meaning in the business context.

3. *Business oriented Intranet* incorporates both formal and informal content and provides direction for their integration in a manner that enhances the business effectiveness. The clear vision of the organisation with regard to knowledge management dictates the selection, distribution, and presentation of information. For example, an organisation may specify unifying themes, such as 'enhance customer access', and provide a forum for linking formal and informal content that relate to such themes, resident in different parts of the organisation. Note that such direction needs to be provided keeping in mind the organisation culture (since it influences how the informal content will be generated and shared) as well as the key business objectives and strategies.

4. *Intranets without any orientation* result when the Intranet incorporates primarily formal information and the organisation provides limited direction for integrating the content. Due to the lack of direction, there may be limited conceptual mapping of the formal information and hence, such information, although technically accessible to all members of the organisation, often remains unusable.

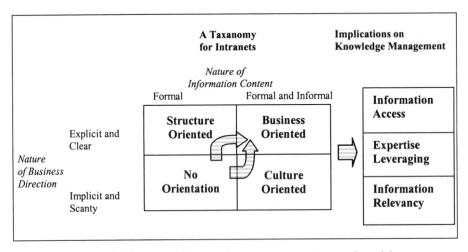

Figure 8.1. Intranet and knowledge management: A research model.

8.3.2. IMPLICATIONS ON KNOWLEDGE MANAGEMENT

The central theme of this study is that the type of Intranet an organisation develops will have significant impact on the type of knowledge management achieved. Here, we focus on three important aspects of knowledge management.

1. *Information access/sharing capability.* This aspect relates to the ease of finding the relationships or linkages between different knowledge components (Davenport and Prusak, 1998; Nonaka and Takeuchi, 1996; Telleen,

1997). In other words, it emphasises the ease of information access from the conceptual rather than from the technical perspective. A mapping of the various components or elements in a knowledge base enables identification of valuable routes for seeking new information and also provides a model for combining information originating from different sources. Such knowledge mapping may be carried out based on broad business themes rather than functional or departmental issues. For example, Hoffmann-LaRoche, a pharmaceutical company, developed their knowledge map so as to help process new drug applications more efficiently and quickly comply with questions about them (Seeman, 1996, 1997).

2. *Expertise leveraging capability.* This refers to the collaboration that can be enabled in the organisation for addressing specific issues. For people to collaborate to solve a problem in organisations, they have to be first aware of where the expertise resides and then understand how such expertise can be accessed (Boland, Tenkasi and Te'eni, 1994; Telleen, 1997). In short, the linkages between the expertise (elements in the knowledge base) and the experts (people) have to be made explicit. This capability reflects the support the knowledge management system provides for knowledge creation or learning (i.e. the process perspective of knowledge management). If the ties are clear and well specified, it facilitates rapid and efficient leveraging of such expertise (Davenport and Prusak, 1998). As Andrew Mahon, senior manager of strategic marketing at Lotus Development Corp, notes, "... what people want from a search query is not the material itself; they want to use the material to figure out who they should call to talk about the problem they have right now" (as quoted in Hapgood, 1998).

3. *Information relevancy control capability:* In any knowledge management system (whether it be paper-based, human-based, or computer-based), the capability to provide relevancy control is a critical success factor (Brookes, 1996). This aspect relates to how well the system processes or categorises the content to provide relevancy information. It assumes importance in this era of push technology when users are bombarded with information that is often not requested and is delivered at the convenience of the publisher. Thus, here the focus is on the system's capability to filter information based on individual preferences and priorities. For example, grapeVINE, a knowledge-based acquisition tool, uses a knowledge chart and user interest profiles to play the role of an automated information gatekeeper (Ruggles, 1997).

Based on the characteristics of the four types of Intranets and the three aspects of knowledge management described above, we extend the following propositions. Given its focus on integrating the formal data, structure oriented Intranets are likely to exhibit information access/sharing capability as well as information relevancy control capability. The mapping of the formal data, as well as a clear definition of the relationship of each element in the knowledge base with the business model, enable structure oriented Intranets to provide easy information-seeking and relevancy control. Culture oriented Intranets, on the other hand, emphasise informal content and provide mapping between people and knowledge elements and hence, are likely to be associated with expertise leveraging capability. In other words, they facilitate making connections and supporting interactions with people rather than documents. Intranets without any orientation are unlikely to be associated with any of the three aspects of knowledge management. Finally, due to their ability to integrate both formal and informal content and provide tight linkage to the business objectives, business oriented Intranets are likely to be associated with all the three aspects of knowledge management. Hence the following three propositions:

Proposition 1: Structure oriented Intranets are likely to be associated with both information access/sharing capability and information pollution control capability.

Proposition 2: Culture oriented Intranets are likely to be associated with expertise leveraging capability.

Proposition 3: Business oriented Intranets are likely to be associated with all the three aspects of knowledge management (information access/sharing capability, expertise leveraging capability, and information relevancy control capability).

8.4. Case Study

8.4.1. RESEARCH METHODOLOGY

Given the lack of theoretical development in this area, the case based methodology (Yin, 1989) was deemed more appropriate for this study. The focus was not so much on empirically validating the stated propositions as on exploring the phenomenon of organisational direction for Intranet management and identifying the salient issues in this area.

Although the case study was based on one organisation, data pertaining to two relatively independent Intranet initiatives were collected. Managers in the two divisions in which the Intranets were implemented were interviewed. The interviews were semi-structured and tape-recorded and later transcribed. Each interview took about an hour to complete. The following issues were dealt with in each interview:

- Key objectives of the Intranet;
- Development and implementation process;
- Role of the top management;
- Intranet usage - problems and issues;
- Future plans.

The managers in the two divisions of the organisation were also queried on their perception of the three aspects of knowledge management, the impact of the Intranet on their immediate business context, etc. In addition, the author was given a brief tour of the two Intranets which enabled the collection of additional data on navigation facilities, ease of use, type of information content, etc. Access was also provided to official documents listing information sharing policies, Intranet development guidelines, IT steering committee meeting minutes, etc.

8.4.2. INTRANET PROJECTS AT CHEMCO

Chemco is a large multinational organisation, operating primarily in the chemicals industry, with offices and production facilities in more than 40 countries. It consists of a number of different product divisions including industrial chemicals, healthcare, and fibres. Its growth has been punctuated by acquisitions across the last two decades and hence, it has a rich and mixed cultural heritage.

Information Technology (IT) management in Chemco is conducted in a partially centralised and partially decentralised manner. IT is a division in its own right and offers services to the other divisions based on a corporate strategic IT plan. The various product divisions have their own IT departments, although the size and capabilities of these IT departments are limited relative to the central IT division. The central IT division's primary role is to set guidelines for IT deployment and to provide leadership to organisation-wide IT projects (e.g. ERP). However, it is also allowed to compete against the divisional IT departments for individual application development projects. The organisation has adopted such a unique approach as a measure of ensuring the internal competitiveness of the IT management. It is in such an interesting context that the organisation initiated its Intranet project.

Two years ago, a business strategy plan envisioned the creation of a transparent information infrastructure that embraced all divisions and national units. The central IT division was the key player behind this plan, although the corporate board, as well as senior managers from the various divisions, participated in the initial meetings and gave the Intranet project the official blessing. CorpIntranet, the organisation-wide Intranet, was designed and developed by the central IT division after a series of meetings with representatives of the various product divisions. One of the product divisions was selected as the pilot site.

However, simultaneously, another product division started its own private efforts in building an Intranet. This Intranet, DivIntranet, was meant as a limited facility for product development teams and marketing managers in the division to interact and share knowledge about new product development initiatives. The managers of the division perceived a business urgency in having such a facility and decided not to wait for the implementation of CorpIntranet but, instead, to build their own Intranet on a limited scale. However, they decided to follow the technical standards set by the central IT division so that the two Intranets could be merged at a future date.

The simultaneous development and implementation of the two Intranets, one built by the central IT division and the other by one of the other divisions, provide an interesting context for examining the key issues in Intranet management. Table 8.1 presents the salient features of the two Intranets. CorpIntranet was developed with the primary focus on the formal information content that can be made available through the integration of the various application systems. The corporate and divisional business models were used for deriving the linkages between data elements. It was decided at a relatively early stage of the project that informal content would be entertained only after the initial system had been built and implemented. Given the dominant role of the central IT division in developing CorpIntranet, the developers were not really conversant with the internal culture of the different divisions and hence, an initial focus on the explicit information base was deemed appropriate. They also established fairly strict guidelines for content management. The design of each page must meet the standards and policies of the central IT division and all content has a content owner who is responsible for every word published on his or her Intranet property. As one manager noted, "our goal is very clear ... we want to focus our attention on the vast formal database that already exists and make it available to everybody. However, we want to ensure that in the process of doing so, we don't forget how the content relates to the organisation's business objectives." Thus, CorpIntranet, in effect, became a structure oriented Intranet as it reflected the content derived by integrating the official information channels of the division. The primary focus was on building the infrastructure and, to a certain extent, the infostructure. There was little effort on the part of the Intranet development team to either define or develop the infoculture.

Table 8.1. Intranet characteristics.

	CorpIntranet	*DivIntranet*
Intranet Scope	Organisation-wide	Limited to one product division
Project Champion	Corporate Management	Divisional Management
Project Leadership	Corporate IT Division Department	Divisional Business
Role of IT Function	Project driver	Facilitator
Nature of Content	Primarily formal	Primarily informal
Integration with Business Applications	Intranet content sourced from 12 IS applications	Poor integration
Content Management	Guidelines strictly enforced	No explicit guidelines or control
Mechanisms for Providing Business Direction	Intranet Content Committee Intranet policy handbook Half-yearly Intranet content audit	One-page Intranet strategy statement Periodic business managers meetings
Intranet Characteristics:		
Infrastructure	Excellent	Barely adequate
Infostructure	Good	Little focus
Infoculture	Little focus	Excellent, already existing

On the other hand, the DivIntranet was very much a grass-roots project with little structure imposed by the IT department. Although the senior divisional managers held the reins for this project, their primary objective was to provide a platform for the members of new product development teams to interact and share knowledge. As such, they did not provide explicit business direction for the Intranet, neither did they allow the IT department to establish guidelines for content management. Indeed, much of the project leadership was with the business managers and the IT department played primarily a facilitating role. As one of the managers noted, "… ownership of the Intranet content is not explicitly spelt out. In fact, we just provide the space for discussion and it is up to individual users (to decide) as to how to utilise the medium." As a result, the informal content on the Intranet developed much faster than the formal content. Everything, from project schedules and market intelligence reports to notices for club meetings, went up on the Intranet. Over a period of time, the DivIntranet evolved into a culture oriented Intranet that truly reflected the infoculture of the division.

Based on our interviews with managers in both divisions in Singapore, it was clear that although the CorpIntranet was deemed to be technically good, its impact on the business had not materialised as expected. Several users noted that while the Intranet had made it easier to acquire operational information, it had not expanded their knowledge horizon in any significant manner (in other words, the Intranet did not open any new avenues of information). The most beneficial aspect of CorpIntranet was the reduction achieved on the extent of document sharing within the division and, to a certain extent, on the overall response time for decision making. On the other hand, most users of DivIntranet felt that their Intranet had significantly enhanced their expertise leveraging capability. Product development teams regularly posted specific project related problems on the Intranet and solutions/suggestions were obtained from offices all over the division. Indeed, DivIntranet users were unanimous in saying that the richness and usefulness of the informal content surpassed their initial expectations. As one product development manager noted, "… I didn't know that there were nine people in my own division who had prior experience with the kind of technical problems I was facing in my project. Most of these people had faced these problems during their tenure with other firms and there was no mechanism at the organisation level to identify or exploit such expertise. The Intranet greatly enabled this process." However, it was clear that the infoculture played a crucial role in ensuring the initial success of DivIntranet.

Managers of the two Intranet projects noted that their ultimate objective was to build an Intranet that combined the rich sources of both formal and informal knowledge bases within the organisation with clear linkages to the business objectives. However, as the case study shows, they took different routes to achieve this: while one focused on the formal content and deployed various mechanisms to enforce content management policies, the other adopted a more laissez faire approach and developed an Intranet that was built around the information sharing culture already practised by the product development teams. Each route has its own advantages and disadvantages. Table 8.2 enumerates these as well as the other key conclusions of the case study.

Table 8.2. Key findings of the case study.

	CorpIntranet	DivIntranet
Proposed Intranet evolution	Structure oriented to business oriented	Culture oriented to business oriented
Perceived advantages	Exploit existing IS applications Relatively easy to quantify benefits Requires limited organisational change management	Exploit existing infoculture Rapid implementation possible Potential benefits may be considerable Direct involvement of users
Perceived disadvantages	May not deliver significant benefits May require considerable time to implement Mechanisms for providing direction are often costly to deploy	Difficult to quantify benefits Calls for significant organisational change management
Perceived impact on knowledge management	Enhanced information access/sharing Limited impact on information relevancy	Enhanced expertise leveraging Limited impact on access to formal control information
Alternate mechanisms for providing business direction	Define and publish formal corporate knowledge maps Appoint Intranet content teams that are managers to promote cross-functional themes closely aligned with various project teams for Intranet content	Promote/facilitate informal user groups Deploy relationship or account

8.5. Implications for Research and Practice

The theoretical framework and the case study presented in this chapter have important implications for both research and practice in the area of Intranet management.

The varied types of Intranets described in this chapter raise interesting questions related to the gradual evolution and growth of Intranets. Organisations need to clearly define the type of Intranet they want to build and how they are going to manage the gradual evolution process. While a business oriented Intranet may be the ideal, the Intranet may take the initial form of one of the other three types and gradually evolve over a period of time into its final form. Further, the framework presented here is an initial attempt at providing a theoretical basis for linking the various types of Intranet with knowledge management. Our focus here has been limited to three key dimensions of knowledge management. Future research may focus on identifying additional aspects and incorporating them into the framework.

Another interesting issue relates to the factors that influence the type of Intranet an organisation develops. Three important organisational factors worth mentioning are: Intranet project leadership, top management attitude towards information sharing, and degree of integration of IS portfolio. First, several functional areas – public relations, corporate communications, IS, marketing, personnel, etc. – have assumed leadership of Intranet projects in various organisations (Hills, 1997; Telleen, 1997). Given the varied focus of the different business functions, the type of Intranet developed may, to a certain extent, be dependant on which function assumes the leadership for the Intranet project. For example, IS dominated projects are likely to lead to structure orientated Intranets given their primary focus on formal data acquired by integrating the applications systems. Second, the development of an appropriate infoculture is a critical part of Intranet implementation. The top management's role in this process cannot be over emphasised. Third, the degree of integration of the IS portfolio (which often is the primary source of formal data for the Intranet) may influence the ease with which different information components on the Intranet can be related and hence, the structure of the Intranet.

This chapter has important managerial implications as well. It may be true that technology push rather than business pull has driven much of the Intranet deployment efforts in organisations (Greenberg, 1998; Telleen, 1997). Indeed, in their haste to deploy the latest sophisticated Internet technology, many organisations have either forgotten, or at least spent limited efforts in providing, a business direction to their Intranet projects. Without proper business direction, the Intranets are not likely to have significant impact on the businesses. Such business direction needs to be provided by deploying a portfolio of organisational mechanisms. In the organisation we studied, the portfolio of mechanisms included Intranet content committee, Intranet strategy statement, Intranet development guidelines, theme based Intranet discussion forums, half-yearly Intranet content audit, focused business managers' meetings, etc. Such mechanisms enable the management of the quality of information delivered over the Intranet. Steps in this direction should also include identifying the people and roles involved in the development and certification of official information, developing an Intranet process and content infrastructure to support these people, and providing them with training.

Organisations also need to clearly define the drivers behind the information access policies, formal and informal (Telleen, 1997). Intranet is an egalitarian infrastructure that does not respect departmental or divisional boundaries. Once the infrastructure is in place, information flow may proceed in ways not intended by the original creators. When such information flow jumps previous management control points, the result can be management ire. In short, organisations are often faced with the prospect of re-evaluating their culture or looking for tools, architectures, and sanctions to shut down many of the Intranet capabilities. Another issue related to this is the need to redesign business processes, taking into consideration the new information flows that are enabled by the Intranet.

Finally, managers should note that both formal and informal information are equally important for deriving the potential benefits from an Intranet. Most organisations neglect this aspect and even if they do incorporate both formal and informal information, they fail to provide any framework for integrating the information content.

8.6. Conclusion

An Intranet is a valuable tool for organising, communicating, and managing organisational knowledge. As such, it is an important component of an organisation's overall Internet strategy. However, an Intranet is not just a technical infrastructure. Organisations need to carefully decide on and implement appropriate policies and guidelines to ensure that the Intranet delivers benefits compatible with the company's strategic objectives. This chapter has presented a theoretical framework that links specific Intranet characteristics with knowledge management. It is hoped that future work in this area may validate this framework and also focus on identifying Intranet additional characteristics and organisational mechanisms for providing business direction.

CHAPTER 9

Ensuring Security and Trust in Electronic Commerce

THOMAS F. REBEL AND WOLFGANG KOENIG

9.1. The Need for Trust and Security

The utilisation of open networks such as the Internet as a platform for communication is steadily increasing. Open and accessible, they allow rapid and efficient world-wide exchanges at low costs. This leads to new forms of business configurations (e.g. "virtual" enterprises, work collaboration across the globe), of private communication (e.g. e-mail) and of organisation of public services (e.g. electronic tax declaration). The Internet will be used for such communication purposes as the use of services on the Net, e.g. online shopping, electronic handling of routine private banking transactions, communication of confidential medical data between physicians, health insurance companies and patients, and communication of transaction data across national borders in global banking.

Where are the perils and pitfalls? One is the lack of trust in open networks. However, in order to own a probative document one has to print it out and sign it by hand. This legally forced breach of media should be stopped as soon as possible. Electronic business transactions are also exposed to misuse such as the manipulation of offers, orders and payments. As long as the risks are as high as they are at present, suppliers and consumers will restrict electronic transactions in open networks to low-value transactions in order to reduce risk. (As examples for the risks in open networks read (Bellovin, 1989) on "sniffing" and (Bellovin and Cheswick, 1994) on "spoofing".) The Internet has to become secure and reliable, otherwise users are unlikely to use the Internet as a platform for commerce in everyday transactions.

What are the requirements for a reliable and trustworthy infrastructure for electronic commerce? Henning (1997) introduces the "four pillars" of secure electronic commerce:

1. *Authentication:* The sender of a document must be identified precisely and without any possibility of fraud;
2. *Confidentiality:* The contents of a message may not be scanned by unauthorised parties;
3. *Integrity:* Changes made in messages without according remarks must be impossible;

4. *Non-Repudiation:* The sender of a message is directly connected to the contents of the message.

Nowadays, integrity and authenticity can be guaranteed by digital signatures. However, public key systems used for digital signatures require a secure technical, organisational, and legal infrastructure to be reliable in the application of encryption in open networks for the purposes mentioned above. This is based in the fact that digital signatures are only technical concepts and their lawful signification depends on whether they are acknowledged as signatures under the present existing law. Lots of states have recognised these problems and passed a multitude of acts in order to solve them.

The objective of the legislator for an initiative of legislation for using digital signatures may be (Utha, 1995):

1. *Relief for commerce* through reliable electronic messages;
2. *Minimisation* of appearance of falsified digital signatures and fraud within electronic commerce;
3. Legal implementation of *lawful relevant standards*;
4. Foundation of *standardised rules* concerning certification and reliability of electronic messages in cooperation with other states.

9.2. The Approaches of Digital Signature Legislation

This chapter addresses the problem of different national regulations on digital signatures and the corresponding public key infrastructure. We introduce the German Digital Signature Act in order to discuss the major issues of such a law. Our purpose is to make a contribution to the forthcoming problem of different national regulation of digital signature acts, which involves the danger that in global electronic commerce the validity of signatures will be regionally restricted.

Worldwide an increasing number of activities concerning the legislation of digital signature acts can be observed. Almost all US-federal states (except Arkansas, Pennsylvania, South Carolina and South Dakota) have passed laws, presented drafts or at least set up commissions in this matter. Outside the USA, this can be also noted within the leading industrial nations. Because of the high significance of this theme for global electronic commerce, supra-regional institutions have also started activities, for example, the European Union, the International Chamber of Commerce and the United Nations.

The goal of laws on digital signatures is to enable the use of a digital equivalent of hand written signatures, so that legally valid contracts can be made over open networks. Following a survey of the Internet Law and Policy Forum (Gidari, and Morgan, 1997), three major approaches can be identified:

*   Prescriptive approach;
*   Criteria-based approach;
*   Signature-enabling approach.

9.2.1. PRESCRIPTIVE APPROACH

The prescriptive approach consists of a detailed framework and regulations related to the security infrastructure. The Utah Digital Signature Act has an outrider position among laws according to the prescriptive approach. The state of Utah was the first legal system in the world to adopt a comprehensive statute enabling electronic commerce through digital signatures (Utha, 1995).

The German Digital Signature Act meets the prescriptive approach. It is the first national act on digital signatures and will be described here in depth.

9.2.2. CRITERIA-BASED APPROACH

The prescriptive approach addresses a public key infrastructure as the fundamental technology to put digital signature into practice. Many legal systems feel the danger of an over-regulated framework. New technologies might be impaired and hindered in their development. To provide more flexibility many states have decided to choose a technology-neutral approach by addressing electronic authentication more broadly.

The predominant model for this approach is the California Government Code, No.16.5 (California, 1997a). Despite having a limited applicability (to communication with public entities), it was the first state to establish five requirements under which a digital signature shall have the same force and effect as handwritten signatures:

1. It is uniquely affiliated to the person using it.
2. It is capable of verification.
3. It is under the sole control of the possessor.
4. It is linked to data in such a manner that if the data is changed, the digital signature is invalidated.
5. It conforms to regulations adopted by the Secretary of State.

The Government Code addresses the Secretary of State to adopt regulations. These regulations are available in the final draft version (California, 1997b). The regulations provide a "list of acceptable technologies" that contains two basic technologies:

1. Public key infrastructure;
2. Signature dynamics.

9.2.3. SIGNATURE-ENABLING APPROACH

According to the signature-enabling approach, any mark with the intent to authenticate its user is an electronic signature. In this context, the notion "electronic signature" is used, representing a genus of the term "digital signature".

The Massachusetts Electronic Records and Signatures Act states that "a signature may not be denied legal effect, validity or enforceability solely because it is in the form of an electronic signature. If a rule of law requires a signature, or provides consequences in the absence of a signature, an electronic signature satisfies that rule of law." (Massachusetts, 1997)

In this case, electronic signature means "any identifier or authentication technique attached to or logically associated with an electronic record that is intended by the person using it to have the same force and effect as a manual signature."

9.3. Cryptographic Applications

The following three measures comply to the four requirements mentioned above:

1. Use of cryptography for encryption;
2. Use of cryptography for digital signatures;
3. Trusted certification authority.

Basically, cryptographic applications can be subdivided into the following categories: hash algorithms, symmetric algorithms, and asymmetric algorithms.

Hash algorithms create "digital fingerprints" of a file, e.g. an e-mail. The fingerprint is a sum generated from the data of the file. If the file is changed, the fingerprint, i.e. the hash value, is changed as well. In this application of cryptography the integrity of a file can be verified. If the same hash algorithm is applied to a file before and after the transfer in an open network, results in the same Hash value, the file is authentic, i.e. unchanged. An example of a hash algorithm is MD5 (Rivest, 1992).

Symmetric and asymmetric algorithms can be used for encryption. Using a special key, the algorithms transform a plain text into an unreadable ciphered text and vice versa. A symmetric algorithm uses the same key for encryption and decryption. An asymmetric algorithm uses different keys for encryption and decryption. The private key is secret and is only used by one person. The public key can be published to other people. These keys are related in a complex way. A message encrypted with a particular public key can only be decrypted by using the corresponding private key. Similarly, data encrypted with a private key can only be decrypted by using the corresponding public key. DES, RC4, and DEA are symmetric algorithms; RSA is the most popular asymmetric algorithm.

We do not want to emphasise the confidentiality of communication. Instead, in this chapter, we concentrate on "pillar" 1, 3 and 4. Therefore, we will briefly introduce digital signatures and certification authorities.

A *digital signature* is the encrypted hash value of a file, where a private key is used to encrypt it. The receiver of the file can decrypt this cipher text with the corresponding public key and verify the hash value. Verification is done by calculating the hash value and comparing it with the value received and decrypted in the signature. The document's integrity is proved if both values are equal.

The public key of the sender can, for example, be looked up in an online directory. But this does not prove that the sender of the message is actually the owner of the public key. There are some scenarios in which fraud is possible, e.g. directories can be faked.

The problem of *authenticity* and the problem of *non-repudiation* can be solved by a certificate connecting the public key to the identity of a person. Such a certificate contains at least the public key of the possessor, the possessor's identity (name or pseudonym), and the digital signature of the issuer of the certificate (the certification authority). One standard for these certificates is the X.509 standard (CCITT, 1988). In general, certificate standards determine what information is stored in a certificate.

There are three basic models that regulate how certificates can be issued:

1. Another user,
2. A certification authority of a private certification hierarchy, and
3. A certification authority of a public certification hierarchy.

These models for certification of the affiliation of a public key with a person are referred to as *trust infrastructures* (also known as "public key infrastructures"), because users trust the issuer of a certificate.

Model A is called the "web of trust". This infrastructure is known from the freely available software Pretty Good Privacy (PGP). In a "web of trust", certificates are issued by other users. By issuing a certificate, a user confirms that he reputes a person as the holder of a certain public key. The basic problem of this approach is that users cannot trust the quality of certificates of people they do not know, because they do not know how they can identify other people. So, one either trusts a signature which is not really trustworthy, or, one can only accept a limited number of signatures from a small number of people known personally.

Trust infrastructures of type B and C are based on the concept of hierarchy. In this case, certificates are only issued by a certification authority. Certification authorities take the role of a *trusted third party* for the relationship between two parties who do not know each other. The certification authority issues certificates (each containing information about the possessor's identity and a public key) to both parties so that each user can be sure about the identity of the opposite user. Trust in the certification authority is determined by their policy of certification, which has to be known to the users, i.e. the customers of the authority.

Basically there are two ways to install a certification hierarchy. The hierarchy can be the responsibility of a company or some other non-public institution (we refer to this as a *private certification hierarchy*), or, the hierarchy is based on an act or some other kind of public regulation (we refer to this as a *public certification hierarchy*). This does not determine who issues certificates, but predicts who establishes the rules and techniques according to which a certification authority performs its business (the certification policy). In a private hierarchy, each authority works according to its own policy. In a public hierarchy, the authorities have to match the requirements established by an act.

An example of Model B is Verisign Inc. The acts discussed here are examples of Model C.

9.4. The German Digital Signature Act

9.4.1. THE PROCESS OF LEGISLATION

The German Bundestag passed the Information and Communication Services Act (IuKDG) in June 1997. The act came into effect in August 1997. The act governs areas as the responsibility of providers, area-specific data protection, and digital signatures. The law is limited to the statement of essential facts which require immediate regulation in order to define the legal framework necessary for the economic development of electronic commerce. In addition, public interests, for example, concerning minors and consumer protection, will be safeguarded. It does not govern any regulations on encryption.

Article 3 of the IuKDG is the act on Digital Signatures. Its basic purpose is "to establish general conditions under which digital signatures are deemed secure and forgeries of digital signatures or manipulation of signed data can be reliably ascertained" (DSA, 1997).

The act describes the framework for the procedures of issuing and using digital signatures. It allows other procedures to issue and use digital signatures than those described in the act. However, these will not belong to the scope of validity of this act and therefore cannot be enforced on account of this act.

The act itself does not determine particular technical and organisational procedures or components. It is specified by an Ordinance on Digital Signature (Ordinance, 1997) and a catalogue of measures.

The technical standards and operational processes of certification authorities are specified in the catalogue of measures (RegTP, 1998). This catalogue includes suggestions on how a certification authority can meet the requirements of the act regarding security and services. Therefore, the catalogue serves as a basis for the approval of certification authorities and the regular review process. The aim is to quicken the process of establishing and reviewing certification authorities according to the Digital Signature Act.

In late September 1998, the Root Certification Authority was implemented after more than nine months of evaluation and implementation. This "Competent Authority" is the RegTP (Federal Bureau of Postal Services and Telecommunication) in Mainz.

9.4.2. THE CERTIFICATION HIERARCHY

Before we describe the procedures and organisational structure of the certifier according to the act, we illustrate the basic concept of the trust infrastructure.

The Digital Signature Act defines the following basic concepts:

A digital signature is a "seal affixed to digital data which is generated by a private signature key and establishes the owner of the signature key and the integrity of the data with the help of an associated public key provided with a signature key certificate of a certification authority or the authority according to §3 (Competent Authority) of this Act." (DSA, 1997)

A certification authority refers to "a natural or legal person who certifies the assignment of public signature keys to natural persons and to this end holds a license
pursuant to §4 (Licensing of Certification Authorities) of this Act."(DSA, 1997)

These two definitions determine a *two layer certification hierarchy* (see Figure
9.1) with a Competent Authority as the root certifier.

The "competent authority" is a public authority. Its purpose is to issue
certificates used for signing certificates, to license certification authorities, and to
monitor those authorities for compliance with the act. The Competent Authority is
not allowed to issue certificates to customers and certification authorities are not
allowed to certify other certification authorities.

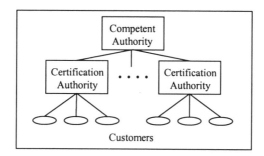

Figure 9.1. The certification hierarchy.

How can the validity of a digital signature be proved in this type of
infrastructure? As shown in Figure 9.2, the digital signature of a document is valid if
it is mathematically correct and if the certificate of the sender was valid at the time
the signature was made. Under which circumstances is a certificate valid? The
certificate of a sender is valid if the signature was made before the certificate
expired (certificates are usually valid for five years). The certificate contains a
mathematically correct digital signature of a certification authority who has attained
a valid certificate from the root certification authority (the Competent Authority). In
the next step, the validity of the certification authority's certificate has to be
examined. The certificate of a certification authority is valid if the original
document was signed before the certification authority's certificate expired, the
digital signature of the Competent Authority on the certification authority's
certificate was mathematically correct, and the certificate of the Competent
Authority was valid at the time the certification authority's certificate was issued.
Finally, the Competent Authority's certificate is valid if the digital signature on the
certification authority's certificate was placed before the Competent Authority's
certificate expired, and the digital signature of this authority on its own certificate is
mathematically correct.

9.4.3. THE COMPETENT AUTHORITY

As we have seen above, the root of the certification hierarchy is the Competent
Authority. The Competent Authority has two basic responsibilities: (a) it signs the
certificates of the certification authorities (so it is the certification authority of

certification authorities); (b) it has to ensure that the certification infrastructure is secure and trustworthy. In this section, we describe the regulations that concern responsibility (b). The activities for issuing certificates will be described in the subsequent section.

Users' trust in the use of digital signatures is mainly determined by the quality and security of certification authorities. The trustworthiness of these authorities depends on different factors, e.g. trust in the organisation of the certification authority, the quality of techniques and processes, the usage of accepted standards, the accordance with laws, a valid contract between authority and user (customer) etc.

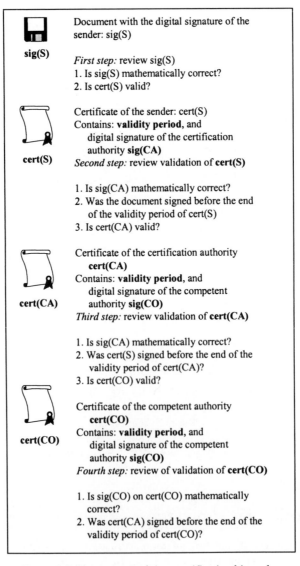

Figure 9.2. The review path in a certification hierarchy.

Therefore, the signature act determines that every certification authority must be licensed by the Competent Authority (§2 SigG (2); (DSA, 1997)). The organisational security concept, the technical components, and the quality of the authority's staff are the subject of a thorough examination preceding the licensing.

The examination consists of two steps. In the first step, the three subjects (concept, components, and staff) are reviewed for their compliance to the act and the catalogue of measures. In the second step the compliance is verified. The evaluation and the verification are conducted by independent reviewers who are certified by the Competent Authority. One Certification Authority cannot be evaluated and verified by the same reviewer.

According to the catalogue of measures, the examination must be completed before the Certification Authority applies for the license. The Competent Authority reviews the application of the Certification Authority based on the results of the examination. If the security concept, the technical components, and the staff of the Certification Authority applying for a certification meet the requirements of the act and the catalogue of measures, the Competent Authority has to license the applicant and issue a digital certificate with the digital signature of the Competent Authority.

The act allows for two types of certificates to be issued: signature key certificates and attribute certificates. The signature key certificates have to include particular information, e.g. the serial number, the expiration date, and the public signature key of the customer.

After the Certification Authority has started its business, the three topics of the examination process will be reviewed periodically, e.g. the organisational concept and the technical components will be reviewed every two years. In case of changes to the relevant three topics made by the Certification Authority, the changes will be subject to a review and an approval.

9.4.4. THE CERTIFICATION AUTHORITY

Once a Certification Authority is licensed it has to offer five specific services. According to the act, the certification authorities may offer more services. However, each authority must offer key creation services, registration services, certification services, individualisation services, directory services, and time stamp services.

We explain these services according to the process of applying for a certificate. In the subsequent section, we only discuss certificates for users. As we have seen above, Certification Authorities are only allowed to issue certificates to users and not to other Certification Authorities.

Assume a person, Mr Jones, needs a certificate. A firm, Smith Inc., is a licensed Certification Authority according to the German Digital Signature Act. First, Mr Jones must use the registration service of Smith Inc. (see Figure 3). The *registration service* has to identify Mr Jones with his passport unless Mr Jones is already the owner of a certificate. In the latter case, he can be identified by his digital signature. We assume that Mr Jones does not have a certificate or a pair of keys. After Mr Jones is identified, the registration service creates a unique name for Mr Jones. The name can be his own name, e.g. "tjones" or a pseudonym, e.g. "MIB1998". The data of Mr Jones is transferred to the certification service.

Subsequently, the *key creation service* creates a pair of keys: a private key handed out to Mr Jones, and a public key stored in a directory. The private key is transferred via a high security channel to the individualisation service. The public key is transferred to the certification service and is deleted from the key creation service.

In the next step the *certification service,* after having received Mr Jones' data and the public key, creates a certificate that contains the following information (DSA, 1997], article 3, §7 (1)):

1. *Name of the owner* of the signature key, to which additional information must be appended in the event of possible confusion, or a distinctive pseudonym assigned to the owner of the signature key, clearly marked as such;
2. *Public signature key* assigned;
3. Names of the *algorithms* with which the public key of the owner of the signature key and the public key of the certification authority can be used;
4. *Serial number* of the certificate;
5. Beginning and end of the *validity period* of the certificate;
6. Name of the *Certification Authority*;

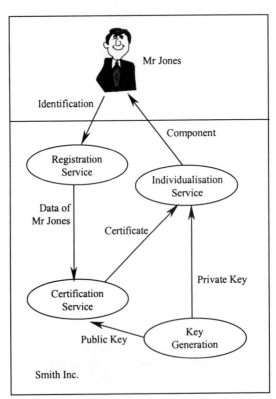

Figure 9.3. Application for a certificate.

7. An indication whether the use of the signature key is *restricted* in type or scope to specific applications.

If Mr Jones wishes to, other parameters can be included in the certificate as well, e.g. rights of disposal. The certificate is sent to the individualisation service.

The *individualisation service* receives the private key of Mr Jones from the key generation service. The private key must be stored on a "signature component", e.g. a smart card, and deleted from all of the Certification Authority's databases. After the private key is stored on the signature component, the component is "locked" with an authentication technique, e.g. a PIN number or a biometric technique like a fingerprint. This authentication technique protects the private key from unauthorised use. The individualisation service signs the component with the private key of the Certification Authority.

The signature component is then transferred to the registration service where Mr Jones is waiting for it. The component contains Mr Jones's certificate, Mr Jones's public key, Smith Inc.'s public key, and the public key of the Competent Authority.

Mr Jones is now able to use his component to sign all kinds of data by putting it in a reader in his computer, identifying himself by a PIN or a fingerprint, and activating the "sign" function of his signature tool.

The *directory service* stores all certificates of a Certification Authority and allows online access for reviewing the validity of a certificate. The process of evaluating the validity of a signature was described above. Therefore, the corresponding certificates in the directory service must be reviewed. The number of steps of reviewing to be taken is dependent on one's personal security needs. At least, the first step, i.e. the reviewing of the correctness of a business partner's certificate, has to be applied. The most important part of the directory service is the revocation list. This list stores all invalid certificates. Reasons of invalidity can be the expiration of the certificate, disclosure of the key, and the loss of the signature component.

Time is an important factor in business and in certification. As we have seen in the discussion of the review of the validity of certificates, the date of signing is relevant. The date on a contract is important in business or the date on which a user performs a transaction, e.g. transfers time-critical data. Therefore, Certification Authorities offer a *time stamp service*. In order to use this service, a user must "hash" a file and transfer the hash value to the time stamp service. The service adds the time the hash value was received and signs this information with its own key. The service therefore proves the hash value (which stands for a certain unique file) was seen at a certain time.

9.4.5. CERTIFICATES ISSUED BY OTHER COUNTRIES

The Digital Signature Act, the Ordinance, and the catalogue of measures contain only very few statements concerning the acceptance of certificates issued in other countries. The act determines that all certificates "shall be deemed equivalent to digital signatures under this act, insofar as they show the same level of security" DSA, 1997. Which certificates meet the requirement will probably be subject to bilateral negotiations between governments

9.5. Conclusion

We have described the status quo of the legislation in Germany as an example of digital signature acts. Certain aspects can be subject to criticism from a legal point of view as well as from a technical point of view, e.g. the discussion concerning the use of biometrical techniques. One of the most important goals for future research on trust and security in electronic commerce is to review the applications and services offered according to this act and create solutions for the problems arising in the real-life markets, courtrooms, and laboratories.

We have also introduced other efforts in digital signature legislation. With regard to the global nature of electronic commerce, there should be a convergence of different laws. International initiatives (such as the European Union or the United Nation Commission on International Trade Law) are attempting first steps for frameworks, guidelines or model laws in order to harmonise international laws on digital signatures. Political, as well as scientific efforts, have to be made to create a global, legal, technical, and business infrastructure for secure and trustworthy electronic commerce.

CHAPTER 10

Small Business and Internet Commerce

What are the Lessons Learned?

SIMPSON POON

10.1. Introduction

Relatively little attention had been given to small business in the study of Information Technology (IT) and organisational change in the 1970s and 1980s. The reason was simple: small businesses did not have complex organisational structures and therefore required little IT support for its internal functions as compared to large corporations. Also, small businesses usually did not have the necessary resources to invest in IT and consequently, their IT systems were simplistic and uninteresting. The Personal Computer (PC) revolution and the era of the Internet have changed this situation considerably.

Although IT systems in small businesses are still small, they are by no means simplistic or unsophisticated from a functionality point of view. For example, there is little functionally a large corporate IT system can do that a PC cannot. The Internet and the low cost of telecommunication now allow a small firm to use the global network, once only the proprietary of large international corporations. Today, a small firm can use its PC to connect to the Internet and transact with other businesses around the world. It can also set up an Internet server to allow its customers to download information, communicate with the firm and to do shopping. With a dedicated communication line (such as an ISDN service), a small business can have a permanent Internet server, with a permanent domain name and all this is achievable using a PC or even a laptop. Based on this revolution, many start to speculate that small businesses will be able to capture the global market, sell to international customers and compete favourably with large corporations. These claims, although technically possible, may have overlooked that technology is all but one part of the success formula. This difference between what is technically possible and the lack of widespread adoption is the classic example of EDI failure among small businesses.

Although on the Internet both a PC and a mainframe computer equally have one Internet address, there are significant differences between a small business and a large corporation from a resource and capability perspective. The Internet does not change the fact that a big company has more resource, funding and market capability. A small business usually targets a niche market with its specialisation and supplies to larger firms (e.g. in retail and manufacturing industries). Small businesses have a simple organisational structure where the owner or management usually have the final decision making power. Most importantly, a small business is vulnerable to failure during its early stage (first two years in business) and many have to battle resource constraints and financial limitations. This is usually not the case of a large corporation. A large corporation usually has significant resources and a comfortable IT budget, a hierarchy of subsidiaries and extensive market networks. This gives it a power advantage over small firms. Notwithstanding this, small firms can still leverage from Internet commerce and be agile competitors. Before knowing how to do this, a small firm should understand what Internet commerce can offer and what others have experienced. This is the key objective of this chapter.

10.2. Small Business Internet Commerce

There are easily as many definitions of Internet commerce as the number of articles written on this topic. In this chapter, Small Business Internet Commerce (SBIC) is defined as *the use of Internet technology and applications to support business activities of a small firm.* Based on this definition, a business activity can be internally or externally oriented and of transactional or strategic nature. This definition is adopted instead of those used in the studies of large corporations because, among small businesses, volume transaction or internal support are not the key application of Internet commerce, simply because of the difference in business nature and organisation structure.

Over the last few years, there have been a number of studies focusing on SBIC. Even among studies that were not deliberately focusing on small firms, it was found that small firms constitute a significant percentage of their samples (e.g. Abell and Lim, 1996; Lederer et al., 1996; Fink et al., 1997). In fact, the percentage of small firms in some samples increases over time (e.g. Fink et al., 1997).

Barker (1994) carried out a study on what small businesses were using the Internet for. Based on Cronin's (1994) Internet usage framework, Barker identified the importance of the Internet from a small business perspective and it is different from that of a large corporation. One of the key differences is that small firms tend to use the Internet not for formal transaction purposes, but for information gathering and socialisation with others on the Net. Large firms, on the other hand, commonly use the Internet for publicity purposes and to obtain vendor support (Quelch and Klein, 1996). It is also identified that there is a difference between the use of the Internet for international marketing between start-ups and large firms.

Apart from surveys conducted on general usage patterns of Internet commerce, there are studies which focus on specific aspects of SBIC. Auger and Gallaugher (1997) carried out a study on factors affecting the adoption of Internet-based sales presence. They concluded that the enablers for small businesses to set up a virtual shopfront are 'low development and maintenance costs', 'the marketing freshness of such a shopfront', 'obtaining and disseminating information', and 'competitive advantage'. At the same time, they also identified factors such as 'difficulty to promote the site', 'limited company resources' and 'poor product match' being the major barriers for such initiatives. Simultaneously, there was development in the area of Internet and marketing. Quelch and Klein (1996) were among the first to address the issue with consideration of small businesses (or start-ups). They concluded that, despite their differences, both large and small firms can benefit from Internet marketing. Hamill and Gregory (1997) studied the use of Internet for internationalisation among small and medium-sized enterprises (SMEs) and found that the Internet could help to overcome psychological, operational, organisational and market barriers. Similar findings were reported in a study of using the Web as a marketplace (O'Keefe and O'Connor, 1997). Poon and Jevons (1997) presented a conceptual discussion on how small business can carry out international marketing through small business alliances.

In terms of longitudinal studies, Poon and Swatman (1998) carried out a study on the difference between expectation and experience of Internet commerce. They found that over a twenty month period, there was a significant difference between expectation and experience, with only a small number of business objectives fulfilled satisfactorily and a larger number falling short of expectation. In addition, Poon (1998), in his major study on factors affecting Internet commerce benefit, concluded that factors such as 'geographic scope of market', 'the structure of the supply chain', 'characteristics of the industry', 'management style', 'ability to innovate' and 'being entrepreneurial' all have a significant effect on Internet commerce benefit.

Sieber (1996) investigated SBIC by focusing on the concept of virtuality. His thesis was that through 'virtualisation' – a process to enable interaction between autonomous companies through distributed IT such as the Internet – small businesses can be strategically stronger. The result shows that through virtualisation, small firms can gain access to new markets by forming strategic alliances with each other. However, many in his sample also admitted that similar alliances could have been formed based on personal relationships without the support of the Internet.

Some studies tried to build frameworks to illustrate the effects of SBIC. Lymer et al. (1997) studied the impact of the Internet on small businesses and constructed a framework which included categories (productivity, information retrieval, communication, knowledge and environment) and levels (business contacts, industry, organisation and task) of impact. They then refined their framework by validating it with cases of SBIC. Rather than focusing on impacts, Barker et al. (1997) constructed a framework to describe the approach a small firm takes on Internet commerce. Essentially, Barker et al divided those who adopted Internet commerce into opportunists and mappers. Opportunists are those who seek new business opportunities based on what the Internet provides and pursue them. These are entrepreneurs who innovate and break free from existing business paradigms. Mappers are those who map the capabilities of the Internet to existing business models. Some mappers focus on the use of the Internet to deliver services and products, others use the Internet for communication and marketing. In addition, they also provided an alternative classification approach which separates SBIC adopters into proactive and passive. Proactive adopters actively look for opportunities and drive the adoption process, while passive adopters take a 'back seat driver' approach.

Most recently, there is a move to study the adoption strategy of SBIC. Cragg (1998) reported a case study of Internet strategy among small firms. Using existing IT strategy frameworks, he analysed the Internet strategies of three firms and suggested the need for further analysis in this area.

10.3. Some Realities of SBIC

Based on the many studies carried out so far, there are a number of realities a small business can expect to encounter when engaging in Internet commerce.

10.3.1. A COMMUNICATION MEDIUM

Among all the studies, a commonly identified usage of the Internet is as a communication medium based on electronic mail (e-mail). The Internet is a good supplement to other communication media such as telephone or fax (Poon and Swatman, 1999). There are many reasons why the Internet can serve this purpose well. Firstly, e-mail provides documentation for each communication; the telephone does not. This can be important when a record of the correspondence is needed. Communication is also essential when an alliance of firms increases in virtuality (Sieber, 1996). In fact, the Internet is thought to be essential in maintaining a reasonable level of interaction within an alliance.

Another reason to use the Internet for communication is because of its non-intrusive nature. Communication can take place without the recipient being actively engaged. This is particularly important when a message is to be delivered instantaneously but the response is expected to be delayed. For small firms that are engaging in interstate or international businesses, this can overcome time zone and geographic differences more effectively than fax and telephone. Communication is also identified by Barker et al. (1997) as an approach to engage in Internet commerce.

A small firm can communicate with its customers, suppliers and those within and outside its industry. However, different studies have identified that communication with customers is better supported by the Internet (Lymer et al., 1997; Fink et al., 1997; Poon, 1998). Relatively few firms are using the Internet to the same extent to communicate with their suppliers. The reasons may be that:

- Most small firms studied so far have been from the non-manufacturing sector and have no traditional suppliers;
- Suppliers to small firms are often larger companies and may prefer to use technology they already know (e.g. EDI).

In addition, small firms have been found to use the Internet to communicate with other potential business partners on the Internet. The usefulness of the Internet for this purpose is dependent on the stage of a business relationship (Poon and Swatman, 1997). The Internet is useful for initial contacts and established relationships. However, at some stage there needs to be a means to allow context rich interaction (e.g. face-to-face) before the business relationship can mature further. Table 10.1 illustrates a generic four-stage framework of a business relationship and the usefulness of the Internet in supporting each stage.

Table 10.1. Usefulness of Internet communication at different stages of a business relationship (Poon and Swatman, 1997).

The stage of the business relationship	→	Usefulness of the Internet to support interaction
Directory search – initial search for partnership	→	High (access directory and initial enquiry)
Getting serious – starting to discuss possibilities	→	Low (often need some kind of rich context interaction)
Focusing on specifics – in-depth specifications	→	Medium (group support and document exchange)
Ongoing relationship – project monitoring	→	High (routine communication and exchange)

It is important to point out that this model is not all-inclusive of Internet-based business relationships. There are examples illustrating that a trusting business relationship can be established based purely on e-mail communication (e.g. ordering from a virtual bookshop).

10.3.2. A MEANS FOR DOCUMENT TRANSFER AND INFORMATION EXCHANGE

Studies have also shown that document transfer and information retrieval/exchange are an important part of SBIC. Often driven by the lack of resources and the busy nature of a small business, the owner and his team attempt to use time as effectively as they can. Given e-mail and other document transfer mechanisms are useful substitutes for postal and fax service, some small businesses find the Internet important as a document transfer mechanism (Lymer et al., 1997; Poon and Swatman, 1999). Although not necessarily a cost-saving method, instant document exchange proved to be important under circumstances such as real-time collaborative design with overseas partners. One example, as illustrated by Poon and Swatman, is that a small firm carried out joint design work by exchanging documents with an overseas developer and conversed with the person over the telephone at the same time.

Information retrieval is also another key aspect of SBIC application. It has been repeatedly identified that information retrieval is the main, if not the most important aspect of business support (Abell and Lim, 1996; Lymer et al, 1997; Poon and Swatman, 1998). In fact, using the Internet to locate information resources is often the first activity of Internet commerce. As more organisations, including government departments (e.g. www.cams.wa.gov.au), are making their information available over the Internet, this time saving feature will be a key to further diffusion of Internet commerce among small firms. Figure 10.1 summarises the stakeholders from whom a small firm gathers information, and with whom information is exchanged over the Internet.

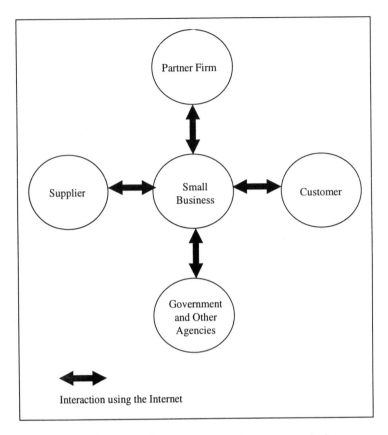

Figure 10.1. Groups that interact with small businesses on the Internet
(Poon and Swatman, 1999).

10.3.3. THE QUEST FOR POTENTIAL LONG-TERM BENEFIT

The media has been quick to report success stories of small firms gaining leverage
from Internet commerce but the reality of how widespread instant success is remains
questionable. In hindsight, it is easy to understand why virtual bookstores and CD
shops are flourishing online but for most non-retailing small businesses, the online
transaction model does not apply. Benefits from Internet commerce can be divided
into four categories – direct, indirect, short-term and long-term (see Figure 10.2).

Based on a multi-case study carried out by Poon and Swatman (1999), small
businesses online have experienced limited direct short-term benefit. Many reports
have suggested that the Internet helps to cut postage and phone tag. Overall this is
not really happening. Many firms found that they could not totally eliminate the use
of mail and the phone. For example, follow-up calls are still necessary after
information or documents are delivered through e-mail. When dial-up costs and
Internet Service Provider (ISP) subscription fees are taken into consideration, the
Internet may not be as economical, and this eclipses direct short-term benefit. The
results from this study indicate that small businesses participating in Internet

commerce aim at longer-term and indirect benefit. The difficulty is, of course, given the resource limitation faced by small businesses, indirect benefit needs to be in some way translated into measurable outcomes.

According to Poon and Swatman, longer-term benefits, such as forthcoming business opportunities and returning customers, are what small businesses hope for. There are also small businesses already positioning themselves to reap the longer-term indirect benefit (Barker et al, 1997). These firms are after acquiring sufficient Internet commerce experience and transforming their businesses into new business initiatives. Basically, many online small businesses are preparing themselves for the ongoing opportunities of Internet commerce and hoping that sometime in the future they will be capturing business opportunities that have been keeping them online.

But, if direct short-term benefit is what a small business is looking for, then it needs to be prepared for a massive business transformation, to the extent that a new business be set up with investments in technology and human resources. This can be a strategic but risky approach, as proven in many early online retailing initiatives.

10.3.4. CUSTOMER VERSUS SUPPLIER RELATIONSHIP IMPROVEMENT

Many examples can be quoted to show that the Internet is key to transforming the supply chain. Indeed, transforming the supply chain is one of the earliest predictions on the impact of Internet commerce (Rayport and Sviokla, 1995; Benjamin and Wigand, 1995). Along a supply chain, a small business situates between its suppliers and customers (see Figure 10.2).

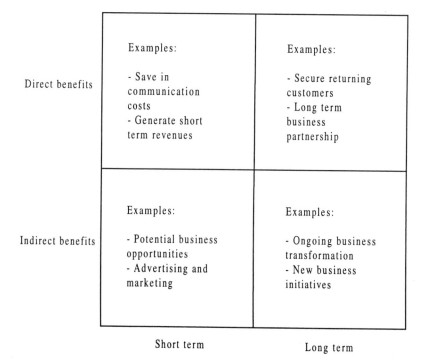

Figure 10.2. Framework of Internet commerce benefits (Poon and Swatman, 1999).

For online small businesses, customer relationship seems to benefit more from Internet commerce than its supplier counterpart (Poon, 1998). This is particularly true among firms in the knowledge-based industry. This may be due to the fact that small businesses are customer-focused and, among non-manufacturing firms, many do not have 'suppliers' in the traditional sense. Consequently, online small firms spend more time improving customer relationships using the Internet. When examining the experience of Internet commerce benefit, the percentage of customers online and how much they use Internet commerce with a small firm is significantly more important than that on the supplier end (Poon, 1998). This means if a small business is to be involved in Internet commerce, it must spend a considerable amount of effort to ensure that the virtual value chain between itself and its customers is well attended to.

10.3.5. THE DIFFERENCE BETWEEN EXPECTATION AND EXPERIENCE OF INTERNET COMMERCE

As there are numerous reports and hypes on what is Internet commerce, small businesses often find it difficult to work out the facts from the fictions. One typical example is to suggest that a small firm can use the Internet to reach out to the global marketplace and open up a worldwide market. Whether this is as easy as it seems is questionable. Reaching out to the global marketplace requires more than just having a Web site. Depending on the product characteristics, it also involves issues such as logistics, delivery, maintenance, support and other services. If a small firm is not properly prepared for international markets, it can jeopardise its reputation as an Internet business, and on the Internet, bad reputation travels faster than in any traditional media.

Based on a study which measures the difference between expectation and experience of Internet commerce, Poon and Swatman (1998) reported that many expectations have not been fully realised after a twenty-month period of Internet commerce experience. Only a small number of expectations turned out to be well achieved. Table 10.2 shows some of the most talked about business objectives of Internet commerce and how well they have been achieved. 'Better marketing and advertising', 'better company image' and 'significant sales through the Net' are among the most disappointing ones. These business objectives have scored high in the study of expectation but dropped significantly in twenty months. 'Forming more extensive business networks', 'obtaining useful expertise' and 'achieving better customer relationship' have been achieved as originally expected. Only two business objectives have exceeded original expectations and they are 'learn more about competitors' and 'saving time to find resources'.

The results from this study indicate that the Internet has so far been an effective information gathering and exchange medium. This is followed by its secondary role as a business networking medium and also as a marketing and trading mechanism. At least this is true among a group of online small businesses whose core business is not retailing. However, continuous development of advanced Internet applications might change this. As large organisations are starting to move away from proprietary inter-organisational systems to intranet/extranet solutions, small businesses will find more business-to-business Internet commerce opportunities with their large organisations. In addition, the change in demographic profile of Internet users means new business opportunities will arise from a broader demographic group.

Table 10.2. Expectation vs experience of Internet commerce (Poon and Swatman, 1998)

Business objectives	Expectation vs. Experience
Better advertising and marketing	✘
Better company image	✘
Trade in a virtual marketplace	✘
More extensive business network	AE
Obtain useful expertise on Net	AE
Savings in communication costs	✘
Better customer relationship	AE
Significant sales through Net	✘
Better supplier relationship	✘
Learn more about competitors	✓
Saving time to find resources	✓
✘ = worse than expected ✓ = better than expected AE = as expected	

10.3.6. HOW IMPORTANT ARE PRODUCT CHARACTERISTICS

The product or service offered by an online firm is often believed to pre-determine Internet commerce success. On the surface this is logical because many firms that sell software and information-based products are prime examples of Internet commerce success. However, whether firms that are selling physical goods will always be the underdog is questionable.

Based on a study by Poon and Swatman (1999) which examined the product characteristics and Internet commerce benefit, it shows that there is no significant difference in experience between those selling physical goods and those selling software and information-based products. Although this could have been a sampling bias, it is important that a small firm should not prejudge itself based on its offering. Indeed, some of the prime examples of Internet commerce success are selling goods that are physical and tangible (e.g. books, CDs and wines). However, if a firm has a local market and 'word-of-mouth' advertising is important, then Internet marketing may not be very useful even though it is selling digital or information-based products. One such example is a small local IT consultancy which offers software solutions to local small businesses. Although the Internet will be useful for exchanging documents with clients and delivering products, 'word-of-mouth' recommendation will still be very important for getting new business. As such, maybe writing a column in the local newspapers about the 'Year 2000' problem can help with the publicity more than advertising on a Web page. If this was a big international software firm distributing a similar product, then the situation could be quite different. Such a firm would have set up an online system on the Web allowing millions of customers worldwide to download updates and enhancements with zero delivery costs. The full cost of delivery is borne by the customer. In addition, it also allows the firm to track all the access details including 'number of times accessed', 'which are the popular products', 'license control' and 'the configurations of the user's system'.

Both being software companies, the market scope and the characteristics of the supply chain make the Internet an effective marketing medium for the international firm but not necessarily for the local one. However, this does not mean the local firm cannot be internationalised with the same approach. It should prepare for such opportunities and be ready when they arrive. At the same time, it should also monitor the reality through customer feedback and market intelligence.

10.3.7. A MATURITY MODEL OF INTERNET COMMERCE IN SMALL FIRMS

As small firms increasingly embrace Internet commerce, I have constructed a maturity model to describe the evolution process (see Figure 10.3). Due to the lack of financial and IT resources, a small firm typically starts small with its Internet commerce initiative, although there are exceptions to this. Many online small firms adopted Internet commerce by simply subscribing to an internet service provider (ISP) to use e-mail and browse the Web. Typical Internet commerce activities at this stage would be information gathering, exploring what is available on the Internet and e-mail communications (often with customers and other online groups). This is the lower left-hand quadrant of the model.

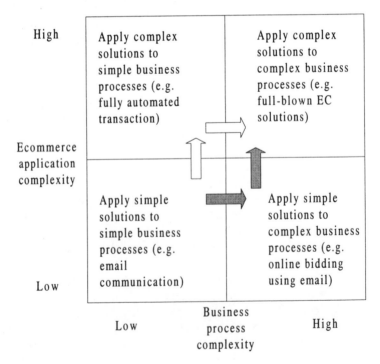

Figure 10.3. An Internet commerce maturity model.

When the small firm starts to find out what Internet commerce is capable of, the next stage is to experiment and find out how to benefit from it. Two approaches are often used. The first approach is to use readily available applications (e.g. e-mail package, Web browser and other freeware/shareware) to support business processes such as receiving orders, customer support, intelligence gathering and document exchange. I call this the 'process-focused' approach. As illustrated by the grey arrows in Figure 10.3, the process-focused approach emphasised exploring how to re-engineer business processes to fit with Internet commerce. The philosophy is to re-engineer business processes first and keep the technology simple. When the business processes have been re-engineered and re-designed, the simplistic technological solution will be replaced by a full-blown one, usually progressively. For small firms adopting the 'process-focused' approach, they follow the grey arrows maturity path. The process-focused approach is typically found in online small firms in which core competence is not IT- or high-technology-based.

In parallel to the process-focused approach, there is the 'technology-focused' approach. Firms that adopt the technology-focused approach started off like their process-focused counterpart – by testing out what can be done with Internet commerce. The difference is in the next stage. Whilst a process-focused firm studies and re-engineers its business processes first, a technology-focused firm advances its technology solution and tests it on simple business processes. The idea is to first build a robust Internet commerce solution without being too hung-up with the business processes, and then extend it to handle more complex business processes later. The white arrows in Figure 10.3 illustrate the evolution path of the technology-focused firms. Firms which adopt this approach are usually from the IT and high-technology industries. They would have already had in-house expertise and equipment to develop such solutions. In fact, many are IT solution builders themselves and therefore doing this is just part of their businesses.

Theoretically, both approaches will lead to the same final stage – a full-blown Internet commerce solution, although more empirical evidence is needed to validate this. In addition, the literature on strategic alignment (e.g. Venkatraman, Henderson and Oldach, 1993; Henderson and Venkatraman, 1994) also warns that there is a risk of failure if the 'technology–business' alignment process is not carried out properly.

Essentially, a firm needs to carry out continuous self-evaluation to decide which approach is best for its situation and to be prepared to switch course if necessary. For example, those who adopted the technology-focused approach may need to find out if the solution developed is helping its business processes to gain strategic improvements. If not, the company needs to go back to its business processes and evaluate what is to be done to achieve such an objective.

In the case of a process-focused firm, it needs to be aware that Internet commerce technology is developing faster than any other IT we have seen before. Both software and hardware for Internet commerce are at the brink of breaking Moore's Law and, therefore, solutions not feasible a year ago may be commonplace now. Therefore, one may need to switch to the technology approach and avoid losing time in the hyper-competitive age of Internet commerce.

In fact, from initial adoption to full-blown Internet commerce solution, it is likely to be a 'zig-zag' path. In addition, a full-blown, high-tech Internet commerce solution may not be for every small business. Some small firms will stay with a technically simple solution if it serves the purpose of the company. Others will only automate some of their business processes to cut down operational costs. In summary, the process of reaching Internet commerce maturity will depend on factors such as: industry characteristics, market demand, competition, affordability of solutions, and most importantly, management vision and the entrepreneurial culture of a firm. Indeed, in the hyper-competitive environment of Internet commerce, the most important asset for sustainability is the ability to implement entrepreneurial ideas and ongoing entrepreneurship.

10.4. Conclusion

In this chapter, I have outlined the current development of SBIC based on recent research carried out on this topic. Although there is evidence that small businesses are adopting Internet commerce, their experiences are sometimes different from what has been speculated. For example, instead of having a worldwide customer base, some small businesses found the experience of marketing over the Internet disappointing and achieved few sales. Essentially, the Internet, so far, has been primarily a communication medium using e-mail and an information exchange and gathering channel. Some firms found that they had improved customer relationships and built up business networks. Many adopted Internet commerce for future and longer-term opportunities because, so far, few had gained any significant short-term benefit.

An Internet commerce maturity model has been developed to describe two common Internet commerce evolution paths and I argued that many small firms are likely to 'zig-zag' between the two.

The evidence leads me to believe that the future of SBIC is bright and many online small firms have already found that the Internet is part of business. However, between now and the age of true global Electronic Commerce, issues such as cross-bordering trading, tangible government support and trusting business partners without face-to-face contact need to be resolved. Hopefully the legal, bureaucratic and business communities will work even closer to make Internet commerce a common way of doing business in the not-too-distant future.

CHAPTER 11

Towards Culturally Aware Information Systems

SCHAHRAM DUSTDAR

11.1. Some Critical Issues in Global Teams

The old boundaries of national economies and markets are bowing to globalisation and traditional offices are giving way to virtual organisational forms. The life-long or long-term employee/employer relationship is breaking down as the workforce establishes dynamic new entities and new organisational forms. Nowadays, everyone will agree that teamwork is becoming more and more fundamental and vital to global business activities. Clearly, when cross-functional and multi-cultural teams are formed and reformed rapidly, the choice of communications and collaboration technology has major implications on the way people work and conduct business. Most people will agree that no computer-mediated technology will substitute face-to-face meetings. But the question is, was that the purpose in the first place? This chapter argues that information systems researchers and practitioners should know the unique qualities of the technologies they use and relate them to the cultural qualities people hold. These cultural issues deal mainly with people's attitude towards time and towards people. Everyone is probably aware that some people tend to be monochronic and some tend to be polychronic. Monochronic people tend to sequence communications as well as tasks. They would not be inclined, as an example, to interrupt a phone conversation in order to greet a third person. Polychronic people can carry on multiple conversations simultaneously, indeed, they would consider it rude not to do so. Monochronic people are committed to the job, whereas polychronic people are group-oriented, tend to be committed to people and have a tendency to build lifetime relationships (Hall and Hall, 1990). These are only some simple examples, which have important implications on information systems design and usage. This chapter argues that cultural awareness is a *fundamental ingredient* for global information systems and technologies that support human collaboration, coordination and communication. The remainder of the chapter is structured as follows: Section 11.2 investigates current information systems and technologies and discusses their characteristics, Section 11.3 introduces a cultural framework for understanding cultural issues in information systems, and Section 11.4 discusses some issues for further research.

11.2. Current Information Systems

It is conventional wisdom that information systems that support teamwork need to integrate *organisational processes* and support *cultural contexts* if they are to be successful. Second, people should not be forced to "feed" the system artificially, i.e. users should work in the "natural" setting and the information system should be "intelligent and flexible" enough to enable the users and the organisations to work. One important goal of future research and development efforts is to support the notion of *cultural and organisational aware* information systems. The figure below illustrates group work in a generic framework. Group work goes through different sets of stages from group set-up, to brainstorming, to discussion of ideas, to actually doing the work with (legacy) applications (action) and finally evaluation of the work being done. Current information systems which are supposed to support collaborative work are called groupware and workflow systems. One of the fundamental problems of groupware/workflow systems on the market today is the lack of integration of this holistic view. Potentially, groupware/workflow systems should *support all stages* and provide *traceability* of discussions and work items from the group set-up process to the evaluation phase. Traditional workflow systems only support processes with the "Action" domain but do not provide support and traceability from, and to, the other important phases of group work. Figure 11.1 illustrates the five phases of group work and shows that groupware is supposed to support mainly brainstorming and discussion, whereas workflow systems are supposed to support action and evaluation. Let us take a closer look at the definitions of groupware and workflow systems.

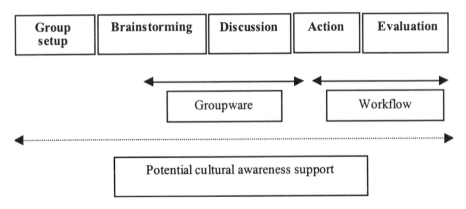

Figure 11.1. Teamwork and potential cultural awareness support.

Groupware has been defined as "technology based systems that support groups of participants working on a common task or goal, and that help provide a shared environment" (Ellis et al., 1991). It naturally includes technologies such as electronic mail, video conferencing, and shared group document editors. Groupware typically does not contain any knowledge or representation of the goals or processes of the group, and thus cannot explicitly help to forward the group process. We say that these systems are not organisationally aware. On the other hand, workflow systems are typically organisationally aware because they contain an explicit representation of organisational processes. Workflow management systems have been defined as "technology based systems that define, manage, and execute workflow processes through the execution of software whose order of execution is driven by a computer representation of the workflow process logic" (WfMC, 1995). Whereas groupware has been criticised because it is not organisationally aware, workflow has been criticised because of its typically inflexible and dictatorial nature compared to the way that office workers really accomplish tasks (Grudin, 1988).

Internet enabled workflow systems are on the rise because software engineers want to propel the market value of their products via integration with the Web. Future workflow systems will soon cover inter-organisational activities and processes including product value-chains on the Internet. Current workflow systems lack the ability to link to the organisations' legacy applications. Instead, most workflow systems move documents around the network. There has been other work attempting to bring together workflow and groupware technologies. Industrial research labs and product teams have made significant steps forward. The interesting work and products of Winograd and Flores based upon speech act theory suggest that any interaction can be viewed as a "conversation" with a protocol structure that can be modelled as a workflow (Flores et al., 1988). The coordinator was a product emerging from this work that had this protocol notion built in.

11.3. Cultural Framework for Information Systems

Now that communication technology is spanning the whole globe, national culture has surfaced as a variable in IS research of many kinds. Following Hofstede (1991), we define 'National culture' as "The collective programming of the mind which distinguishes the members of one country from another". That is, national culture is taught from early infancy. It does not encompass personality, nor, on the other hand, human nature.

One of the theories on national culture that is widely adopted by IS researchers is Hofstede's framework of five dimensions of national culture (Hofstede, 1980, 1991). Hofstede's main findings are that the attitude of people towards their jobs and employers can be classified along a number of "dimensions of culture". These were originally empirically derived in a comparison among IBM employees from many nationalities. They have been found to be quite useful for describing intercultural communication (Gudykunst and Ting-Toomey, 1988, Pedersen and Ivey, 1993). Hofstede's dimensions constitute the framework for our research model. They are: (a) power distance, (b) individualism versus collectivism, (c) masculinity versus femininity, also termed competitiveness versus cooperativeness, and (d) uncertainty avoidance. A fifth dimension was found with South-East Asian cultures: (e) long-term versus short-time orientation. The first three dimensions represent three fundamental *relationships between people*: vertical, horizontal, and gender-related. The latter two can be seen as the western and eastern version of a culture's *orientation towards time*. The fifth dimension, long-term orientation, did not figure in Hofstede's original data because the original questionnaires, having been drawn up by a team without South-East Asian members, did not contain questions addressing this dimension. It was discovered later, using a questionnaire designed by South-East Asians. The particulars can be read in Hofstede (1991). All five dimensions are orthogonal; that is, a country's score on power distance has nothing to do with one's score on individualism, masculinity, uncertainty avoidance, or long-time orientation. To see how this framework can help explain communication during meetings, let us return to the Dutch expatriate quoted in the introduction. The Netherlands and the USA are both countries with low power distance, high individualism, and low uncertainty avoidance. But the USA is considerably more masculinist in its national culture than the Netherlands. This difference can account for the Dutchman's comment. Two of the five dimensions usually breed most problems in organisations if people who cooperate differ along them. These are power distance and uncertainty avoidance (Hofstede, 1991). An instance of this in the IS field is described in Barret et al. (1996) in an account of a cross-cultural IS development team. To our knowledge, specific research about the influence of national culture on communication during meetings has not been carried out, although much anecdotal evidence exists. Hofstede's dimensions are being used for training intercultural consultants, however, indicating their relevance in this context (see, for example, Pedersen and Ivey, 1993, Brislin and Yoshida, 1994). Pedersen et al. introduced the concept of a 'synthetic culture', a script for an extreme manifestation of only one of the five dimensions. For instance, a synthetic culture can be 'high power distance' or 'long-term oriented'. Experiments in which meeting participants enacted extreme manifestations of one of the dimensions showed a marked effect of enacted national culture on both the process and the outcome of meetings (Hofstede, 1996). Although Gudykunst and Ting-Toomey (1988) give many clues, we have, so far, not found a comprehensive treatment of floor control issues during meetings in a cultural perspective. What is very clear from both literature and practice is that culture clash can lead to severe communication breakdowns in any cross-culture conversation.

Among groupware systems, videoconferencing represents a challenging category for researching cultural issues in information systems because they provide visual clues in communications. In the reminder of this chapter, we therefore focus on videoconferencing as an example to see whether videoconferencing systems and procedures can be adapted to the particular cross-cultural setting they are used in so that the occurrence of culture-clash related misunderstandings is minimised.

11.3.1. USING VIDEOCONFERENCING IN CROSS-CULTURAL BUSINESS TEAMS

One basic manifestation of cultural values is transparent when we deal with the concept of 'floor control'. A meeting is a group setting in which only one participant can speak, or 'have the floor', at any point in time. So, informally, 'the floor' means 'the temporary monopoly for distributing signals to the other participants'. A more precise definition of the concept of 'floor' in videoconferencing can be found in Dommel and Garcia-Luna-Aceves (1997, p. 23): "Floors are temporary permissions granted dynamically to collaborating users in order to mitigate race conditions and guarantee mutually exclusive resource usage". This second definition shows that more than one 'floor' can exist at a moment in time in an electronic meeting. One person could have the audio floor, while another one has a whiteboard floor or a minutes floor. However, there will almost always be a main speaker at any point in time, and the loose definition, which captures that concept, will suffice for the present chapter.

How the floor is taken and lost, or granted, is crucial for a meeting's process and outcome. A meeting needs a *social protocol*, part of which is a floor control mechanism in order to proceed in a manner that is satisfactory to the participants. For instance, a chairman may be appointed whose task it is to keep a first-in, first-out queue of people who have indicated a wish to speak by raising their hand. Alternatively, a participant with a high prestige may grant the word and the others will just wait until they are addressed by this high-status person. Or everybody may just try and get a word in, using their voice and body posture to indicate the urgency of their contribution. It is not hard to see how differences in culture can affect the floor control mechanism that is chosen. For example, participants from countries with low power distance will expect that anybody can take the floor whenever they want, unless other arrangements - such as appointing a floor-granting chairperson - have been made explicitly. The floor control mechanisms are engrained in national culture.

Distributed collaborative systems such as videoconferencing systems must indicate something about the social world they represent, in particular, who is on the system, what are the others currently doing and in which context. These *social activity indicators* (Ackerman and Starr, 1996) are becoming increasingly important the more people from various cultural and professional backgrounds have to collaborate. Furthermore, the lack of social activity indicators in collaborative systems slows down the process of establishing a critical mass of users. Dealing with floor control issues, two areas have to be discussed: floor control policies and floor control mechanisms. Policies describe how conference participants request the floor and how the floor is assigned and released. In the context of desktop videoconferencing systems, the simplest form of floor control would be if only one conference participant had the floor at any given time and the floor was handed off whenever requested by other participants. Floor control mechanisms are low-level means used to implement floor control policies (Reinhard et al., 1994).

In the following section, we summarise our findings gained from several years of videoconference usage with people from countries with low power distance and high individualism on the Internet. We discuss some issues that are crucial in point-to-point and multipoint desktop videoconferences and give some suggestions for dealing with problems that we encountered. The videoconferencing tools on the Internet can be classified as (a) video-tools, (b) audio-tools, and (c) shared whiteboards. These tools are *not integrated*; i.e. it is not possible to use an audio-tool to transmit video either from point-to-point or to multi-point. The same is true for video-tools and shared whiteboards. One of the first things one says after establishing a videoconference link is the question: "Can you hear me and/or can you see me?". This circumstance makes it impracticable to establish a videoconference without using a telephone as a *backup medium*. We shall first account a number of experiences in an informal way, ordered by type of communication medium. This is done in order to capture as much richness as we can. Then, we shall try to interpret these in the light of the five culture dimensions and see whether we can find evidence that relates to our research framework.

Regarding *audio*, we can say that in a point-to-point telephone conversation, the listener will frequently hum or say 'yes' to indicate he or she is listening and hears what is being said. In a multi-point telephone conference, this is not so easy. The listeners tend to be silent. This may leave the speaker wondering how what he has said has been received. This is especially disturbing for 'political' persons, who rely on atmosphere and eye contact to assess how their messages are received. The next thing one encounters is the problem of *concurrent speaking*. Generally speaking, network bandwidth is limited. Since audio and video streams are sent over the Internet the traffic is a problem. Therefore, audio and video data packets get lost. In the case of audio packet loss, one will feel very disturbed and the conversation will decrease in quality. It was mentioned above that collaborative systems lack "*social activity indicators*". Due to the fact that the videoconferencing tools are not integrated, it is difficult for conference participants to check which of the participants is having, for example, audio or whiteboard only. However, the audio tool shows which conference participant is speaking. In the popular Mbone videoconferencing tools for the Internet there is a "meter" below the loudspeaker symbol that moves according to the speakers' volume. Another useful feature is the "mute" button. There are cases in which a conference participant needs some "private" time or simply does not want to transmit audio from his or her site.

The *video* component in a videoconference is often viewed as the crucial component. As stated above, network bandwidth is limited in most of the cases. Over the Internet, data packets get lost. In cases of video packet loss, human perception is not so sensitive as is the case with audio packet loss. If video packets get lost the motion of the other videoconference participant(s) is "jerky". Nuances in facial expression will be lost and it will not be possible to infer how the others respond to what is being said. On the other hand, one can stare at a particular participant unnoticed, and still infer things from, for example, fidgeting. A problem which occurs in multipoint videoconferences is the missing link between audio- and video tools. In large videoconference settings with some 10 conference participants one can hardly tell who is currently speaking, even when one enlarges the thumbnail video of the anticipated conference participant manually by clicking on it. In this context, one of the main problems desktop multipoint videoconference participants have to deal with is how much "*real estate*" the video for each conference participant gets on the users' computer monitor. As one can imagine, it is very difficult to have all video windows open, even if the user has a 21 inch monitor. One has to think of also having the necessary audio and shared whiteboard windows open concurrently. A feature which one can find in face-to-face meetings but which is missing here is the possibility of directing audio or video streams to one member or to a subgroup of the conference participants only ("side chatting"). In a face-to-face meeting you can turn to your neighbour and have a short chat. Using desktop multipoint videoconferencing this ability gets lost.

Figure 11.2 also illustrates the problem of "*conference participants' context*". The window below shows (at least) two conference participants sharing one videoconference workstation. Communication and collaboration using one workstation with two participants can be quite disturbing and might happen often in business scenarios. In this area, we suggest that desktop videoconferencing participants have at least two video cameras installed so that the conference partners have more clues on the organisational- and personal context.

Figure 11.2. Context of videoconference participant.

Finally, the shared *whiteboard* heavily depends on cultural issues. Whiteboard applications usually have some drawing and writing tools and some shared document space. The whiteboard tools also display who is actually drawing at the moment. However, in some cases it makes a lot of sense to "anonymise" the results by not showing which participant wrote on the whiteboard. If a contribution is anonymous, those who read it will tend to take it at face value. If it is not, it will be interpreted politically, on the basis of the reader's relationship to the author. Another issue that sufaces in whiteboarding, or in simple e-mail, is use of language. For instance, whether a non-native English speaker has been taught British or American English makes a great deal of difference in the style they have learnt to adopt. Misunderstandings can arise because participants unknowingly offend the receiver. For example, USA inhabitants frequently do not bother to put any header (such as 'Dear X' or even 'Hi X!') above their e-mail messages. Receivers in many countries (cultures) will not be favourably struck by what they perceive as a lack of respect or manners.

11.3.2. SOME CULTURAL IMPLICATIONS FOR VIDEOCONFERENCING ON THE INTERNET

This section tries to illustrate some implications of these findings. For the sake of clarity, they will be sorted by dimension of culture, although this is rather artificial. After all, any person is a 'living mix' of all five dimensions, also each person has a number of personal characteristics and a personal history. The mix of all of these can lead to different behaviours than can be explained by only one dimension of culture.

Power distance

Low scores on power distance will lead to equal distribution of speaking time and spontaneous "taking the floor" by all. Given the audio quality that is reached with current technology, this will lead to packet loss. Videoconference participants with low power distance will have to get used to waiting for a silence before they talk. High scores will lead to unequal distribution of speaking time, with subordinates only speaking when a superior explicitly grants them the floor. If the status of participants is not clear, communication will be tentative until clarity is reached. If the participants in a meeting are of similar power distance, there will not be any problems, as long as they know each other's relative status; participants will then know their place. However, if they differ along the power distance axis, those low on power distance will tend to take the floor uninvited, and to assume that others will do the same. This can lead to frustration. To tackle this issue, one could think of a feature such as a "*speaking time meter*" which shows to all conference participants the length of time taken to speak to the group of participants. Currently, no such thing exists, but it is technically easy to implement in a video- or audio-conference. A session chair could use such a device to ensure participation from everyone. In fact, it is this sort of innovation that electronic media can bring.

Individualism

Individualists will all freely express their opinions with a focus on the task at hand. They may be of diametrically opposed opinions without having any personal antipathy. They may invest considerable energy into forming and negotiating *ad hoc* coalitions. In order to do so, they will occasionally engage in 'side-chatting' in small groups. As stated above, current videoconferencing tools do not allow for this. Individualists who are, moreover, low on power distance will frequently bump into each other's statements. This will be awkward in electronic meetings. Collectivists of a single in-group will all express similar views, with a view to preserving group harmony. To them, expressing a different view equals an attack to the group. Collectivists from different in-groups will most likely either not express any opinion at all for fear of saying the wrong thing, or they might fiercely attack outgroup participants who express deviant views.

Masculinism

Achievement-oriented (masculinist) participants will not hesitate to engage in open, up-front conflict when there is a difference of opinion. Cooperation-oriented (femininist) participants will avoid open conflict, but rather they will try to resolve differences of opinion by compromising, and will mediate.

Uncertainty avoidance

Speakers high on uncertainty avoidance will wish to set formal rules for the meeting, including floor control regulation. They will be emotional in their statements, possibly exaggerating. Those low on uncertainty avoidance will be calm, possibly "dull", will like to explore divergent ideas, and will be tolerant of individuals who deviate from any rules. Differences in uncertainty avoidance are known to be the cause of much aggravation in organised life. In a setting of mixed uncertainty avoidance, it is probably a good idea to lay out the rules of the meeting very clearly at the outset to avoid ambiguity.

Long-term orientation

As to long-term orientation, speakers who are short-term oriented will be much concerned with issues of "face": not insulting somebody, reciprocating compliments, and the like. Long-term oriented speakers will not offend others either, unless their own objectives for the meeting are at stake. Table 11.1 summarises the hypotheses ventured above.

Table 11.1. Characteristics of meetings according to extreme manifestations of national culture dimensions.

	Implications for floor control	
Dimensions of culture	*Low*	*High*
Power distance	Spontaneously taking the floor	Unequal distribution of time, with superior controlling the floor
Individualism	Non-verbal signals important. Deviant views lead to strong feelings, and often to withdrawal.	Free opinion sharing. Quality of signals not so important. Interruptions will occur, or could be blocked. Side chatting occurs.
Masculinity	Compromise and mediation	Open up-front conflict
Uncertainty avoidance	Calm meetings. few policies	Participants want formal rules for the meeting. Strong non-verbal support for utterances.
Long-term orientation	Much concerned with saving "face"	Achieving objectives more critical, even if it means being impolite.

11.3.3. DISCUSSION

So far, we have been concerned mainly with the perspective of a participant who has the floor, or would wish to take it. But, in an actual meeting, most participants are just listeners most of the time. It is only after having listened that they decide whether to take the floor and what to say or write and it is especially for a listener that an electronic meeting differs from a face-to-face meeting. For instance, consider a meeting where the participants are unknown to each other. Somebody issues a statement. A listener will not only listen to the content of what is being said. Depending on their culture, listeners will also wish to know something about the speaker in order to be able to interpret what is being said. Table 11.2 predicts that people high on individualism and low on the other dimensions will readily engage in communication on the basis of the utterances only, without knowing who is talking. In fact, this coincides with the success of the Internet, where "nobody knows you're a dog", in Anglo-Saxon countries. The table also predicts that listeners will feel uncomfortable in settings where the clues they culturally wish to have about a speaker are not provided. There are two ways to respond to this uncertainty. Either one could adapt the communication medium to include the necessary clues (the "social identity clues mode", or "clues mode" for short), or one could deliberately leave them out, forcing communication on the basis of ideas only (the "Mind mode"). In the context of videoconferencing, clues mode would necessitate giving explicit information about status and group membership (through institutional and educational background or *curriculum vitae* information). Gender can be seen, as well as some limited information about social identity through hair-do, clothing, pronunciation, vocabulary, verbosity. Mind mode would lead to the use of whiteboarding techniques, so that contributions could be made anonymous.

In an actual electronic meeting, actual groupware tools will be used. What floor control policies and mechanisms should these possess, according to our findings and hypotheses? Table 11.2 provides an overview of the proposed floor control policies and mechanisms.

Table 11.2. Implications of culture for floor control policies.

Dimensions of culture	Implications for videoconferencing sessions	
	Low	High
Power distance	'Wish to interrupt' indicator for listener that floor holder can choose to acknowledge or disregard	Show people's responsibilities, privilege of floor-granting
Individualism	Enhance video quality, provide background for participants	Allow side-chatting
Masculinity		Possibilities for non-verbal displays of strenghth are limited
Uncertainty avoidance		Have a formal protocol
Long-term orientation		

Videoconferencing in particular, and groupware generally, should, if possible, accommodate all possible mixes of culture. It is up to the participants to choose how to use them. Let us imagine a multi-cultural videoconference with participants from all synthetic cultures who do not know each other well. There are two chairpersons: one is the regular meeting chair, the other is a technical chair who knows about the software. The meeting could start with a little 'looking around' introduction in which all participants tell and show the others where they are, if their camera can be moved. This will allow the participants to do whatever their synthetic culture has taught them to do: be polite, "come on strong", obtain information about the others' status or group membership. Then, the technical chair could explain how the meeting will proceed and give examples of the features offered by the software. Prior consultation between the general chair and the technical chair would have set the guidelines here. Depending on the meeting's aim, the general chair can distribute the floor or 'I wish to interrupt' buttons could be used; anonymity of contributions could be an option, speaking time could be regulated, side-chatting could be disabled. Also, the technical chair could give some advice about how to enhance communication, such as getting proper lighting for one's face, speaking clearly, not moving about too vehemently when speaking. Thus prepared, the participants can start the meeting. It will be rather more orchestrated than a face-to-face meeting. Among other things, the time slot for the meeting is likely to be quite strict so that the meeting's end-time is pre-determined. The general chair will take this into account and do whatever is necessary to wind up the meeting in time.

11.4. Future Research

Research on desktop videoconferencing and its application in collaborative work processes is interlinked with research on other information processing, communication and coordination activities. Together with an Internet connection, the MBone desktop videoconferencing tools provide the user and the organisation with the possibility to communicate, collaborate, and coordinate on a global scale. However, the tools need to be integrated into organisational information systems such as workflow and groupware systems, word processing, project management software and spreadsheet applications and, most importantly, they need to support "social protocols" and be *culturally aware*. Desktop videoconferencing is not a substitute to face-to-face meetings, but it "forces" people to change decision making processes, collaboration, coordination, and communication patterns.

Among the organisational issues, questions of *floor control policies* and the necessary support for cross-cultural communication and collaboration have to be resolved. This research area needs interdisciplinary efforts since multimedia and CSCW (computer supported cooperative work) themselves are interdisciplinary fields. Future research should consist of both controlled experiments and observation of non-controlled videoconferences. As Ishii et al. (1995) state, we are interacting not *with* computers, but *through* computers. This should gradually lead to a new and better understanding of cultural issues as dependent variables in desktop videoconferencing. Social protocols will have to emerge surrounding videoconferences. Gradually, the integration of videoconferencing tools with other essential groupware and workflow systems will become a reality for global business teams on the Internet.

CHAPTER 12

The Online Stock Broker

An Investigation of Electronic Contracting on the Web

SUBHASISH DASGUPTA

12.1. Introduction

We have been witnesses to the invention of the World Wide Web and its amazing growth in this decade. With this growth, electronic commerce and transactions on the Internet has increased. Approximately 2.7 billion dollars worth of transactions took place over the Internet in 1997, and the number is expected to climb to 5 billion dollars in 1998 (Guay, 1998). This phenomenal increase in electronic commerce has not been restricted to any particular industry and this buying trend has affected both products and services. People are buying products from web shopping malls, travel services from Internet-based travel agencies, and financial services from banks and brokerage houses. One such service, which has experienced unprecedented growth in the USA, is online stock trading. In fact, more people trade securities than purchase books, CDs or any other product online.

The online brokerages are in the midst of phenomenal growth. Average daily online trades in the last quarter of 1997 were 153,000. The majority of trades involved stocks not funds. In the first few months of 1998, 4.6 million individuals traded stocks online - an increase of over 150% in the last six months of 1997 alone. By the year 2002, more than 20% of American households are expected to invest electronically. Online trades accounted for 17% of total retail trades in 1997; this figure will approach 30% in 1998 (Dreyfuss 1998).

Commerce is defined as the trade between different parties (Webster Dictionary 1998). An essential part of commerce is the ability of parties to enter into an official or legal agreement to exchange goods or money. As commerce has moved to the World Wide Web, the ability to provide agreements has been moved to this new medium. Since the Web provides an electronic medium to trade, contracts executed in it are called electronic contracts. An industry which has seen a major change due to the phenomenal growth of the Internet is stock trading. Now, people can buy and sell securities directly over the World Wide Web using online stock trading sites. In this chapter, we look at electronic contracting in the present model for online stock trading in the USA. We also investigate the various issues critical to the continued success of the industry.

This chapter is organised as follows. First, we define electronic contracts and provide a classification of electronic contracts. Next, we provide a description of the traditional stock trading systems followed by online stock trading systems and electronic contracting in these systems. After that, we provide reasons for the success of these systems and its limitations and a conclusion.

12.2. Electronic Contract

Electronic contracting involves the exchange of messages between buyers and sellers, structured according to a prearranged format so that the contents are machine processible and automatically give rise to contractual obligations (Baum 1991). According to Runge (1998), electronic contracting comprises of two activities. The first activity includes electronic agreement or contract negotiations. The second activity is the signing of contracts, which have been previously negotiated or exchanged electronically.

Like any other contract, an electronic contract involves two or more parties. The electronic contract can take different forms: explicit and implicit. This classification is characterised by the medium used for execution of the contract and its implementation. The two forms are described below:

- *Explicit electronic contract*: An explicit electronic contract is one in which the parties involved sign a traditional or a non-electronic contract. The implications of this agreement are then carried over to an electronic medium like the World Wide Web.
- *Implicit electronic contract*: An implicit electronic contract is one in which the contract is signed electronically by the parties involved on the Web. In many cases, some kind of guarantee is required so that one of the parties does not balk from the contract. In electronic retailers like amazon.com and priceline.com, a credit card provides guarantees that a customer will buy the product. On the other hand, there are some electronic contracts that do not involve a guarantee, like signing up with a web portal like Yahoo! which allows the user to customise information available to them from the web portal. In this case, the web site exercises control by using cookie technology. Moreover, the goods traded on Yahoo! are not tangible like the books traded in Amazon.com and airline tickets in priceline.com.

12.3. Traditional Stock Trading System

A traditional stock trading system has three major players: the investor, broker and stock exchange. According to Picot et al. (1998), there are three steps involved in the intermediation process in which an investor is able to buy or sell his or her investments in a stock market.

- Since the investor is not allowed to deal directly in the stock exchange, he or she has to hire an agent to get access to a security market arena.
- The second is the exchange itself, which provides the environment in which

organisation and control mechanisms are in place for the transaction arena.

- The third step of intermediation takes place through the price discovery process, which adjusts the orders of the investors through the interaction of trading participants.

There are two types of stock exchange organisations based on the price discovery process used: the market maker system like the one practiced on the London Stock Exchange and the auction system like the one practiced on the Chicago Mercantile Exchange (Cohen et al., 1986; Picot, 1998; Stoll, 1992). According to Picot (1998), the major difference between these systems lies in that two orders may directly meet in the auctions system, whereas in the market maker system, direct order matching is impossible. In the market maker system, the market maker intermediates between the quotes for bids and asks. His revenues result from the spread between bid and ask. Between the auction and the market maker systems, there is a continuum of hybrid systems that match bids and asks.

Figure 12.1. Traditional stock trading system.

Information systems based stock exchanges became popular with the NASDAQ (National Association of Securities Dealers Automated Quotation). The National Association of Securities Dealers (NASD) used "pink sheets" for quotations prior to the information systems. The pink sheets were inefficient because the papers had to be printed every single day and timely price information was impossible. The Securities and Exchange Commission (SEC), which is the regulatory agency in the USA, demanded in 1970 that the quotation pink sheets be replaced with an information system providing real time quotation information. The NASDAQ that was established in 1971 enabled brokers to observe quotations from different market makers in real time on the computer screen.

In addition to computer-based exchange systems, additional systems are needed to send orders to the exchange and to publish information about executed transactions, like price and volume. According to Picot (1998), there are two types of systems classified according to their function:

- *Order routing systems.* Order routing systems are responsible for the electronic transmission of an order to the relevant receiver. The relevant receiver could be the broker or the broker's representative on the trading floor or automated exchange system.

- *Clearing and Settlement Systems.* When an order is executed by two parties; the broker representing the seller and the broker representing the buyer. The clearing and settlement system manages the transfer of securities from the buyer to the seller. The system allows the transfer process to be efficient, since these procedures are particularly time-consuming and error-prone.

The different systems that are part of the online stock trading system are provided in the next section.

12.4. Electronic Contracting in Online Stock Trading Systems

In the traditional method of stock trading, investors call brokers for advice and placement of orders. The cost for a trade is generally a minimum amount plus a percentage of the total value of the transaction. One brokerage firm, Charles Schwab, introduced a business model that allowed investors and brokers to place their trades using a virtual private network for trading. Online trading systems allow investors to place their trades on the World Wide Web. Brokerage houses have set up web sites that handle all aspects of the transaction.

The process of online stock trading can be broken down into three distinct activities. The first activity involves an electronic agreement between a buyer and a broker (and similarly between a seller and an agent). The second encompasses an electronic agreement between agents representing the buyer and the seller to transfer stocks from the seller to the buyer at a mutually acceptable price. The third activity is the execution of the contract, in which the order completion information is relayed back to the buyer and the seller. Let us look at the different activities in detail.

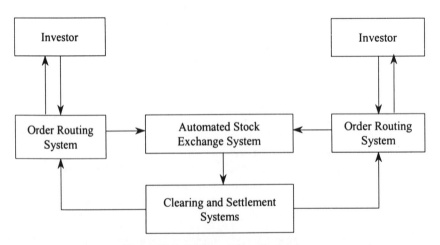

Figure 12.2. Online stock trading system.

12.4.1. INVESTOR-BROKER

The process of online stock trading starts with the investor signing up with an online brokerage house. Some online trading systems allow investors to complete the entire application form over the Internet while others require a copy to be mailed to them using traditional mail. The use of an explicit electronic contracting system like this is prevalent in most online brokerages. The form is a contract that allows the firm to trade as an agent for the investor at a preset trading price. After the successful completion of the application process, the client may start trading. When the investor places a trade using the online system - the investor is effectively signing an electronic contract with the agent (their broker) to buy (or sell) a certain number of stocks at market price (called a market order) or at a client-given price (called a limit order). The agent handles the next step in the process.

12.4.2. STOCK EXCHANGE

The agent or the broker electronically transmits the order to the exchange where the price discovery process takes place. Exchanges provide the organisation and the operation of a trading arena in which their members can achieve profits. Despite the heterogeneity of trading processes there exists a homogeneous governance structure. A number of studies have espoused the benefits of information technology investments in stock exchanges. In a stock market, communication takes place between participants. Since all participants act strategically, and since the communication is not frictionless, the use of coordination mechanisms incurs costs known as transaction costs. Investments in information technology allow for a more efficient communication and potentially greater coordination of the market participants, thereby reducing transaction costs (Picot et al, 1998).

Each exchange has a different system for price discovery, that is, to determine the price between the buyer and seller; as mentioned earlier, these prices are called bids and asks. In online stock trading systems, the automated exchange mechanism remains the same as discussed in our earlier section on traditional stock exchanges. As we discussed earlier, there are two fundamental types of exchange mechanisms: the market maker system and the auction system, and there are other hybrid forms of price discovery, which lie in the continuum between the market maker and the auction system.

In an electronic exchange (like the NASDAQ), the price discovery process takes place electronically. Brokers establish an electronic contract for sellers and buyers. The contract culminates with the execution of the trade or the transfer of shares from the seller to the buyer.

12.4.3. BROKER-INVESTOR

The brokers relay the confirmation of the trade execution back to the investor (buyer). The settlement date is three days from the date of the trade. By this time, the investor has to provide adequate funds for the completed transaction. The buyer transfers money from his or her account in cash, if cash is available or by using a traditional instrument like a check, and this completes the trade. The entire process is handled by the settlement and clearing system. The broker for the seller transfers the securities to the broker for the buyer. The money realised from this transaction is given to the seller.

12.5. Reasons for Success

What has fueled this increase in the electronic web-based stock trading? The success of online brokerages in the US can be attributed to four reasons: (1) resolution of Internet security concerns of users, (2) investor power, (3) reduced cost of trading due to competition, and (4) the state of the economy. We discuss each of these issues in detail below.

12.5.1. SECURITY

Investors access accounts using a password. SSL encryption protection is provided. While existing models of electronic commerce require investors to make payments over the web by credit card, online stock trading is different. For settlement of a trade in which the investor buys stock, the brokerage house extends a line of credit for a period of three days by which time the investor has to provide enough money to pay for the transaction. The investor generally uses traditional instruments like checks that are mailed to the financial institution. This environment does not require investors to use their credit cards or to provide and transmit personal information over the Internet.

12.5.2. INVESTOR POWER

Online brokerage systems give investors the ability to do all the transactions on their own, thus giving them a feeling of power. An increase in the number of market information sources on the Internet is also contributing to this surge in investor trading. The individual investor utilises the immense amount of market data available on the Internet to execute more transactions than the average institutional investor. In fact, there are a group of individuals who trade during the day and perform a large number of transactions in a day. They are called day traders. It is quite possible that online stock trading is giving rise to a new breed of customer - the impulsive buyer, or in our case, the impulsive trader. A new generation of investors may find themselves trading not because they really want to, but because they cannot resist the urge.

12.5.3. COMPETITION

Only 17 online stock-trading firms existed at the start of 1997. As of June 1998, there are 52 firms in the US. With the increase in the number of firms, competition has also increased. Online stock-trading firms are not only competing against traditional full service brokerages but also amongst themselves. The online investor is now reaping the benefits of increased competition. The average commission during the last quarter of 1997 had fallen to $15.95 compared to $52.89 in the first quarter of 1996 (Dreyfuss, 1998). A list of 12 US online trading firms and their charges per trade is given in Table 1. These firms account for 90% of all trading accounts on the web.

Table 12.1. Top US online brokers.

Web Site	Brokerage	Price per trade in USD (market orders)*
www.ameritrade.com	Ameritrade	8.00
www.datek.com	Datek Online	9.99
www.discoverbrokerage.com	Discover Brokerage Direct	14.95
www.dljdirect.com	DLJDirect	20.00
www.etrade.com	Etrade	14.95
www.fidelity.com	Fidelity Investments	14.95
www.ndb.com	National Discount Brokers	14.95
www.quickwaynet.com	Quick & Reilly	14.95
www.suretrade.com	SureTrade	7.95
www.schwab.com	Charles Schwab	29.95
www.waterhouse.com	Waterhouse Securities	12.00
www.webstreetsecurities.com	WebStreet Securities	14.95

*Prices are as of 20 June 1998, and are subject to change. Prices vary for limit orders. Restrictions on number of shares and a required minimum of trades may apply.

12.5.4. ECONOMY

Another reason for the success of online trading systems is the state of the US economy. The US stock market has grown over 20% in each of the last three years (1994-1997). Individual investors have seen their investment grow at a rate rarely seen in the past. This growth has attracted new, as well as smaller, investors to the stock market. These new entrants have embraced the low fees charged by online brokerages. Moreover, with increased amounts of information, including market data, company data, analysis, and reports available on the Internet, even the price-sensitive investor has moved to the online broker.

12.6. Limitations

Online stock trading systems have limitations. The two important limitations are discussed below (1) The capacity of online systems, and (2) the cost and quality of customer support services.

12.6.1. TIME

Online stock trading systems emphasise an explicit electronic contracting system in which users sign a contract using traditional means. This makes the entire contractual process time consuming. It is extremely important for online brokerages to determine ways in which electronic contracts can be made implicit.

12.6.2. CAPACITY

On one November day in 1997, when the New York Stock Exchange Dow Jones Stock Index plunged approximately 550 points, the trading volume on all major stock exchanges in the US was more than 50% above the daily average. Due to this unusually heavy traffic, a large number of online trading customers could not access the web sites of their brokerages. Most online trading brokerages should enhance their systems to provide services to their customers on these high volume days.

12.6.3. CUSTOMER SUPPORT SERVICES

Although trading is performed over the Web, some important transactions, like opening an account and confirming payment, are generally done by calling the brokerage's customer service centre. A large number of online trading services are very poor in replying to email inquiries from their customers, and customers find themselves calling the customer service centre. Company personnel operate these centres, and the labor costs associated with operating such centres are high.

12.7. Conclusion

In this chapter, we have investigated the role of electronic contracting in online brokerage services in the US. We have defined different types of electronic contracts: explicit and implicit. In online trading, we have found that most of the initial contracts made between an investor and an online brokerage are explicit electronic contracts. Contracts made while trading are all implicit contracts. In addition, we have looked at the reasons for their success and the limitations they will have to overcome for continued growth.

On the whole, the future of the online broker looks bright. There are some critics of the present system who think otherwise. Some question the viability of online brokerages at current price-levels for placing trades. They argue that, due to competition, companies are charging prices that will not allow many of them to survive. But, as we have seen in this chapter, the present state of the online stock trading systems provides valuable lessons for other electronic commerce and electronic contracting systems.

CHAPTER 13

Consumer Information Search and Decision Making in the Electronic Commerce Environment

REX EUGENE PEREIRA

13.1. Introduction

Marketing managers in the consumer goods industry face a new frontier of electronic information and commerce. Understanding buyer behaviour in this new marketing channel is crucial. Projections about the diffusion of electronic commerce have been breathtaking. It is estimated that by the year 2000, business-to-consumer electronic commerce will account for a sales volume of 80 billion dollars a year and business-to-business electronic commerce will account for a sales volume of 300 billion dollars a year (Al Gore, USA Vice President in his report to Congress, 1998). The past few years have seen a rapid growth in the variety of products carried by the electronic shopping malls on the World Wide Web. Simultaneously, technological advances have resulted in increasingly complex products. Consumers, who are becoming more mature, sophisticated, and intelligent, are demanding higher levels of product information before making purchasing decisions (Beninati, 1994; Whittemore, 1994). Rapid advancements in Web technology have offered a solution to this dilemma in the form of computerised decision aids that use software smart agents to provide an intelligent interface to the consumer. These computerised decision aids improve transactional efficiency by providing merchandising and sales information to consumers, offering sales support, and facilitating sales promotions, while at the same time, enhancing the consistency, availability, and quality of support to consumers. These computerised decision aids have the potential to empower consumers by enabling them to make informed decisions about the marketplace.

The providers of these computerised decision aids inherently assume that these computerised decision aids are useful and desirable. To be useful as alternative sources of product information, consumers must choose to incorporate these computerised decision aids in their decision making process, and to rely upon the information and recommendations presented. Consumers will be more likely to develop new patterns of information search and decision making strategies involving new information technologies if the time and energy expended in these activities is perceived to be judicious and beneficial (Russo, 1987; Russo and Leclerc, 1991).

As marketing managers aim to provide consumers with information on which to base their decisions, the question of how to provide such information arises. Specifically, marketing managers have to select the type of information system they want to utilise in order to deliver the most appropriate information to consumers. One of the main objectives of marketing managers is to present consumers with information on which to base their decisions (Anderson and Rubin, 1986). The information presented has to be such that it allows consumers to make decisions and select products that best match their tastes and needs (Bettman, Johnson and Payne, 1991). Otherwise, consumers' incentive to seek out information will be minimal (Alba, Lynch, Weitz, Janiszewski, Lutz, Sawyer, and Wood, 1997). Presenting such information is not simple. On the one hand, a vast amount of information could be relevant, even very relevant to some consumers. On the other hand, presenting superfluous information might impede consumers' ability to make good decisions (Bettman, Johnson and Payne, 1991). If consumers were predictable and all alike, presenting information would present no problem – marketing managers could provide only the information that is deemed most relevant by all the consumers. However, because of the heterogeneity between and within consumers, almost none of the potentially available information is universally perceived as relevant. What is a key datum for a certain consumer at a certain point in time may be perceived as superfluous information by other consumers and even by the same consumer at a different point in time. The task facing marketing managers is not simply to present consumers with every piece of information, but rather to present consumers with information that is appropriate for their current needs. The objective is to help consumers be appropriately selective in their information acquisitions (Hoffman and Novak, 1996a, 1996b; Alba, Lynch, Weitz, Janiszewski, Lutz, Sawyer, and Wood, 1997). Since there is an abundance of potentially relevant information and since consumers have limited cognitive resources available to process this information, there is a need for marketing managers to choose wisely which information to present, and how to present it. The central goal of the current research, therefore, is to examine how the design of communication systems impacts consumers' ability to use the information provided.

The issue of information overload has occupied marketing managers for some time now, as it relates to all forms of marketing communications. The relevance and scope of this problem has increased tremendously with the prevalence of electronic information, computers, and computer networks (Alba, Lynch, Weitz, Janiszewski, Lutz, Sawyer, and Wood, 1997; Hoffman and Novak, 1996a; Gupta, 1995; Hoffman, Novak and Chatterjee, 1995). The wealth of available information makes it clear that information providers need to help consumers sift through and manage the information. This is necessary so that consumers can find the information they need without being "drowned" in it (Alba, Lynch, Weitz, Janiszewski, Lutz, Sawyer, and Wood, 1997). Since providing information becomes a central activity for many organisations, their survival depends on their understanding of how to help consumers acquire and use the information. The goal of the current research is to understand how query-based decision aids (QBDA) influence consumer decision making, to examine their advantages and disadvantages, to relate these to different aspects of information systems, and to shed some light on the relationship between the availability of these decision aids and consumers' use of information systems.

I focus my research efforts on attempting to understand the role which QBDA on the Web play in this information search process. By QBDA, I refer to the search and decision making tools available on the Internet, such as those provided by Personal Logic (www.personalogic.com), Microsoft Carpoint (carpoint. msn.com), and Bargain Finder (bf.cstar.ac.com/bf). These tools support the decision making process of consumers who are shopping on the Web. Some of them support common multi-attribute heuristics such as elimination by aspects and the conjunctive rule. The use of QBDA seems to have both advantages and disadvantages. In terms of benefits, the use of QBDA allows consumers to deal with information systems that better fit their individual informational needs and are more flexible (Kleinmuntz and Schkade, 1993; Schkade and Kleinmuntz, 1994). In terms of costs, the use of QBDA requires the user to invest processing resources in managing the information flow and in specifying the query criteria.

13.2. Influence of Computerised Decision Aids on Decision Making

Power, Meyaraan and Aldag (1994) investigated the fit of specific types of computerised decision aids with various decision problem situations. They found that users who had access to computerised decision aids in their choice tasks considered fewer alternatives, took more time making decisions, used more analytical tools and had poorer decision quality as compared to users who did not have access. Users who had access to the computerised decision aid had positive attitudes toward it. Users would seriously limit their search behaviour and had significantly altered choice behaviour. They did not observe significant interaction effects between problem structure and the use of the computerised decision aid.

Hill, King and Cohen (1996) investigated the perceived utility of computerised decision aids by consumers. They investigated the effects of the type of computerised decision aid format (autonomous versus dominant) and the provision of educational information on the perceived utility of the computerised decision aid by consumers. They found that the selection of an appropriate format depended upon the nature of the product being selected, whereas the inclusion of educational information enhanced the perceived utility of the computerised decision aid regardless of the type of product being purchased.

Todd and Benbasat (1992) investigated the influence of a computer-based decision aid on the extent of information used by subjects and the resulting decision quality. They found that subjects who had access to the computer-based decision aid did not use more information in their decision making as compared to subjects who did not have access to the computerised decision aid. They found that overall, subjects behaved as if effort minimisation was an important consideration. They conclude that in the design of computer based decision support systems it is important to consider the decision maker's trade-off between improving decision quality and conserving effort. Effort played a mediating role in determining the effectiveness of a computer based decision support system (DSS).

Todd and Benbasat (1996) investigated how cognitive effort interacts with task complexity and the presence of computerised decision aids to influence the formulation of mental models by subjects. They found that two types of cognitive effort influenced decision making. The first was the effort associated with building or formulating a model. The second was the effort associated with utilising that mental model in the solution of a problem. Kotteman and Davis (1991) investigate the impact of decision conflict on the user acceptance of multi-criteria decision making aids. They found that decision conflict played a major role in the strategy selection and the selection of the multiple criteria decision making technique to be employed.

Olson, Moshkovich, Schellenberger and Mechitov (1995) investigated the influence of the method in which preference information is elicited, and the structure of alternatives presented on the results from using various multi-criteria decision making aids. They found that two systems based on the multi-attribute value theory model were just as diverse in their conclusions as were results between AHP and the multi-attribute value theory models. Accuracy of information reflecting decision maker preference was found to be an important consideration. Feedback capable of assuring the decision maker that the information provided is consistent is a necessary feature required of computerised decision aids applied to selection problems. The study also found that the way in which information is elicited influenced the result more than the underlying model. Elicitation procedures that are more natural for the user are likely to be more accurate.

Mackay, Barr and Kletke (1992) investigated the influence of computerised decision aids on problem-solving processes. They found that the effects of computerised decision aids on the problem solving process was contingent on a number of factors. They found that the simple explanations of decision aid familiarity and task familiarity were misleading. Interaction effects were significant in the time needed for problem solving and the time required to identify a solution.

13.3. Information Search

Information search is an integral part of the decision making process for most consumers considering the purchase of a major durable such as an automobile. Understanding the determinants of information search and their interrelationships presents a very complex problem. Comprehensive theories of consumer decision processes (Bettman, 1979) recognise the importance of this component and incorporate it as a construct in models of the decision process. It is crucial to further our understanding of why we observe different amounts of search across consumers and how these amounts of search are influenced by other salient decision process constructs. Comprehensive models of information search date back to Howard and Sheth (1969). Models of the determinants of information search effort have been presented by Punj and Staelin (1983) and Srinivasan and Ratchford (1991). The academic importance of studying search is evident from its role in most macro models of consumer behaviour and the streams of research on information search, the economics of information, and normative and descriptive models of search.

Consumer information search refers to pre-purchase information seeking. The focus of this research has been on external information assessed in making choices but has typically stopped short of discussions of what consumers do with the information gathered. The dependent variable is usually the amount of search, rather than the resulting choice outcome or preferences for alternatives. A number of factors, such as prior experience and knowledge, have been investigated for explaining variations in search patterns among consumers. Most of the research takes the perspective of the consumer seeking the best value for money. The cost-benefit approach to search has been verified by a number of researchers (Furse, Punj and Stewart, 1984).

From the extensive research in the field, the broad conclusions are that consumers go through limited search for information. There is wide variation in the amount of search undertaken across different consumers. While a number of factors have been hypothesised as explaining the variation in search behaviour, the variance explained has been insignificant. Ratchford (1980) provides one explanation for low pre-purchase activity. Assuming a random selection of alternatives in the marketplace, he demonstrates that the benefits from additional search drops rapidly with the amount of search. Measures of search quality would need to incorporate the context effects, that is, the types of alternatives that are discovered in the search process, as well as the methods used to minimise search.

One major assumption inherent in the literature is that search leads to choice, and that the benefit of this activity is the act of making the right choice. An entirely different focus is derived by Downs (1964). Commenting on the value of the unchosen alternative, he develops the hypothesis that people derive value from an unchosen but desirable alternative, even if they do not actually make use of it. Such a focus would point to search as building up a set of acceptable alternatives and then narrowing down the number of alternatives being considered.

13.3.1. NORMATIVE MODELS OF SEARCH

Normative models have been derived from economic theory, and postulate how consumers should search for information. The foundation for this work was laid by Stigler (1961), who postulated that buyer search behaviour would have an important impact on competitive price structure in the market. Stigler analyses the behaviour of an imperfectly informed consumer interested in purchasing a homogeneous good. In his model, only a single attribute, price, varies across the set of firms/products. Once a consumer samples a firm, all relevant information, in this case price, is known. The model also assumes that the dispersion of prices is known and, since search is a costly activity, the consumer must select a strategy for acquiring information. Stigler suggests that consumers set a fixed number of alternatives to examine, then buy the lowest priced alternative. Based on this model, a number of research propositions between cost of search and optimal amount of search were derived.

A number of researchers have examined the other facets of search behaviour. Hagerty and Aaker (1984) develop a normative model of consumer information processing based on search. Their model is a micro level model and attempts to predict which attribute will be processed, based on the assumption that consumers attempt to maximise the expected value of sample information. Their model is based on four assumptions:

1. In choosing between alternatives, the consumer will select the alternative with the highest utility. The utility of the alternative is assumed to be represented by an additive compensatory model of attributes.
2. Consumers do not know the value of the attribute levels of an alternative, but have a prior multivariate normal distribution of them with known means, variances and covariances.
3. The covariation between alternatives is assumed to be zero, implying that information about one alternative does not provide information about other alternatives in the market.
4. The correlation among the attributes is allowed, assuming that halo effects may exist and affect valuation.

The consumer makes consecutive decisions about whether to process information, and which information to process. An information unit is defined as an information piece concerning one alternative for one attribute. There is a cost of processing this information, which is constant. The consumer expects that after processing the information, there will be a reduction in the variance of the attribute value. This model is used to derive a number of propositions about when processing will take place (and, conversely, when to stop searching for information), and to predict which information will be processed. For example, the model implies that attributes having a higher variability are likely to be processed earlier. Since their model assumes that the consumers know the distribution of the alternatives in the marketplace by attributes, their formulation suggests that determinance of attributes presents the logical choice for a rational consumer to use. This is also experimentally supported by Meyer (1981), who found that subjects searching for an apartment to rent tended to process the attribute with the highest variability.

A similar model, but with a different research focus has been postulated by Shugan (1980). In his model, the consumer is viewed as sampling product pair differences by attributes. This framework is used to develop the number of comparisons that need to be made and the cost of using different decision rules to make a decision. The focus of his work is on computing the difficulty of choice in comparing alternatives whose attribute utility levels are known. Unlike other work on search, Shugan suggests that the cost of search is also influenced by the choice rule used, and not only the value and the number of alternatives in the choice set.

13.3.2. DESCRIPTIVE MODELS OF SEARCH

Descriptive models are posited to capture the search process in terms of a representation of the cognitive processes that underlie search, and to represent this framework in a form that is amenable to modelling and prediction. Meyer (1981) develops a comprehensive model of search. This model is based on the following process description. The decision maker is sampling sequentially from a distribution of alternatives, each alternative being characterised by a bundle of attributes. At each inspection, complete information is revealed about all or some of the attributes for the alternatives selected. In addition, each selection entails a cost, which is fixed and includes both cognitive and other costs. On each inspection, the consumer may either choose one of the alternatives or delay the choice and continue to search further.

The model further assumes that all the information on an alternative is gained through overt examination/inspection. The focus of the model is on processing by alternative. The mathematical model is built around propositions that relate the utility of any new alternative to the inspection costs and attribute importance times the attribute value. The key part of the model deals with assigning values to the attributes before inspection, and updating these after each search. This model breaks up the utility into its riskless value, its dispersion, and the interaction between these two terms. The chapter details propositions and cites empirical work which supports the relationship between attribute variability and utility evaluation, the formation of perceived utilities for unfamiliar alternatives, and the existence of a reservation price in the search process.

13.3.3. RESEARCH ON INFORMATION SEARCH

The conceptual models of search view this as a stage wise process, and assume that the valuation will change depending upon the type of information that is encountered. Further, the search depth will be influenced by the information that is sampled and the derivations made about the alternatives available. Both the normative models as well as the descriptive models assume that the linear compensatory model captures the valuation of the alternatives. These models differ in terms of the assumptions made about what the consumers know about the alternatives in the marketplace. Meyer postulates this as learning during the search, where the risk adjusted value increases. Hagerty and Aaker assume that the consumer knows the means and the dispersions about the attribute, and can therefore act in a way that would minimise search costs. The emphasis in these models is on the context effects and the rationale for the search. The sequence in which the information is acquired is presumed to implicitly influence the uncertainty and is purposive. Beyond attempting to minimise the variance, there is a random component in terms of what will be discovered, and this component is not entirely controlled by the consumers. The pattern of information received may influence the search and this is termed as order effects.

Prior research on search behaviour has primarily studied the determinants of search effort (Srinivasan and Ratchford, 1991; Punj and Staelin, 1983), determinants of search strategies (Furse, Punj, and Stewart, 1984; Kiel and Layton, 1981), and the determinants of the outcome of the search process. Zettelmeyer (1997) examines how the nature of relationships among manufacturers, retailers, and consumers evolves as a function of technology-based reductions in search costs. In their extensive review of the literature, Beatty and Smith (1987) list seven categories of variables that affect search; market environment, situational variables, potential payoff, knowledge and experience, individual differences, conflict and conflict resolution, and cost of search. They then list 60 variables that have been identified in various studies as determinants of search. Most of the research in consumer search has focused on pre-purchase events – that is, information gathering relevant to a specific consumption problem (Furse, Punj, and Stewart, 1984; Punj and Staelin, 1983; Srinivasan and Ratchford, 1991). This conceptualisation embraces the traditional decision making perspective, whereby a buying problem is recognised and search activity follows to help solve that problem. In a pre-purchase context, the extent of search is determined, in part, by the buyer's short-term involvement with the consumption problem resulting from risk perceptions. Other factors influencing pre-purchase search include the market environment, situational factors, and product familiarity. The consumer's primary motive for pre-purchase search is to enhance the quality of the purchase outcome, increase product and market expertise, and heighten satisfaction with a purchasing job well done (Punj and Staelin, 1983).

Previous research on search strategies has found that consumers employ information search strategies which can be distinguished by the amount of search effort and decision time. Kiel and Layton (1981) sought to more fully examine the richness of the pattern of information search. The literature suggests that there are rather distinct patterns of information search, at least among purchasers of durable goods. Most of the research to date has examined search for high-cost items such as appliances and automobiles. The amount of search activity a consumer actually engages in, is a function of a number of factors. Punj and Stewart (1983) suggest that an interaction of situational and individual difference characteristics may produce distinctive patterns of search and decision-making. Chaiken (1980) has suggested that a distinction should be made between heuristic and systematic processing in choice behaviour, in order to understand how various factors influence decision-making and information search strategies. In the systematic processing mode, decision makers actively attempt to comprehend and critically evaluate information about relevant attributes of alternatives. In the heuristic mode, decisions are based on a more superficial assessment of cues. The systematic mode requires detailed processing of information content, whereas the heuristic approach emphasises the role of simple schemas or cognitive heuristics. Chaiken (1980) has suggested that heuristics are most likely to be used by individuals with low involvement in the decision, by those who do not have the ability or expertise to engage in systematic processing, and by those faced with tasks or distractions that are difficult for them. This view is consistent with the interaction framework of decision-making proposed by Punj and Stewart (1983). Research by Chaiken (1980) has supported the suggestion that heuristic processing is more likely in low involvement settings. Punj and Staelin (1983) have offered an empirical test of the proposition that product knowledge in memory consists of two unique components:

1. Knowledge of specific attributes associated with product alternatives, as well as general shopping procedures for the particular product;
2. A general knowledge structure about the product and/or purchase decisions in general.

The former construct would tend to decrease external search, while the latter would tend to increase external search – at least up to a point, since it provides a frame of reference for new product information.

Empirical research on consumers' information search behaviour has been extensively covered (Beatty and Smith, 1987; Newman, 1977; Punj and Staelin, 1983; Srinivasan and Ratchford, 1991; Urbany, Dickson, and Wilkie, 1989). Much of the past work on consumer search has been based on psychological models of information processing, with variables such as beliefs and attitudes (Beatty and Smith, 1987; Duncan and Olshavsky, 1982), involvement (Beatty and Smith, 1987), and knowledge (Alba and Hutchinson, 1987; Brucks, 1985; Johnson and Russo, 1984; Urbany et al., 1989). This behavioural stream of research provides us with excellent descriptions of the psychological processes that accompany search. The two categories of search that have been studied are internal search and external search.

Internal and external search are two steps that are generally posited to precede a purchase decision (Bettman, 1979). These are important aspects of the process by which consumers make decisions. Howard (1977) has suggested that pre-purchase behaviour can be classified into three categories: extensive problem solving, limited problem solving, and routinised response behaviour. A person's current stage depends primarily on familiarity with the product class and the available alternatives. Similarly, Bettman (1979) proposes that consumers search for information in pursuit of particular goals, and that this search may be internal (memory) or external. Furthermore, he suggests that an internal search is usually performed initially, and is followed by external search if there is insufficient information in memory to make a decision. The greater the importance of the purchase decision, the greater will be the amount of external search undertaken.

Little is known about internal search. A number of studies suggest the very plausible hypothesis that experience leads to knowledge, which gives rise to internal search in future. Studies using behavioural process methods have found that consumers acquire less information when alternative names are present than when they are not. This suggests that more internal search is taking place when alternative names are present, i.e. when the subject's knowledge is increased. One might infer from these findings that more internal search is taking place after knowledge has been gained through previous experience. There have been numerous empirical studies on the determinants of external search. Most previous studies have used self-reported search behaviour collected some weeks or months after the search and have used "amount of search" as the dependent variable. At least one study reported "little or no correlation" between the observation-based and survey-based scores of in-store information-seeking by buyers who said they shopped only in the store of purchase where they had been observed (Newman, 1977). This result is consistent with work suggesting that individuals have great difficulty in accurately recalling the cognitive processes they have used.

Given that it is so difficult to measure external search, it is not surprising that the determinants of search are not well established empirically. The cost-benefit concept drawn from economic theory (Stigler, 1961) provides the primary theoretical basis for most empirical studies (Punj and Staelin, 1983; Srinivasan and Ratchford, 1991). This concept implies that a person will continue to acquire and process information until the costs of additional acquisition and processing outweigh the expected benefits. Thus, other things being equal, product importance would imply higher benefits and, hence, more search. Similarly, learning and experience would imply smaller expected benefits for additional external search.

13.4. Consideration Sets

13.4.1. FORMATION OF CONSIDERATION SETS

The theoretical construct of a consideration set is those alternatives that the consumer seriously considers for purchase when making his purchase decision. The concept that consideration sets can contain more than one alternative, but not necessarily all alternatives, is real, important to practical applications, and consistent with prevailing views of how consumers process information. Such behaviour on the part of consumers can be explained by consumers' balancing of consumption utility and evaluation cost. Thus this phenomenon is consistent with Payne's (1982) cost-benefit framework to explain human decision making.

Peter and Olson (1990) view consideration sets as being composed of:

1. A set of familiar alternatives evoked from memory;
2. Alternatives found through intentional search;
3. Alternatives found accidentally.

Hauser and Wernerfelt (1990) and Roberts and Lattin (1990) provide reviews of research relevant to understanding the role and rationale for consideration sets. They note that the existence of consideration sets is a logical outcome of theories in economics and psychology and has strong empirical support. Research in the economics of information search suggests that consumers will continue to search for information as long as the expected marginal returns from search exceed the marginal cost of further searching. "Phased" decision strategies have been suggested as characteristic of human decision-making in a number of contexts where consumers have to cope with complexity (Bettman, 1979). More direct evidence for the existence of consideration sets is provided by the work of Nedungadi (1990) and Ratneshwar and Shocker (1991). Nedungadi (1990) was able to demonstrate an effect on probability of choice by changing the probabilities of alternative consideration, without altering alternative evaluations. Ratneshwar and Shocker (1991) examined the nature of categorisation of alternatives in memory. Their study provided evidence that the presentation of different specific usages cued different "typical" alternatives. Researchers using the "substitution-in-use" approach to product-market structure (Srivastava, Alpert and Shocker, 1984) have found a high level of agreement among subjects in the alternatives they would consider for different uses. This suggests that, when usage and awareness are controlled, there may be some similarity in the content, and possibly the structure, of consideration sets. Taken together, these findings suggest that consideration sets are real, dynamic, changing with time and usage occasion, and affected by consumer contexts and purposes.

Most individual-level models of alternative choice have ignored the effects of consideration sets and focused instead on the role of alternative evaluations in determining choice from within a given, researcher-specified set of alternatives. Prior determination of the consideration set, which results in restricting a choice model to considered alternatives only, should improve the predictability of choice models. A practical benefit from the incorporation of consideration sets is more accurate prediction from choice models that recognise the two stages involved. The concept of a consideration set is useful to marketers as it can aid in defining a market and investigating its structure (Ratneshwar and Shocker, 1991). Much research dealing with consideration sets has focused on descriptive aspects (notably size) and ignored their specific content and structure. Nedungadi (1990) has been an exception, using structure to predict the effects of "prompting" on the formation of the choice set.

Ratneshwar and Shocker (1991) have demonstrated different content and structure of consideration sets as a function of intended usage. The structure of such sets as a function of order of entry of the alternatives in the set has been demonstrated at an aggregate level by Hauser and Wernerfelt (1990). Srivastava, Leone and Shocker (1981) and Ratneshwar and Shocker (1991) have also provided evidence that consideration sets could include alternatives with different physical characteristics, but which deliver the functional benefits required by a particular usage.

The consideration set is a concept that is both intuitively appealing and practically useful. This notion was formalised as the "evoked set" by Howard and Sheth (1969) as part of their model of buyer behaviour. Consumer researchers have further developed the evoked set construct and empirically investigated it as a relevant component of the buying process. The basic idea is that when choosing to make a purchase, consumers use at least a two-stage process. Consumers faced with a large number of alternatives first use a simple heuristic to screen the alternatives from the feasible set and then reduce the number of alternatives which they will seriously consider prior to making their decision to a relevant set which is referred to as the consideration set. Purchase or consumption decisions are then made from alternatives in this consideration set. Self-report methods are the most commonly used approach for set assessment, and the unaided format is more common because it reduces artificially created awareness which could inflate reported consideration set size. The predictive power of choice models could be improved by distinguishing a first stage in which the consideration set is built, and a second stage in which a choice is made from among the alternatives in that consideration set (Roberts, 1989; Roberts and Lattin, 1991).

There exist several operational definitions of the notion of a consideration set. Howard and Seth (1969) defined a consideration set as a set of alternatives that consumers bring to mind in a particular choice situation from which they will make the final choice. Alba and Chattopadhyay (1985), on the other hand, define a consideration set as the total set of alternatives a consumer would consider buying. A distinction between memory-based and stimulus-based consideration sets is proposed by Alba, Hutchinson, and Lynch (1991). The former consist of those alternatives which are retrieved from memory whereas the latter refers to those sets which are formed when all the alternatives are available in front of the consumer. According to Shocker et. al. (1991), a consideration set is purposefully constructed and can be viewed as consisting of those goal-satisfying alternatives that are salient or accessible on a particular occasion. This viewpoint is similar to Alba, Hutchinson and Lynch's (1991) definition of memory-based consideration sets. It is from the consideration set that a consumer will make the final choice. It is therefore critical that a marketing manager is able to place his alternative in the consumer's consideration set because unless the alternative is included in the consideration set, it might not be chosen (Nedungadi, 1990).

Despite the considerable research conducted in the choice area, research on consideration sets has been limited. Hauser and Wernerfelt (1990) showed that across different product categories, consumers generally consider between two to eight alternatives, which is far fewer than the total number of alternatives available. The explanation for the existence of these smaller sets is rooted in theories of economics and psychology (Hauser and Wernerfelt, 1990; Roberts and Lattin, 1991). Research in the economics of information search suggests that consumers will continue to search for information as long as the expected marginal returns from that search exceed the marginal cost of further searching. That is, consumers will consider an additional alternative as long as the marginal benefits (in terms of making an optimum choice) exceed the marginal costs (in terms of searching for information about that alternative and comparing it with other alternatives). In psychology, the process of retrieving a few items relevant to an immediate purpose into the short term memory from a larger set stored in long term memory is similar to the process of reducing the entire set of alternatives to considering only a few alternatives. Empirical support for this comes from a study by Ratneshwar and Shocker (1991) who found that providing consumers with different usage situations led to their recalling different "typical" alternatives. This highlights the point that although consumers were aware of a larger set of alternatives, the number of alternatives they retrieved for any one occasion was smaller. Because retrieving alternatives from memory is critical to the formation of consideration sets, the role of memory in the formation of consideration sets is discussed next.

13.4.2. MEMORY AND CONSIDERATION SETS

Memory plays a key role in the formation of consideration sets because if consumers cannot recall an alternative, that alternative will not be included in the consideration set. Those consideration sets that consumers form by retrieving a set of alternatives from memory are referred to as memory-based consideration sets. Memory-based consideration corresponds to "top-of-mind" awareness, which has been reported to be a good predictor of alternative choice and usage. However, consumers can also form consideration sets from the alternatives available in front of them. These consideration sets are classified as stimulus-based (Nedungadi, 1990). As pointed out by Alba, Hutchinson and Lynch (1991), few decisions in the real world are purely stimulus-based. They usually include some memory component. For instance, viewing some alternatives may remind consumers of some other alternatives (Nedungadi, 1990) for which they may then search.

Explaining the role of memory in the formation of consideration sets, Holden and Lutz (1992) proposed that consideration sets are categories which consumers form in situations to satisfy certain goals (i.e. the benefits that consumers desire). Thus, they are referred to as goal-derived categories. To understand how goal-derived categories are formed, it is critical to know what elements consumers can use to retrieve alternatives from memory. Knowing the kinds of information consumers store about the various alternatives in their memory is very important. Summarising various conceptualisations that have catalogued a variety of features linked to an alternative in memory, Holden and Lutz (1992) proposed that memory be considered as an associative network with links to various associates such as attributes, goals, attitude, product category and choice situations. In examining the role of memory in alternative consideration, the authors suggest that it is necessary to examine those associates that lead to retrieval of the alternative. Each associate might have stronger links to some alternatives than others; thus any given associate can retrieve some alternatives with greater probability than others (Holden and Lutz,

1992). From the above discussion, it is clear that if choice is memory-based, the organisation of memory constrains the retrieval of alternatives, membership in the consideration set, and thus choice.

13.4.3. SCRIPT LITERATURE

Script literature illustrates how people represent events in memory and how they form a category of alternatives associated with each event. Studies in development psychology have demonstrated that people develop general, sequentially correct representations of many familiar routine situations. This knowledge, termed an event schema or a script, is developed primarily by experiencing the event and is originally derived from plans that are carried out in order to achieve a goal. An event representation is formed when a particular plan has been carried out enough times for it to become routine. The representation is a generalised structure made up of slots (or categories of event information such as actors, actions, and props) that are filled according to the requirements of a particular event. Associated with these open slots are a range of more or less probable alternatives, called slot fillers.

An important question relates to how consumers form categories when they encounter an unfamiliar situation. Essentially, new events are interpreted in terms of what is already known about previous events by searching for an already established event representation that shares important aspects of the new event. Consumers can thus form categories for partially unfamiliar situations. Having examined how consumers form categories of alternatives associated with events, the issue of how they retrieve alternatives from such categories to form consideration sets is examined next. The retrieval process is important because not all the alternatives associated with an event will be retrieved for inclusion in the consideration set.

13.4.4. TAXONOMIC VERSUS AD HOC LITERATURE

Barsalou (1983) explained the retrieval of alternatives from memory with the help of a comparison-network model. This model posits that people have a very flexible knowledge about a category. That is, they can represent the same category by different concepts in different situations. A concept is a person's cognitive representation of a category on a particular occasion. In this model, concepts and properties are represented as nodes (or points) in memory and the associations between concepts and properties are represented as pathways that carry spreading activation. These associations between the concept and different properties can vary in their strength depending upon the extent to which the property is related to the concept. The stronger the association, the greater the likelihood of the property being retrieved when a cue of the concept is given. This relationship between a concept and a property has a parallel in the relationship between the consideration set and the alternatives included in it. The strength increases as a function of how frequently and recently an association has been active in working memory.

According to the comparison-network model, activation of the category will lead to the activation (hence, retrieval) of stronger associations only. Well established taxonomic categories have strong concept-to-instance associations (i.e. associations between the category of alternatives that form the consideration set and the individual alternatives included in the set). The direction of the linkage is from the category to the individual alternatives included in the category. These associations enable category concepts to easily activate category instances. Well-established taxonomic categories also have strong instance-to-concept associations (i.e. associations between the individual alternatives included in the consideration set and the category of alternatives that forms the consideration set). The direction of the linkage in this case goes from the individual alternatives to the category. These associations enable instances to activate their category concepts. Such "bottom-up" associations are useful for categorising single instances into their appropriate category. Ad hoc categories on the other hand, are those that people rarely or very infrequently think of. They are not well established in memory simply because of the lack of development and the strengthening of the two kinds of associations discussed above. Thus, these categories have weak concept-to-instance associations (i.e. category-to-alternative associations) because the consumer has not encountered the situation frequently. As a result, there is no ready set of alternatives available that can be retrieved given the category cue (Barsalou, 1983). Hence, retrieving instances from ad hoc categories should be more difficult than retrieving instances from taxonomic categories.

Secondly, ad hoc categories have weak instance-to-concept associations. Because the ad hoc category is not frequently formed, consumers do not have the opportunity to evaluate the relevance or appropriateness of different alternatives for the category, and the result is that alternative-to-category associations are not well established. Consequently, even though the alternative name may be provided to the consumers, they will find it relatively difficult to think about the infrequently encountered situations in which this alternative could possibly be considered. If ad hoc categories have poor category-to-alternative association, one can ask how people retrieve exemplars from these categories? One possibility is that a generate-test procedure is employed (Barsalou, 1983, 1991). In other words, the associative structure of related, well-established categories may be used to generate possible instances of a poorly established category. As each item is retrieved, it is tested for membership in the poorly established category.

13.5. Order Effects

A number of research streams have shown that sequence or order effects moderate the relationships between the constructs of interest. A common example of this is the need to randomise the order of presentation of stimuli in research designs. Order effects have been documented in perception formation. Rumelhart and Anderson's (1978) model of accretion, tuning and restructuring uses the idea that initial information can affect the manner in which the subsequent information is learnt. Bruner, Goodnow and Austin (1956) investigating concept identification suggest that the learner uses some aspects of the first few instances encountered to form a set of hypotheses. Subsequent information is used to confirm these hypotheses. In these concept transfer studies, both the size and variability of the learning set have been manipulated. While sets containing low variability showed higher abstraction of the central tendencies and lower training time, sets with higher variance lead to best transfer. The "Law of Primacy" has been shown to be applicable in relating the effectiveness of advertising and communication to the order of presentation. Order effects have been studied in the context of the biases on judgment, with the effects being sometimes in favor of the first (primacy effect) and sometimes in favor of the last information seen (recency effect). Nisbett and Ross (1980) point out that primacy effects may be the rule in serial information tasks, and that recency effects are rare. People have limited information processing capacity but they are adaptive. The nature of the judgment task determines to a large extent how people can and do deal with the task. For example, if the information is presented sequentially, this induces a judgment strategy that is different to that used when the information is presented simultaneously. Shugan (1980) notes that the exact order in which the alternatives are compared may affect both the potential cost of comparing alternatives, as well as the average binary cost of the comparison. Buyukkurt (1986) summarises the theoretical reasons for expecting order effects. The following are among the reasons that have been hypothesised:

1. The change in meaning hypothesis, where sequential presentation of information may change the meaning because of the impressions caused by those presented first.
2. The attention-decrement hypothesis which implies that more attention is paid to information presented first.
3. The people as theorist explanation where the first information is used to form the hypothesis about subsequent information.

There exists adequate face validity in assuming that order effects would change perception, preference and, therefore, choice of alternatives. Two points about order effects need to be mentioned. First, these effects have been investigated under conditions where the stimuli are given. This difference is not a matter of semantics. Being given the freedom to choose, and exploring choice within that context, is likely to be different from being given a set of stimuli from which choice is made. In the former, we might expect that the search will be purposive, while in the latter condition, no statement about the reason for the effect can be made. Second, the strength of these effects is likely to be weak.

13.6. Problem Structuring

A number of research streams in the marketing, economics, and decision sciences literature have attempted to model choice behaviour. These research streams have used experimental, as well as survey, data to develop verbal and mathematical models to describe and predict this behaviour. For example, in the marketing literature, these models span those dealing with micro-details of choice (Howard and Sheth, 1969; Bettman, 1979) to those attempting to explain relationships between two or more elements of the process. While the differences between these models is greater than the similarities, the common characteristic of the choice process is thought to have three simple stages. The first stage is the problem definition stage wherein a need deficiency is identified. This motivates the consumer to choose a product class that may satisfy the need. The next stage consists of information search to generate alternatives that are acceptable, given a need. This information search is therefore purposive, and is bounded by the problem the consumer faces. The final stage is the evaluation of the alternatives generated, leading to a choice of one of the alternatives. Most of the models that have been developed to describe and predict choice behaviour assume that the consumer faces a structured problem. Structured problems are those that can be explicitly stated in a language, implying that a theory concerning their solution is available. Simon (1978) distinguishes between well-structured problems and ill-structured problems in three ways. First, the former assumes that the criterion for defining the goals is clearly defined. Second, for well-structured problems, the problem instructions contain enough information to solve them. Third, the set of possible alternatives remains the same at each stage of the problem. The assumptions that underlie the use of structured problems to model choice are:

1. The consumer has a stable utility function, at least for the choice situation in question.
2. The consumer is aware of all the alternatives in the market.
3. The consumer has complete information by attributes of the alternatives in the market.

The major advantage of using these assumptions to model choice is tractability. Unstructured problems present a truer picture of the decision processes but have messy problems associated with heterogeneity among consumers (using different rules for information integration), differences in alternatives and attributes considered (because of experience etc.) and differences in the importance weights (if conceptualised as being independent of the search set). Logically, over time, for the same set of problems, the consumer will move from treating them as an unstructured problem to treating them as a structured problem. While learning over repeated questions is one method of studying unstructured problems, there are many instances where repeated purchases may not take place, and where such a structuring is done during the problem resolution (for example, purchase of a computer, buying a house). An alternative conceptualisation of structuring the task is to examine other facets of the problem. One such facet is the type of uncertainty faced by the consumer.

13.7. Types Of Uncertainty

The classical definition of uncertainty as being unmeasurable risk is attributed to the seminal work of Knight (1971). Three types of uncertainty that consumers face in making a choice are identified. The first type of uncertainty takes place because of the problem definition itself. For example, in the choice of an airline, the consumer's program may be contingent on another's convenience (meeting schedules, etc.) for which complete information is not available at the time of making a choice. In this situation, the focus is on resolving the uncertainty through an assessment of the risk. The second type of uncertainty occurs when the suitability of a particular solution for a choice task is not clear. This could be due to a lack of experience in the choice task. For example, think of the problem confronting a consumer whose car has just started malfunctioning. The decisions will involve first understanding possible reasons for the failure, and then taking remedial action. Often a good deal of learning about priorities and trade-offs of dimensions may take place only after inspection of available alternatives. Thus, when being constructed at an early choice decision stage, the net may not adequately capture the decision maker's actual choice, which may be influenced by his/her learning and dynamic changes taking place at a later stage of the choice decision. These dynamic changes of decision plan over time and their implications on an individual's choice prediction are important issues to be addressed. Search, in the context of reducing these types of uncertainties, would involve changing attributes used in the evaluation, setting boundaries, cutoffs and importance weights on the attributes, etc. Search would consist of two stages, where the first stage would involve gathering information to develop an understanding of the solution space (what are the important attributes, which ones need to be traded off, etc.), followed by an evaluation of the alternatives presented. Over the search process, the attributes that are important, the weights to give to the attributes, whether to use some as cutoffs, etc. are developed. Modelling this type of choice situation would involve models where importance weights and the valuation of attributes is done dynamically.

Finally, there are uncertainties that the consumer faces regarding the types of alternatives available. This is the simplest of the three types of uncertainties to study. It assumes that the consumer has knowledge of the attributes that will be used to evaluate different alternatives. The importance of these attributes is driven by the task and by prior experience. Essentially, the consumer undertakes search to develop and choose an acceptable alternative. The concern, in this choice task, is how the consumer deals with limited information on alternatives. The third type of uncertainty may arise because of lack of experience in the particular task, or because the alternatives themselves keep changing, making it impossible, and even undesirable, to collect complete information on all alternatives available.

13.8. Theoretical Development of Hypotheses

In this section, I discuss the underlying theories which support the hypotheses which were tested. The nature of QBDA in the electronic commerce environment is significantly different from the use of search and decision aids in other environments in two specific ways. The ability to store and process large quantities of information is greatly increased given the use of computers in the electronic commerce environment. The use of hypertext significantly changes the way users navigate the environment and examine data for the alternatives. The use of QBDA enables consumers to quickly and easily identify alternatives which match their preferences.

This research focuses on the following types of consideration sets:

1. *Stimulus-based as opposed to memory-based.* The objective of this research is to study consumer behaviour when the consumers are making their purchases at the electronic shopping malls. Accordingly, the objective is to study the effects that a stimulus, such as a query based decision aid, has on

the formation of the consideration sets of the consumers. While prior memory structure may play some role in the formation of the consideration sets, this dimension is not explicitly manipulated in this study.

2. *Brand level as opposed to product level.* The specific product category I am studying is the purchase of cars on the Internet. The specific purpose of this study is to examine the formation of the consideration set of the consumers and which alternatives are included in the consideration sets. Because consideration sets are goal-derived categories (Holden and Lutz, 1992; Ratneshwar and Shocker, 1991) whose members are drawn from different product categories, it is important to study the process at the product level first. However, since the study is specifically designed to examine the purchase of cars on the Internet I am examining it at the brand level. Thus this study will have significant implications for brand managers.

3. *Plan based as opposed to non-plan based.* This study focuses on those consideration sets that are plan-based since the study specifically examines the purchase of cars on the Internet. This is as opposed to the formation of the consideration set in a non-plan situation in which the consumer decides to purchase a car and then finds himself at a dealer's site and attempts to form a consideration set.

The four phases of the purchase decision, the corresponding elements of uncertainty and the psychological response of the decision maker are illustrated in Table 13.1.

Table 13.1. Phases of the purchase decision.

Description	Focus of uncertainty	Psychological response
Pre-decision	Desirability of alternatives	Decision conflict
Post-decision, pre-purchase	Desirability of chosen alternative versus foregone alternatives	Apprehension
Post-purchase, pre-use	Desirability of foregone alternatives Adequacy of chosen alternative	Performance anxiety
Postuse	Consequences of performance	Regret, (dis)satisfaction

This research focuses on the pre-decision and to some extent on the post-decision, pre-purchase phases of the purchase decision process and hence the issues being studied relate to decision conflict and the formation of the consideration set. The pre-decision phase of the decision process consists of a difficult choice between close alternatives. Little beyond decision difficulty is evident in this phase. The main psychological response of the subjects relates to decision conflict. The post-decision, pre-purchase phase of the decision process introduces the purchase consideration of foregone alternatives on the part of the consumer. This results in regret and/or hindsight. In this phase, the consumer experiences the fact that the purchase decision will leave the unchosen alternatives "on the table". This state of anticipated regret (to distinguish it from the realisation of regret) leads to a general feeling of apprehension on the part of the consumer. This apprehension on the part of the decision maker can lead to cognitive dissonance and result in reduced satisfaction with the decision. As originally described by Festinger, dissonance is a "psychologically uncomfortable tension state". In the current context, it represents an apprehension over the chosen alternative and is closely tied to a psychological construct "consideration of future consequences". A choice does not necessarily involve consequences and can often be reversed. Hence, it fits into the post-decision, pre-purchase phase of consumption.

At any given purchase decision, consumers do not consider all the alternatives available. Consumers typically consider a much smaller subset in their purchase decision. Consider, for example, how consumers might deliberate when trying to decide which brand of a particular product to purchase. Assume that the consumer is browsing the Web sites of the product manufacturers in order to obtain information about the various alternatives. In such stimulus-based choice contexts, a large variety of alternatives is generally available, both within and across product categories, that satisfy the same consumption or purchase purpose. Unlike the purely memory-based conditions investigated in some past research on consideration sets (Alba and Chattopadhyay, 1985; Nedungadi, 1990; Ratneshwar and Shocker, 1991), the consumer can readily perceive or view the various alternatives. However, it is expected that careful consideration will not be given to all of the available alternatives, or even to all of the familiar ones, because of the cognitive processing demands of doing so. Instead, the consumer is likely to engage in a multi-stage choice process whereby a small set of options is identified and a final choice is made after more detailed consideration through a process referred to as the phased narrowing of the consideration set (Levin and Jasper, 1995; Hauser and Wernerfelt, 1990; Kardes, Kalyanaraman, Chandrashekaran, and Dornoff, 1993; Roberts and Lattin, 1991).

The model which represents the dependencies between the variables is illustrated in Figure 13.1. The theoretical explanations for the expected directions of the dependencies follows.

13.8.1. INFLUENCE OF QBDA ON MEDIATING VARIABLES

Influence of the QBDA on size of the consideration set
The attractiveness of the opportunity to inspect an expanded number of alternatives is dependent in part on the consumers' ability to sort efficiently through a potentially daunting amount of information. A particular advantage of the QBDA is that it provides consumers with the ability to screen information efficiently so that consumers can focus on alternatives that match their preferences. In most product categories, consumers have prior beliefs and preferences about alternatives (Hauser and Wernerfelt, 1990; Roberts and Lattin, 1991; Simonson, Huber, and Payne, 1988). Consumers use this information to make purchase decisions more efficiently by forming a small consideration set and then evaluating alternatives within this subset in greater detail. The savings in search costs involved in using this multi-stage process often overwhelms the potential opportunity cost of overlooking the "best" alternative that would have been selected by carefully inspecting the entire universe of alternatives. The use of the QBDA enables consumers to easily locate alternatives which match their preferences. It is expected that this will result in the

consumers seriously considering a larger number of alternatives in their purchase decision.

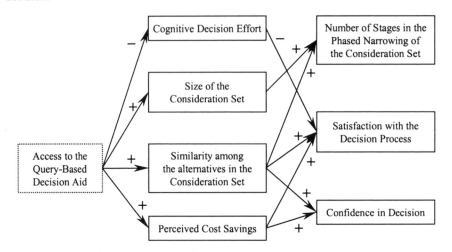

Figure 13.1. Influence of QBDA on decision making in electronic commerce.

Reduced cognitive search effort implies that the decision maker is likely to evaluate a larger number of alternatives from within the feasible choice set prior to making his purchase decision. Economic theories of information search postulate that consumers will evaluate a larger number of alternatives as long as the expected benefit of evaluating each additional alternative exceeds the additional cost of evaluating the additional alternative (Hauser and Wernerfelt, 1990; Kardes, Kalyanaraman, Chandrashekaran, and Dornoff, 1993; Roberts and Lattin, 1991). Inasmuch as the cost of searching for and evaluating new alternatives continues to increase, a point is reached at which the expected cost of considering additional alternatives is greater than the potential increase in benefits. At this point, the consumer terminates the search for additional alternatives. I expect that the reduced cognitive search effort associated with access to the QBDA will result in an increase in the number of alternatives which the decision maker evaluates and seriously considers for purchase. These arguments lead me to expect that the size of the consideration set will be larger among the subjects who have access to the QBDA as compared to the subjects who do not have access to the QBDA.

Influence of the QBDA on similarity among alternatives in the consideration set

When the consumer has access to the QBDA, he is easily able to locate alternatives which match his preferences. The alternatives which he considers for purchase are likely to be similar to the preferences he expressed in the query and hence they are likely to be similar to each other. This leads me to expect that the similarity among the alternatives in the consideration set will be higher in the case of subjects who have access to the QBDA as compared to subjects who do not have access to the QBDA.

Influence of the QBDA on perceived cost savings

Electronic commerce has the potential to differ markedly from conventional channels in search costs (Alba, Lynch, Weitz, Janiszewski, Lutz, Sawyer, and Wood, 1997; Bakos, 1997; Lynch and Ariely, 1998). This will enable consumers to make more effective comparisons of price and quality across products and across the merchants' Web sites. Such lowering of consumers' search costs causes retailers to view electronic commerce with trepidation. They fear that electronic commerce will intensify competition and lower profit margins by expanding the scope of competition from local to national and international (Quelch and Klein, 1996). If there are differences among the merchants in an assortment of complementary products, the electronic commerce channel could be more effective than existing modes of retailing in conveying those points of differentiation. This is primarily due to the presence of QBDA in the electronic commerce environment which allow consumers to quickly and easily identify alternatives which match their preferences. Bakos (1997) provides several arguments supporting this conjecture. It is expected that this will lead to a greater degree of expectation by the consumers that the selected alternative is a good bargain from among the available alternatives and will result in a higher perception of cost savings associated with their choice. This leads me to expect that the perceived cost savings will be higher among those subjects who have access to the QBDA as compared to subjects who do not have access to the QBDA.

Influence of the QBDA on cognitive decision effort

It is expected that subjects who have access to the QBDA will easily be able to locate alternatives which closely match the preferences they specify in their queries. This will result in reduced cognitive search effort. Reduced cognitive search effort refers to the expectation that the goal-directed search for specific information is expected to be much more efficient and effective if the decision maker uses a QBDA which will enable him to easily locate and evaluate alternatives which match his preferences. The use of the QBDA provides the decision maker with the capability to screen information efficiently so that he can focus on alternatives that match his preferences. It is expected that this will enable the formation of consideration sets that include those alternatives best suited to a decision maker's personal tastes with relatively little cognitive effort. This leads me to expect that subjects who have access to the QBDA will perceive a reduced cognitive decision effort as compared to subjects who do not have access to the QBDA.

13.8.2. INFLUENCE OF THE QBDA ON THE DEPENDENT VARIABLES

Influence of the QBDA on the number of stages of phased narrowing of the consideration set

In recent years, there has been a growing awareness of the importance of pre-choice behaviour in decision making (Payne, Bettman, and Johnson, 1993). This has led to the development of process tracing approaches to study the cognitive processes underlying multi-attribute choice. The single most unique feature of the process of phased narrowing is that, unlike other process tracing methods, it requires decision makers to use a series of discrete steps in narrowing the consideration set to the final choice. Prior research on consideration sets has not traced the decision process as the subject moves from one set to another. Nevertheless, we are encouraged to do just that by Beach (1993) and Beach and Potter (1992) who demonstrate that the screening of choice options (the initial stage) is qualitatively different from choosing the best option (the final stage). Various researchers have speculated that consumers use a fixed number of stages of phased narrowing to proceed from the "awareness set" to the "consideration set" to the "choice set" to the "final choice" (Levin and Jasper, 1995; Nedungadi, 1990; Roberts and Lattin, 1991; Shocker, Ben-Akiva, Boccara, and Nedungadi, 1991). The uniqueness of the approach which I have used in this research is that the subjects are allowed to narrow their initially constructed consideration sets at their own pace without any restrictions being placed on their decision making process. This allows me to study the influence of similarity among the alternatives in the consideration set and the size of the consideration set on the consumers' decision making much more effectively since it provides a natural replication of the process by which consumers make their decisions.

In the earlier discussion of the influence of the QBDA on the mediating variables, I concluded that subjects who have access to the QBDA are expected to have a larger number of alternatives in their consideration sets. Therefore, it is expected that they will need a greater number of stages in the phased narrowing of the decision process in order to arrive at their final choice.

In the earlier discussion of the influence of the QBDA on the mediating variables, I concluded that subjects who have access to the QBDA are expected to have a greater degree of similarity among the alternatives in their consideration sets. Since the alternatives are similar, it is expected that the selection of the optimal alternative from the choice set will require a finer level of discrimination to sequentially eliminate less desirable alternatives from the consideration set. This is expected to result in an increase in the number of stages in the phased narrowing of the consideration set.

These arguments lead me to expect that subjects who have access to the QBDA will require a greater number of stages of phased narrowing of the consideration set in order to select one alternative from the consideration set as compared to subjects who do not have access to the QBDA.

Hypothesis 1a: Subjects who have access to the query-based decision aid will experience a larger "number of stages in the phased narrowing of the consideration set" as compared to subjects who do not have access to the query-based decision aid.

Hypothesis 1b: The variable "number of stages in the phased narrowing of the consideration set" mediated by the variables "similarity among the alternatives in the consideration set" and "size of the consideration set", is not significantly related to the variable "access to the query-based decision aid".

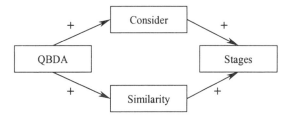

Figure 13.2. Influence of query-based decision aids on number of stages of phased narrowing of the consideration set.

Influence of the QBDA on confidence in the decision

It is expected that the use of the QBDA will enable consumers to screen the alternatives by attribute. This will create a more manageable information environment. But it may also result in some attractive options going unnoticed. It is expected that the subjects who have access to the QBDA will experience a greater, but illusory, sense of confidence in choices made from incompletely constructed consideration sets.

In the earlier discussion of the influence of the QBDA on the mediating variables, I concluded that subjects who have access to the QBDA are expected to experience an increased perception of cost savings in their selected alternative. This will increase the confidence the subjects have in their final decision.

Paese and Sniezek (1991) found that the greater the amount of relevant information the decision maker has, the greater is his confidence in his judgment. In the context of the current research, subjects who do not have access to the QBDA do not have the information that indicates the degree to which each alternative they are evaluating matches their preferences. Hence, it is expected that the confidence they will have in their final decision will be less than that of the subjects who have this information available to them.

These arguments lead me to expect that subjects who have access to the QBDA will experience a higher confidence in their decision as compared to subjects who do not have access to the QBDA.

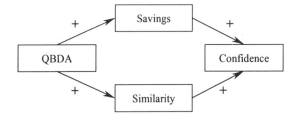

Figure 13.3. Influence of query-based decision aids on confidence in the decision.

Hypothesis 2a: Subjects who have access to the query-based decision aid will experience a higher "confidence in the decision" as compared to subjects who do not have access to the query-based decision aid.

Hypothesis 2b: The variable "confidence in the decision", mediated by the variables "perceived cost savings" and "similarity among the alternatives in the consideration set" is not significantly related to the variable "access to the query-based decision aid".

Influence of the QBDA on satisfaction with the decision process

As noted by King and Hill (1994), it is necessary that the consumer's involvement with the decision process be distinguished from his experience with the outcome of the process (that is, the product or brand selected) since the consumer's degree of satisfaction with the process may influence his ultimate decision regarding purchase of the product. The current study focuses on understanding the effects of the access to the QBDA on the perceived satisfaction with the decision process. In other words, I was not interested in subjects' reaction to the particular alternative they selected, but rather how useful they perceived the decision process to be in selecting an optimal alternative. Thus, all questions relating to perceived satisfaction with the decision process were stated to specifically reflect this orientation.

In the earlier discussion of the influence of the QBDA on the mediating variables, I concluded that subjects who have access to the QBDA are expected to experience an increased cost savings in their chosen alternative. It is expected that this will lead to a greater perception of equity in the purchase transaction. It is expected that this will result in a greater degree of satisfaction with the decision process (Oliver and Swan, 1989a, 1989b).

A major determinant of the satisfaction which a consumer derives from the purchase of a product is the belief that he has exhaustively searched the set of acceptable alternatives such that there is no regret regarding a missed opportunity (Gilovich and Medvec, 1995). When the subject is using the QBDA, he is easily able to locate alternatives which closely match his preferences. This increases the likelihood that he will focus his search efforts on a set of alternatives which closely match the preferences he expresses in his query. Thus, there is less likelihood that the subject will experience a feeling of regret over alternatives which were not considered in his purchase decision.

These arguments lead me to expect that subjects who have access to the QBDA will experience a greater degree of satisfaction with the decision process as compared to subjects who do not have access to the QBDA.

Hypothesis 3a: Subjects who have access to the query-based decision aid will experience a greater "satisfaction with the decision process" as compared to subjects who do not have access to the query-based decision aid.

Hypothesis 3b: The variable "satisfaction with the decision process", mediated by the variables "perceived cost savings", "similarity among the alternatives in the consideration set" and "cognitive decision effort" is not significantly related to the variable "access to the query-based decision aid".

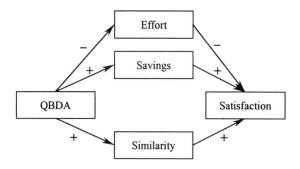

Figure 13.4. Influence of query-based decision aids on satisfaction with the decision process.

13.9. Description of Variables and Operationalisation of Constructs

13.9.1. INDEPENDENT VARIABLE BEING MANIPULATED

This refers to whether the subject had access to the QBDA or did not have access to the QBDA to assist him in the decision making process.

13.9.2. MEDIATING MEASURES

Cognitive decision effort (EFFORT)

Cognitive decision effort refers to the psychological costs of processing information. Cognitive decision effort refers to the ease with which the subject can perform the task of obtaining and processing the relevant information in order to enable him to arrive at his decision. The following scale items were used in the measure for the construct EFFORT. The respondents were told to mark each of the responses on a 7-point Likert scale ranging from "Strongly Disagree" to "Strongly Agree".

1. The task of selecting a car model using this system was very frustrating.
2. I easily found the information I was looking for **(r)**.
3. The task of selecting a car model using this system took too much time.
4. The task of selecting a car model using this system was easy **(r)**.
5. Selecting a car model using this system required too much effort.
6. The task of selecting a car model using this system was too complex.

The value of Cronbach α for the construct EFFORT was .92.

Size of the consideration set (CONSIDER)

This is the number of alternatives that the subject seriously considers for purchase when making his choice. The theoretical construct of the consideration set comprises the specific brands, models, or alternative designs of a specific product that the consumer is willing to consider for purchase. This variable is operationalised as the number of alternatives which the subject seriously considers for purchase in the first stage of the phased narrowing of the decision process.

Similarity among the alternatives in the consideration set (SIMILARITY)

This refers to the degree of similarity among the alternatives in the consideration set following the initial construction of the consideration set. The subject is initially asked to assign importance weights to each of the attributes he would consider when purchasing the product. Based on this information and the preferences which the subject expresses in the query, the system computes a similarity score for each of the alternatives in the database. This similarity score reflects the extent to which each alternative matches the preferences expressed by the subject. This is measured on a scale of 0 (completely different) to 100 (completely similar). The similarity measure reflects the mean and the dispersion of this similarity score for all the alternatives in the consideration set. The values are combined using a linear additive multi-attribute model.

Perceived cost savings (SAVINGS)

This reflects the degree to which the subject feels that the use of the system has helped him to realise significant cost savings in his purchase decision. The following scale items were used in the measure for the construct SAVINGS. The respondents were told to mark each of the responses on a 7-point Likert scale ranging from "Strongly Disagree" to "Strongly Agree".

1. By using this system to select a car, I was able to obtain the best value for my money.
2. The use of this system has enabled me to save a lot of money in purchasing a car.
3. If I had not used this system I would have obtained a better deal for my money **(r)**.

The value of Cronbach α for the construct SAVINGS was .94.

13.9.3. DEPENDENT MEASURES

Confidence in the decision (CONFIDENCE)

This refers to the confidence expressed by the subject that he has selected the best alternative from the set of feasible alternatives. The following scale items were used in the measure for the construct CONFIDENCE. The respondents were told to mark each of the responses on a 7-point Likert scale ranging from "Strongly Disagree" to "Strongly Agree".

1. I am confident that I selected the best car model to suit my needs.
2. I am confident that I selected the car model which best matches my preferences.
3. I am **not** confident that I selected the best car model **(r)**.

The value of Cronbach α for the construct CONFIDENCE was .73.

Satisfaction with the Decision Process (SATISFACTION)

This represents the decision maker's subjective state of satisfaction with all aspects of the decision process immediately after the decision has been made. The following scale items were used in the measure for the construct SATISFACTION. The respondents were told to mark each of the responses on a 7-point Likert scale ranging from "Strongly Disagree" to "Strongly Agree".

1. This system is one of the best ways to select a car.
2. If I could do it over again, I'd rather not use this system to select a car **(r)**.
3. I am **not** happy that I used this system to select a car **(r)**.
4. This system was very useful in helping me to select the best model of car to suit my requirements.
5. If I had to select a car in future, and a system such as this was available, I would be very likely to use it.
6. If my friend was searching for information in order to purchase a car, and I knew that a system such as this was available, I would be very likely to recommend this system to him.

The value of Cronbach α for the construct SATISFACTION was .86.

Number of stages in the phased narrowing of the consideration set (STAGES)

This reflects the number of stages of phased narrowing which is required for the subject to narrow his choice from the set of feasible alternatives to his final choice. This process is achieved by initial construction of the consideration set followed by sequential elimination of alternatives from the consideration set through a process referred to as phased narrowing of the consideration set.

13.10. Research Methodology

13.10.1. INDUSTRY SELECTION

Several criteria had to be satisfied by the product selected for the experiment. First, the product had to be identified as being predominantly a search product. In addition, it was desirable to identify a product with which most subjects were familiar. Ideally, subjects should have had some purchase and/or usage experience with the product. This was particularly important for the product used in the training task since the function of the training task was to familiarise subjects with the computer software and the decision environment. Selection of a music CD was chosen for the training task since it was composed of search attributes, and because virtually all subjects could be expected to have some experience in the selection or consumption of this type of product. Hence, the subject could concentrate on becoming familiar with the computer-assisted decision process.

The cognitive search effort effects can be tested in choice settings where the cost of goods/services is substantial enough to warrant involved search for, and evaluation of, alternatives, as opposed to using simple heuristics and/or variety seeking behaviour. Further, the choice situation should encompass an environment where the alternatives available keep changing across different choice situations or the frequency of purchase is low. These conditions are necessary to capture search and evaluation under conditions of uncertainty in a realistic manner. For these reasons, the automobile industry is an appropriate setting for this decision making task. Given the rapid changes that take place in the automobile industry, most car purchases would entail some amount of search to uncover what information is currently available. Some of the advantages which this industry provides are that it provides a natural setting and the choice task is familiar. In choice processes that underlie the selection of cars, consumers go through the process of searching extensively for information prior to making a choice. Online information on car models and prices are now commercially available to consumers on the Web. The user friendly nature of the Web software allows users to scan huge databases of information and points to a more extensive use of cheap and efficient search for products and services in the future.

13.10.2. DEVELOPING THE CHOICE SCENARIOS

In order to develop the choice scenarios, I interviewed several managers and consumers at two automobile dealerships in a major city in the southern United States. Several MBA students were interviewed, and this data is used to provide guidelines in structuring the experimental design. The design of the decision support system which is available on the Personal Logic Web site (www.personalogic. com) was closely replicated. This Web site supports the sales of automobiles through the medium of the Internet.

13.10.3. FACTORS CONTROLLED IN THE EXPERIMENT

The results of the pre-tests point out the need for experimental control. In order to test the hypothesised effects, the following factors were controlled in the experiment:

Information presentation format and graphics

The use of a local Web site for each alternative enabled effective control of the information presentation format and graphics on the Web sites so that this would not influence the decision making of the subjects.

Information content of the Web sites

For each alternative which the subject examined, the information content provided was the same. That is, the attributes on which information was provided was consistent across all the alternatives. I developed the entire software system using PowerBuilder software and was thus able to control the information which was presented to the subjects for each alternative.

Download time of the Web pages

Since software was developed to simulate the Web browser environment, the download time of the Web pages was constant for all the alternatives. This could have been a major influence on the decision making process of the subjects because the Web sites for many of the car models are located on servers all over the world (Germany, Japan, Italy, France, UK, Korea, USA, Canada). The use of Web sites and a database query system located on a single server which was located in the same physical vicinity where the subjects were undertaking the experiments eliminated this factor as a source of variability in the subjects' responses.

Number of alternatives in the feasible set

The subjects were told to make their choice from among the set of alternatives which were presented to them. This set was the same, regardless of the treatment condition, and included all the 400 car models currently available in the USA. The manipulation which was done was with respect to whether or not the subjects were provided information which indicated the degree to which these car models matched their preferences, and whether the list of alternatives was sorted with respect to this similarity score. These are precisely the effects of the presence or absence of the QBDA.

Choice situation

All the respondents were given only one choice situation, a setting where they were asked to select a car to purchase from among the cars in the database. This choice set included all car models currently available in the USA.

Number of attributes for each alternative

When making the query the respondent had a choice of a fixed set of attributes. He could set values and ranges for some or all of the attributes in the choice set. These attributes are the same set of attributes used in the car selection task by Personal Logic (www.personalogic.com). The attributes used included body type, fuel efficiency, safety record, price, maintenance costs, performance (in terms of acceleration, braking distance), car manufacturer, and country of manufacture. The subjects could specify preferences for various subcategories within these broad categories.

Source of information

This was confined to a search of the Web sites which represented the type of design and information content which the car manufacturers provide on their Web sites. The design of the Web sites for all the alternatives was similar to enable me to provide consistent information about all the alternatives to the subjects.

Market segment

The sample is based on a convenient sample of MBA students. This represents a fairly homogeneous market segment for the decision making task. These controls limit the generalisability of the research, but are necessary to test the effects of interest.

13.10.4. SUBJECTS

The experimental subjects were MBA students from a large university in the southern United States. The use of students as subjects in experiments to study the purchase of cars has been done previously (Levin and Jasper, 1995). A total of 175 subjects participated in the experimental procedure. Two subjects were eliminated from further consideration due to equipment failure or incomplete task performance resulting in a final pool of 173 subjects. Subjects were recruited on a voluntary basis, and were offered extra credit in their course as an incentive for participation in the experiment. Due to the nature of this investigation, and because the subjects demonstrated a fairly wide range of computer experience, use of a convenient sample of students was justified. During the initial briefing, the students were told that the expected duration of the experiment was approximately 45 minutes, and that this experiment was about purchasing cars on the Web.

Preliminary discussions with some students indicated that most MBA students had previously purchased or actively participated in the purchase decision of an automobile. 96.3% of the respondents indicated that they currently owned a car. 90.8% of the respondents indicated that they had purchased a car within the previous five years. The average number of cars purchased by each respondent within the past five years was 1.62. 68.5% of the respondents indicated that they had been window shopping for a car within the past year. One major concern in any research is the credibility of the choice task. Since the data indicated that most MBA students had actually purchased a car or had actively participated in a car purchase decision, this indicates that the choice task which they were asked to perform is credible. Furthermore, students are likely to use the Web to search for information prior to purchasing a major consumer durable such as a car. This is because they have easy access to the Web in the universities and have vast experience in using this medium to search for pre-purchase information for various products. The subjects indicated that they used the Web extensively to search for information prior to purchasing several products, and in many cases actually completed the entire purchase transaction on the Web. Thus, the subjects were familiar with the choice task. As familiarity with the choice task and the attributes of the alternatives have been hypothesised as influencing information search and decision making, these effects would be minimised in this setting. Thus, this is an appropriate sample for this research.

13.10.5. CHOICE ENVIRONMENT

A laboratory experiment served as the vehicle for testing the stated hypotheses. The experiment was conducted in a behavioural decision laboratory at a major university in the southern United States. Eight workstations in a behavioural laboratory provided a controlled environment where subjects participated in the experiment. An interactive software system running on personal computers was used to collect the information. The package was designed to be user friendly, with complete details/instructions provided on the system. A software program developed in PowerBuilder was the main instrument used in data collection. The database used to store the details of the alternatives was Oracle. The PowerBuilder software enabled the establishment of a connection from the Web to a database which contained the data for the queries and thus simulated the Web browser environment. This program used a structured database and interactively displayed the desired information, recording unobtrusively the data selected.

13.10.6. CHOICE PROCEDURES

Subjects, who were randomly assigned to treatment conditions, were ushered into a behavioural decision lab and seated in front of a computer terminal, where the monitor screen instructed them to enter a pre-assigned user ID and password.

Subjects were then presented with a series of screens which introduced the nature of the experiment and provided instructions regarding the use of the computer to complete the experimental tasks. The experiment was divided into training and experimental sessions. I used the training methodology advocated by Green and Srinivasan (1990). The training session was designed to train the subjects to understand each task demand and also how to handle potential problems which may arise. Subjects completed a training task (selection of a music compact disc). The subjects in each of the two treatment groups (those who had access to the QBDA and those who did not have access to the QBDA) were asked to perform the choice task after being given the appropriate training for that task. The main experimental session required the subjects to select a car from the set of hypertext links to car models they were presented. After completion of the selection task, subjects were presented with questionnaire items designed to measure their assessment of the satisfaction they experienced with the computerised process in selecting that alternative, the confidence they had in their decision, as well as several questions which served as manipulation checks.

To investigate the relationship between the specific characteristics of the computerised decision aid and the satisfaction which the subject experiences with the decision process, two versions of an interactive, computer-driven decision aid were developed. Each version contained a database of attribute-value information for 400 car models which are currently available in the USA. Beyond the common database, the versions varied by whether or not the subjects had access to a QBDA which enabled them to specify their preferences and provided them with information which indicated the extent to which each alternative matched their preferences. This resulted in two distinct types of decision environments. Extensive pre-testing was conducted to check the effects of the experimental manipulation on the mediating variables.

The design of the decision support system for subjects who had access to the QBDA was identical to the system designed by Personal Logic (www. personalogic.com) which is currently being used to sell cars on the Internet. The initial few screens of the decision making task are used to elicit a preference structure from the decision maker about the specific product he would like to purchase. The decision maker is asked to assign weights to each of the attributes which he considers important in the purchase of that product. He is then asked to specify values or ranges for some or all of the attributes that he would like in the specific brand he purchases. The system uses the information entered on these screens to compute a similarity score for each of the alternatives in the database. This similarity score represents the degree to which that particular alternative matches the preferences expressed by the decision maker. A score of 0 indicates that the alternative does not match the query on any attribute. A score of 100 indicates that the alternative matches the query on all attributes. From the next screen, the subject begins the selection process. If the subject is in the treatment group that has access to the QBDA, the next screen lists all the alternatives in the database sorted in descending order of the similarity score for each alternative. This similarity score is indicated on the screen. If the subject is in the treatment group which does not have access to the QBDA, the next screen lists all the alternatives in the database sorted randomly, without providing any information with regard to the extent to which each alternative matches his preferences. The subject is asked to browse through this list. If the subject clicks on any alternative, he is taken to the Web site that contains detailed information about that alternative, including a photograph. The subject is told to select the alternative currently being evaluated for further processing in his decision process if he would seriously consider purchasing the alternative. Otherwise, he can reject this alternative from further consideration in his decision process. Either way, he is returned to the screen that lists all the alternatives. The subject can browse this list and view the detailed information about as many alternatives as he wishes. When the subject indicates that he has evaluated a sufficient number of alternatives, the next screen provides the subject with the list of alternatives that he selected for further processing in his decision process. The process of sequential elimination of alternatives from the consideration set is followed iteratively and the subject is allowed to narrow the consideration set in stages at his own pace without any restrictions being placed on his decision making by the system. After several stages of phased narrowing of the consideration set, the subject arrives at his final decision with regard to which alternative he would like to purchase.

13.11. Establishing Reliability and Validity of the Research

13.11.1. DEVELOPMENT OF THE RESEARCH INSTRUMENT

Existing literature was used as the source of measures for the constructs defined in the theoretical model as far as possible. Where I was unable to find suitable measures for the constructs, new measures were developed and tested for reliability and validity.

The initial list of scale items was developed utilising an exhaustive search of the literature as well as by analyzing the data from the case studies. The instrument was then reviewed by professors who have done work in this area. Following the review an analysis of the extent of consistency among them was performed. At this point, special care was taken that in the instrument each construct was measured by multiple scales, none of which was nominal. Following the development of the instrument, with multiple scale items per construct, "content validity" (Venkatraman and Ramanujan 1987) was established.

Once all the scale items were developed, the instrument was divided into individual scale items and respondents were asked to draw scale items at random out of a bucket and place them on cards labelled with the constructs – a procedure outlined in Moore and Benbasat (1991). This was done with two categories of people: (i) faculty members and (ii) PhD students. They were asked to go through this sorting procedure. Statistical tests were performed to calculate the placement accuracy and how it changed over different revisions of the instrument.

When the instrument was being pre-tested, particular attention was paid to the understandability of words, question difficulty, and length. The participants in the pre-testing process were asked to verbalise their thoughts so that a match between their thoughts and the researcher's intentions could be established. Finally, as recommended by Peter and Churchill (1986), wherever feasible items were not grouped by construct category the direction of several items was reversed to improve the psychometric properties of the instrument.

The format of the instrument, specifically the layout and the wording of the scale items, was designed using the total design method of Dillman (1978).

13.11.2. SAMPLING DESIGN

Since the objective of this research is to study consumer decision making at the unit of analysis of the individual consumer, a crucial issue lies in way the sample is selected. I used a convenient sample of MBA students at a major university in the southern United States. An important consideration is the likely variability across contexts in the relationships among the constructs (Jaworski and Kohli 1991). Given the large sample size and the fact that subjects were randomly assigned to the various treatment conditions, it was ensured that most of the threats to the internal validity of the study were eliminated. If factors such as purchasing context, and the decision making systems that are used to arrive at the decisions, are considered at the individual level this can have a significant impact on the nature of the decision making process. As far as possible, several factors were specifically considered in order to ensure that the individuals selected for inclusion in the sample could be compared to each other. I had selected all respondents from MBA classes at a major university in the Southern United States. This homogeneity helped in removing any variance that might be caused by the nature of the decision making process used and the information sources utilised in arriving at the final decision.

13.11.3. STEPS IN ESTABLISHING RELIABILITY AND VALIDITY

This research set forward two goals: The first goal was to build a framework to understand how the use of the QBDA on the Internet influences the decision making behaviour of consumers making their purchases in this environment. The second goal was to measure (in a reliable and valid manner) and subsequently test the relationships between the presence of QBDAs and the satisfaction and confidence in the purchase decision. The procedure used was essentially iterative. Scale items were developed and tested for reliability and validity before they were used in estimating relationships or testing hypotheses.

The first stage required establishing face validity for the framework developed. The second stage required purifying the scale items of the research instrument that could be used to measure the constructs corresponding to the independent variables (access to the query based decision aid) and dependent variables (confidence in the decision, decision accuracy, number of stages in the phased narrowing of the consideration set and the satisfaction obtained from the purchase). This purification could be accomplished by testing for reliability and validity (at the mono-method level) using data collected from pilot experiments. The third and final research stage required testing the relationships postulated by the framework through a series of experiments. In terms of the instrument used to test relationships and hypotheses, a refinement and purification process was conducted along two dimensions: remove unreliable and invalid scale items and introduce scale items that measure the mediating and the dependent variables.

13.11.4. THREATS TO VALIDITY

In the previous section, an overall picture of the methodological approach that was utilised was presented. In this section, the threats to reliability and validity that the research design and methodological approach poses are discussed. Specifically, the way these threats were dealt with are discussed in some detail.

There are two major categories of threats to validity that could arise in this study: the threat posed by the use of individual subjects (there are four kinds of such threats), and the threat posed by using an experimental study (there are nine kinds of such threats). Table 13.2 illustrates how these threats to the validity of the study were addressed in this research.

Table 13.2. Threats to validity and how they were addressed.

Kind of threat	*How addressed in this research*
Use of individual subjects	
Motivational barrier (Huber and Power 1985; Lee 1989)	Strict confidentiality. Subjects were provided extra credit for participating in the experiment.
Perceptual and cognitive limitations (Huber & Power 1985; Lee 1989)	Research instrument rigorously pilot tested
Perception bias	Test for independence between mediating and independent variables
Lack of information (Huber and Power 1985; Lee 1989)	MTMM design: multiple sources of information (Campbell and Fiske 1959).
Experimental studies	
Validity criteria of Cook and Campbell (1979)	
Statistical conclusion validity	Sample size was calculated using power tests. Factor analysis assumes multi-variate normality. Checked skewness and kurtosis of indicator variables, examined residual plots (Venkatraman and Ramanujan 1987).
Internal validity	Correlations between constructs. To rule out alternate explanations, the individuals to be assigned to the treatments were selected at random.
External validity	I performed the experiment using MBA students, 96 % of whom have purchased a new car within the previous 5 years.
Validity criteria of Bagozzi (1980)	
Theoretical meaningfulness of concepts	Drawn from prior research and case studies
Observational meaningfulness of concepts	Extensive pilot testing with potential respondents.
Convergent validity	MTMM approach; exploratory and confirmatory factor analysis
Discriminant validity	MTMM approach; exploratory and confirmatory factor analysis
Nomological validity	Mediating variable regression using standardised terms.

In the following subsections of the chapter, I discuss how the various threats to validity that arose from the use of an experimental methodology were dealt with.

13.11.5. THREATS INTRODUCED BY THE USE OF INDIVIDUAL SUBJECTS

The use of individual subjects introduces two significant threats to validity (Phillips 1981):

1. Subject's inability to make complex judgements;
2. Subject bias or ignorance.

Additionally, Lee (1989) identifies three categories of threats that arise from the use of individual participants:

1. Motivational barriers;
2. Perceptual and cognitive limitations;
3. Lack of information.

The key research issue in addressing these threats to validity and successfully utilising such a design lies in the selection of the individuals for assignment to the treatments. Phillips and Bagozzi (1986) advocate "the extent to which the subject participated in the decision making with respect to the issues covered in the experiment" as an indicator of subject qualification.

To counteract the motivational barrier threat, the promise of strict confidentiality was made to each potential respondent. Participants were guaranteed that their responses to the questions on the research instrument would not be disclosed to any person other than the researcher under any circumstance. This helped potential respondents to be honest – without the fear that their individual responses would be seen by others. To decrease the cognitive burden on the respondents, I extensively pre-tested the instrument, paying particular attention to the understandability of words, scale item difficulty, and length. The participants in the pre-testing process were asked to verbalise their thoughts so that a match between their thoughts and the researcher's intentions could be established.

A final threat to validity was that of perception bias. This refers to the fact that respondents might report values for the scale items corresponding to the independent variable that have been influenced by the mediating variables. Perception was addressed by ensuring that the measures for the independent variable and the mediating variables were independent of each other. The subjects were not informed of the treatment condition which they were in. This helped to counter the validity threats in terms of perception bias.

13.11.6. THREATS INTRODUCED BY THE EXPERIMENTAL STUDY

One of the primary purposes of this research was to create reliable and valid scale measures. A major threat to validity arises from the use of experimental studies. The subsequent sections discuss how the six threats to validity that arise from using an experimental study (Bagozzi, 1980) are addressed. In this study, the operational basis for addressing the six threats to validity follows the approach taken by Phillips and Bagozzi (1986). For purposes of completeness, the description of how the threats to validity are addressed has been augmented by specifying how the threats can be addressed from a statistical point.

Convergent and discriminant validity at the mono-method level of analysis

Convergent validity (reliability and uni-dimensionality) at the mono-method level of analysis refers to the degree of agreement in individual subjects' responses to different instrument items designed to measure the same concept (Phillips and Bagozzi 1986). Individual respondents are viewed as the method and different instrument items are viewed as different operationalisations within the same method. Discriminant validity at the mono-method level of analysis is the extent to which a concept differs from other concepts. Discriminant validity is achieved if the separate measures of each true score converge within components and the true scores are unique from each other. Convergent and discriminant validity are established using reliability analysis, exploratory factor analysis and confirmatory factor analysis.

Convergent and discriminant validity at the multi-method unit of analysis

Convergent validity at this level is assessed by constructing a MTMM matrix of correlations (Campbell and Fiske 1959). For convergent validity to be established:

1. Correlations between subjects reporting on the same trait must be positive, statistically significant, and sufficiently large (Campbell and Fiske 1959);
2. All variation and covariation in the MM matrix must be due to the traits alone except for random error.

Discriminant validity at this level of analysis refers to whether a particular concept differs from other concepts when measured by different methods.

The question that needs to be answered while addressing convergent and discriminant validity is: "Do each of the scale items measure only a single construct and do they measure the construct they are intended to measure?". Factor analysis is the tool that can be employed on the set of scale items measuring the independent and mediating variables to answer this question. As each item represents an independent attempt to measure a particular construct, all items of a scale should load on one factor if they are to satisfy the requirement of convergent validity and should load weakly on all other factors if they are to satisfy the requirements of discriminant validity.

Factor analysis results provide only necessary conditions for assessing validity. Hence, they must be augmented by using the MTMM matrix of correlations analysis. In this study, several procedural issues involved in constructing the MTMM matrix and establishing convergent and discriminant validity at the multi-method level of analysis arise. The most important is that the MTMM approach requires that the number of methods measuring each trait be a constant for each unit of analysis.

Nomological validity at the multi-level level of analysis

Nomological validity relates to the degree to which the predictions from a theoretical network are confirmed. Since the scale items in the measurement instrument needed to be purified (following the use of the procedure recommended in Churchill 1979), nomological validity at the multi-method level of analysis could only be assessed when the criteria for convergent and discriminant validity were satisfied.

Typically, confirmatory factor analysis (Bagozzi 1980) is used to test for nomological validity. Mediating variable regression is the appropriate technique to test the hypotheses embodied by the framework and establish nomological validity at the multi-method level of analysis.

13.12. Results

13.12.1. TESTING OF HYPOTHESES

The experiment was administered to 173 MBA students. 87 subjects were assigned to the treatment condition that had access to the QBDA. 86 subjects were assigned to the treatment condition that did not have access to the QBDA. The allocation of subjects to the treatments was done at random. Following extensive pre-tests and the procedures required for instrument purification, the measures used were found to have values for Cronbach α ranging from .73 to .94. Hence, I concluded that the measures have high reliability. Table 13.3 shows the values of Cronbach α for the measures used. Factor analysis of the data indicated that the scale items loaded onto the constructs were *a priori* expected to load on (there were no cross-loadings). Furthermore, the number of factors that emerged was identical to that expected *a priori*. As all the scale items loaded correctly on the constructs in the theoretical framework, there is statistical evidence to support the claim that the scales have adequate uni-dimensionality, convergent and discriminant validity at the mono-method level of analysis. I concluded that the measures used had high validity.

Table 13.3. Reliability of measures used.

Acronym	Measure	Cronbach α
EFFORT	Cognitive decision effort	.92
SATISFACTION	Satisfaction with the decision process	.86
CONFIDENCE	Confidence in the decision	.73
SAVINGS	Perceived cost savings	.94
STAGES	Number of stages in the phased narrowing of the consideration set	
SIMILARITY	Similarity among the alternatives in consideration set	
CONSIDER	Size of the consideration set	
QBDA	Access to the query based decision aid	

The influence of the QBDA on the mediating and dependent variables was tested using a single factor ANOVA with the factor being QBDA. The factor QBDA was coded as present or absent, and coded as a dummy variable. I followed up the single factor ANOVA tests by regressing the dependent variables on the variables QBDA, CONSIDER, SIMILARITY, SAVINGS, and EFFORT. I used linear regression models. The variable QBDA was coded as present or absent, and coded as a dummy variable. The measure used for the variable CONSIDER was the number of alternatives in the first stage of the phased narrowing of the decision process. The measure used for the variable SIMILARITY was the degree of similarity among the alternatives in the consideration set in the first stage of the decision process. This was measured on a scale of 0 (completely different) to 100 (completely similar). The measures used for the variables SAVINGS and EFFORT were represented as the mean-centered scores of the 7-point Likert scale items that were used to measure these constructs. The measure used for the variable STAGES represented the number of stages in which the subject carried out the sequential elimination of alternatives from the initially constructed consideration set until he arrived at his final choice. The measures used for the dependent variables SATISFACTION and CONFIDENCE were represented as the mean-centered scores of the 7-point Likert scale items that were used to measure these constructs. The regression analyses included the data from all the subjects. I tested for interaction effects between the mediating variables that would increase the predictive power to explain the variation of the dependent variables. No significant interaction effects were identified. Tests for correlation among the mediating and the dependent variables indicated no significant correlations.

Table 13.4. Correlations between the constructs.

	EFFORT	*SATISFACTION*	*CONFIDENCE*	*SAVINGS*
EFFORT	1.00			
SATISFACTION	-.1546	1.00		
CONFIDENCE	.0947	.0443	1.00	
SAVINGS	-.2027	.1973	.1498	1.00

*** Significant LE .01 (2-tailed)   ** Significant LE .05 (2-tailed)

Table 13.5. Results of single factor ANOVA tests where the factor is QBDA.

Dependent variable	Mean of sample with access to the query based decision aid	Mean of sample without access to the query based decision aid	$F_{1,171}$	Significance level
SIMILARITY	87.38	76.31	13.125	.001***
CONSIDER	10.54	8.87	2.152	.116
SAVINGS	4.062	3.667	3.595	.057**
EFFORT	2.92	3.70	10.401	.002***
CONFIDENCE	4.8	4.25	2.146	.118
SATISFACTION	4.649	3.983	5.419	.023**
STAGES	4.27	3.81	3.725	.058**

To rule out any potentially confounding effects due to non-random assignment of the subjects to the treatment conditions, the sample means for computer familiarity and experience with their previous car were statistically compared across cells. Results of these tests indicated that each cell contained subjects who, on average, had the same level of computer familiarity and experience with their previous car. In addition, subjects were distributed approximately equally across cells by gender. Hence, effects identified in the experimental data can be assigned with greater certainty to the experimental variables under investigation.

13.12.2. INFLUENCE OF THE QBDA ON THE MEDIATING VARIABLES

Influence of the QBDA on size of the consideration set

I found a weak influence of the variable QBDA on the variable CONSIDER. The pattern of means was as predicted. The mean value for the variable CONSIDER for the sample which had access to the QBDA was 10.54. The mean value for the variable CONSIDER for the sample which did not have access to the QBDA was 8.87. A single factor ANOVA was conducted to examine the influence of the variable QBDA on the variable CONSIDER. This showed a weak influence ($F_{1,171}$ = 2.152, p < .12).

Table 13.6. Results of the regression analysis.

Depend. variable	Statistical significance		Predictors					
	R square and adjust.R square	F-statistic and signific. level	β coeff. for QBDA t-statistic signif. level	β coeff. for EFFORT t-statistic signif. level	β coeff. for CONSID t-statistic signif. level	β coeff. for SIMILA t-statistic signif. level	β coeff. for SAVING t-statistic signif. level
EFFORT	.560 .528***	$F_{2,170}$= 8.092 .001***	β = .363 t = 6.497 .001***		β = .355 t = 6.405 .001***		
STAGES	.711 .681***	$F_{2,170}$= 10.368 .001***			β = .485 t = 4.803 .001***	β = .119 t = 2.181 .115	
CONFID	.426 .401***	$F_{2,170}$= 5.030 .009***				β = .142 t = 3.774 .027	β = .328 t = 6.930 .005***
SATISFY	.762 .725***	$F_{3,169}$= 9.659 .001***		β= -.284 t =-4.86 .006**		β = .223 t = 3.241 .028**	β = .439 t = 4.484 .001***

I was unable to obtain a significant result that the access to the QBDA would result in increased size of the consideration set. Though the sample means are in the direction hypothesised, the single factor ANOVA test failed to yield a result at a reasonable level of significance. This was because the variance in each of the samples for this variable was very high, resulting in a high sum-of-squares error term. This resulted in a low F-statistic.

Influence of the QBDA on similarity among the alternatives in the consideration set

I found a significant influence of the variable QBDA on the variable SIMILARITY. The pattern of means was as predicted. The mean value for the variable SIMILARITY for the sample which had access to the QBDA was 87.38. The mean value for the variable SIMILARITY for the sample which did not have access to the QBDA was 76.31. A single factor ANOVA was conducted to examine the influence of the variable QBDA on the variable SIMILARITY. This showed a significant influence ($F_{1,171} = 13.125$, $p < .01$).

Influence of the QBDA on perceived cost savings

I found a significant influence of the variable QBDA on the variable SAVINGS. The pattern of means was as predicted. The mean value for the variable SAVINGS for the sample which had access to the QBDA was 4.062. The mean value for the variable SAVINGS for the sample which did not have access to the QBDA was 3.667. A single factor ANOVA was conducted to examine the influence of the variable QBDA on the variable SAVINGS. This showed a significant influence ($F_{1,171} = 3.595$, $p < .06$).

Influence of the QBDA on cognitive decision effort

I found a significant influence of the variable QBDA on the variable EFFORT. The pattern of means was as predicted. The mean value for the variable EFFORT for the sample which had access to the QBDA was 2.92. The mean value for the variable EFFORT for the sample which did not have access to the QBDA was 3.7. A single factor ANOVA was conducted to examine the influence of the variable QBDA on the variable EFFORT. This showed a significant influence ($F_{1,171} = 10.401$, $p < .01$). I followed up the single factor ANOVA test by regressing the variable EFFORT on the variables CONSIDER, SIMILARITY and QBDA. I used a linear regression model. I obtained a significant explanation of the variation in the variable EFFORT (R square = .560, adjusted R square = .528, $F_{2,170} = 8.092$, $p < .001$). Of the variables used in the regression, the variables QBDA ($\beta = .363$, $t = 6.497$, $p < .001$) and CONSIDER ($\beta = .355$, $t = 6.405$, $p < .001$) were found to have a significant influence on the variable EFFORT.

13.12.3. INFLUENCE OF THE QBDA ON THE DEPENDENT VARIABLES

Influence of the QBDA on the number of stages in the phased narrowing of the consideration set

Hypothesis 1. I found a significant influence of the variable QBDA on the variable STAGES. The pattern of means was as predicted by hypothesis 1a. The mean value for the variable STAGES for the sample which had access to the QBDA was 4.27. The mean value for the variable STAGES for the sample which did not have access to the QBDA was 3.81. A single factor ANOVA was conducted to examine the influence of the variable QBDA on the variable STAGES. This showed a significant influence ($F_{1,171} = 3.725$, $p < .06$). I followed up the single factor ANOVA test by regressing the variable STAGES on the variables QBDA, CONSIDER, EFFORT, SAVINGS, and SIMILARITY. I used a linear regression model. I obtained a significant explanation of the variation in the variable STAGES (R square = .711, adjusted R square = .681, $F_{2,170} = 10.368$, $p < .001$). Of the variables used in the regression, the variable CONSIDER ($\beta = .485$, $t = 4.803$, $p < .001$) was found to have a significant influence on the variable STAGES. The variable SIMILARITY ($\beta = .119$, $t = 2.181$, $p < .12$) was found to have a minor influence on the variable STAGES. The variable QBDA was found to have no influence on the variable STAGES in the regression.

Because of the theoretical support for, and the intuitive appeal of, the proposed relationships between the mediating variables in the model and the variable STAGES, evidence of strong effects was not surprising.

Influence of the QBDA on confidence in the decision

Hypothesis 2. I found a weak influence of the variable QBDA on the variable CONFIDENCE. The pattern of means was as predicted by hypothesis 2a. The mean value for the variable CONFIDENCE for the sample which had access to the QBDA was 4.8. The mean value for the variable CONFIDENCE for the sample which did not have access to the QBDA was 4.25. A single factor ANOVA was conducted to examine the influence of the variable QBDA on the variable CONFIDENCE. This showed a weak influence ($F_{1,171}$ = 2.146, p < .12). I followed up the single factor ANOVA test by regressing the variable CONFIDENCE on the variables QBDA, CONSIDER, EFFORT, SAVINGS, and SIMILARITY. I used a linear regression model. I obtained a significant explanation of the variation in the variable CONFIDENCE (R square = .426, adjusted R square = .401, $F_{2,170}$ = 5.030, p < .01). Of the variables used in the regression, the variables SAVINGS (β = .328, t = 6.930, p < .01) and SIMILARITY (β = .142, t = 3.774, p < .03) were found to have a significant influence on the variable CONFIDENCE. The variable QBDA was found to have no influence on the variable CONFIDENCE in the regression.

The influence of the QBDA on the dependent variable CONFIDENCE was as predicted. The relationships are both theoretically grounded and intuitively appealing.

Influence of the QBDA on satisfaction with the decision process

Hypothesis 3. I found a significant influence of the variable QBDA on the variable SATISFACTION. The pattern of means was as predicted by hypothesis 3a. The mean value for the variable SATISFACTION for the sample which had access to the QBDA was 4.649. The mean value for the variable SATISFACTION for the sample which did not have access to the QBDA was 3.983. A single factor ANOVA was conducted to examine the influence of the variable QBDA on the variable SATISFACTION. This showed a significant influence ($F_{1,171}$ = 5.419, p < .03). I followed up the single factor ANOVA test by regressing the variable SATISFACTION on the variables QBDA, CONSIDER, EFFORT, SAVINGS, and SIMILARITY. I used a linear regression model. I obtained a significant explanation of the variation in the variable SATISFACTION (R square = .762, adjusted R square = .725, $F_{3,169}$ = 9.659, p < .001). Of the variables used in the regression, the variables SAVINGS (β = .439, t = 4.884, p < .001), SIMILARITY (β = .223, t = 3.241, p < .03) and EFFORT (β = -.284, t = -4.867, p < .01) were found to have a significant influence on the variable SATISFACTION. The variable QBDA was found to have no influence on the variable SATISFACTION in the regression.

Because of the theoretical support for, and the intuitive appeal of, the proposed relationships between the mediating variables in the model and the variable SATISFACTION, evidence of strong effects was not surprising.

13.13. Conclusions and Discussion

This research developed and tested a model for understanding the influence of QBDAs on consumer decision making in the electronic commerce environment. The results show that the use of well designed QBDA leads to increased *satisfaction with the decision process,* and increased *confidence in judgments.* The *number of stages of phased narrowing of the consideration set* was higher in the case of subjects who had access to the QBDA. The mediating variables through which this influence occurs are *size of the consideration set, similarity among the alternatives in the consideration set, cognitive decision effort,* and *perceived cost savings.* The size of the consideration set and the similarity among the alternatives in the consideration set were higher in the case of subjects who had access to the QBDA. Subjects who had access to the QBDA perceived an increased cost savings and a lower cognitive decision effort associated with the purchase decision. The subjective reports showed that subjects who had access to the QBDA both liked the interface more and had more confidence in their judgments compared to subjects who did not have access.

13.13.1. ACADEMIC CONTRIBUTIONS

The phenomenon of consumers purchasing products on the Web is relatively new. In this business model, consumers select items to purchase from electronic shopping malls by making queries to databases using software tools such as software smart agents. A large proportion of the purchase transaction is conducted via computers without the consumer ever having face-to-face contact with the sales personnel. This has raised a host of interesting research issues which need to be investigated. Research that should shed light on such issues is already underway (e.g. Degeratu, Rangaswamy and Wu's (1998) study of electronic commerce for grocery items; Lynch and Ariely's (1998) study of electronic commerce for wines; and Shankar and Rangaswamy's (1998) study of electronic commerce in the travel industry).

This research significantly extends previous research in several ways:

1. The influence of QBDA on satisfaction with the decision process, confidence in the decision and the number of stages in the phased narrowing of the consideration set has not been examined previously.
2. The fact that "similarity among the alternatives in the consideration set" acts as a mediating variable between "access to the query-based decision aid" and the dependent variables has not been examined previously. Prior research (Stone and Schkade, 1991) has treated it as an independent variable and manipulated it explicitly by creating sets of similar and dissimilar alternatives and observing consumer decision-making in each treatment condition. In my research, this variable is manipulated implicitly depending on whether or not the subject has access to the QBDA.
3. The measure used to compute the variable "similarity among the alternatives in the consideration set" is new. It takes into consideration both the mean and the dispersion of the attribute values among the alternatives in the consideration set and combines these values using a linear additive multi-attribute model.

4. The process of phased narrowing of the consideration set has been done in a completely natural manner without any restrictions being placed on the number of stages in which the subject can narrow his choice to arrive at his final decision. This represents a more natural replication of the process by which people make their decisions. Previous researchers (Levin and Jasper, 1995) have restricted the phased narrowing of the consideration set to a fixed number of stages.

13.13.2. MANAGERIAL IMPLICATIONS

This research has significant managerial implications in terms of providing guidelines for the design of Web sites in order to optimise the interface between the decision maker and the system.

1. The design of the user interface, with a view to optimising the satisfaction of consumers who are making their purchases via the Web, is a critical issue. By the year 2000, the volume of business-to-consumer electronic commerce is expected to be $80 billion a year, and the volume of business-to-business electronic commerce is expected to be $300 billion a year. The electronic commerce channel is likely to emerge as a significant channel for conducting sales transactions and will significantly alter the structure of most industries. Given the recent emergence of the electronic commerce phenomenon and the rapid spread of the Internet and electronic commerce, it is imperative that a research agenda be immediately established to understand how this will influence consumer behaviour and market structures. Designers of Web sites need to understand the cognitive and perceptual rules that prompt consumers to make electronic detours in their search for goods and services. Ultimately, this research should help designers of Web sites to make accurate generalisations about the effects of computerised decision aids on strategy selection so that they can then design their Web sites to provide the optimal interface for a given task environment.

2. The Web is increasingly being used by consumers to search for information prior to the purchase of major consumer durables such as cars. In 1997, 2% of the car sales in the US originated from a single Web site, Auto-by-Tel (www.autobytel.com). DealerNet (www.dealernet.com) has become a major player in the car sales market and a majority of car dealers in the USA have registered their online dealerships with this Web site. Bud Mathaissel, Chief Information Officer of Ford Motor Corporation, expressed the opinion that he expects a significant proportion of new car sales to be transacted via the Web by December 1998 and that this would increase dramatically over the next two years. Thus, this research has significant managerial implications.

3. Given the large number and variety of decision aids currently emerging on the Internet, it is imperative that we investigate how these decision aid formats impact consumer satisfaction and confidence in the decision. The fact that the mere provision of information on the Web page which indicates the extent to which each alternative matches the consumer's preferences has a significant impact on consumer satisfaction and confidence is worth noting.

Cognitive effort and perceived decision accuracy are important determinants of how the search aids (QBDA) are used. While designers of Web sites can use this knowledge to their advantage, ignoring it may lead to the tools being used in unanticipated and undesirable ways. Designers of Web sites who take a non-directive approach to the design of their Web sites risk foregoing the improved decision quality benefits and are instead more likely to see efficiency benefits. Only by designing Web sites efficiently, using the reduction of cognitive effort as a key lever, will the use of the decision aids for the purpose of electronic commerce result in increased decision making effectiveness. Documenting the performance of these computerised decision aids in varied environments should help identify the conditions under which they can be used to a decision maker's advantage and when they might create system-induced errors. Understanding when problematic interactions are likely to occur should focus research attention on corrective mechanisms to mitigate the potential for error. In addition, it is of interest to investigate the users' viewpoints with regard to the computerised decision aids to discern a computerised decision aid's likelihood of acceptance.

4.   Many merchants who have set up electronic shopping malls on the Web fear that the reduced cognitive search effort associated with this environment will lead to increased price competition and lower profit margins. This is in line with arguments proposed by Bakos (1997), Lynch and Ariely (1998), and Alba, Lynch, Weitz, Janiszewski, Lutz, Sawyer, and Wood (1997). This may lead merchants to adopt a strategy of providing a less than optimal Web site so as to make it difficult for consumers to use this medium to obtain price comparisons, quality comparisons and comparisons across Web sites. I have found that the presence of QBDA on the merchants' Web sites has led to an increased perception of cost savings among the consumers who use these decision aids to search for pre-purchase information. This has led to consumers experiencing a greater satisfaction with the decision process. This will lead to the consumers using this channel more extensively to search for pre-purchase information and, ultimately, even making their purchases through this channel. Thus, merchants who adopt the strategy of not providing the optimal interface to consumers on their Web sites will risk losing a substantial portion of the business which would be transacted via this channel.

5.   The fact that many Web sites such as Auto-by-Tel (www.autobytel.com), Microsoft Carpoint (carpoint.msn.com), and Personal Logic (www. personalogic.com) provide a consolidated source of information about products from many manufacturers significantly increases the benefits that consumers obtain from using these Web sites to search for information. This has resulted in the rapid adoption of these Web sites by consumers in their search for pre-purchase information on various products.

13.13.3. IMPLICATIONS FOR CONSUMER POLICY

Widespread availability of electronically provided product information has the potential to significantly enhance consumers' ability to cope with complex product environments, thereby facilitating the decision process. However, because of their ability to influence consumers' choice process, such systems should be subjected to careful scrutiny. Electronically provided information is not currently regulated with respect to its veracity or objectivity. Since the majority of these systems are sponsored by parties with a vested interest in selling products, it is plausible that the information presented is likely to be biased in favour of the sponsor. If the integrity of the information is compromised, the strategic position of the consumer is likely to be weakened, rather than improved, through interaction with the computerised decision aid.

Because of their dual power to both empower as well as abuse the consumer, these issues must be addressed by consumer advocates and policy makers alike in the near future. Future regulatory legislation should address the issues of information veracity and system integrity, particularly in the case of systems which offer product solutions. Until regulation of such systems occurs, caution must be exercised in advocating their use. The future challenge in developing consumer oriented computerised decision aids does not reside in technological advances, but rather in developing systems that are useful and appealing to the intended consumer. These steps are necessary to avoid consumer perceptions of non-utility and, ultimately, non-use of the computerised decision aids.

13.13.4. DISCUSSION

The environment in which consumers encounter information has a substantial impact on the way this information is evaluated and integrated. Specifically, user interfaces which provide consumers with control over the content, order, and duration of product-relevant information cause information to have higher value and to become increasingly usable over time. The experiments presented here demonstrate that the provision of QBDA has a significant impact on consumers' ability to integrate information, understand inputs to their judgments and to be confident about their judgments. In addition, consumer satisfaction with the decision process was significantly increased. Although the current work was carried out in the context of electronic communications, the applicability of the current research reaches beyond computerised interfaces. The same conceptual principles should extend to the analysis of any communication medium conveying information to be integrated over time.

The presence of QBDA can help consumers integrate information and express utilities in a more consistent and accurate manner. These decision aids also allow for a better match between evaluative judgments and underlying utilities. The provision of the QBDA allows consumers to discern better which alternatives are better suited to their true underlying utilities.

My research has shown that the presence of QBDA significantly increases satisfaction with the decision process. However, it has been noted that although some decision aids may improve decision making, abuse is possible (Todd and Benbasat, 1994). In particular, Widing and Talarzyk (1993) have shown that the decision aid most likely to be a part of an electronic commerce environment (i.e. a cutoff rule that allows formation of a consideration set containing only those alternatives that pass consumer-specified attribute cutoffs) can lead to sub-optimal decisions in efficient choice sets. In addition to this, a separate stream of research has shown that a second likely characteristic of an electronic commerce environment, i.e. a visually rich presentation, can distort the decision process by diverting attention away from information that is most important for the task at hand (Jarvenpaa, 1989, 1990).

It is important to note that the provision of QBDA is not a panacea, and some caution should be exerted when utilising them. In particular, one should pay attention to the processing demands of the information system (Carroll, 1997), the experience of the consumer with the information system, and the learning process over time. The need for the consumer to explicitly specify his preferences increases the cognitive load on the consumer and may have the effect of reducing decision quality and satisfaction with the decision process.

13.13.5. LIMITATIONS

As with any experimental investigation, there are a number of limitations present in the current study. I restricted my research to the selection of cars on the Web. Clearly, a variety of choice situations as well as products must be investigated before generalisable comments can be made to guide the development of computerised decision aids. Another limitation of the present study is the size and composition of the group which participated in the study. The sample is homogeneous, and presumably has greater than average cognitive capabilities. A larger and more diverse sample would have facilitated investigation of several intriguing results and would have offered greater opportunity for generalisation of the findings. The respondents were placed in a choice task that implicitly demanded and facilitated search, and an analytical approach. However, since the hypotheses which were developed dealt with the specific effects of the manipulations, these factors only point to the difficulty in the generalisation of these results to different segments of the market and to different choice situations.

13.14. Directions for Future Research

The current research has examined issues regarding the influence of QBDA on decision making and their impact on different aspects of performance and satisfaction with the decision process. Much more work needs to be done on examining the influence of these QBDA on consumer preferences. Some of the potential research areas are discussed below.

13.14.1. INFLUENCE OF QBDA ON DECISION STRATEGIES

The electronic commerce area is a rapidly emerging paradigm and marketing researchers need to focus their research efforts to fully understand consumer behaviour in this paradigm. A potential area for further research is to examine how the use of these decision aids, such as software smart agents and database query engines, impacts the decision strategies which consumers adopt when they are shopping on the Web (Alba, Lynch, Weitz, Janiszewski, Lutz, Sawyer, and Wood, 1997). Several researchers (Biggs, Bedard, Gaber and Linsmeier, 1985; Stone and

Schkade, 1991) have found that the greater the similarity among the alternatives, the greater will be the tendency of subjects to use compensatory decision strategies. Based on these findings, I anticipate that subjects who have access to the QBDA will use compensatory decision strategies, whereas subjects who do not have access to the QBDA will use non-compensatory decision strategies.

13.14.2. DECISION AIDS PREFERENCE IN USER INTERFACES

The experiments presented in this chapter examined the influence of QBDA on different aspects of task-related performance. In particular, it was shown that the use of QBDA could have significant benefits regarding aspects of the task such as confidence in the decision and satisfaction with the decision process. However, the experiments presented in this chapter forced subjects to use computerised interfaces for some time and measured the outcomes of this experience. In the real world, consumers are not randomly assigned to treatment conditions, and it is an open question whether they will demand a greater availability of QBDA in conditions where the current research shows they are beneficial. In other words, for many marketing applications, the important question is not whether a particular interface causes higher performance if used, but rather whether it is used at all. Therefore, in order to understand the role of QBDA on consumer decision making, we need to study preferences and not just performance. Preferences for interfaces are particularly important in situations where there are multiple information providers that offer similar content in their information systems. Perhaps, because in most such cases consumers do not get feedback on their performance levels, it is likely that their decisions about which interface to use will be based on preferences for simplicity. Therefore, the goal of information providers is not only to provide consumers with useful information that could facilitate good decisions but also to get consumers to adopt their services and continue to subscribe to them and use them in the long term.

13.14.3. MOTIVATION AND SEARCH EFFORT

Aside from resulting in differences in the ability to process and integrate the same information, there is a question with regard to whether the use of QBDA would increase consumers' motivation to search for and understand information. Though motivation is a very relevant and important aspect, it cannot account for the results obtained in this research. Regardless of the applicability of motivational factors for the current results, motivational factors could still play an interesting role in other applications of QBDA. Pleasurable activities are likely to result in a higher tendency to engage in these activities. Therefore, much as consumers who enjoy shopping spend more time at it than those who do not, one can ask whether the use of QBDA will enhance the pleasure of information search and thus increase search time. Some evidence in this direction has come from work on optimal stopping rules (Saad and Russo, 1996) which demonstrated that under conditions that allow more free search, people examine more information before they feel they have sufficient information to make a decision. In addition, the ability to have control over the different aspects of a situation has been shown to increase the pleasure of the event itself (Shapiro,

Schwarz and Astin, 1996). Understanding such motivational factors is crucial because, in the long run, it will determine consumers' ability to fully utilise electronic communication channels. While electronic communication channels have the potential to significantly decrease search costs, increased motivation can ultimately result in increased overall search effort and search time.

13.14.4. USE OF QBDA IN DIFFERENT INFORMATION ENVIRONMENTS

QBDA can select information and merchandise for the consumer, thereby virtually eliminating search costs with little active intervention by the consumer. Ample evidence exists to suggest that information is not simply acquired in reaction to pre-defined preferences, but that it also helps decision makers define their own values and preferences as they engage in the process of acquiring information (Tversky, Sattath and Slovic, 1988; Payne, Bettman and Johnson, 1993). In other words, the information itself changes the way preferences are constructed, therefore one cannot define the decision space in advance. There exist potential liabilities for QBDA in dynamic environments in which innovation can change the correlation structure of alternatives in the environment. As long as the information environment is stable and does not change much, the structure of preferences can be expected to have some stability. Hence, in such environments QBDA can be beneficial. However, in situations in which information changes over time, consumers served by QBDA alone would be unlikely to notice the changing correlational structure of the environment. In these environments, additional mechanisms would need to be built into the system to continuously update the knowledge base. Expert systems could play a vital role in these decision environments.

13.14.5. PLANNING UPGRADE PATHS

Under some circumstances, it might be better to have a simple user interface that does not require much effort to learn and use. The advantages of such interfaces are primarily at the initial stages of usage, when experience is low and therefore complexity is high. Over time, however, as experience accumulates, the advantages of more powerful and flexible interfaces become more apparent. Therefore, electronic merchants have the problem of providing either a good solution for the short term in the form of simple user interfaces or, for the long term, in the form of complex user interfaces. Ideally, a smooth upgrade path for user interfaces could be planned. This way, consumers could start with simple systems that would progress to become more complex and powerful. The difficulty in designing such user interfaces is that as the learning of the simple interface increases, it is more difficult to undo this learning. Paradoxically, learning of a complex interface might be more difficult after using a simple interface than after having no experience at all. In other words, the initial stages of experience can have a particularly large impact on learning and to some extent stabilise the process. Therefore, when the environment changes, consumers might tend to under-utilise these changes and not alter their search strategies accordingly. The challenge for marketing managers is to provide consumers with information systems that change over time such that they fit the consumers' short term needs without sacrificing their long term interests.

CHAPTER 14

Fiddlers on the Wire

*Music, Electronic Commerce and Local Economic Development on a
Virtual Cape Breton Island, Canada - A Case Study*

MICHAEL GURSTEIN

14.1. Cape Breton Island

Cape Breton is an island off the easternmost tip of North America, attached by a causeway to mainland Nova Scotia, Canada. The main population centre, the Cape Breton Regional Municipality (CBRM, also known as Sydney, the name of its largest individual settlement), is at the easternmost tip of the island, reflecting its origins as a European-facing seaport and supplier of coal, and then steel, to Europe and especially Great Britain. The CBRM has a population of 125,000 out of the total island population of 175,000, and a provincial Nova Scotia population of approximately 850,000. Sydney is some 275 miles (5 hours by car) from the provincial capital, Halifax (population 350,000), which is a regional service and professional hub. The closest major urban centre is Montreal, some 800 miles west, or Boston, some 800 miles (1250 kilometers) to the southwest.

In the latter part of the 19th and early part of the 20th century, Cape Breton was among the most prosperous and industrially active parts of Canada with booming coal mines, a rapidly expanding steel industry, and significant fishing and agricultural sectors. Since its "glory days" supplying the British navy in World War I, however, the industrial sector in Cape Breton has been in gradual but continuing decline. Employment in mining has been reduced from a high of 15,000 men to the current 1600 (another downsizing to 500 was recently announced) and in the steel works from 10,000 men to the current 1200. This decline, which has accelerated in recent times, has been partially balanced by increases in the service industries and tourism but the region has experienced gradual population erosion and an aging of the labour force. The current unemployment rate is 20+% with a significantly lower "participation" rate than the rest of Canada, suggesting a "real" unemployment rate in the 40% range.

Available resources are few - the scenery and related amenities are world class, but the season is short and it would be difficult to see how an economy could be built on this single pillar. The region has never achieved a managerial or significant service economy commensurate with its level of industrial development. The traditional rivalry with Halifax, the provincial Capital, has paralleled the very high concentration of information intensive activities in Halifax including administration, professional services, research and management. This has left the Cape Breton economy with little to build on in the emerging information sector and with a very meagre local market and skill reservoir.

Cape Breton, however, is the "ancestral home" of a uniquely pure form of Scottish style Celtic music and other features of traditional Gaelic culture. As an artifact of its relative isolation and limited economic prospects, many of the elements of pre-Jacobean Scottish culture which have been lost in Scotland have survived in Cape Breton over the some 250 years of settlement. Scots musicians or musicologists find in Cape Breton tunes and fingerings which have long disappeared in "the home country" (MacInnes, 1998). Cape Breton musicians have become nationally, and even internationally, recognised and are becoming a new "coal bed" from which wealth is being extracted for the larger community.

14.2. Economic Development and Cape Breton Island

The key problems for economic development for Cape Breton, as for many similar rural and remote regions, are the limitations of location: distance to markets; lack of a local human resource pool with a range of commercially useful experience and skills; limited access to technical and marketing information; and absence of risk capital (Gurstein, 1996).

The University College of Cape Breton was established in the late 1960s after considerable local agitation, and represented the amalgamation of the Extension wing of a regional university with a local technical college. As a "University College", it combines both degree-granting undergraduate programs in the liberal arts, humanities and sciences with technical programs in several areas including telecommunications, environmental engineering and geomatics.

A Chair in the Management of Technological Change (MOTC) received funding in 1992. The Chair was part of a national program for promoting, as a research and pedagogical priority, the discipline of the "Management of Technology".

The awarding of the Chair to UCCB more or less coincided with the beginning of an accelerated decline in the local economy. Inevitably, there were immediate and irresistible demands that the Chair become engaged in practical activities to respond to the employment crisis in the region - training programs, economic development planning, small enterprise counselling and mentoring, and regional strategic planning among others. It was widely recognised that existing resources and enterprises would provide no medium or longer-term economic security for the region and that there was a need to embrace new technologies and new business models, and the opportunities for enterprise and job creation which these might present.[1]

Where other available economic resources have failed, Cape Breton communities were coming to see information and communications technologies (ICT) as offering some potential for ensuring a degree of on-going sustainability of

---

[1] For a similar program and case see Pigg (1998).

livelihoods. Local residents were coming to understand that the local economic context was such that one must find a new type of livelihood, different from the resource based employment of the past, or, with a dwindling social safety net, there was little alternative but large-scale migration to urban/metropolitan centres. Accompanying this, of course, would be individual/family disruption and loss of non-transportable capital (home and land, family support network, cultural connections) (Landry, 1997; Bibby, 1995).

The truly exciting opportunity of ICT is that the limitations presented by an "unfavourable" location, in theory at least, could be overcome by the technology. Thus, the opportunity for marketing at a distance, creating and maintaining product loyalty "virtually", surmounting steep costs for market entry, and finding openings for radically new enterprises by individuals with imagination and skill, are among the economic opportunities enabled by ICT. (Gurstein, 1999)

Unfortunately, as with many other relatively isolated resource based communities, Cape Breton had become a context with few resources for commercial experimentation and market "research". Business methods and attitudes had grown stagnant and rigid; Cape Breton business, to a degree, suffered from a lack of creative contact with outside influences; and it lacked a tradition of entrepreneurial risk taking. The Chair could respond to this by acting as a kind of Research and Development division for local enterprise. It brought to the region an objective "outsider's" perspective on the local situation, some knowledge and awareness of the rapidly emerging opportunities presented by ICT, a degree of flexibility and responsiveness to the immediate problems, and a facilitated access to the range of resources available through the University College.

14.3. The Centre for Community and Enterprise Networking

The Associate Chair (A/MOTC), whose co-sponsor is the local economic development authority, Enterprise Cape Breton Corporation (ECBC), is directly concerned with responding to the local opportunities by looking for technology based alternatives to employment being lost from traditional sector jobs. The immediate "research" challenge, faced on the appointment in 1995 of the A/MOTC, was to respond to the very high unemployment in fishing and industrial communities; among young people looking to work and stay in their communities; and among the older unemployed requiring retraining and then needing opportunities to put their new training to work.

Through the framework of the Chair, start-up funding was obtained for a research, development and enterprise incubation centre, the Centre for Community and Enterprise Networking (C\CEN). The Centre's rationale was that even where there is knowledge of the opportunties presented by ICT, as was beginning to emerge in Cape Breton at that time, there is a need for a focussed effort to develop specific activities and enterprises to take advantage of these resources (Gurstein and Dienes, 1998; Gurstein 1999).

C\CEN identified community applications of ICT for non-metropolitan areas as an area of possible opportunity for Cape Breton. Among other activities, C\CEN "invested" in providing its mostly locally hired staff with up-to-date technology training and tools. It then looked to support these staff members when they undertook to develop technology-enabled enterprises which might provide employment for themselves and others in the local community (Gurstein, Lerner and MacKay, 1996; Gurstein and Andrews, 1996; Dienes, 1997).

In this, C\CEN was not undertaking "research" in the traditional sense of pushing forward the state of the technical art. Rather it was making a one-time only investment in ensuring that the region would "stay in the game". The intent was that Cape Breton would have access to the skills and opportunities to develop commercially competitive technology based enterprises similar to those developing at such a breakneck pace in other areas (Piore and Sable, 1984) - a form of "putting the coal back into the ground".

C\CEN focused on the Internet because this technology has opened an opportunity for change in the way the economy is structured—locally, regionally, nationally and internationally. Tools like e-mail and the World Wide Web make long-distance (and even local) communication faster and less expensive. Community access to the Internet might be able to facilitate non-metropolitan areas such as Cape Breton Island to become full and equal participants in the global information economy (Schuler, 1996; Scott, Diamond and Smith, 1997).

14.4. Electronic Commerce and Economic Development

Almost all of the discussion and developments concerning "electronic commerce" have focused on the opportunities that the technology presents for individual commercial enterprise or as an adjunct and facilitator for growth for larger businesses (Hagel and Armstrong, 1997). What has not yet been extensively explored is how ICT, and particularly the Internet, can be used to support the broader "social" goals of economic development in lagging regions or for providing employment opportunties to marginal populations or the currently unemployed. (Gurstein 1998; Orenda, 1998).

The case discussed in this chapter describes efforts undertaken between 1995 and 1997 to explore how ICT and, specifically, various activities within the broad framework of e-commerce, might be used to support local economic development efforts in an economically marginal region such as Cape Breton. More particularly, how the techniques of e-commerce might be used to enhance the utilisation of the most significant local resource, "Cape Breton Music".

One of the emerging themes of e-commerce is that of "virtual communities" i.e. a group of individuals who invest a degree of emotional involvement and time in interacting electronically with others around a common interest. By establishing such a community, with the elements of trust and co-ownership that are associated with it, opportunities arise for commercial relationships to develop or to be enhanced. (Our project developed simultaneously to, but independent of, the work of Hagel and Armstrong (1997) but we were aware of the more theoretical discussions of virtual community as, for example, those of Rheingold (1993).)

This case study describes the development of a "virtual community" built around a common interest in, or love for, the Cape Breton variety of Celtic music and the economic activities and economic development opportunities that grew out of this "community". What is of particular interest in this case, is that the benefits, which have arisen through the development of the "virtual community", have been quite widely distributed within the broader physical community of Cape Breton Island. In addition, there is currently an attempt to directly translate these benefits into local employment opportunities (within a context of severe unemployment and very limited employment alternatives).

14.5. CB-Music@chatsubo.com

Music, and particularly Celtic music, with the associated Gaelic culture, and all of these with their links to tourism, has now become the primary "resource" of Cape Breton Island and the overall largest employment sector - greater than steel making and coal mining combined. Recently, local development strategies have been revised to accommodate this.

As a first effort in determining how to use the tools being offered by ICT to support the expansion of the economic development opportunities presented by Cape Breton's music and culture, an electronic mailing list (e-list) on the subject of Cape Breton music was established. CB-Music@chatsubo.com has been active since 1995 and currently has over 400 subscribers.

Cape Breton Music On-Line (CBMO) and the A/MOTC host this list. A local Web design company maintains the list and provides technical support. The list attracts subscribers interested in Cape Breton's music legacy, as well as individuals with an interest in the contemporary music that has been influenced by this culture. Participants discuss all aspects of the music scene, past, present, and future: including performers, performances, history and musicology, venues and Cape Breton music as a sustainable resource for the Cape Breton economy. Among those active on the CB-Music list are several quite well known musicians and the mother of perhaps the second most nationally well-known CB Musician. It has also become a communications medium for those active in the "industry" including agents, technicians, teachers, commercial representatives and others.

In the fall of 1997, a survey was conducted to analyse the economic impact of the CB-Music List. These figures highlight specific economic spin-offs created by the list.

Average amount spent yearly per person on music products and events	$122.36
Average amount spent on travel per day by those whose vacation travel in Cape Breton resulted from participation on the CB-Music list	$310.59

The start-up and on-going operations costs for the "e-list" were extremely low:

- A call to an Internet Service Provider (ISP) who put the list online for a very modest fee and undertook for a similarly modest fee to provide on-going maintenance and technical support (such lists can now be established at no charge through several online service providers in return for the right to add an advertising banner to each message forwarded through the list).
- A brief introduction to be circulated to prospective subscribers and a second one as a welcome to individuals as they subscribed was prepared. The proposed list was added to a roster of other lists managed by this service provider (a very minor technical procedure) and, in this way, a new listserv (the most common form of e-mail software is called "Listserv" and the spelling has come to represent all e-lists), "CB-Music" was born.

This list, being "unmoderated", is for the most part self-policing. If off-topic messages are posted (the acceptable topics are outlined in the "welcome") the members of the list will usually and quite gently (for this list at least) remind the sender of the inappropriateness of the message and no second reminder is usually necessary.

Information concerning the list and how to subscribe to it was circulated to whomever it was thought might be interested but, in particular, it was sent to an e-list of "new lists" which is maintained as a public service by volunteers at the University of North Dakota. This list of new lists circulated the information to their some 20,000 subscribers, with the likelihood that it would then be forwarded on to thousands of others on other lists where there might also be an interest.

By chance, one of the principals in the host ISP was himself a local music producer and a very active participant in the local music community and he agreed to be an initial co-host of this list. He also undertook to introduce the list to his friends and associates which immediately gave the list broad credibility as a source of information and means for communication concerning Cape Breton music. No similar means for electronically distributing information about the music or its participants existed at that time (Hagel and Armstrong, 1997).

In two years of operation, the hosts of the list have only had to intervene once when an individual quite innocently posted slightly off-coloured humour to the list. Simply informing him that this was not acceptable resulted in an end to the problem. On two other occasions, the list "hosts" have had to intervene to bring a technical problem to the attention of the technical service provider. Other than this, the list has required effectively no maintenance and no intervention to stimulate or redirect discussion towards the desired topic areas.

The list has been remarkably successful. There has been a stream of very lively and informed discussion and camaraderie around the shared interest in CB Music:

- An average of 20 messages have been posted per day over the life of the list.
- There are some 30 regular contributors and another 20 contribute less regularly (these figures are, at 10-15%, about average for participation levels based on the experience reported on the list moderators e-list (List-Moderators@ lists.ironclad.net.au).

- The numbers of subscribers have ranged between 360 and 420 with the numbers increasing during academic term and declining during summer months as students get university accounts and then retire them.

Little effort has been made to publicise the list since the first announcements. There is, however, a steady replacement of those who leave the list as there appears to be a considerable "word of mouth" and the list is frequently referred to publicly in discussions of CB Music by musicians, promoters and enthusiasts.

There are subscribers from some twenty countries including France, Iceland and Portugal, but the bulk of the subscribers are Canadian - 50%, with the next largest group being from the US - 40% and with roughly 40% of subscribers having ".edu" (education) accounts indicating a student or faculty member. (These estimates are based on an analysis of the e-mail addresses of subscribers.)

It is not possible to identify the number of Cape Bretoners subscribing but it would, on the basis of comments on the list and from e-mail addresses, appear to be in the 30% range, with an additional 10% being other Nova Scotians (many of the non-Cape Breton Canadian subscribers indicate in their postings some sort of link to Cape Breton, primarily either themselves or their parents being CB emigrants).

The list has drawn the attention and participation of a range of people including CB-Musicians, agents, promoters, music company representatives, record dealers. music school owners, and ordinary fans. The topics discussed have been generally music related and of the "fan list" variety (gossip about performers, information on up-coming performances, and personal comments on performances) but also deeper discussions on musical form (several musicologists subscribe and occasionally participate), the instruments (primarily the fiddle) and the tunes, along with more formal announcements and "forwards" concerning performance dates, comments and reviews.

Other topics have dealt more broadly with Cape Breton culture including such areas as step-dancing, the Gaelic language (which has been maintained as a living language in certain parts of the island and which several of the performers use in their songs), and even discussions of the unique form of housing occupied by the miners of Cape Breton in mining communities around the Island. The list has stayed quite close to Cape Breton Celtic music with occasional forays into discussions of, and comparisons with, Newfoundland music, Scottish Celtic music and Celtic music, as played in the United States and elsewhere in Canada, as it might relate to CB-Music. The list has not dealt in any depth with other varieties of music found in Cape Breton, for example, the music of the MiqMaq First Nations community, the music of the Acadians, or the very active "new" (contemporary) music scene on the Island.

14.6. CB-Music and Local Economic Development

The list has made some useful contributions to overall economic development of the region, which of course was the original intention.

Two anecdotes concerning the list: at the time of Celtic Colours, a major international festival of Celtic music recently initiated in Cape Breton, an individual approached a list host wondering if a meeting could be arranged as he had encountered the individual on the e-list and would like to continue the conversation. The individual involved was a veterinary technician and his wife was a veterinarian living in Pennsylvania. Although he had, for a long time, had an interest in music, he had not even heard of CB music when he noticed a mention of the list on the "new list" circular. Curious, he subscribed to the CB-Music list and had been subscribed almost from the beginning. He had now bought a number of CB music CDs, attended several concerts of CB musicians and had decided with his wife to take a long weekend and fly up from Pennsylvania to Cape Breton to attend Celtic Colours. He was planning to spend his next two-week summer vacation in Cape Breton and expected to enroll in a fiddle course on the Island while he was there. He now considered himself a major "fan" of Cape Breton music.

A second individual, also from the United States, was planning a trip to Cape Breton and found the list by doing a Web-search on the island. He subscribed and sent an inquiry to the list concerning the kinds of things he and his wife should do during a week's summer vacation on the Island. Other subscribers to the list inundated him and his wife with information, suggestions and even invitations "to drop in for tea". He was so taken with this that he and his wife decided to forego the trip to New England that they had planned for the second half of their vacation and made reservations to spend a second week in Cape Breton.

Our estimate, based on the survey which is analysed below, was that the list resulted in an annual direct contribution of approximately $40,000 (an average of $100/subscriber) to the economy of Cape Breton. This was derived from performances, CDs, travel/tourism or courses which were "purchased as a direct consequence of participation in the CB-Music e-list" (from the survey). There was also the likelihood of this increasing over time as the CB-Music "virtual community" came to include more participants (or former participants). Remembering that many of those currently active on the list are students suggests that "winning" them as enthusiasts for CB-Music and Cape Breton Island tourism would have increasing economic benefits as their income grew subsequent to the completion of their education.

The building of a "virtual CB-Music community" based on a shared interest in or family connection to Cape Breton and its culture also has the effect of maintaining linkages which otherwise would atrophy over time. The possible benefit of linkages such as these, for example, providing reinforcement for the very active campaign by local Cape Breton economic development authorities to have former "Cbers" and others retire to the island, is potentially very significant. Also, reinforcing the image of Cape Breton as a place with a desirable lifestyle and culture might have the effect of inducing a "foot-loose" Lone Eagle (an individual who is able to locate and work from anywhere he/she chooses) or entrepreneur looking for a desirable location for a new enterprise, to learn of or look more favourably on Cape Breton as a possible site.

The "cost" of the creation and maintenance of the list, including archiving, is somewhat less than $1000 p.a. in time and fees. Roughly two hours were spent setting up the list initially, with a cash outlay of $100 and a cost of approximately $10/month to maintain the list. Hosting the list, including reviewing and supporting the list (helping people to subscribe and unsubscribe mostly), has required roughly one hour per month. The result is a rather startling return (to the economic well being of the Cape Breton Island community) on investment of 4000%!

Among the other contributions of the list to local economic development activity were: providing the initial means for marketing a local summer school for Cape Breton music, including assistance in the recruitment of a number of students, some from very substantial distances; assisting a local music distributor to develop their market for the sale of Cape Breton Music tapes; assisting a local Cape Breton dance instructor to develop a market for her services in the Eastern United States; assisting in distributing information concerning up-and-coming younger Cape Breton musicians and thus helping them to make contacts for performances elsewhere in Canada and the US; and providing a means for distributing information about up-coming performances of Cape Breton music and thus increasing the attendance at these concerts and festivals.

No	Question	Average
	Survey Results	
1	Length of time as member of CB Music discussion list.	13.896 months.
2	Number of purchases of Cape Breton Music recording (video, book, etc.) directly resulting from list membership. Cost of purchases.	3.7555 (Can)$78.035
3	Number of performances, workshops or festivals attended featuring Cape Breton artists resulting from list membership. Cost of attending events.	1.283 (Can)$44.331
4	Number of days involved in making new/revised travel plans for Cape Breton Island. Amount of money spent per day. Amount of money spent per visit.	1.830 (Can)$35.682 (Can)$310.595
5	Courses/classes relating to Cape Breton music resulting from list (fiddle, Gaelic, Irish stepdancing). Cost of instruction.	(Can)$28.533
6*	Number of people who have altered their retirement plans and moved to Cape Breton Island as a result of the list.	8%* (of sample)
7*	Number of people who persuaded others to alter retirement plans and move to Cape Breton Island.	11%* (of sample)
8	Number of businesses developed as a result of the list.	1

*Using the economic markers as indicated in *An Interim Economic Evaluation of the Retirement Cape Breton Program*, a report prepared by ECBC with cooperation from CBCEDA, assumptions can be made regarding the economic benefit of CBMO.

Attracting 123 expatriate Cape Bretoners to retire on the Island has resulted in a positive economic impact. Annual household expenditures by this group has generated an estimated $559,100 in household income which supports up to 37 full-time equivalent jobs. The survey indicated that 8% (based on the sample) of the list members would alter their retirement plans and move to Cape Breton and 11% had persuaded at least one other person to alter their retirement plans and move to Cape Breton as a result of the list. The following assumptions can be made:

$$400 \times .08 = 32 \text{ members} + 400 \times .11 = 44 \text{ others} = 76 \text{ in total}$$

$$\$559,100/123 = \$4,545.53 \text{ per expatriate}$$
$$\$559,100/37 = \$16,191.81 \text{ per one full-time equivalent job}$$

So, 76 individuals retiring on Cape Breton Island would result in a yearly household income of \$345,460.28 (76 × \$4,545.53), which would support up to 21 (\$345,460.28/16,191.81) full-time equivalent jobs.

14.7. CB-Music On-Line (CBMusic.Com)

An additional CB-Music related project has developed in association with the list.

A young Cape Bretoner with a passion for CB music was identified through his very active participation on the CB-Music list. He was hired as a summer intern by C\CEN to develop an online facility to support CB music which would be a not-for-profit "portal" available to inform and promote CB-Music over and above the existing commercially oriented Web sites, which were developing at the time (1996). The individual working with C\CEN had a family relationship to one of the most successful of the local CB music groups and much of his involvement with the music was initially linked to this relationship. In addition, he developed a partnership with a somewhat older and very well respected session guitar musician who was looking to develop a somewhat more stable lifestyle.

Within this framework, the initial CBMO Web site was established with the help of C\CEN's technical resources. The individuals who were driving the development were able to work as part of C\CEN's technology and community economic development team where they learned a number of useful technical skills with respect to managing and further developing the Web site, as well as certain business related skills and techniques. In addition, they were assisted in the development of an initial proposal and in receiving sufficient funding to support the completion and marketing of their proposal.

At the beginning, it was not clear what such a facility might look like but there was the notion that some sort of virtual "Centre" for Cape Breton music might be developed which would interact with and support the music. In turn, this "Centre" might be able to leverage off the music to develop a sustaining enterprise and employment for this young man and possibly others, and also to provide a bridge between the burgeoning music industry locally and the world of online commerce.

The proposal for CBMO (see the Appendix) is an attempt to turn the CB-Music Web site, which was initially sponsored by C\CEN, into an on-going and sustaining enterprise and employment opportunity for the site developers. In fact, it should be noted, there are very important and interesting links already between the music and the local online industry. The leading local Internet oriented service company was founded by a musician cum sound engineer and a lighting technician who worked most actively providing lighting for various of the music performances and particularly the annual CB music showcase, the Summertime Review.

The two CBMO partners also have been working with a local Community Economic Development organisation, which has helped them with their start-up management requirements such as bookkeeping, payroll, and tax planning. CBMO has now obtained one year of financial support from the local tourism development authority on the basis that they will provide on-going online support to the development of the local music industry as a tourism resource. For example, they have contracted to develop an up-to-date calendar/schedule of events, Web sites for local musicians, a single "portal" for CB-Music with links to the Web sites of CB-musicians, and links to other businesses with an interest in CB-Music such as local CB-Music schools, festivals, event sites, and technicians (cbmusic.com).

14.8. Conclusion

The ICT and Cape Breton Music project grew out of recognition that the old resources, which had sustained the local Cape Breton economy, were not going to suffice into the next century. There was a belief that perhaps the new ICTs might provide a means to enable local commercial activity to overcome the geographical distance and isolation barriers to more conventional forms of economic development. There was also the expectation that the new technologies might enhance and support the development of existing resources and particularly the very rich resource "vein" or opportunity presented by the outstanding music and cultural traditions of the island.

As an initial step, an e-mail list was established to provide a forum for the discussion of the music. The e-mail list, somewhat unexpectedly, has evolved into a "virtual community", including many of the characteristics of such communities as identified by Hagel and Armstrong (1997).

As a second step, C\CEN incubated an enterprise which would provide ways of using the new technology opportunities as they developed to support and promote the CB-music "industry". This enterprise is working to develop innovative strategies to link to the industry and to become financially sustainable and, although it has gone through an initial round of funding and achieved a measure of activity, it is still looking to achieve a firm financial footing and on-going sustainability.

As the once profitable resource based industries of Cape Breton Island have become increasingly exhausted, local economic development agencies look to information and communication technology as an employment solution. The CB Music project has taken advantage of this change in focus. The project has provided employment. It encourages the purchase of and participation in local production. It provides a bit of nostalgia for expatriates and also nurtures the desire to return home. It opens the door to new visitors and encourages locals to take pride in the endeavours of the local musical community.

A key element in the development of the CB Music project was the role of C\CEN. C\CEN was providing, before it was wound down because of financial limitations, developmental and incubation support to several enterprises, including CBMO, which were looking to use the new technologies for the support of local economic development.

In the on-going and accelerating race to maintain and expand a technology base on which a more internationally competitive, efficient and creative national economy can be built, there is an important role for technology enterprises, even in non-metropolitan regions. This is particularly significant if they can support the creation of a "cluster" of firms or activities which are sufficiently numerous; well supported by appropriate research, development and training; and successful at developing and maintaining markets (and thus employment) to be capable of self-generating growth.

Such a "cluster" creates local opportunities for developing "spin-offs", "break-aways", technical support and service enterprises where the "rhizomatic" propagation of new ideas and new enterprises becomes possible. This is happening where such clusters have developed as, for example, in Silicon Valley, the Greater Boston area, the Research Triangle of North Carolina, and even where such clusters are forming around music production studios, and optical technologies in Arizona. Based on the experience so far with the Cape Breton Music project and with the burgeoning activity in the Cape Breton music sector overall, it is possible that such a "cluster" might develop in Cape Breton based on the CB-Music resource.

While it is somewhat exceptional to have access to a world class resource such as CB-Music, it is not inconceivable that other regions having similar difficulties in keeping up with the economic race may find similar local resources which can be enabled and enhanced by means of the new technologies. Regional cuisines, crafts, dance and other folk traditions - even new types of enterprises - which produce distinctive local products can be imagined. The net makes possible the entering onto the global market of local enterprise and where local economic activity may be uncompetitive and ineffective in local or regional competition, it may find markets and outlets on a global level.

In the case of the CB-Music list, the economic benefits, which flowed from the list, were quite widespread. This includes the performers whose performances and discs were promoted; the tourism operators and local merchants who benefited from the additional tourism traffic; those involved in various parts of the music industry who benefitted from the additional visibility, and several with specific benefits such as the music school developer and the online CD merchant who were able to promote their local business using the list.

While such "successes" may be limited and result in only partial solutions to local economic problems and disparities, they are nevertheless doorways through which local communities can gain knowledge and experience. In this way, they can begin to have confidence in their capacity to participate in the emerging technology intensive global economy and the often bewildering world of "electronically enabled commerce".

Appendix: Cape Breton Music On-Line (cbmusic.com)

This experimental Web site is meant to strengthen the Cape Breton musical community by facilitating communication within the industry and promoting the music to local and international audiences.

1. What is CBMO?

This project is using modern information technology in a creative, yet practical, way to enhance the gathering, organizing, and marketing of Cape Breton music. It will be operated as a self-sustaining virtual resource accountable to the community with a major focus on awareness, education, and preservation of Cape Breton's music and culture. It will also foster partnerships between musicians and companies in the music industry.

Technological advancement has sometimes led to the disappearance of local culture for a more "mass media" dominated music scene. CBMO will reverse this trend by giving Cape Bretoners the ability to channel our talents in new and exciting directions, and will give us an opportunity to access the world market place. This will be a great way to attract visitors to the region and give them the chance to plan their trip around the unique musical entertainment of our region. This site will facilitate cooperative competition by working with the musicians and in conjunction with pre-existing sites and services in the public and private sector. It will not replace, threaten, or exploit any of the current stakeholders in the music industry. It will unify resources in order to develop and stimulate the community's economy and strengthen Cape Breton Island's musical reputation in the international scene.

2. Who is CBMO?

CBMO was conceived from an e-mail list that deals with our Island's music community. To join the list, visit The Cape Breton Music Mailing List Administration page. It is a community of musicians and friends of the music community that have the chance to share their talent and comments with the rest of the world. If you have any thoughts or ideas that would make this site a better place, do not hesitate to share them with us. We want to help as many people as possible become familiar with the power of the Internet as a promotional tool and use it most effectively by getting as much feedback as possible.

CBMO is creating an increasingly organised presence for Cape Breton music and culture on the Internet while teaching musicians the power of this information resource and marketing tool. CBMO is a Web site devoted to Cape Breton music. It is a dynamic virtual resource accountable to the community and focuses on awareness, education, and preservation of Cape Breton's music and culture. It helps foster partnerships between local musicians and the international music industry by providing access to an interactive discussion forum, up-to-date contact directories, marketing opportunities, and information on funding sources and performing rights societies.

Technological advancement has historically led to the disappearance of our local culture for a more "mass media" dominated scene. CBMO helps to reverse this trend by giving us the ability to channel our talents in new and exciting directions.

Our mandate is to research and develop innovative applications of information and telecommunications technology to stimulate local economic development through partnerships with private, government, and education sectors.

The CBMO Web site enables members of the music industry, music fans, and potential visitors to view a wide selection of information about our Island's performers, organisations, and events.

3. Project Objectives

In order to provide a gateway to the multi-faceted resources available and coordinate the development of guidelines for presentation and management of information, CBMO:

- Utilises new technology to maintain a comprehensive Web site for Cape Breton Music;
- Provides the latest news on Cape Breton music and musicians;
- Publishes an e-mail digest of Cape Breton music news;
- Maintains an updated comprehensive calendar of Cape Breton Music events;
- Provides an updated music mall with banner advertisements;
- Works toward down-streaming Cape Breton Music 24 hours a day;
- Incorporates online music instruction of Cape Breton music;
- Gathers contact information on musicians and music groups;
- Provides training and consultation through workshops to the various levels of organisations;
- Promotes public access to CBMO resources;
- Coordinates digitisation of music-related documents;
- Commissions music theme for the site;
- Utilises the Internet as well as traditional means to market the site;
- Encourages musicians to take advantage of new technology;
- Develops strategic partnerships to encourage the exchange of information resources;
- Improves the audio-visual quality of the site: i.e. logo, graphics, layout, streaming audio, etc.;
- Incorporates a searchable database.

4. Project Description

- *Weekly E-zine*: compile site updates and local music news into a promotional e-mail message that will be distributed to e-lists and newsgroups throughout the Net.
- *Promotion/Marketing*: promote the site and develop mutual links with other online resources.
- *Sponsorship*: actively seek out potential sponsors and advertisers for the site.
- *MIDI/Audio Workshops:* programs to teach musicians various ways to get their music on the Internet.
- *Graphic and Database Design:* contract a third party to design and develop a professional graphical interface for the site and a searchable, relational database for our directories and calendars.

- *Digitisation*: make available music archival facilities.
- *Musician Data Entry*: musicians and music industry people enter their information on our directory database.
- *Calendar Data Entry*: venues, community groups and tourism organisations, etc. and continuously update our events calendar.
- *CAP Site Contact*: set up communication links with the different CAP sites across the province.
- *Group Workshops:* help organisations in the music industry to use information technologies to increase their marketing skills.
- *Musician Workshops*: introduce Internet promotion, marketing and research skills to musicians.
- *On-line Instruction:* begin developing an online music instruction program
- *Record Theme Music:* commission original music for CBMO
- *Streaming Audio*: broadcast Cape Breton Music to the world through RealAudio technology.

CHAPTER 15

Consumer Adoption of Electronic Commerce

The US Perspective

GERHARD STEINKE

Electronic commerce in North America, as well as around the world, has experienced dramatic growth during the last year. While electronic commerce encompasses a large variety of components, our focus is on consumer-to-business transactions, as exemplified by consumers purchasing goods electronically via the Internet or World Wide Web.

Consumers can buy nearly everything online - from books to airline tickets and stocks. Home computers, the availability of Internet service providers, and the variety of services offered by companies on their Web sites have made electronic commerce an attractive alternative to the traditional tasks of in-person or telephone shopping.

Statistics released by the Computer Industry Almanac Inc. in February 1999 claimed that the number of Internet users worldwide rose from 61 million in 1996 to over 147 million by the end of 1998, with over half of these users in the US. Their report predicts that the number of Internet users worldwide will increase to 320 million by the end of 2000.

The growth in business on the Internet has also exhibited tremendous growth. Forrester Research predicts that consumer electronic commerce in the US will increase from some 8 billion dollars in 1998 to 18 billion dollars in 1999 and 33 billion dollars by the year 2000. An example of a company experiencing tremendous growth is Amazon.com. Amazon.com's sales jumped from $148 million in 1997 to $610 million in 1998 and they increased the number of customer accounts from 1.5 million in 1997 to 6.2 million in 1998. In a one-month period (November to December 1998), Macys went from 382,000 unique user accounts to 1,330,000 - a change of 246%.

Yet there are serious concerns which need to be addressed if electronic commerce is to become a common worldwide reality:

1. *Affordability and Access.* Access to the Internet and electronic marketplace requires financial resources—which many cannot afford.
2. *Education and Training.* An education and training process is required to help people access the Internet.
3. *Legal.* Governments need to cooperate to provide the legal undergirding, which will ensure the fulfilment of electronic contracts.

4. *Security.* Security concerns must be addressed.
5. *Privacy.* As they enter the electronic marketplace, many consumers are concerned about privacy issues.

In this chapter, I examine these five areas, with special reference to policies and actions of the Federal Trade Commission (FTC) in dealing with the privacy issue.

15.1. Affordability and Access

One must admit that the cost of admission to the electronic marketplace is high - too high for a large percentage of the world's population. The computer connects only 1% of the world's 6 billion people. Many, including Bill Gates, argue that information technologies will help the poor become literate and enable them to enter the information marketplace. The geographical barriers and isolation can be reduced. Yet most people in this world cannot afford the required components such as a computer, Internet access, or even a credit card. It is estimated that about one third of the homes in North America have a personal computer - a much higher percentage than anywhere else in the world. Michael Dertouzos states: "The rich, who can afford to buy the new technologies, use them to become increasingly productive and therefore even richer while the poor stand still. Left to its own devices the information revolution will increase the gap between rich and poor nations and between rich and poor people within nations" (Dertouzos, 1999).

A 4Q 1998 report from the Organization for Economic Cooperation and Development (OECD) estimates that 80% of global e-commerce revenues emanate from the United States. The Second Annual Ernst & Young Internet Shopping Study reports that 10% of US households shop online (close to 10 million households). A study by Pew Research Center found that 11% of the US population bought a product or service online during the past 30 days (November 1998) in the US. According to a February 1999 report released by Jupiter Communications, only 10% of the population in the UK, Germany and France are online as compared to 28% of all US households now use the Internet. Much of the rest of the world is far behind.

It is obvious that to purchase one must have money. According to the Second Annual Ernst & Young Internet Shopping Study, 46% of the online shoppers have over $50,000 annual income and 94% have some college education. A poll commissioned by ITAA and conducted by Wirthlin Worldwide found that those earning more than $60,000 were three times more likely to have made an electronic purchase than those earning $15,000-$30,000. (Yet those with higher incomes also were far less likely to trust their online vendors with personal information.) In the 1998 Georgia Tech Internet Survey, 30% of the users reported that they spent more than $500 on Web purchases.

The main means of completing an Internet transaction is with a credit card. While credit cards are relatively common in North America, only 2% of the world's population have credit cards. For example, less than 8% of all Germans use credit cards. In the US, 35% of the population do not have bank accounts. So businesses must address issues such as: How does a business accept payment in multiple currencies? Can a business accept cheques?

In addition to the affordability of the infrastructure is the question of products and services that are available via the Internet. The top market on the Internet, ranked in terms of online dollar volume, is leisure and travel. Only a small percentage of the world's population has the means to afford to enter this market. Other top markets are computer hardware, apparel, books and software.

The other component related to cost is that the cost of doing business electronically is significantly lower. *Manufacturing News* (17 March 1998) claims that whereas the traditional distribution channel adds 135% to the cost of a manufactured item, the direct link between consumer and manufacturer will only add 10%. Whereas a traditional bank transaction costs over a dollar, an e-commerce transaction will cost about a penny. Similarly, while traditional airline tickets currently cost $8, an e-ticket should only cost $1. This means that those who are able to do business electronically will receive products for a lower price, contributing to increasing the gap between the well off and those less well off.

Efforts must be made to prevent "economic segregation" which limits the future of electronic commerce. Although the cost of personal computers is continuing to decline, it will be some time before personal computers are as common as television sets and Internet access as common as television reception.

15.2. Education and Training

Consumers must be educated in how to use the computer and the Internet most effectively. Not only is some technical know-how required in operating a computer, the Web with its vast and ever-changing resources is a maze, easily creating frustration and fatigue.

The consumer and the business operating the Web site, joined by an electronic commerce transaction, have separate goals and expectations. The consumer wants to gather information in order to make a decision, which may lead to the purchase of a product or service. The merchant's concern is receiving payment for the goods or services rendered. There must be a valid payment method and an assurance that the buyer cannot claim not to have ordered the product once it has been delivered (non-repudiation). The international dimension adds another level of uncertainty and anxiety in terms of trusting each other to meet the other's expectations - particularly when the legal basis is not clear. In addition, merchants want data on their customers. This leads to the privacy concerns described below.

Much more education of both the merchant and the consumer is required. In the US, the FTC has made education a major initiative. The FTC has developed a "Rules of the Road" business guide to help educate entrepreneurs and has designed a continuing legal education course for lawyers who counsel new Internet businesses. Their Web site, www.ftc.gov, contains advice and other information for both businesses and consumers. They claim to receive 2.5 million hits per month.

There is a Web site, www.consumer.gov, geared to consumers to provide electronic commerce information. This is a "one-stop" consumer site for 12 US federal agencies. Among other educational initiatives, the FTC has created "teaser" Web sites that mimic fraudulent advertising sites with examples of false promises and so forth. At the end, they provide an explanation as to what makes the material illegal.

So, in addition to the issue of affordability and access to the Internet, there is the need for training and education. The current generation of children may soon understand commerce on the Internet as we understand shopping in a store.

15.3. Legal

There is a serious lack of a predictable legal environment governing electronic transactions since existing laws often do not address issues created by the rapid advances in technology. This is not only for transactions within a country, but is particularly true for international activity, where concerns about enforcement of contracts, liability and intellectual property protection cause consumers to limit their transactions. Firms operating on the Internet may be situated in one or more countries - and thereby beyond the reach of any one country's legal system.

In the US, the Federal Trade Commission (FTC) Act contains the following provisions that are being used to regulate electronic commerce: Section 5 prohibits unfair or deceptive acts or practices in, or affecting, commerce; Section 12 of the FTC Act prohibits dissemination of false advertisements. These statutory provisions provide the FTC with law enforcement authority over many sectors of the economy - electronic commerce and commercial activities on the Internet fall within the scope of this mandate. In addition, there is a "Mail and Telephone Order Merchandise Rule" which was created to deal with orders for merchandise using the telephone. The term telephone is defined so broadly that orders placed by fax or by computer through telephone modems also apply.

The US government is actively monitoring electronic commerce activities. The FTC has increased the personnel assigned to monitoring and enforcing electronic commerce from 22 full-time equivalent (FTE) persons in 1996 to 42 FTEs in 1997 and 66 in 1998. Also, this year, the Bureau of Consumer Protection has dedicated 56 FTEs (16% of its budget) to monitoring consumer protection related to electronic commerce. The Bureau of Competition has 10 FTEs assigned to monitoring anti-competitive behaviour and assisting consumers as they engage in electronic behaviour.

The Draft Model Law of the United Nations Commission on International Trade Law for Electronic Commerce was issued in 1996. Its objective is to provide the basis of an electronic contract's enforceability. It must be adopted by member countries of the United Nations in order to be effective.

In addition to legal issues, the loss of taxation revenue for business conducted via the Internet concerns many governments. Ernst & Young is forming a coalition to help US companies formulate policies to provide input to the European Union on taxation issues.

Related security and privacy issues are described below. In the world of the Internet, legal, political and geographical boundaries are blurred. There is no telling where the consumer or the business is physically situated. The question of where to go to resolve disputes between consumers and businesses and who has jurisdiction is a tough one.

15.4. Security

Security is a huge concern - and even more so when consumer and business are situated in different countries. Consumers are concerned that their information is transmitted and stored securely and accurately. According to a November 1998 IntelliQuest survey, 75% of consumers worry about the security of their credit cards.

Merchant sites are also concerned about security. They require that the information they receive is accurate and reflects the communication from the customer. Systems to ensure that these objectives can be met are being implemented using technologies like credit card authorisation networks, digital certificates, etc.

We want to emphasise security issues from the consumer's point of view. Security of the telecommunication network is required. Security of the systems attached to the networks is required. There must be the means for authenticating and ensuring confidentiality. For example, personal information may be captured or changed as it passes along networks. Worse still, personal information may be taken from a merchant's database. Others may impersonate you electronically. Or, for some reason, the system you wish to access may not accept communication from you.

Consumers have little knowledge (and it is very difficult to discover) of the level of security which different merchants employ. The requirements for security are usually stated in vague terms. For example, Amazon.com advertises the "guaranteed safety of transactions" and "all transactions are backed by a security guarantee protecting shoppers from unauthorised use". Companies have to balance security expenditures with other needs and priorities based on risk analysis and return on their investment.

Gaining in popularity is the partnership of ISPs (Internet Service Providers) and Web housing services with EC solution providers to enable individual merchants to set up a shop quickly on the Web. For example, Yahoo!Store allows a business to set up a "cyber-store" in a few minutes for $100.00 per month. If it is that easy for businesses to sell over the Internet, what assurance does the consumer have that the products ordered will be delivered and the information provided will indeed be secure? Does the underlying service provider carry any responsibility?

Security concerns relate to the legal issues discussed earlier and the privacy issues in the next section. I believe the reputation of the business will drive businesses to continuously increase their security measures.

15.5. Privacy

For many who consider buying something online, the privacy issue is the major concern - although this may differ by country and culture. Privacy is linked toward our concept of personal freedom and our ability to control what others know about us. Electronic commerce enables the collection and reuse of information - in a much more efficient manner than possible before, and with less opportunity to be anonymous.

More than 70% of users are so concerned about privacy that they refrain from monetary exchanges on the Web, according to Stanton McCandlish, program director at the Electronic Frontier Foundation in San Francisco. (www.eff.org). According to a November 1998 IntelliQuest survey, 58% of consumers worry about receiving junk email which inhibits their online shopping. At least 4 states in the US have passed legislation to curb junk email. So, only if the privacy issue is properly addressed will electronic commerce reach its potential.

In the US, it is the FTC that has the mandate of consumer protection. One of the roles of the FTC is to "foster the development of electronic commerce by acting to prevent fraud and deception". The FTC released a substantial report to Congress in June 1998, entitled "Privacy Online".

A European directive that recently went into effect restricts the gathering and distribution of personal data and prohibits transmission of data to countries that do not have similar laws. This will affect American electronic commerce sites that have, or plan to have, European customers. Since it is unrealistic to expect countries to come to similar policies on privacy and data collection, it probably means that companies must tailor their policies to fit those of the country they want to do business with. Ira Magaziner, President Clinton's former technology advisor, predicts that companies may provide a "privacy picture or symbol" if they are following certain privacy principles.

First, there is concern with regard to the privacy of the data used in creating transactions. This refers not only to the security of a credit card number, but the management of the other data involved in the transaction, e.g., name and address, product ordered, history of transactions, etc. Such information has been used for many years by businesses such as department stores, credit card companies, catalogue merchants, etc. Yet, the fact that it is gathered electronically makes this data much easier for merchants to use. Whereas one could go into a store and pay cash for a product, thereby remaining anonymous, this anonymity is much more difficult (if not impossible) to achieve electronically.

Second, Internet marketers have the ability to gather information that is not explicitly given by the consumer. Information such as the previous Web pages visited, when, for how long, etc. can be collected. This is possible with the use of "cookies". In August 1998, companies including GeoCities and Ticketmaster announced that they would begin tracking users' movements on Web sites (Schroeder, 1998). This information can be used to tailor each person's Web options and future marketing. For example, when you visit an online bookseller, your access is personalised to the extent that they recommend books you may be interested in purchasing - based on past books you have purchased or other criteria. Some people may find this beneficial, whereas others see this as an invasion of their privacy. But, what if the fact that you purchase certain types of books is passed to a third party, e.g. a travel service that can now recommend specific travel destinations and options? The marketing potential is endless. This kind of information is not available to those selling in a real store.

Third, there is a vast amount of information about consumers available - from public and proprietary sources - over both proprietary computer networks as well as the Internet. Consumers are often not aware of all of this information and have only very limited means to verify and correct errors. The transfer and access of such personal information by third parties leaves many consumers extremely uncomfortable.

The European Union has adopted a directive that prohibits the transfer of personal data to countries that, in its view, do not extend adequate privacy protection to EU citizens.

Vice President Gore, in a speech at New York University's commencement on May 14, 1998, announced plans for a Web site sponsored by the FTC which would enable individuals to prohibit companies from pre-screening their credit records without their permission. It would also prevent driver license data from being sold to data miners and allow individuals to have their names and addresses removed from datamailing and telemarketing lists. This provides some relief to privacy concerns - but lacks legal backing.

The FTC conducted a survey of over 1,400 Web sites in March 1998 and found some disturbing results. The vast majority of Web sites (over 85%) collect personal information from consumers. Only 14% of the commercial Web sites provided the consumer with any notice with respect to their information practices, while only 2% provided notice by means of a comprehensive privacy policy.

Particularly troubling are the statistics the FTC discovered regarding the collection of information from children. Of the Web sites for children, 89% of those surveyed collected personal information from children. While half of the children's sites provided some form of disclosure of their information practices, few sites took any steps to provide for meaningful parental involvement in the process. Interestingly enough, 23% of the sites told children to seek parental permission before providing personal information. While 7% said they would notify parents of their information practices, less than 10% provided for parental control over the collection and/or use of information from children.

At the FTC's Public Workshop on Privacy in 1997, a national survey was presented which reported that 97% of parents whose children use the Internet object to the release of children's information to a third party. 72% object to collecting real names and addresses which would be used internally. The online privacy of children is obviously a significant concern for parents.

The FTC issued an opinion letter last July 15, 1997 which states that the release of children's personally identifiable information online, without providing parents with adequate notice and an opportunity to control the information, may result in sufficient injury or risk of injury to meet the unfairness standard in Section 5 of the FTC Act (described above).

To pre-empt legal regulations (and in conjunction with the FTC), in December 1997, fourteen companies of the individual reference service industry (IRSG) agreed to a set of principles to self-regulate themselves as to the availability of information. These IRSG principles should lessen the risk that information held by these services will be misused - although they left out some important issues for consumers (e.g., there is no provision for consumers to verify the information held about them). This self-regulation is intended to address public concerns and pre-empt government regulations and legislation. Yet, it seems that this self-regulation is not yet working, according to the June 1998 FTC report.

On 7 October 1998, eight major Web companies (Microsoft, Excite, Lycos, Infoseek, Snap, Netscape, Yahoo! and America Online) announced an initiative to educate consumers about privacy rights and encourage companies to post clear and easily accessible policies dealing with the collection of personal data. Using primarily banner ads, these companies expect to reach 85% of the American online audience. Again, the goal is to pre-empt government legislation.

In light of some of their findings, the June 1998 FTC report states that they will soon make recommendations because "it is evident that substantially greater incentives are needed to spur self-regulation and ensure widespread implementation of basic privacy principles".

The use of third parties or intermediaries is a solution to the privacy issue. CoolSavings (www.coolsavings.com) is a Web-based marketer that distributes coupons on behalf of retailers and merchandisers. They attribute the willingness of visitors to sign on and provide personal data to the fact that consumers trust them more than they would trust the advertiser. Perhaps people think that Coolsavings will, upon request, delete their information faster and more permanently than a specific subscriber would.

If consumers know an organisation's privacy policy, they can then make an informed decision on whether they want to conduct business with that organisation. Certainly one still needs to develop that trust relationship to believe that the written policy is also implemented.

The non-profit TRUSTe initiative (www.truste.org/) has provided a model for a privacy policy on a Web site. It should describe what information is collected, how it is used, how a user can opt not to give information and how to change the information that has been collected (see www.cnet.com/privacy.text.html as a good example of such a privacy policy).

As consumers get to know an organisation's privacy policy, they are able to decide whether to do business with that organisation or not. Hopefully, being in favour of privacy is good for business.

15.6. Conclusion

Electronic commerce around the world will continue to grow dramatically. Many consumers (and businesses) will benefit. But, at the same time, we must provide the means and infrastructure so that more people around the world can enjoy the privilege of gaining access to the electronic marketplace. In addition, governments must work together to provide a proper legal basis which extends into the international realm. Certainly continued emphasis must be given to security measures that ensure protection and give assurance that information is kept secure and private. The development of electronic commerce and its use by continued consumers is at a critical juncture. Companies must address the issues that concern consumers so that the electronic marketplace can continue its rapid growth and progress.

CHAPTER 16

Electronic Commerce in Israel

AVI SCHECHTER, MAGID IGBARIA AND MOSHE ZVIRAN

16.1. Introduction

The rapid growth of the Internet as a strategic business tool is mainly attributable to its strength as a medium of communication between the customer and the organisation. By moving the workplace to the customer's site in a digital economy, electronic commerce (e-commerce) via the Internet enables businesses easy access to potential customers, lowers their costs and increases their attractiveness (Lederer et al., 1997), thereby addressing the needs of both the sellers and the buyers.

Connecting different countries, languages and cultures, the Internet is also a global information system. The little research that has been done on the subject suggests that cultural differences between international users of information systems may be converging; though empirical findings have indicated some differences. The work of Hofstede (1980, 1983), for example, supports the view that research in one culture may not be applicable to another.

During the 1990s, Israel, a small, developing country in the Middle East with a population of six million, enjoyed a period of thriving economic development, unprecedented in its history. This growth may be attributed to several causes: an influx of well-educated immigrants that swelled Israel's already highly educated population by 15%; the de facto cancellation of the Arab boycott; and substantial long term investment in research and development. Despite the present slow down, the forecast for the years 1999-2000 is optimistic, assuming the government implements a restraining policy and cuts its expenses without increasing the tax burden. The business sector is expected to grow by an average of 6% per annum, enjoying a high volume of foreign investments. Domestic consumption will increase by 5% per annum, exports by 8.5% per annum, and unemployment will decrease to 6.3% of the working population by the end of the period.

Studying the e-commerce of a small country like Israel is particularly useful when we consider the increasingly popular perception that small organisations or countries may not be at an economic disadvantage. Ein-Dor et al. (1997) and Igbaria and Zviran (1996) determined that information technology industries of small countries might actually have a distinct advantage over larger competitors. This research also addresses the problem of the dearth of information on e-commerce outside the USA. Apart from providing data on Israel's e-commerce infrastructure in general and its ability to enhance e-commerce in particular, we believe our model will be applicable to research on other countries too. In our review of the literature, we found no similar research or model of Internet site analysis.

Based on economic and qualitative variables, the model describes and tests the qualitative and quantitative usage of the Internet by the Israeli business sector. In this examination of Israel's e-commerce infrastructure, we make empirical comparisons of different Web sites, analysing the types and levels of links between economic and qualitative variables relating to e-commerce and information systems.

16.2. Method

The research sample was formed from 1128 companies that represent the Israeli economy: 670 public quoted companies registered in the Tel-Aviv Stock Exchange (TASE); and the 458 top Israeli companies listed by Dan and Bradstreet. This research population was divided into three sectors: private, public and companies that are traded in TASE. From these three sectors, a cross-section of 64 companies was created of these three sectors, as depicted in Table 16.1.

The groups were selected on the basis of the following criteria:

- To satisfy the need for future comparison with other Western countries;
- To satisfy the need to examine a large number of companies affecting the economy and representing all the important and influential sectors;
- The possibility of obtaining reliable and freely available financial information.

Towards the end of 1997, we began our search for the Web sites of the companies included in the research population, making the appropriate recordings in the research questionnaire. Web sites not located during the first search were searched for repeatedly until the end of the research period. The probability of a site not being located was therefore very low. The research phases were as follows:

- *Phase A:* Measurement of the economic and qualitative variable range to determine the variable distribution limits and research framework.
- *Phase B:* Factor analysis of all the qualitative variables to neutralise any question that does not match the main trend factor of the category to which it has been allocated, and allocating it to the trend to which it more correctly belongs. Here, we follow Lederer et al. (1997), who employed factor analysis to screen questions in their research on the correlation between information systems strategy and benefits from e-commerce.
- *Phase C:* Categorisation and unification of the questionnaire data and subjects, in order to create a single variable for each trend factor created in every category according to factor analysis results and neutralising non-matching questions/data.
- *Phase D:* After obtaining the unified variables, the following steps were taken:
  - Examining the correlation between economic and qualitative variables such as "Is there any relation between the company's type, number of

employees, business turnover, etc.", and qualitative variables such as graphic design, Web-site performance, etc.
  – Examining a possible correlation among the various qualitative variables.

The analysis of the findings and the correlation described above were carried out using one-way ANOVA, crosstabs and two-tailed correlation.

16.2.1. THE RESEARCH QUESTIONNAIRE

The research questionnaire is based on the questionnaires designed by Baroudi and Orlikowski (1988) and Doll and Torkzadeh (1988), combining suitable analysis, content and quality components to examine the parameters comprising the Web site and user interface. The full questionnaire contains 13 sections that focus on: general and economic data, definition of the Web site's type, site's traffic capacity, possibilities to transfer information at the user-Web site interface level, way of locating the site, data on the site's character type and quality, Web site arrangement, Web site design, terminology type and quality, capability to learn the site's operation, site's technical capabilities, language, and user's satisfaction from the site. The questions were answered on a scale of 1-7, "1" being "very little" and "7" representing "very much", depending on the level of importance the respondent accords.

16.2.2. THE RESEARCH SAMPLE

Table 16.1 describes the distribution of the entire research population of 1128 companies. 18.8% of the traded companies, i.e. 126 of them, and about 40% of the top 458 companies appear on the Internet. Altogether, 27.2% of the research population companies appear on the Internet. If we take out the cross-section group, the figure drops to 21.5%, i.e. only 243 companies of the total research population appear on the Internet.

Table 16.1. Research sample distribution.

Source	Entire Sample	Number of companies appearing on the Internet	Proportion (%)
Stock Exchange	670	126	18.8
Top 458	458	181	39.5
Total	1128	307	27.2

Table 16.1 shows that the percentage of the top 458 companies in Israel with Web sites is more than double that of the traded ones. This may be explained by the fact that companies registered at the TASE, as per TASE's publications, include shell companies (having no physical activity volume), companies dealing purely in financial operations, and holding companies (companies that hold shares of other companies). Such companies usually do not operate a Web site. Moreover, 64 of the top 458 are also traded and appear as such in Table 16.2. According to Table 16.2, the percentage of Web sites among the private companies is three times higher than for the public companies, i.e. 48.1 % compared to only 16.6%.

Table 16.2. Distribution of Web sites of the top 458 companies

Company type	Number of Web sites	Proportion (%)
Public	30	16.6%
Private	87	48.1%
Public traded	64	35.4%
Total	181	100.0%

The sample of the top 458 companies is divided into three main sub-groups:

- Public companies not traded on the Stock Exchange;
- Private companies, accounting for almost 50% of the top 458 group;
- Companies that are both public and traded; these large economic leaders appear in both the top 458 and traded groups.

16.2.3. RESEARCH HYPOTHESES

Businesses today use strategic information systems in order to improve their comparative advantage and ability to survive in the rapidly changing and keenly competitive environment (Landau and Zviran, 1997), recognising the Internet as an important tool in this context. Taking the view that organisations generally prefer the strategy of focusing on specific products rather than spreading their expenses and that the classic value-added chain is changing and its components are no longer attractive for achieving competitive advantage (Thornton, 1994), we consider the e-commerce framework suggested by Wigand and Benjamin (1995). The first of the five basic assumptions of this framework is that "every individual and organisation will be connected to the Internet", which leads to the inference that the more users of e-commerce there are, the more the natural balances of a free market can operate without artificial interference or manipulation. Organisations which in the past were conservative regarding development, applications, application compatibility and information systems in general, are now rushing to buy almost anything that comes to hand just not to be left behind (Wanninger, 1998). This leads us to our first hypothesis.

Hypothesis 1. Commercial organisations in general and in Israel in particular, recognising the commercial potential of the Internet, will aspire to be represented on the Web and operate in the framework of e-commerce.

The second hypothesis is based on the economies of scale philosophy: the bigger the organisation the more resources it can invest in information technology. In his book, *The Productivity Paradox*, Eric Brynjolfsson (1993), in examining whether the investment in information systems increases the productivity of the organisation, claims that Internet activities and e-commerce are innovations that cannot be separated from information technology as a whole. It is, moreover, logical to assume that economies of scale will influence the extent of usage, level and quality of information systems in general and Internet activities in particular. Internet activity is not generic to every business. In his research on computerisation in Israeli industry, Ragowsky (1986) found a direct connection between the size of the organisation and the use and quality of its information systems. From this, we derive our second hypothesis.

Hypothesis 2. There is a distinct positive correlation between an organisation's business variables and the extent of usage, level and quality of its Web site. The larger the organisation (turnover, profit, number of employees) the higher the quality of its Web site.

Acknowledging that the traditional value chain is undergoing change and becoming more and more direct, the second basic assumption of the e-commerce framework suggested by Wigand and Benjamin (1995) is of a fast, user-friendly, interactive and multimedia connection to the Internet. Hoffman et al. (1995) claim that creating the correct link between supplier and consumer by means of an integral marketing approach with built-in technical tools will produce the platform on which e-commerce can be built. Wanninger (1998) presents what he sees as the four supporting pillars of e-commerce. The fourth of these deals with the electronic service environment occasioning the link between supplier and consumer, which is crucial, in his opinion, to providing an atmosphere of reliability and security for the end user. Hence, our third research hypothesis.

Hypothesis 3. Organisations using a Web site will take full advantage of the Internet's power and employ the most advanced technological tools to create an interface between them and the user, emphasising two-way interaction and feedback in order to improve their competitiveness.

The view of the Internet as providing an active infrastructure for a mass media marketing and distribution network can be seen in the Many to Many model of Marketing Communication (Hoffman et al, 1995), and in the research of Anderson and Rubin (1986) and Hoffman et al. (1995). Landau and Zviran (1997) also point to the use of the Internet as a competitive marketing and distributing tool allowing the transfer of large volumes of information at relatively low cost. The proliferation of the Internet and the possibility of appropriately directing the organisation's products or services to the relevant consumers open yet further possibilities for increasing competitive advantage. Thus, Strongeslove (1995) claims that to achieve a competitive advantage organisations should plan their new information systems to accommodate the new reality in which the supplier has to provide ever more easily available, targeted and organised information. From this, we derive our fourth hypothesis.

Hypothesis 4. Players will expand their use of the Internet, with its broad scope and cost-saving advantages in comparison to other marketing and distribution channels, using multiple data, information and screens.

Miller et al. (1993) claim that commercially oriented organisations that are technologically well equipped will find it profitable to engage in e-commerce because of the ease with which it integrates into the natural working environment of these organisations. Transaction Cost Theory explains how information systems and e-commerce lower the costs of internal coordination and communication and improve the competitiveness of the organisation. Lederer et al. (1997) found that organisations active in the electronic marketplace see it as an "enabler", improving competitiveness and profitability through product differentiation, targeting the product and thereby increasing sales. Zeithaml (1996) claimed that industrial or manufacturing enterprises make use of the Internet to develop marketing channels, sales and services to a greater extent than companies from other sectors of the economy. Cornin and Taylor (1992) and Bitner and Hubbert (1990) found that manufacturing enterprises see quality of service as a business interest and providing a high level of service as a vital part of their business strategy and marketing effort. All this leads us to our fifth hypothesis.

Hypothesis 5. Organisations and sectors rich in information systems will be the first to use the Internet as a tool for e-commerce. The quality and frequency of their use will be higher than organisations and sectors poor in information systems.

A sub-hypothesis to the above is – manufacturing organisations and companies will use the Internet more as a marketing tool and as a basis to render value added services to the customer than other organisations and companies.

16.3. Findings

16.3.1. SPECIAL FEATURES ANALYSIS RESULTS

This section describes the special features and the use of technology enabling e-commerce. The advantage of using the Internet and its suitability to e-commerce derive from its capability to transfer messages and information via advanced technology at low cost to a broad range of end users. However, in practice, Israeli Web site holders make little use of the Internet's advanced capabilities other than e-mail. That is, companies use the one-to-many marketing model suitable for physical trade, instead of the many-to-many model specially designed to optimise the possibilities of creating a new, efficient and cheap method of e-commerce via the Internet. We propose that the ability to create an infrastructure and open a user interface by means of Web sites is low and limited and does not enable a high level of e-commerce and, in fact, they are used as uni-directional advertising and information channels. In order to examine this issue, we started out by checking the purpose of the sites. The data presented in Table 16.3 indicate that only 4% of all the sites examined offer e-commerce, the remainder restricting themselves to advertising and the provision of information.

Table 16.3. Distribution of Web site purposes.

Web site use type	Proportion (%)
Information	40.4%
Sales	3.7%
Advertising	20.2%
Presence	35.7%

Another indication deriving from an analysis of the relationship between the Web site's purpose and the company's trade on the stock exchange shows a significant correlation between these two variables, at the level p=0.0416 for 124 companies as shown in Table 16.4.

Table 16.4. Relationship between the Web sites and company type.

Web site purpose/company type	Advertising	E-commerce sales	Information
Traded company	18	1	51
Not traded company	6	4	44
Total	24	5	95

These findings support the conclusion that the Web site's main purpose is providing information, advertising and demonstrating a presence and not to conduct e-commerce via the Internet.

16.3.2. QUALITATIVE FEATURES

In this section, we present the results of a 12-feature trend factor analysis of business Web sites. The aggregated result presented in Table 16.5 for each feature or quality variable is based on several questions.

Table 16.5. Description and comparison of qualitative data on the research sample.

Feature	Feature degree Top 458	Feature degree Stock exchange	Total research sample
Dynamism and interactivity	3.65	3.19	3.52
Motion	6.04	5.75	5.88
Feedback	4.94	5.35	5.10
Characters	3.12	2.79	3.04
Dense/spaced screen	4.03	4.19	4.12
Screen – information organisation level	5.94	5.78	5.81
Graphic design – general	4.69	4.26	4.53
Graphic design – use of audiovisual and video aids	5.35	4.64	5.01
Terminology, terms and messages	5.86	5.55	5.70
Learning	3.76	3.90	3.81
Site's capability – response, speed	5.56	5.54	5.52
User interface	4.82	4.32	4.61
Total	57.33	55.26	56.65

As we can see, the quality variables range from 2.79 to 5.78 in the traded companies sector and 2.69 to 6.04 in the top companies. In order to examine whether there is any difference between the populations or result ratings, we made the following calculation. We took the sum of the variables range and the total final features and multiplied it by the range to see where each population stands in relation to the maximal result (by this method, summing up the 12 questions on a scale of 1-7 gives a range of 0-84 scores). Each component that passed the statistical factor analysis and was unified into a given feature was given the same weight as the other variables. The results demonstrate that the top 458 population accumulated 57.33 of the 84 possible scores, i.e. 68.25%, and the traded companies accumulated 55.26 of the 84 possible scores, i.e. 65.7%. This difference may lead to a conclusion that the top 458 Web sites were of a somewhat higher quality than the traded companies, but not unequivocally. Another reasonable inference is that the cost of creating a Web site is a negligible expense when considered in relation to the large business turnovers of these companies. Israeli Web sites are built using fairly standard models, and they are information rather than e-commerce sites, which would require interface and integration with the proprietor's information systems or connection to a charging, clearance and distribution system.

Thus, on the one hand, the data demonstrates that the Internet penetration threshold required to fulfil the needs of the Israeli economy is low, and economic size does not afford any advantage in creating a quality Web site with e-commerce capabilities. On the other hand, Israeli companies are conducting little or no e-commerce, and the main infrastructure is designed to convey information and establish a presence over the net.

Table 16.6 rates the qualitative features according to measurement range size. The most salient aspect of the data presented is that the features fall into three groups.

Table 16.6. Rating of features by level.

Feature	Total research sample	Rating	Success percentage from total range 1-7
Motion	5.88	1	84%
Screen – information organisation level	5.81	2	83%
Terminology, terms and messages	5.70	3	81.4%
Site's capability – response, speed	5.52	4	78.8%
Feedback	5.10	5	72.0%
Graphic design – use of audiovisual/video aids	5.01	6	71.5%
User interface	4.61	7	65.8%
Graphic design – general	4.53	8	64.7%
Dense/spaced screen	4.12	9	58.8%
Learning	3.81	10	54.4%
Dynamism and interactivity	3.52	11	50.2%
Characters	3.04	12	43.4%
Total	56.65	84	67.4%

The features included in the range 5-6 on a scale of 1-7 are motion, information organisation level, terminology, Web-site ability, feedback, and graphic design (50% of all the features). The features in the range 4-5 on a scale of 1-7 are learning, dynamism and interactivity, and characters (25% of all the features). Twelve features under the range 5-6 (the rating range is between 5.88 for the highest feature and 3.04 for the lowest).

The differences get progressively smaller as we proceed down the range, but if we look at the differences between the features of the highest group and the lowest one, the difference is significant – almost double. It is noteworthy that the cornerstone user interface feature - dynamism and interactivity – is rated eleventh, i.e. in almost the last place. This reinforces our observation that the basic communication model for building an interface and infrastructure for e-commerce is not employed properly.

16.3.3. ECONOMIC FEATURES

Analysis by Sector

In the one-way ANOVA analysis carried out on the sector variable and the 12 qualitative variables, a significant correlation was found between the sector variable and number of screens, usage of terms, use of means (audio, video, etc.), organisation of information and organisation of screens. In examining the data distribution over the various sectors, we learn that there is no uniform trend of a sector leading in all or most features. Each sector shows predominance in a different feature. Following is a summary of the significant correlations between the qualitative variables and the sector variable. We found a significant correlation of $p = 0.00066$ for $N = 124$, when analysing the bi-directional variance between sector type and site destination. This analysis indicates that 77% of all sectors use the Internet merely for disseminating information, 4% for sales and 19% for advertising. We found only five companies selling via the Internet – four commercial companies and an insurance agency.

The data show no significant differences in the distribution of the results among the various sectors. The conclusion is that there is no substantial difference between the level of the sites in the various sectors. All the companies made the same use of the Internet and there was no qualitative or content advantage of the home page Web sites of one sector over the others. The correlations found suggest that analysis by sector might elicit qualitative trends at a high level of significance and enable characterisation of trends within the sectors. The implications of the findings of the sector variable analysis with regard to the research hypotheses are as follows.

Hypothesis 2, suggesting a significant positive correlation between economic parameters and degree of Web site usage, level and quality, was partially supported. We found a significant correlation for five of the 15 qualitative features (33%). The types of correlations found indicate that a "features/variables basket" may be used to locate qualitative and usage trends in business Web sites.

Hypothesis 4, assuming that organisations using the Web will expand usage with multiple screens and data, was supported. The distribution of number of screens in the various sectors indicates three sector groupings:

- Up to 15 screens (low use of the site to distribute information) – companies dealing in manufacturing; metal and metal products; computers and computer services; real estate and development (4 of the 8 sectors).
- 16-26 screens (medium use of the site to distribute information) – banks, insurance companies and agencies (2 of the 8 sectors).
- 26-40 sectors (substantial use of the site to distribute information) – electronics, electrical appliances and optics; trade (2 of the 8 sectors).

Analysis by Stock Exchange Trade

The ANOVA results show a significant correlation between the stock exchange trade variable and the following qualitative variables: terminology, terms and messages, dynamism and interactivity, number of screens. We also found a significant correlation of $p = 0.00003$ for $N = 236$ between Web-site type and the stock exchange trade variable.

Table 16.7. Distribution of Web-site types according to stock exchange trade.

Web-site type	Company not traded on stock exchange	Company traded on stock exchange
Independent site	58	71
Site under construction	1	2
URL only	8	23
Sub-site of another Web-site	17	20
Site/homepage appearing in an index	31	5
Total	115	121

The data appearing in Table 16.7 indicate that 60% of traded companies have a Web site and 40% appear on the Internet in other ways. By comparison, 50% of top 458 companies have Web sites and 50% appear in various other ways. The bi-directional difference analysis shows a significant correlation between stock exchange trade and the site's destination – $p = 0.0416$, for $N = 124$. Of the traded companies, 51 used the Internet for information purposes, 18 for advertising and one for e-commerce. As for the non-traded companies, 44 had Web sites for information, four for e-commerce and 6 for advertising. The stock exchange trade findings have the following implications regarding the research hypotheses.

Hypothesis 2, proposing a significant positive correlation between economic parameters and qualitative parameters pertaining to the degree of usage of the Web site and its quality, was partially supported. Four of the 15 qualitative parameters (27%) showed significant correlations with the economic parameters.

Hypothesis 3, proposing that marketing on the Internet will be interactive and employ high technology tools that create a bi-directional interface, enabling feedback between the user and the Web site, was refuted. According to our findings, there is a significant but low correlation with the ability to create a dynamic interactive interface. The interface exists but is not sufficient to establish an infrastructure for e-commerce.

Hypothesis 4 was proved valid; the companies use multiple screens to transfer information and data to the users. We also found that traded companies use less screens that non traded ones – 14 screens compared to 30 screens, respectively.

The research findings show that the Web site of a company not traded on the stock exchange is superior to the site of a traded company in that it transmits a higher volume of information, using an average of 30 screens. The user interface is of a low level, though superior to the level of the traded company, the terminology level is higher than that of the traded company, and the number of fonts is three on average.

Analysis by Annual Turnover

Significant correlations with annual turnover were found for the following parameters: number of fonts used on the Web site, terminology, level of terms used and messages, number of screens. When correlating turnover with Web site ownership, at a significance level of $p=0.00675$ for $N=231$, we found that 20.3% of the companies with a turnover between $10 million and $100 million have Web sites, accounting for 42% of all the companies owning Web sites. Of the companies with Web sites, 19.5% have a turnover of $100 million to $1 billion and represent 57% of the Web-site owners. The findings for the two groups at either end of the turnover scale were as follows: 5.6% of all companies have a turnover up to $1 million and account for 13% of the Web-site owners; the group of companies having a turnover over $1 billion represent 8.2% of all the research companies and 15.3% of all the companies owning Web sites.

We also found only two groups under the category of companies mentioned on a Web site other than their own: companies with a turnover of $10-100 million and those with $100 billion. These companies are also notable for appearing in indexes (except for three companies in the over $1 billion group). Of the companies having a Web site or being mentioned in any way whatsoever over the Internet, 83% are in the $10 million to $1 billion turnover range.

The analysis indicates three significant correlations between qualitative features and annual turnover, providing further reinforcement for Hypothesis 2. Site size, measured by the number of screens, is also a significant variable: the larger the turnover, up to $1 billion, the higher the number of screens used and the larger the information distribution (see table), providing support for Hypothesis 4.

The foregoing leads to the conclusion that for companies in the $0 to $1 billion turnover range, which covers 95% of all the companies in the Israeli economy, the larger the turnover, the better the quality features of the Web site. That is, the better the usage of terms and the extent of information transfer, and the larger the number of fonts in the site.

Analysis by Annual Profit/Loss Level

Three qualitative parameters were found to correlate significantly with the annual profit/loss variable - number of screens, learning quality, number of fonts used, thus partially corroborating Hypothesis 2. The correlation of the company's profit with the number of screens it uses and the amount of information it transfers to the user also provides corroboration of Hypothesis 4. For companies with a profit range up to $1 million, the larger the profit, the better the quality of the Web site in terms of learning features, information volume transfer and number of fonts.

16.4. Discussion

This preliminary research builds an empirical model to describe, analyse and evaluate the e-commerce infrastructure in Israel, also examining and analysing the user interface level and quality. We believe this model, together with its diagnostic tool - the questionnaire - will serve as a new framework for future research. The research had three principal aims:

- To test and analyse the economic and business parameters (turnover, profit, number of employees, etc) vis-a-vis the qualitative variables of the information systems comprising the e-commerce infrastructure of the population under investigation;
- To examine the level and quality of the user interface and its components;
- To identify the analysis components and qualitative variables that best describe the Web site's level and quality.

The model presented in this research enables the handling of data for macro comparisons, between countries and between sectors as well as micro handling in terms of level and quality of the individual Web site's components. Here we analyse the research hypotheses related to the three principal research aims.

Hypothesis 1 maintains that commercial organisations in general and in Israel in particular, recognising the commercial potential of the Internet, will aspire to be represented on the Web and operate in the framework of e-commerce. This hypothesis was proven true only partially and to a small degree, insofar as only 27.2% of all the research companies are represented on the Internet. It was also found that the private sector uses the Internet to a greater degree than do the public and traded sectors. Companies having an independent Web site were even fewer – 16% of the research population, the others appearing on an information home page, in indexes or on parent company sites. We estimate that this low representation is due to the fact that using the Internet implies a substantial change in the company's attitude and strategic thinking.

According to a study conducted by *CIO Magazine* in March 1995, 50% of the 500 largest companies in the USA had a Web site. At that time, the Web was largely considered a toy for "just playing or dabbling". The situation in the USA in 1995 was very similar to that prevailing in Israel in 1999. Thus, for example, Web sites of banks in the USA enable a far wider range of transactions than do the very much more limited Israeli bank Web sites. Though certain Israeli companies develop technology for the Internet and others seriously wish to use it for conducting their business, the awareness of the Internet as a commercial channel worthy of massive organisational investment is still quite limited. Thus, we have a duality in the perception of the Internet's content and potential in the Israeli economy. On the one hand, the media frequently reports on the Internet and Israeli companies who succeed in selling Internet technology, thus giving the impression that the Internet plays an important role in the Israeli economy. On the other hand, close inspection of the actual use Israeli companies make of the Internet shows that it is indeed used mainly for "just playing or dabbling". Companies that recognise the Internet as a commercial channel are present on the Web in a partial way, appearing on information sites. The general trend is to watch and wait for the first success, after which other companies follow suit.

Having recognised the research population's trend and the extent of this trend, Hypothesis 2 examines the correlation between economic and qualitative variables, proposing a distinct positive correlation between an organisation's business variables and the extent of usage, level and quality of its Web site. The larger the organisation in terms of turnover, profit, number of employees, it claims, the higher the quality of its Web site.

The business Web site needs to have the qualitative features necessary to create a user interface to support the e-commerce value chain and establish a direct and effective connection between the site and the user. Interactivity, user satisfaction, and effective content and graphics are among the qualitative criteria the site and its interface have to meet. In our examination of the qualitative components, grouped into several categories, we found no differences among the various sectors of the research population and no particular qualitative characteristic distinguishing a given sector. Nor did we find any uniform trend of any given group of qualitative features being consistently correlated with a particular business parameter. The groups of qualitative variables are wide and include: number of screens, number of fonts, terms and terminology, dynamism and feedback, screen organisation, use of multimedia, information transfer, characters, user interface, information organisation, and others. The absence of statistical correlations between qualitative features (general graphics, capabilities, Web site motion, e-mail) and economic parameters indicates that the quality variable is low in analysis and comparison capability. However, to establish its suitability for research purposes, the components of the quality variable should be re-examined sequentially.

Hypothesis 2 is based on the size advantage concept – will an economically larger organisation have a quality edge over a smaller organisation? Ragowsky (1986) found that there is a correlation between the organisation's size and the use and quality of its information systems. In our research, we did not find a correlation between the organisation's size and quality, and level of use of its business Web site. However, we did find a correlation between organisation size and appearance on the Internet, i.e. the larger the organisation, the higher the probability that it has a Web site. The meaning of these findings is that size advantage does not provide a qualitative advantage. Our conclusion is that the Internet enables small and medium-sized companies to try to bridge the gap between them and the large companies. At the same time, the large companies recognise the risk of losing their competitive edge and use the Internet in order to maintain the gap. This confirms the claim of Lederer et al. (1997) that organisations will prefer a strategy of increasing competitiveness via the Internet.

After examining the first two research hypotheses, we consider the user interface, to which we relate in our third hypothesis: organisations using a Web site will take full advantage of the Internet's power and employ the most advanced technological tools to create an interface between them and the user, emphasising two-way interaction and feedback, in order to improve their competitiveness. The research findings show that the user interface of the Israeli companies is weak and not exploited. According to our findings, 96% of the Web sites of Israeli companies restrict themselves to information and advertising and do not deal in e-commerce at all. The results relating to Hypothesis 1 concerning the level and quality of the user interface show that Israeli companies do not yet consider the Internet as a tool for improving competitiveness. They do not yet see it as an economic channel with business potential. Among the reasons for this perception are the following.

- Until December 1998 the large credit card companies in Israel refused to recognise the Secured Socket Layer (SSL) security protocol.
- The average Israeli surfer is afraid of purchasing over the Internet by credit card.
- The Israeli companies do not recognise the Internet as an economic channel uniquely equipped to improve their performance.

When examining Hypothesis 3, we traced five influential user interface components: user satisfaction from the site and its features; site capability; use of multimedia; graphics; text – terms and terminology. These are the components to which the organisation should relate if it wishes to create a site with an effective high quality interface that enables utilisation of the Internet's potential. Not using them is a kind of technological declaration that the site is not intended for e-commerce. We also found strong positive correlations of the user's satisfaction from the site with features such as dynamism, feedback and use of multimedia to support the interface.

Hypothesis 4 is concerned with the extent and volume of information transfer: Players will expand their use of the Internet, with its broad scope and cost-saving advantages in comparison to other marketing and distribution channels, using multiple data, information and screens. Our findings that companies use the Internet to distribute information confirm this hypothesis, and provide support for the statement in Hoffman et al. (1995) on the multi-dimensionality of the information distribution model. Relating back to the discussion of our findings concerning Hypothesis 3, Israeli companies do not use the Internet as a multi-dimensional distribution channel. With their uni-directional and static user interfaces and the limited end-user targeting, which make marginal use of the Internet's vast technological capabilities, most Web sites are designed for information distribution only. It is not surprising then that 96% of the Web sites are little more than a relatively cheap substitute for other advertising and information dissemination media such as the press, radio and TV.

The results on the extent of information distribution confirm Hypothesis 4. There is a clear and positive correlation with all the economic features, except for organisation size, as measured by number of employees. Private companies transfer more information than public companies and traded ones. The larger the information turnover, the greater the quantity of information transferred to the user. Also, manufacturing companies transfer more information than service or other companies.

Hypothesis 5 states that organisations and sectors rich in information systems will be the first to use the Internet as a tool for e-commerce. The quality and frequency of their use will be higher than organisations and sectors poor in information systems. A sub-hypothesis to the above is that manufacturing organisations and companies will use the Internet more as a marketing tool and as a basis to render value added services to the customer than other organisations and companies.

This hypothesis was not clearly proven, but we did find that organisations and sectors rich in information systems will appear over the Internet to an extent proportional to their size and even more, whereas organisations and sectors poor in information systems will appear in proportion to their size or less. As for the sub-hypothesis, the findings clearly showed that manufacturing organisations account for 47% of all the companies appearing on the Internet, compared to service companies (34%) and others (19%). The manufacturing companies are higher in quality and extent of use and interface level than the other companies in the Israeli economy, in support of Hypothesis 5.

16.5. Conclusion

This study aims at laying the foundation for an empirical research framework to examine and analyse e-commerce. The study presents an initial research tool to analyse and evaluate Web sites via a questionnaire. The questionnaire is valid and reliable, but it was not examined psychometrically. Further research is required to create a more powerful research tool.

The research population is representative of the Israeli economy, and the sub-populations - stock exchange traded companies and the top 458 companies - are comparable to similar populations in other, mainly Western, countries. Thus, it may serve as the basis for future research on the infrastructure of e-commerce in Israel and abroad, as well as to generalise on other populations, taking the usual precautions advised in conducting inter-cultural research.

Integrating research and data from the USA, companies and business organisations may be seen as entering the Internet in the following stages.

- *First stage.* Presence or preliminary penetration, via an information or advertising Web site, without connecting back to office systems or other information systems. The Web site in this case is a stand-alone system.
- *Second stage.* The companies move from the first stage to the second by connecting the Web site, partially or wholly, to information systems at the organisation. At the same time, new companies enter the first stage.
- *Third stage.* The Web site becomes an integral part of the company's sale array. Some companies even conduct their entire activity over the Internet, like Amazon and Dell.

In 1995, 50% of the largest 500 companies in the USA sat waiting on the fence, while the other 50% appeared on the Internet, though they did not necessarily conduct e-commerce. In Israel, during 1997-98, 16% of all companies owned independent Web sites, and 4% enabled electronic trade via the Web. It seems that the Israeli economy is still sitting on the fence, waiting for one of its number to pioneer the breakthrough into e-commerce.

There is a significant advantage to financial size (turnover) for appearance on the Internet. Companies with a turnover above $10 million appear more than do those with lower turnovers. It would seem that large organisations will be the first to enter, more or less according to the stages described above, though the organisation's size would seem to have little bearing on site quality. At the same time, the low entrance threshold will enable small and medium-sized companies to bridge the gap vis-a-vis large companies and organisations with considerable advantages in other areas. We may deduce, therefore, that if the expected potential of the Internet is realised, and if the small and medium-sized companies recognise this potential and exploit the low threshold advantage, there may well be changes in the structure and type of companies leading the world economy.

Sectors rich in information systems appear in proportion to their size or above this level, and their activity over the Internet is large in proportion to their size. Sectors that are not rich in information systems appear in proportion to their size or to a lesser extent.

This main conclusion of this research is that the usage of Internet sites in Israel is still in its initial stages and, despite its status as a high-tech leader, the level of e-commerce in Israel is comparatively low.

CHAPTER 17

Electronic Commerce in China

TED CLARK

17.1. Introduction

China is one of the largest countries in the world. It is only slightly larger than the United States in geography, but the 1998 population of 1.3 billion was more than four times that of the U.S. There are 31 provincial-style entities (including Taiwan) and 517 cities. Over recent years, China's economy has been growing very fast as the country has gone through a process of opening up to the outside world. By 1996, according to International Monetary Fund data, China's domestic economy was more than four times larger than it was in 1978, and was roughly 50% the size of the US economy. In other words, by 1996, the country had, amazingly, met Deng Xiaoping's stated economic reform objectives - to have doubled and then redoubled the size of the domestic economy in less than 16 years.

Politically, the economic reforms introduced in China have been explained and rationalised as 'market socialism'. Market socialism is the 'socialist' version of economic liberalisation, wherein a basically socialist economic system (state planning, public ownership) is retained, but the beneficial elements of the market system are incorporated so as to improve economic performance and increase social welfare. However, a decade and a half of piecemeal reform has created an incoherent morass of half-reformed enterprises and multi-layered government authority. The government appears to genuinely believe that information systems can help to solve its economic and coordination problems. In particular, 'informatisation' has been put forward as a substitute for legal and institutional reforms. While privatisation, price rationalisation, and other more difficult structural reforms have been stalled or shelved, informatisation is promoted as the tool for macroeconomic control.

The history of electronic commerce in China is tightly linked with government politics and with the debate over the role of information technology, telecommunications, and electronic commerce as enablers of economic growth, political and economic control, and/or political fragmentation and instability. The history of electronic commerce development in China is an interesting one, and is filled with unexpected turns and events as politics and economic forces have resulted in several transformations of the political and regulatory landscape of the nation.

To understand the evolution and future of electronic commerce in China, it is essential to begin with examining the basic frameworks and value propositions that have been used to justify investments in information technology and liberalisation of communications networks in China. The lessons learned from understanding China's experiences provide some interesting parallels for other countries who are in the process of liberalising their communications infrastructures and evaluating the political implications of alternative forms of regulation and ownership of telecommunications and information network infrastructures.

17.2. The Role of Information Technology Infrastructure in Society

The growing convergence of computers and telecommunications and the unprecedented opportunities that come with them have given rise to conflicting views on the role and impact of information technology on society. Snow (1988) describes telecommunication, including all forms of information networks (e.g. the Internet), as the central nervous system of a contemporary society and a precondition for growth and welfare. From an international point of view, a sophisticated telecommunications and information infrastructure can become a critical source of competitive advantage of a nation (Porter, 1990). The correlation between investments in telecommunications and information infrastructure on economic development is widely acknowledged for developing countries, although there is much debate on whether investments in telecommunications and information technology infrastructure are enablers of economic development or are a result of economic growth. However, there is much less agreement on the political and economic control implications of these information infrastructure investments.

The debate has leaned heavily towards the "controlling" versus "liberating" potential of these new technologies. Some analysts have argued that information technology and networks are essentially a reinforcement and continuity of pre-existing forms of control (Attewell and Rule, 1984; Beniger, 1986; Gandy, 1993; Pfeffer, 1978; Zuboff, 1988). In surveying a number of studies on information technology, Attewell and Rule found that most of the available research pointed to reinforcement of the existing power structure in organisations. Similarly, in his search for the origins of the "Information Society," Beniger argues that generalised control shifted progressively after World War II. In his view, the convergence of telecommunications, computing, and mass media has lead to a restoration of economic and political control that was lost to local levels of society during the industrial revolution. Zuboff (and others) have also found that computer networks have reinforced the ability of managers in hierarchical structures to monitor their subordinates.

Some authors have argued instead that information technology and networks are weakening hierarchies and central control on behalf of decentralisation (Bailyn, 1989; Eccles and Nolan, 1993; Johansen and Swigart, 1994; O'Hara-Devereaux and Johansen, 1994; Perin, 1988; Davis and Davidson, 1991). From this perspective, decision making in organisations is becoming increasingly decentralised. Johansen and Swigart see computer networks enabling the migration of production from the traditional workplace to an emerging "virtual workspace." Davis and Davidson describe the rise of global communication networks as closely linked with the rise of a global "anytime/anyplace economy." Eccles and Nolan maintain that the transition to an information-based economy has resulted in information technology and networks transforming organisational structures from traditional functional hierarchies to informal networks "floating on top of formal hierarchies."

Others see the potential of information and communications networks in more ambiguous terms (Ganley and Ganley, 1989; Malone, Yates, and Benjamin, 1994; Malone, 1987; Malone and Smith, 1984). In their view, communication networks have a vast but contradictory potential. Malone, Yates, and Benjamin (1994), for example, argue that new information technologies are making both markets and hierarchies more efficient. The increased efficiency is mostly born out of the considerable reduction in coordination costs that new information networks can provide. They sustain, however, that ("without changing anything else") the reduction of coordination costs should increase the proportion of economic activity coordinated by markets - which are more communication intensive than hierarchies. But market growth leads to an increase of economic actors, which in turn requires an increase in the amount of communication required by the market to operate efficiently. Based on historical evidence, Malone and Smith (1984) argue that "this change favoured hierarchies over markets."

This trend towards the reinforcement of hierarchies stands in contradiction with the position of those that argue that increased concentration of power at the top of the political system is doomed to failure because of insufficient ability to process the needed information. These advocates of power decentralisation argue that the amount of information required to treat each input and output in a fully disaggregated fashion and to allocate society's resources efficiently is beyond the control of central planners of a large economy. For this line of thinking, new information technology does not provide a solution to the problem because there is still the need of a huge pool of human resources to supply, manage, and classify correctly the large amount of information required (Putterman, 1995).

Most of these analyses are articulated from an economic point of view. But, for most governments around the world - and in particular for Asian ones - considerations related to economic growth, and national competitiveness and efficiency are not dealt with in a socio-political vacuum. In countries undergoing transition from a planned to a predominantly market economy, like China, economic development is as closely linked to issues of equity, social welfare, and politics as it is to market efficiency, productivity, and national competitiveness. In this regard, new information technology and communication networks seem to offer the tools (if not the illusion) to achieve at the same time both growth of market forces and central control and monitoring of the economy and the polity. China is not the only country in Asia that holds this particular position on the potential of information technology and new communication networks. Other governments in the region (e.g. Singapore, Vietnam, Malaysia, Indonesia, etc.) share similar views on the matter (Petrazzini and Lovelock, 1996).

Following this perspective, senior Chinese government officials see new information and communication networks as providing benefits from both an economic and a socio-political point of view. On the one hand, advanced networks can offer a powerful coordination tool to resuscitate the state from its fading role as a mediator and arbiter of economic activities in society. A centralised and powerful state can not only play a crucial role as a mediator in the marketplace, but it can also institutionalise exchange transactions and minimise transactions costs (Dugger, 1993). On the other hand, a much praised spill over effect in the implementation of enhanced national communications is the significant increase of political monitoring and control. Although increased networking could provide a national platform for the organisation and dissemination of political dissidence, government officials in Beijing believe that an adequately designed network will serve first and foremost the interests of the central government.

For Beijing, information technology and communication networks are a new solution to an old problem. The objectives and the processes mirror those that were the core of imperial power, but now information technology and networks are seen to allow for a crucial tightening of the administrative process. In the current times of high inflation, institutionalised corruption, multi-layered bureaucracy, and increasing political disaggregation, information technology has come to be seen by the Chinese leaders as a key tool for combating these rising problems. In other words, the pre-eminent role that information technology and networks have come to play in Chinese modernisation has its roots in the preceding economic reforms and the subsequent reconceptualisation of both economic and political administration.

17.3. Alternative Forms of Information Infrastructure Regulation

Telecommunication and information infrastructure development are critical for economic growth, as well as an important part of the security of the nation. Most countries have tightly regulated the ownership and control of these strategic assets. Until the 1980s, almost all countries outside the US viewed government ownership of a monopoly telecommunications provider as the only reasonable approach for management and control of telecommunications. The Internet was viewed by most PTTs[1] as an unwelcome form of competition for the existing telecommunications infrastructure and services. Pressures technology innovation (including the Internet) combined with the economic development needs for improved communications infrastructure capabilities have resulted in many countries pursuing various forms of liberalisation of communications infrastructure ownership and regulation over the past two decades (Bradley and Hausman, 1989; Petrazzini, 1995; Petrazzini and Clark, 1996).

The worldwide movement towards liberalisation in telecommunications services is gaining steam and the process seems irreversible. Yet, pace and scope of market opening has diverged considerably among countries. This is particularly true in the case of less developed countries (LDCs), where liberalisation - encompassing both competition and privatisation - ranges in practice from the fully private and

---

[1]PTT officially means Post, Telegraph, and Telecommunications. However, it generally refers to any government owned telecommunications company, even if postal or telegraph services are not included.

competitive Chilean market to the state-owned monopoly markets of many Asian, African, and Latin American nations (Petrazzini, 1995).

There have been a large number of statements arguing that privatisation and competition in telecommunications markets bring a considerable number of benefits to consumers and the economy by improving the overall performance of the industry. Rigorous evidence across cases and industry indicators in support of such statements have been less common, especially for LDCs (Petrazzini and Clark, 1996). Traditionally, policy makers view telecommunications liberalisation as a trade-off of costs and benefits. It is commonly assumed that labour and incumbent operators would bear the costs of liberalisation due to job and market share losses, while consumers and the economy in general would enjoy the benefits through increased teledensity, lower prices, improved quality and diversity of services, as well as a modernised network. In discussing the impact of liberalisation, it is important to distinguish between two very different forms of opening up telecommunications markets. Privatisation liberalises telecommunications ownership and investments by partially or completely separating ownership of telecommunications from the government. Introduction of competition in various segments of the market (cellular, local, domestic long distance, international, and value-added services) represents a different form of liberalisation, which is independent of financial liberalisation. There are clear benefits of increased liberalisation (both in the form of competition and privatisation), but they are not always consistent with the traditional view of costs and benefits resulting from these policy decisions in LDCs (Petrazzini and Clark, 1996).

Telecommunications regulation is the imposition of rules by the government on the telecommunications industry with the effect of controlling the market structure and the industrial behaviour (Hills, 1991). The objective is to ensure that telecommunication, as a critical resource of the society and a vital component of the economy, is used efficiently, is developed fully and its costs and benefits distributed fairly.

A continuum between total control and free market operation can be considered. At the one end, the state assumes provision of all telecommunications facilities and services. The monopolistic telecommunications provider, who is also the regulatory agency, is a government department. The government has complete control of the planning, implementation and provision of telecommunication. At the other end, telecommunications are completely provided by the market with the invisible hands of supply and demand, which determines the allocation of resources and levels of services and facilities.

Historically, telecommunication has been under heavy state control with most PTTs supplying and controlling telecommunications facilities and services. Today, governments are relaxing regulation in the telecommunications markets and various levels of competition in one form or the other are being introduced. Although it is believed that liberalisation fosters competition and a competitive environment leads to economic efficiency, technological innovation and increased welfare, the extreme case of non-interventionist free market operation has not occurred, even within the highly competitive US market.

For China, the debate on privatisation and liberalisation of telecommunications ownership and regulation occurred globally at the same time as the country was making the transition from state-ownership of almost all enterprises to evolving into a much more capitalistic market economy. However, allowing competition into the telecommunications section was considered unacceptable as this represented an important area of national security as well as economic and political control for the nation. Even in 1998, foreign ownership of telecommunications services companies is still prohibited, but the past decade has seen multiple forms of domestic competition emerge in the rapidly growing telecommunications and information networking (i.e. Internet) market.

17.4. China's Telecommunications Infrastructure and Policies

Following the "Open Door Policy" in 1979 and the introduction of the ideology of "Market Socialism" by Deng Xiaoping in the early 90s, China has placed a high priority on the development of telecommunication and information industries. As Hu Qili, Electronic Minister, pointed out on 14 June 1994, "Promoting information services and integrating them with industrialisation will greatly enhance the quality of China's national economy." With over 1.2 billion people, nearly 10 million square kilometres and many ethnic groups and languages, tensions between the centre and periphery, fragmentation and warlordism have been an issue in national agenda (Ure, 1994, 1995). Telecommunication development improves the infrastructure for bureaucratic and economic coordination and control at the national level, allowing senior officials in Beijing to monitor economic growth and to ensure compliance with national ideology and official guidelines. An effective national information infrastructure is thus perceived by the government as important in all aspects of public administration. Informatisation is perceived as a tool for macroeconomic control (Clark, Lovelock, Petrazzini, 1996). Jin (1995) echoes that the telecommunication industry is the nervous system of the national economy and would improve macroeconomic adjustment.

Economic reforms have also had significant destabilising political effects. Economic growth and diversification has resulted in a dramatic increase in the number of social and political institutions that operate at the crossroads of economics and politics, making the Chinese political scene more complex and more difficult to monitor and manage. For Beijing, the overall outcome of the process has been an unwanted but sustained decentralisation of political power and an increasing tension between the centre and periphery of the national political system. It was within this environment that China's leadership began to see possibilities in the application of information and telecommunications technology to bring both the national economy and polity under some kind of systematic central control.

At the economic level, extensive wiring of the nation and aggressive incorporation of information technology provides a basis for increasing economic coordination and control at the national level while achieving improved efficiency and performance of the productive system.[2] At the same time, the introduction of distance insensitive technology increases the potential of Beijing to effectively monitor economic growth and compliance with official guidelines in rather remote and previously isolated regions of the country.

At the political level, a networked nation provides the required infrastructure to regain central control of political institutions and organisations. Information networks also open a valuable avenue to integrate political mandate and economic development. In China, significant economic and social leaps forward can be achieved as the simple result of the sizeable human and institutional resources available. Yet experience has taught government officials that those initiatives are illusory unless all parts involved in the task are led by a strong authority at the top of a clearly defined hierarchy (Petrazzini, 1995). When such authority is missing, different institutions throughout the nation will fight rather than cooperate - even if they agree on a common goal. Government officials believe that information networks will allow leaders to sit in Beijing, yet "be present" in each and every politically sensitive spot through the nation, appeasing political unrest and leading major national crusades.

Pressed by the increasing forces of economic decentralisation and political disaggregation and, perceiving in the new information and communication technology the vast potential for tackling many of these problems, Beijing launched, in 1993, a high level national networking initiative that came to be known as "The Golden Projects." The Golden Projects can thus be viewed as both a major thrust forward to develop an information highway in China to improve the efficiency of the economy, and as an effort to use information technology to centralise information and coordination over business and political activities within the nation.

The initiation of Deng's economic reform and open-door policies created the environment for the rapid expansion of China's telecommunications capacity. As early as 1980, expansion of the network was seen as necessary for promoting a more vigorous domestic economy. By 1985, telecommunications investment exceeded 1% of GNP for the first time. Although China still trailed many other nations in this regard, investment levels continued to rise and, progressively, infrastructure deployment began to be funded from a diversity of new sources such as private companies and individuals.

China's telecommunications network consists of public and private networks. The usage of the terms 'public' and 'private' is, however, different in China from elsewhere. Both public and private networks are owned by the State or the public. The public networks are those run by the Ministry of Posts and Telecommunications (MPT), while private networks are simply those not operated under the MPT.

By 1980, China lagged well behind international standards. Public telephone service was almost non-existent. Practically no telephone service was provided to households except for high-ranking government officials. In a country with

---

[2] If, in a broad sense, business re-engineering is defined as the merger of process innovation and information technology innovations to achieve significant improvements in performance, then this national initiative can be seen to reflect the reforms carried out, albeit at a different scale, by the corporate community in their recent "re-engineering" wave.

approximately 250 million households only about 1,000 urban households had their own telephone. Many small towns had no phone service at all. Foreigners in China attempting business were consistently frustrated by the difficulty of making a telephone call. In the early 1980s, more than one-third of all calls never got through because of overloading of the ancient telephone exchanges. The situation did not really begin to improve until well into the early 1990s. By 1993, with reliability in the network as a target for improvement, provincial capitals and large cities were registering call success rates in excess of 70 percent - including in peak hours. In 1987, AT&T customers placing calls to Shanghai had to dial an average of five times to complete one call. By 1995, most callers were reported to be getting through on the first try.

Even so, networking in China was still quite limited in the mid-1990s. Computer penetration was less than 1 per every 400 people, and telephone penetration was still only 3 per 100 residents. Most businesses in the major cities did have telephones by 1995, but outside the largest cities, even basic telecommunications facilities were generally unavailable. By 1995, more than 500,000 of the 800,000 villages in China did not even have access to a single telephone. In the banking industry, inter-provincial networking had just begun in 1995. Even in 1995, cheques written on a branch of the same bank often could not be deposited in a different province for that same bank, as there was no arrangement established for inter-provincial clearing of cheques for most banks across China. Business travellers frequently carried large sums of cash to complete business transactions and to pay for hotel and food expenses as credit cards were uncommon, and, even if available, were only accepted for payment if the card had been issued in a local provincial bank. Thus, the Golden Projects represented an ambitious effort to develop a networked information highway in a nation where even basic communications linkages often did not exist.

17.5. The Emergence of China's Golden Projects

Since the late 1980s, a competing ministry, the Ministry of Electronics Industry (MEI), had been trying to break the communications monopoly held by the MPT, unsuccessfully arguing in favour of domestic competition for telecommunications services. However, by the early 1990s, MEI had changed tack: data communications - information - was the new crucial ingredient to being internationally competitive, and the data communication demands, both for international and domestic business, were going to grow exponentially as China re-integrated into the international economic community. With the public telephone network already painfully overloaded, waiting lists for a household telephone exceeding 12 million, and the MPT already committed to ambitious growth targets, it was suggested a second network was required to facilitate the growth of data communications. Thus, in 1993, Hu Qili, Minister for the Electronics Industry (MEI), went before the State Council to sell them the idea of the 'Three Golden' projects - China's version of the 'information superhighway'. He sold the State Council on the importance of data communications, not competition or liberalisation, and emphasised that, although telephones were under the jurisdiction of the MPT, computers were traditionally the preserve of MEI.

In late 1994, the State Council formally approved the creation of two new telecom entities in China. One of the entrants, Ji Tong Communications Co., was a corporate arm of MEI. Licensed in 1994, Ji Tong was seen as the 'builder' or integrator of the new network. The other challenger, China United Telecommunications (known also as Unicom, or Liantong in Chinese), was set up in July 1994 with the intention of offering long-distance data communications to compete with the MPT. Of course, digital communications being what they are, who can tell what is data and what is voice?

In selling the 'Golden Projects' to the elders of the State Council, Minister Hu provided a further incentive: computer information systems tend to be centralised, allowing for greater administrative control. Thus, Zhu Rongji's call for a national public economic information network later became the 'Golden Bridge Project'; Chairman Jiang Zemin's call to facilitate a genuine Central Bank in China became the 'Golden Card Project' and Vice Premier Li Lanqing's initiative to link the Ministry of Foreign Trade and the Ministry of Custom's import/export trade management system, so as to reduce smuggling and regain some administrative control over the coastal ports, became the 'Golden Customs Project'.

One of the primary selling points for the Golden Projects was that they would enable the China government to increase its control over the economy and of commerce in general. For example, the US Federal Reserve has the ability to fine-tune the US economy through tiny interest rate adjustments to maintain economic stability. In China, information on economic performance and development are so inaccurate and delayed that any efforts to manage China's economy are more like aiming a rudderless boat than fine-tuning a high performance machine. By providing the various government Ministries with better information and feedback loops, the government would be better able to take actions that would influence national policy and economic development without requiring ownership of all of the means of production in the nation. In fact, in a modern economy, the possession of information is often more important as a means of control than the ownership of productive enterprises.

Many other government agencies responded to the success of the MEI in getting the Golden Projects approved and funded, with the State Council approving at least nine other Golden Projects in the following two years. Each of these Golden Projects involved the use of information technology and networking to improve economic development or control in China (Lovelock, Clark and Petrazinni, 1996). Although most of these projects were justified publicly as a means of improving economic performance for the nation, nearly all of these later Golden Projects maintained some form of improved control or access to information for the central government.

One exception to the control orientation of most of these initiatives was the "Golden Intelligence Project" which is also known as China's Education and Research Network (CERNET). Aimed at supporting research and development among China's academic community, CERNET was the first Internet network project in China. All CERNET Internet users had to register with the Government and academic Internet access was largely limited to faculty and research staff (Lovelock, Clark and Petrazzini, 1995). Although CERNET had been in operation prior to the Golden Projects being introduced, the credibility of becoming one of the Golden Projects enabled CERNET to become a nation-wide backbone with gateways to the global Internet by 1995, including eight regional networks and over 1,000 campus networks (Li, Wu and Liang, 1995).

Responding to the threat of competition from MEI and other ministries under these Golden Projects initiatives, the MPT began rapidly to upgrade its services. In October 1994, it launched a high-quality, dedicated line communications service, ChinaDDN, for transmitting digital data at high speeds and also upgraded its existing packet-switched data network, Chinapac. In 1996, MPT introduced its own Golden Internet project that expanded the services offered by CERNET and provided Internet access to any business or residential customers that were able to pay for the services. Thus, by 1996, with Ji Tong and Unicom together committed to building the 'Golden Bridge', China was suddenly constructing three different national information data communications and Internet backbone networks.

By 1998, the rivalry between the MPT and MEI had become intense and services provided by the two government agencies almost completely overlapped. However, the MPT officially regulated all telecommunications facilities and services in the nation and was strongly opposed to allowing increased competition. The China State Council was often asked to mediate in disputes between the two government ministries, and thus, decided to resolve the debates by merging the two ministries into a single Ministry of Information Industries (MII). There would still be competition between the networks managed by this combined ministry, but the MII was charged with gradually separating the regulatory and operating roles of the government ministry to allow fair and equal terms of interconnection and competition to develop under an impartial regulator. Although this merger of competing infrastructure providers has decreased the level of competition for basic telecommunications services in China, the market for Internet services and access remains highly competitive and fragmented in 1999. In spite of various government efforts to manage the growth and access to the Internet, the growth in demand and services on the WWW is expanding at a very rapid rate across China.

17.6. The Internet and Electronic Commerce in China

The Internet has already challenged traditional concepts of telecommunication and national boundaries in electronic commerce and idea distribution and sharing. This worldwide trend has impacted the development of the Internet in China too. The government faces a dilemma between 'liberating' and 'controlling'. On the one hand, it values the development of the national information infrastructure for economic modernisation. On the other hand, it worries about the 'pollution' of national ideology by unwanted political ideas from foreign countries or even the underground rightist political parties.

The construction of a national 'firewall' is one option to limit the flow of unwanted political ideas from foreign countries. China Internet Corporation (CIC) was established in Hong Kong in late 1995 as an Internet Services Provider (ISP) partially owned by the Xinhua News Agency, the official news reporting agency in China (Clark and Sviokla, 1996). CIC wanted to become the business information gateway between China and any foreign countries, with the network operating as a form of Intranet within China that provided a "firewall" to the public Internet of the outside world. Xinhua argued that control of information was very important in China and that their role as the official new agency was an excellent fit with the needs of the nation for controlling Internet access and content within China. CIC proposed to develop an Internet services network across China dedicated to the needs of business (Clark and Sviokla, 1996). However, the stated goals of information censorship and control resulted in one cartoonist for the Financial Times describing the CIC service as "an information superhighway without the information" (Beave, 1995). In early 1996, the efforts by the State Council to limit access to the Internet and strengthen controls over international information links and flows seemed to fit well with this "firewall" strategy of CIC for Internet development in China (Crothall, 1996). However, the importance of the Internet for businesses, including the businesses of other government Ministries, was sufficient to overcome these efforts to limit access and information. By the end of 1996, most of these government controls and restrictions had been lifted, or, at least, were generally ignored by businesses in China.

CIC was never strongly accepted by the business sector in China, but the problem was not one of political censorship. Censorship and government control of information are generally assumed and accepted in China. CIC's problem was that it was unable to compete cost effectively with the MPT and MEI Internet service offerings. Both MPT and MEI were much more concerned about competing with each other than with the need to control information flows within China. After all, information censorship was the responsibility of Xinhua and of other agencies, not of MPT or MEI. They were happy to cooperate with Xinhua, but not if this resulted in higher costs that might leave them less cost competitive than their domestic infrastructure rivals. In addition, neither MPT nor MEI wanted to allow Xinhua to control the future of China's rapidly growing Internet market.

In addition to Xinhua, other Ministries also began offering their own Internet access services, and some private companies began offering connections to the Internet as well. Most of these private ISPs were essentially just reselling bulk access to the Internet provided by the MPT or MEI, but they were able to resell these services as dial-up connections (e.g. using a modem to call the ISP instead of having a direct private line or packet switched line connection). Since the MPT and MEI were both more focused on selling Internet services to business customers, they were willing to provide dedicated connections to these ISP resellers, who then offered dial-up services at very attractive prices to consumers and smaller business customers.

These competitive ISPs often operated without any official license, and would occasionally be shut down by the government (*Asian Wall Street Journal*, 1996). However, the smaller ISPs continued to grow due to the high demand for Internet services from both businesses and consumers and because of the very attractive prices that they were able to offer for these potential customers. The official price of an Internet connection from the MPT in 1996 was $75 USD per month (Lovelock, Petrazzini and Clark, 1996). By 1999, intense competition had reduced the price for dial-up Internet connection to $40 USD per month from the MII and $12 USD per month from some of the smaller ISP resellers.

Internet users in China in early 1999 are estimated at 2.1 million users with 1.2 million Internet accounts and 400,000 dedicated leased-line connections to the Internet (Leung, 1999). Many accounts in China are used by multiple users due to the high cost of Internet services (even $12 USD per month is a lot of money for most Chinese families). Even though the cost of services is still expensive relative to average income in China, the usage of the Internet is expanding at almost 20% per month in China from 1996 to 1998, and Yahoo believes that China could eventually represent 20% of the global Internet market, with some industry experts projecting China will have more than 280 million Internet users by the year 2010 (Leung, 1999).

However, there is still a battle within China over economic development and information control. The Internet is enabling government ministries to better access to information to manage and govern the nation. At the same time, political activism is increasing as well, and the Internet is perceived as a destabilising force within China. In a speech on 23 December 1998, President Jiang Zemin threatened computer programmers as well as artists and writers with stiff jail sentences if they "endangered state security." Public crackdowns on cyber-dissidents have attracted lots of attention internationally and are an indication that the Internet has been taken seriously as a threat and a destabilising force in China. Even so, usage of the Internet continues to expand rapidly and there are no expectations that China will pull the plug on its Internet connection.

The continuing growth in Internet usage, in spite of government restrictions on access and policing of emails and WWW usage patterns, actually has little to do with the political or free speech aspects of the Internet. Political dissidents and hackers create a lot of noise and international interest, but the fundamental driver of Internet growth in China is that the Internet has becoming increasingly important for businesses in China as they compete in a global economy.

Since international telecommunications costs are still very high in China, multi-national and domestic firms have learned to use the Internet extensively to reduce the costs of communications with trading partners. In addition, the use of the WWW and transmission of images as email attachments have enabled firms in China to provide services to customers worldwide and to overcome the disadvantages of being across the world from their customers.

For example, one firm has been able to use image transmission of clothing offered by its customers' competitors to create local prototype clones of these fashion apparel items. The firm can then model these cloned apparel items to prospective customers on the WWW within a day of receiving the initial transmission of a competing fashion offering. The entire transaction of receiving the image of a competing product to prototype modelling and even buyer order of the product specified can take place without any physical interaction between buyer and manufacturer. For an electronics equipment manufacturer, receiving electronic and physical computer drawings of plastic and electronic part specification via the

WWW has enabled them to reduce response time for orders from overseas customers by as much as a week, which can be critical in the fast moving consumer electronic market. For more and more firms, doing business on the Internet has become a vital part of business operations.

In the early days of China's economic development into a free market economy, business managers used to say that if you built a road into a village, economic development would follow. In the 1990s, this saying was amended to state that if you could get a telephone into a village, the businesses would come and they would get the road built. Today, if you can get a telephone and a link to the global Internet community via dial-up connection, you can start doing business globally even before the road gets built. For example, some manufacturers in central China were once considered too far away from a major airport to be viable partners or suppliers for multi-national firms, as their executives would have to spend too much time travelling to get to the city where these firms are located.

Today, firms that are far from major airports are able to communicate with their customers and partners through WWW connections and have been able to largely overcome the barriers of distance for connecting to their suppliers. This has become especially important as the labour cost differential has increased between the major areas of economic development and the more rural interior and western cities of China. For the textile manufacturer that receives design images from its customers and then shows models wearing the prototypes on the WWW, this is critical because their location is more than five hours away from the nearest major airport. This means that they would be at a serious disadvantage in getting buyers to see their products and capabilities when a physical visit to the factory was required, but in the electronic commerce environment, they are as close as the factory next door and more responsive as well.

Thus, electronic commerce is alive and well in China, and doing business on the Internet is one of the primary reasons for the fast growth of the Internet in China. At the same time, we are not likely to see much development in retail electronic commerce in China until 2002 or beyond. There are several reasons for the slower development of the consumer WWW market in China. First, much of the Internet information is still in English, which is not commonly spoken in China. Second, there is little tradition of any form of mail order or indirect sales of goods in China. Quality is often poor for goods, so consumers want to be able to physically see and inspect the products they buy. There is little recourse for buyers who have been cheated, although laws in China have recently been passed to protect consumers. This situation should improve over the next five years. Finally, in China, income levels for consumers are still limited, and a large portion of most families' income is spent on essential goods and services. The Internet is not as useful a tool for shopping for basic necessities as it is for finding interesting, but non-essential, luxuries.

However, there are many applications where consumers in China are actually business producers as well. The official government estimate of the total number of businesses in China is more than 300 million businesses, including every family farm and street vendor as an independent business. Since agriculture is still a major source of employment in China and the Internet can provide access to pricing on goods in other regional markets within China, there is a lot of interest in Internet access, even in remote farming villages. There is a real possibility of cybermarkets developing across China for small businesses that use the technology to overcome the barriers of distance even within the nation (Clark and Sviokla, 1996).

In summary, electronic commerce is alive and well in China. The retail market has not yet developed in any substantial way, but business-to-business usage of the WWW is enabling firms in China to compete effectively in the global marketspace (Rayport and Sviokla, 1994).

CHAPTER 18

An Action Research Report of an E-Commerce Firm in South Korea

OOK LEE

18.1. Introduction

This chapter describes an aspect of electronic commerce; that is, advertising in South Korea. Since South Korea is a developing country, its national IT infrastructure is not developed sufficiently to support all aspects of electronic commerce as in developed countries such as the USA. Nevertheless, there are many new organisations that are trying to do business in cyberspace in South Korea. Firstly, this chapter introduces the IT environment of South Korea and the inevitable choice of direct e-mail advertising as a chief marketing tool for these cyber businesses. Secondly, the action research method used in this research, the inevitable choice of this particular research method, is described. Thirdly, the attitude towards direct e-mail advertising by end-users of cyberspace in South Korea is identified by presenting the results of an online survey with intensive interviews and a simple questionnaire, which was conducted by the action researcher as a part of the action research plan. The analysis is done qualitatively, largely due to the small sample size. Lastly, a South Korean firm's struggle to implement and run a direct e-mail system is chronicled based on the observation of the action researcher. This example shows that, in a country with a less developed IT infrastructure, there are a lot of pitfalls for an e-commerce company to overcome in order to succeed.

18.2. National IT Infrastructure and Electronic Commerce

It is obvious that an e-commerce business in a developed country would be different from one in a less developed country. Here, "development" refers mainly to the level of national IT infrastructure development. National IT infrastructure can be defined as the vision of broadband communications that are interoperable as if a single network, easily accessible, widely distributed to all groups within a society that brings business, education, and government services directly to households, and that facilitates peer-to-peer communication within the society (Kraemer et al., 1996). This idealistic vision, however, is hard to achieve for countries with less economic resources. Nevertheless, South Korea embarked on building its national IT infrastructure in 1994 which was officially called the "Korea Information Infrastructure (KII)" project (Jeong and King, 1996). The Korean government committed itself to promoting industries such as computer makers, telecommunication network builders, value-added service providers, multimedia firms, cable TV industries, and Internet-related companies. Since all these projects could not succeed without a substantial investment and consumer demand, the recession, which started in 1994, halted all these initiatives. With the current economic hardship situation, the South Korean government's ambitious plan needs to wait until it sees the fruits of its investment.

In the meantime, e-commerce firms in South Korea have to struggle with a national IT infrastructure which is not yet adequate for effective commercial activity. The following are aspects of e-commerce in a developing country which need to be addressed:

1. *How to create a sustainable e-commerce venture with a less developed national IT infrastructure.* Effective e-commerce activity requires a well-developed national information technology infrastructure, such as well-connected fibre optic computer networks that cover the entire country, easily available computers, and an affordable cost of network use among ordinary citizens of the country. Until now, there has been no attempt to address the difficulties facing e-commerce activities in those less developed IT infrastructure-based countries which, in fact, comprises much of the world. Before the rest of the world is wired as much as the USA, those firms that try to conduct business through the Internet will face different and difficult challenges compared to their counterparts in developed nations.

2. *How to conduct marketing for the venture.* Not only is it very difficult to establish a functioning e-commerce firm, it is even more difficult to market on the Internet. The product of an e-commerce firm is usually advertised in banner-style advertisements on Web pages, which are common and are considered to be a working solution in developed countries. However, in less developed countries such as South Korea, few people are surfing the Internet. The number of people who can afford to surf the Internet for a lengthy time is limited due to the outdated practice of the government-owned monopolistic phone company. Thus, in this environment, an e-commerce company that wants to sell a tangible product, such as computer hardware components or software items, has no choice but to create a Web page to sell those products and face the problem of how to advertise their Web pages to the small number of Web surfers in Korea. Furthermore, those e-commerce companies that sell intangible goods face an even more difficult challenge in advertising their products. In short, any e-commerce company in Korea faces the same problem in marketing; that is, how to advertise effectively in an environment in which there are only a small number of people using the Internet. Fortunately, e-commerce companies have found a way to penetrate the cyber-market through direct e-mail advertising. This direct e-mail advertising campaign is particularly useful for e-commerce companies that cannot afford their own Web page for commerce but it could cause a serious backlash from consumers who think

that their privacy is violated. However, an empirical study conducted to identify consumer attitudes toward direct e-mail advertisements, presented later in this chapter, shows that they are somewhat effective and do not cause such a serious negative reaction as in the USA.

3. *How to establish a workable payment method.* This matter is a serious obstacle in the development of e-commerce, even in developed countries such as the USA, since consumers are worried that their credit card numbers might be stolen or they may not get the ordered goods after payment. In less developed countries, such as South Korea, the consumers are, of course, worried when they order a product online; not because of the possibility that their credit card numbers might be stolen, but because the cash they have already paid might be stolen, i.e. the goods might never arrive. The reason is simple. In a less developed country like South Korea, many people do not have credit cards and, even those who do, prefer to pay in cash for low-priced goods. For this reason, most online payment is made as follows. Firstly, the customer goes to the bank and arranges a wire-transfer of cash to the designated bank account of the vendor, which is an e-commerce firm. Secondly, the firm's employee goes to the bank to verify if a certain customer's cash was transferred. Lastly, if the money transfer is confirmed, the firm sends the goods that were ordered by the customer. With this kind of payment method, consumers are naturally worried since, in actual incidents, some firms took the money and ran, i.e. the goods that were paid for never arrived.

18.3. Action Research as a Research Method

I chose to conduct this research on the effectiveness of a direct e-mail advertising business by using the action research method since I was asked to be a technical advisor to the firm on a contract basis. That is, I was to conduct the feasibility test and give continuing advice on the implementation of the direct mail system and its maintenance. Action researchers can take into account the full richness of organisational interactions (Kock, 1997). Action research studies are characterised by the researcher applying positive intervention to the client organisation, while collecting field data about the organisation (Lewin, 1946; Peters and Robinson, 1984; Jonsonn, 1991). This characteristic of action research provided a particularly solid ground for my decision to use action research method in this study. I have tried to follow the model established by Susman and Evered (1978) in which the action research comprises five stages: diagnosing, action planning, action taking, evaluating, and specifying learning. During the diagnosing stage, I conducted a survey of online consumers in order to assess the feasibility of a direct e-mail advertising business. During the action planning and action taking stages, I recommended that the firm should implement the DM system and I oversaw the implementation process. During the evaluating and specifying learning stages, I evaluated the performance of the firm. This resulted in many problems which, in turn, became valuable sources for how to conduct e-commerce in South Korea.

18.4. Cyberspace Consumers

As many firms throughout the world try to conduct business on the Internet, the importance of marketing on the Internet has become an important issue to IS scholars and practitioners alike (Copfer, 1998). Some businesses are interested in setting up a Web site to expand their reach to customers in addition to the physical entity in the real world, whereas others try to establish a presence on the Internet without having any physical entity in the real world. In both cases, firms need to conduct marketing research in order to solve vexing questions such as who the customers are and how to advertise effectively (Mosley, 1998).

In this chapter, I define those consumers who are using the Internet and/or an online information provider, such as America Online, as cyberspace consumers. Cyberspace consumers are attractive targets for almost all kinds of products. More and more people are spending their waking hours surfing the Internet, which means that companies should advertise in this medium since the consumers' precious attention span is being used here just as in TV and radio.

Thus, how to advertise effectively in cyberspace has become a very important issue. To advertise effectively, a business should choose the right kind of tool in order to reach enough customers with a reasonable amount of time and money. Direct e-mailing has attracted attention from businesses or individuals who are interested in finding an inexpensive advertising tool on the Internet (Allen, 1998). However, this tool has some negative side effects, such as violation of privacy, which can result in a consumer boycott of the product, not to mention the possible legal restrictions imposed on this kind of advertising. Given these concerns, I advised my client firm that unless there was empirical evidence indicating the effectiveness of direct e-mail advertising, the firm should not use it. So, I investigated attitudes toward direct e-mail advertising with an empirical study of users of a South Korean online service (Chollian Service) using the qualitative methods of intensive interviews and a simple questionnaire. The results reveal how cyberspace consumers feel about direct e-mail advertising

18.5. Internet Business Marketing

Many businesses now have Web pages which were made for a variety of purposes. For example, big corporations created Web pages to promote a corporate image; thus, these Web sites are not for trading goods and services. On the other hand, some firms created Web sites for the purpose of selling goods and services, such as books, computers, flowers, etc. Among them some exist only on Web sites, i.e. no physical entity exists, while others have physical entities with Web sites used for additional business from cyberspace consumers. Except for corporations that created Web sites for public relations purposes, all other Web sites are engaged in a profit-making venture, which consequently needs sophisticated marketing strategies and tools (Hansen, 1998). Thus, Internet marketing can be defined as a marketing strategy and tool that is designed to enhance product purchase on the Internet.

Cyberspace consumers have some distinctive characteristics compared to real-world consumers. The main difference is that cyberspace consumers choose only the

Web sites of interest to them, which means that unlike TV, radio or print advertising, it is difficult to promote a product to unsuspecting mass customers. In other words, people who are interested in adult-related products will go to those Web sites without wandering into some other Web sites like one selling flowers. Thus, making people aware of the existence of particular Web sites, even though they are not of interest to the consumer at the moment, is not easy. There are some technological breakthroughs, such as PUSH technology, which do provide Web site information to the consumer who seems to have a potential interest in a particular area (Burke, 1997). But even with PUSH technology, one can only push things after the information regarding the customer's behavior is gathered. Thus, with many thousands signing up on the Internet every day, the PUSH technology has its limits.

Nowadays, Internet advertising is often done with banner advertisements which take a small space on a Web page and are supposedly noticeable and, hopefully, actually read. But banner advertisements can only appear on Web pages that a particular consumer reads, i.e. if a Web site is not visited by consumers then the advertisement becomes simply obsolete. There has to be a better way to market a product on the Internet in order to reach more people, possibly in mass numbers.

18.6. Direct E-Mail Advertising as a Tool for Internet Marketing

Direct e-mail advertising can be a good solution to the problem that banner advertisements cannot reach mass customers. Direct and bulk e-mailing literally means sending bulk or a mass number of e-mails directly to unsuspecting cyberspace consumers (Gustavson, 1997). The product that is advertised by direct e-mail can be anything. This means that, unlike PUSH technology, which advertises only products considered to be of interest to consumers whose online browsing behavior is known, direct e-mail advertising can send promotion messages for any product to almost anybody who has an e-mail address. Thus, direct and bulk e-mailing is more or less similar to direct marketing in real-world shopping. In direct marketing, shoppers are either called or sent so-called junk mail by the direct marketer.

Some merits of direct e-mail advertising are as follows:

1. Unlike direct marketing, which can be expensive, the cost of bulk e-mailing is very low since sending e-mail to any number of people in the world does not cost a dime, at least for the use of the communication line. In other words, Internet communication is free. All the firm has to pay is a local phone bill and, if the firm does not own a server, the Internet service provider, which charges by the time spent online not by the number of e-mail messages. (Sometimes, Internet service providers charge just a flat fee per time period, say per month.)

2. E-mail can cause a direct response from consumers since, unlike junk mail in real world marketing, people tend to read e-mail, even those that are advertising (Martin, 1998). Junk mail can be thrown out without even considering what the content could be but junk or spam e-mail is harder to delete without reading. Most people tend to read e-mail before they delete it. Once they read it, the information which is contained in the e-mail

advertisement can be very effective in terms of getting attention from a potential customer.

But bulk e-mailing has its negative side effects. For example, unsolicited e-mail can be considered a violation of privacy and can be considered unlawful. Some states in the USA have already banned unsolicited e-mail (Markoff, 1998; Wang, 1998). Thus, potential consumers can be discouraged from buying the product which was advertised due to negative feelings toward unsolicited e-mail advertising.

18.7. An Empirical Example: South Korean Survey

A survey of users of Chollian, a South Korean online service firm, was conducted. This firm provides information on entertainment, business, education, news, etc. to online subscribers as well as providing Internet accounts. The total number of subscribers is estimated to be two million and fees are paid in proportion to the amount of online time spent by the user. This service is now clogged by unsolicited direct bulk e-mail which advertises all types of products, such as videotapes, computers, books, etc. The main reason for the recent boom in junk e-mail is the fact that several small companies started to operate as direct bulk e-mailers for anyone who wanted to advertise to online subscribers of the Chollian service. These firms charge by the number of e-mails, about USD20 per one million e-mails. Unlike some states in the USA, the government's position on this kind of advertising is not clear. It has a law against online fraud and sexual harassment but no specific law against spam mail (except that if an online service company's own computer becomes victimised by mail bombs, the police can arrest the mail bomber on the grounds of harming unlawfully an online service company's business).

I sent questionnaires to about 2,000 email addresses, of which 41 questionnaires were completed and returned by e-mail. The reason for the low response rate could be the fact that people have to use their online time to reply, which means there is a cost involved to answer questions that are not very beneficial for them. In addition, since this online survey was done via direct e-mailing, people could regard my questionnaire as just another junk advertisement and ignored it. Since 41 responses was too small a sample to be analysed quantitatively, I decided to conduct qualitative analysis by interviewing the respondents online. I sent a detailed follow-up letter to each respondent and they replied with detailed explanations. Sometimes, we met during an online chatting session and exchanged ideas. Thus, this result combines the questionnaire and intensive interviews with some cyberspace consumers in South Korea.

Following are the results of each question in the questionnaire.

1. *What is your attitude toward direct e-mail advertising in general?*
   (a) *Favourable*   *2%*
   (b) *Unfavourable*   *91%*
   (c) *Don't Care*   *7%*

It is clear that most people do not like this kind of advertising. People naturally find that their privacy is severely violated when an unknown party sends unsolicited e-mail to them.

2. *Have you ever been interested in a product or service because it was advertised in a direct e-mail?*
    (a) Yes   87% (please state your reasons)
    (b) No   13%

The most striking finding of this survey is the fact that even though most people object to direct e-mail advertising, they are still interested in the products that are advertised. After intensive interviews with the respondents, I realised that direct e-mail advertisements are actually read no matter how much they are disliked. By reading or just skimming e-mail advertisements, people find there are some items that are interesting or cheaper. However, this attitude did not lead to actual purchasing action, as shown in the next question.

3. *If you said yes in question 2, answer the following. Have you purchased a product or service that was advertised in a direct e-mail?*
    (a) Yes   5%
    (b) No   95% (please state your reasons)

It is clear that the interest generated by e-mail advertising did not make people buy the product. A few people actually purchased products such as computer software, hardware, compact disks, magazines, etc. (nothing was of very high value). After intensive interviews with the respondents, I discovered that the major reason that interest in the product did not lead to actual purchase was because of the payment method problem in South Korea. Few people use credit cards and even people who do use credit cards tend to prefer cash when it comes to paying for inexpensive products. The payment method in South Korea cyberspace is to transfer cash through a bank account and receive goods later, which of course makes the purchaser nervous about committing to buying on the Internet or online.

4. *Have you ever got any negative impression of a product or service because it was advertised in a direct e-mail?*
    (a) Yes   12% (please state your reasons)
    (b) No   88%

Surprisingly, people answered that they got a negative impression of the product only because it was advertised in direct e-mail. After intensive interviews with respondents, I realised that there had been quite a few incidents of fraud in this kind of commerce activity due to problems in payment and delivery, and these incidents were known widely through TV news and newspaper coverage. Therefore, it is natural that some people do not trust products advertised in direct e-mail.

18.8. Analysis of the Results

By conducting follow-up interviews through e-mail exchange and online chatting, I was able to gather in-depth reasons for their behaviour regarding direct e-mail advertising. The following is a summary of reasons for each behaviour.

The reasons why people were interested in the product:

1. The product or service was one that people were interested in buying anyway.
2. E-mail advertising informed of the otherwise unknown existence of a product or service, i.e. were it not for direct e-mail, people may not have known of the existence of the product or service.
3. The announcement of the product is timely, i.e. the product was a necessary item at that very moment.

The reasons why people got negative impressions of the product:

1. People feared that unsolicited e-mailers might be criminals trying to sell products with defects or with legal problems, such as stolen property.
2. People thought that the e-mail advertisement itself sounded too good to be true. A bargain that is too good makes people suspicious of the quality of the product.

The reasons why people would not take a purchase action even if they were interested in the product or service:

1. In South Korea, most people use not use credit cards so the usual payment method for online customers is through bank account transfer. In other words, the advertiser gives the bank account number to the prospective buyer who sends cash through a bank-to-bank wire system. This means purchasing an item involves a cumbersome payment mechanism, which can discourage potential customers to take actual purchase action.
2. People are afraid that even if they pay the price, the product might not be delivered. The potential for fraud is great and there are, in fact, many cases of such fraud because people do not use credit cards for transactions. If they did use a credit card and no product was delivered, the customer could challenge the transaction through the credit card company. In most online shopping cases in South Korea, cash is transferred through wire service which has no means of recovery.

18.9. A Direct E-mail Advertising Firm's Struggle

As indicated previously, after conducting an empirical study on the attitudes of consumers toward direct e-mail advertising, I recommended to the firm that the direct mail business plan should go ahead. At least I had found that people paid attention to e-mail advertising, which could be considered a good sign for an advertising firm. The first thing that the firm had to do was to develop a system to handle direct and bulk e-mailing for advertising. The firm decided to develop an information system that did so-called "direct bulk mailing", which is popular in the USA for advertising on the Internet. This kind of information system could be purchased with a hefty price from existing direct e-mail service companies. However, the firm thought that it could create its own direct e-mail system which could be superior to others that were used currently by direct e-mail service firms.

Thus, the firm decided to develop a direct e-mail system from scratch. The firm hired two programmers who were skilled in utilising the IYAGI communication software. This software is a kind of communication terminal emulator that works by connecting users to a host computer via a modem. IYAGI software has a facility that allows users to program functions of the communication emulator, such as making scripts for automatic dialling and inputting to the host computer. In other words, the hired programmers wrote IYAGI software scripts so that the communication software itself called and connected to the host computer and sent commands, such as writing a letter and e-mailing it. This communications program has been so popular among Korean Internet users that virtually all of them have a copy of this software.

The target audience for this direct e-mail advertising campaign was the users of commercial online services, such as Chollian, Hitel, and Unitel, which make up most of the online services in Korea. In Korea, those companies that provide Internet access only are not very popular due to high telephone fees (there is no unlimited local call rate in Korea). Thus, users of the Internet in Korea usually sign up for online information service providers, which are similar to America Online. These users are estimated to be over three million and, instead of cruising Internet Web sites, many users of these Information/Internet Service Providers (I/ISPs) are examining information items such as education, vacancies, adult information, and chatting services. Therefore, there are two ways to reach these users via e-mail. The first is to send e-mail that is local to that specific service, i.e. Chollian e-mail can be only sent to another Chollian users. The second is to send Internet e-mail to all the users of every major I/ISP. But, unfortunately, as was mentioned before, the government has passed a law to make it an offence to mass mail on the Internet. In other words, if one sends too many e-mails through the Internet to a certain I/ISP, such as Chollian, and Chollian feels that its service is being slowed down due to this massive mailing, it can report the incident to the government, which is empowered to arrest the mass Internet mailer.

For this reason, the firm chose the first option which was to develop mass mailers to each major I/ISP such as Chollian, Hitel, and Unitel. Since they could not use Internet mailing technique, they had to rely on the communication software IYAGI's script language. In other words, they programmed, using IYAGI script language, an automatic e-mail writing and sending procedure for specific I/ISPs such as Chollian. This project took three months to complete and working versions for three major I/ISPs were released in November 1997. The systems analysis and design were done by the founder of the firm who had extensive background in system development. The working version looked fine once the coding was done. It could send 10,000 e-mails per hour which was the theoretical limit on the performance of the direct mailer, i.e. performance of the direct mailer could be much slower depending on circumstances. In short, the whole system analysis, design and coding took about six months due to highly motivated employees who worked more than 12 hours a day. In December 1997, the service finally began to send out advertisements in a direct e-mail form.

The fatal mistake was that the firm never tried to test the system in extreme conditions such as periods of high traffic, which are typically between 7:00pm and 11:00pm. During these hours, the performance of the system drastically downgraded from 10,000 mails to 100 mails per hour. In other words, one of the most coveted characteristics of the firm's service was the fastest delivery of advertising and, due to the slowing down of the system, customers simply could not take advantage of it. Besides, people who did not like direct e-mail advertising started complaining about it to the authorities of these I/ISPs. Subsequently, the firm received warnings from the I/ISP administration, such as cutting off the firm's account permanently. The firm had to have an account with those I/ISPs because local mailing was only allowed for the users who had an account with that I/ISP. Furthermore, since the direct mailing was done via a modem and thus took a significant amount of telephone usage time, the telephone bill was mounting. The firm had to pay all those hours of modem usage without discount, which cost thousands of dollars per month.

After three months of operation, with about 1,000 clients, the firm had no choice but to scale down the operation due to financial burdens, such as a huge telephone bill, an I/ISP bill (the firm also had to pay for the online service fee since it needed its own account to send e-mail locally to the users of the service), and personnel costs (two programmers and one administrator). The I/ISP even threatened to launch a lawsuit against the firm, which was very similar to what America Online did with direct e-mail advertisers.

18.10. Lessons on Electronic Commerce in Developing Countries

The conclusions drawn from this action research could be applied in countries with less developed national IT infrastructure only. While being aware of the special situation in South Korea, the following points from this study can be highlighted:

1. Direct e-mail is effective since people are generally interested in products or services advertised, even though, in general, they do not like to see advertising in their e-mail accounts. But there is also a negative effect as people think their privacy is violated so advertised products could be unfairly ignored or not given full consideration. Direct bulk e-mail is at least working as a marketing tool in terms of getting people interested in products or services. However, this interest in products or services does not necessarily extend to purchasing, as shown in the evidence presented. This is largely due to the negative perception of direct e-mailers as potential law-breakers. This is quite understandable considering the anonymity of e-mailers and the pay-first-deliver-later payment method, which is the dominant method of online shopping payment in South Korea.

2. The difficulties that the subject firm faced while implementing its direct e-mail system indicates that inattentiveness to testing could cause serious harm for the success of an information system project. Testing should have

been done in all possible conditions, such as a heavy network traffic situation. The firm also should have tested how the cost accumulates as the system is being deployed and run. Often system coders ignore this important factor, which can result in abandoning the system even though it was correctly implemented. Unless there is thorough testing that involves endurance under extreme condition and cost accumulation, the success of the system can not be achieved.

Despite these concerns, when Korea's national IT infrastructure is more developed, the subject firm's chance of financial success can be easily foreseen.

18.11. Conclusion

Consumers who are surfing the Internet, defined in this chapter as cyberspace consumers, are good targets for any kind of advertising. It has been demonstrated that direct e-mail advertising can be used effectively as a tool for Internet marketing, even though legal and ethical issues create negative consequences. Despite the hostile attitude toward direct e-mail advertising, cyberspace consumers become interested in the product advertised by e-mail. However, due to a variety of reasons, very few purchases are actually made in South Korea. The reason for this is the inferior national IT infrastructure, which is vividly demonstrated by the direct mail firm's experience. The lessons from this firm's experiences can be applied to e-commerce activity in other countries with a less developed national IT infrastructure.

Bibliography

Abell, W. and Lim, L.: 1996, Business use of the Internet in New Zealand: An exploratory study, www.scu.edu.au/ausweb96/business/abell/paper.htm.

Ackerman, M. S. and Starr, B.: 1996, Social activity indicators for groupware, *IEEE Computer*, 29(6), 37-42.

Adam, N., Dogramaci, O., Gangopadhyay, A. and Yesha, Y.: 1998, *Electronic Commerce: Technical, Business, and Legal Issues*, Prentice Hall, New York.

Adam, N., Gangopadhyay, A. and Holowczak, R.: 1998, A survey on research on database protection, *Proceedings of the Conference on Statistical Data Protection*, January.

Adam, N. and Jones, D.: 1989, Security of statistical databases with an output perturbation technique, *Journal of Management Information Systems*, 6(1).

Alba, J. W. and Chattopadhyay, A.: 1985, Effects of context and post-category cues on recall of competing brands, *Journal of Marketing Research*, 22(August), 340-349.

Alba, J. W. and Hutchinson, J. W.: 1987, Dimensions of consumer expertise, *Journal of Consumer Research*, 13(4), 411-454.

Alba, J. W., Lynch, J., Weitz, B., Janiszewski, C., Lutz, R., Sawyer, A. and Wood, S.: 1997, Interactive home shopping: Incentives for consumers, retailers, and manufacturers to participate in electronic marketplaces, *Journal of Marketing*, 61(3), 38-53.

Allen, L.: 1998, Using the Internet can augment advertising and marketing, *Austin Business Journal*, 30 January, 17(48).

Allport, A. D.: 1989, Visual attention, *in* M. I. Posner (ed.), *Foundations of Cognitive Science*, MIT Press, Cambridge, MA.

Anderson, P. M. and Rubin, L. G.: 1986, *Marketing Communications*, Prentice Hall, Englewood Cliffs, NJ.

Applehans, W., Laugero, G. and Globe, A.: 1998, *Managing Knowledge: A Practical Guide to Internet-Based Knowledge Management*, Addison Wesley, New York.

Asian Wall Street Journal, 1996: China takes superhighway less traveled on Internet, 1 February.

Attewell, P. and Rule, J.: 1984, Computing and organizations, *Commmunications of the ACM*, 27, 1184-92.

Auger, P. and Gallagher, J. M.: 1997, Factors affecting the adoption of an Internet-based sales presence for small businesses, The Information Society, 13(1), 55-74.

Baecker, R. and Small, I.: 1990, Animation at the interface, *in* B. Laurel (ed.), *The Art of Human-Computer Interface Design*, Addison Wesley, pp. 251-267.

Bagozzi, R. P.: 1980, *Causal Models in Marketing*, Wiley, New York.

Bailyn, L.: 1989, Towards the perfect workplace? *Communications of the ACM*, 32(4), 460-71.

Bakos, Y. J.: 1997, Reducing buyer search costs: Implications for electronic marketplaces, *Management Science*, December.

Barker, N., Fuller, T. and Jenkins, A.: 1997, Small firms experiences with the Internet. *Proceedings of the 20th ISBA National Conference*, Belfast, Northern Ireland.

Barker, N.: 1994, The Internet as a Reach Generator for Small Business, Unpublished Masters Thesis, Business School, University of Durham (September).

Barner, R.: 1996, The new millenium workplace: Seven changes that will challenge managers and workers, *Futurist,* 30(2), 14-18.

Baroudi, J. and Orlikowski, W.: 1993, A short-form measure of user information satisfaction: A psychometric evaluation and notes on use, *Journal of MIS,* 4(4), 44-59.

Barret, M., Drummond, A. and Sahay, S.: 1996, Exploring the impact of cross-cultural differences in international software teams: Indian expatriates in Jamaica, *in* J. D. Coelho et al. (eds), *ECIS Proceedings of the European Conference on Information Systems,* pp. 347-356.

Bauer, C.: 1998, *Internet und WWW für Banken,* Gabler, Wiesbaden.

Bauer, C.: 1998, Using reference models to develop WWW-based applications, *Proceedings of the 9th Australasian Conference on Information Systems (ACIS '98),* University of New South Wales, Sydney, Australia, pp. 14-25.

Bauer, C. and Scharl, A.: 1999, Acquisition and symbolic visualization of aggregated customer information for analyzing Web Information Systems, *Proceedings of the 32nd Hawaiian International Conference on System Sciences (HICSS-32),* Maui, USA.

Baum, M. S. and Perrit, H. H.: 1991, *Electronic Contracting, Publishing and EDI Law,* Wiley, New York.

Beach, L. R.: 1993, Broadening the definition of decision making: The role of pre-choice screening of options, *Psychological Science,* 4(4), 215-220.

Beach, L. R. and Mitchell, T. R.: 1978, A contingency model for the selection of decision strategies, *Academy of Management Review,* 3, 439-449.

Beach, L. R. and Potter, R. E.: 1992, The pre-choice screening of alternatives, *Acta Psychologica,* 81, 115-126.

Beatty, S. E. and Smith, S. M.: 1987, External search effort: An investigation across several product categories, *Journal of Consumer Research,* 14(1), 83-95.

Beave, R.: 1995, Cartoon for article, Net for China: No smut, no politics, no decadent culture, *Financial Times,* 10 July.

Beck, L. L.: 1980, A security mechanism for statistical databases, *ACM Transactions on Database Systems,* 5(3).

Bellovin, R.: 1989, Security problems in the TCP/IP protocol suite, *Computer Communications Review,* 19(2), 32-48.

Bellovin, R. and Cheswick, W.: 1994, *Firewalls and Internet Security.*

Beniger, J. R.: 1986, *The Control Revolution: Technological and Economic Origins of the Information Society,* Harvard University Press, Cambridge, MA.

Beninati, M. D.: 1994, Vision for the new millenium, *Discount Merchandiser,* 34(May), 46-47.

Benjamin, R. and Wigand, R.: 1995, Electronic markets and virtual value chains on the information superhighway, *Sloan Management Review,* 36(2), 62-72.

Berger, M.: 1996, Making the virtual office a reality: Sales and marketing management, *SMT Supplement,* June, pp. 18-22.

Bernard, R.: 1996, *The Corporate Intranet: Create and Manage an Internal Web for your Organization,* Wiley, New York.

Bettman, J. R.: 1979, *An Information Processing Theory of Consumer Choice*, Addison Wesley, Reading, MA.

Bettman, J. R., Johnson, E. J. and Payne, J. W.: 1991, Consumer decision making, *in* T. S. Robertson and H. H. Kassarjian (eds), *Handbook of Consumer Behaviour*, Prentice Hall, Englewood Cliffs, NJ, pp. 50-84.

Bhimani, A.: 1996, Securing the commercial Internet, *Communications of the ACM*, 39(6), 29-35.

Bibby, A.: 1995, *Teleworking: Thirteen Journeys to the Future of Work*, Calouste Gulbenkian Foundation, London.

Bichler, M. and Nusser, S.: 1996a, W3DT – The structured way of developing WWW-sites, *Proceedings of the 4th European Conference on Information Systems*, Lisbon, Portugal, pp. 1093-1101.

Bichler, M. and Nusser, S.: 1996b, Modular design of complex Web-applications with W3DT, *Proceedings of the 5th Workshops on Enabling Technologies: Infrastructure for Collaborative Enterprises (WET ICE '96)*, Stanford, USA, pp. 328-333.

Biggs, S. F., Bedard, J. C., Gaber, B. G. and Linsmeier, T. J.: 1985, The effects of task size and similarity on the decision making behaviour of bank loan officers, *Management Science*, 31(8), 970-987.

Bitner, M. and Hubbert, A.: 1990, Encounter satisfaction versus overall satisfaction quality, *in* R. Rust and R. Oliver (eds), *Service Quality: New Directions in Theory and Practice*, Sage, London, pp. 72-91.

BITS, Open Financial Exchange and Integrion: 1998, BITS, Publishers of Open Financial Exchange and GOLD Team Announce Timetable for the Publication of Converged Specification, Press Release, Washington, USA, 7 April, www.ofx.net/ofx/pressget.asp?id=17 (01/99), www.integrion.com/news/story040798.html (01/99).

Bloch, M., Pigneur, Y. and Sergev, A.: 1996, Leveraging electronic commerce for competitive advantage: A business value framework, *Proceedings of the 9th International Conference on EDI-IOS*, Bled, Slovenia.

Boland, R .J., Tenkasi, R. and Te'eni Dov: 1994, Designing information technology to support distributed cognition, *Organization Science*, 5(3), 456-475.

Booz, Allen and Hamilton: 1996, Consumer Demand for Internet Banking, New York, USA.

Borok, L. S.: 1997, Data mining: Sophisticated forms of managed care modeling through artificial intelligence: Review, *Journal of Health Care Finance*, 23(3), 20-36.

Bosco, P.: 1995, Branchless banking: First direct holds the phones, *Bank Systems and Technology*, 26-27 November.

Bradley, S. P. and Hausman, J. A.: 1989, Future Competition in Telecommunications, *Harvard Business School Press*, Boston, MA.

Bressand, A. and Distler, C.: 1995, *La Planete Relationelle*, Flammarion, Paris.

Brislin, R.W. and Yoshida, T.: 1994, Improving Intercultural Interactions, Sage, Thousand Oaks, CA.

Brookes, C.: 1996, Gaining Competitive Advantage Through Knowledge Management, www.gvt.com/gaining.htm.

Brucks, M.: 1985, The effects of product class knowledge on information search behaviour, *Journal of Consumer Research*, 15, 117-121.

Brynjolfsson, E.: 1993, The productivity paradox of information technology, *Communications of the ACM*, 36(December).

Burke, R.: 1997, Do you see what I see? The future of virtual shopping, *Journal of the Academy of Marketing Science*, 25(4).

Burn, J. M., Marshall, P. and Wild, M.: 1999a, The emperor has no clothes: Time to address the virtual organisation, paper presented at the *Information Researchers Management Association Conference (IRMA99) on Managing Information Technology Resources in Organisations in the Next Millennium*, 16-19 May, Hershey, PA

Burn, J. M., Marshall, P. and Wild, M.: 1999b, Managing change in the virtual organisation, paper presented at the *7th European Conference on Information Systems: Information Systems and Change (ECIS'99)*, 23-25 June, Copenhagen Business School, Denmark.

Business Week: 1997, A census in Cyberspace: World Wide Web, 3 years old, now has 40 mil users, almost enough to attract enough advertising and sponsors to support the Internet, 5 May.

Byrne, J.: 1993, The virtual corporation, *Business Week*, pp. 36-41.

California: 1997a, California Government Code §16.5, www.ss.ca.gov/digsig/ code165.htm.

California: 1997b, California Secretary of State: Final Draft of California Digital Signature Regulations, 18 November (www.ss.ca.gov/digsig/finalregs.htm).

Campbell, D. T. and Fiske, D. W.: 1959, Convergent and discriminant validity by the multitrait-multimethod matrix, *Psychological Bulletin*, 56, 81-105.

Carroll, J. M.: 1997, Human-computer interaction: Psychology as a science of design, *Annual Review of Psychology*, 48, 61-83.

Caudill, E.: 1997, *Darwinian Myths – The Legends and Misuses of a Theory*, University of Tennessee Press, Knoxville, USA.

CCITT: 1988, Recommendations X.509, *The Directory - Authentification Framework*.

Chaiken, S.: 1980, Heuristic versus systematic information processing and the use of source versus message cues in persuasion, *Journal of Personality and Social Psychology*, 39(November), 752-766.

Chesbrough, H. W. and Teece D. J.: 1996, When is virtual virtuous? *Harvard Business Review*, January-February, pp. 65-73.

Chin, F. Y. and Ozsoyoglu, G.: 1979, Security in partitioned dynamic statistical databases, *Proceedings of the IEEE COMPSAC Conference*, pp. 594-601.

Choi, S., Stahl, D. O. and Whinston, A. B.: 1998, Intermediation, contracts and micro-payments in electronic commerce, *International Journal of Electronic Markets*, 8(1), 20-22.

Churchill, G. A.: 1979, A paradigm for developing better measures of marketing constructs, *Journal of Marketing Research*, 16, 64-73.

Clark, T. E., and Sviokla, J.: 1996, China Internet Corporation, *Case Paper*, Hong Kong University of Science and Technology, 20 March, No. 9-39601, pp. 1-19

Clark, T. H., Lovelock, P. and Petrazzini, B. A.: 1996, China's golden projects: Re-engineering the national economy, *Case Paper*, Hong Kong University of Science and Technology, 1 March, No. 9-39602, pp. 1-19

CMP: 1998, *Intranet Trends: Second Wave*, CMP Media Inc., Enterprise Consulting Group, New York.

Computer Industry Almanac, www.c-I-a.com, 10 February 1999.

Cook, T. D. and Campbell, D. T.: 1979, *Quasi-Experimentation: Design and Analysis Issues for Field Settings*, Houghton Mifflin, Boston.

Cope, N.: 1996, *Retail in the Digital Age*, Bowerdean, London.

Copfer, R.: 1998, Marketing in an online world, *American Salesman*, 43(3).

Cowe, R.: 1998, Bringing home the bacon, *The Guardian*, 10 October, p. 26.

Coxe, W.: 1980, *Marketing Architectural Service and Engineering Service*, Wiley, New York, USA.

Cragg, P. B.: 1998, Clarifying Internet strategy in small firms, *Proceedings of the 9th Australasian Conference on Information Systems, Vol. 1,* Sydney, Australia, pp. 98-107.

Cronin, J. and Taylor, S.: 1992, Measuring quality service: Re-examination and extension, *Journal of Marketing*, July, 55-66.

Cronin, M. J.: 1994, *Doing Business on the Internet: How the Electronic Highway is Transforming American Companies*, International Thomson Publishing, NY, USA.

Cronin, M. J.: 1998, Ford's intranet success, *Fortune*, 137(6), 158-159.

Crothall, G.: 1996, Beijing moves to take control of Internet access, *South China Morning Post*, 24 January, Hong Kong.

DAS: 1997, *Digital Signature Act*, Article 3, Information and Communication Services Act, Bonn, www.iid.de/rahmen/iukdgebt.html.

Dasgupta, S.: 1998, Electronic contracting in online stock trading, *International Journal of Electronic Markets*, 8(3), 20-23.

Davenport, T.H. and Prusak, L.: 1998, *Working Knowledge: How Organizations Manage What They Know*, Harvard Business School Press, Boston, MA.

Davidow, W. H. and Malone, M. S.: 1992, *The Virtual Corporation*, Harper Business, New York.

Davidson, P.: 1998, On-line ads beginning to click: AOL's sales blossom in growing trend, *USA Today*, Arlington, 24 February.

Davis, S. M. and Davidson, B.: 1991, *2020 Vision*, Simon & Schuster, New York.

Degeratu, A., Rangaswamy, A. and Wu, J.: 1998, Consumer choice behaviour in online and regular stores: The effects of brand name, price, and other search attributes, *Working Paper*.

Denning, D. E.: 1980, Secure statistical databases with random sample queries, *ACM Transactions on Database Systems*, 5(3).

Denning, D. E., Denning, P. J. and Schwartz, M.D.: 1979, The tracker: A threat to statistical database security, *ACM Transactions on Database Systems*, 4(1).

Denning, D. E., Schlorer, J. and Wehrle, E.: 1982, Memoryless inference control for statistical databases, *Technical Report*, Purdue University.

Dertouzos, M.: 1999, The rich people's computer, *Technology Review*, www.techreview.com/articles/jan99/dertouzos.htm, January-February.

Devlin, J. F.: 1995, Technology and innovation in retail banking distribution, *International Journal of Bank Marketing*, 13(4), 19-25.

Dienes, B.: 1997, *WiNS'97 Final Report*, Centre for Community and Enterprise Networking, University College of Cape Breton, Sydney, NS.

Doll, W. and Torkzadeh, G.: 1988, The measurement of end-user computing satisfaction, *MIS Quarterly*, June, 259-274.

Dommel, H.-P. and Garcia-Luna-Aceves J. J.: 1997, Floor control for multimedia conferencing and collaboration, *Multimedia Systems*, 5, 23-38.

Downs, A.: 1961, A theory of consumer efficiency, *Journal of Retailing*, 39(Spring), 6-12.

Dratva, R.: 1994, WWW-based home banking services in Switzerland: A case study, *Proceedings of the 2nd International World Wide Web (WWW) Conference: Mosaic and the Web*, Chicago, USA.

Dreyfuss, J.: 1998, A new world - New options, *Money.com,* 1(1), 16-20.

Driver, J. and Baylis, G.: 1989, Movement and visual attention: The spotlight metaphor breaks down, *Journal of Experimental Psychology: Human Perception and Performance*, 15(3), 448-456.

Dugger, W. M.: 1993, Transaction cost economics and the state, *in* C. Pitelis (ed.), *Transaction Costs, Markets and Hierarchies*, Blackwell, Oxford and Cambridge, MA.

Duncan, C. and Olshavsky, R.: 1982, External search: The role of consumer beliefs, *Journal of Marketing Research*, 19(February), 32-43.

Duncan, J.: 1984, Selective attention and the organization of visual information, *Journal of Experimental Psychology: General*, 113(4), 501-517.

Eccles, R. G. and Nolan, R. L.: 1993, A Framework for the design of the emerging global organizational structure, *in* S. P. Bradley, J. A. Hausman, R. L. Nolan (eds), *Globalization, Technology and Competition: The Fusion of Computers and Telecommunications in the 1990s*, Harvard Business School Press, Boston, MA.

e-Commerce Times: 1999, Selling on the Internet: How to get started and how much does it cost?, www.ecommercetimes.com,

Ein-dor, P., Myers, D. M., and Raman,K. S.: 1997, Information technology in three small developed countries, *Journal of MIS*, 13(4), 61-89.

Ein-dor, P., Segev, E. and Orgad, M. 1993, The effect of national culture on IS: Implications for international information systems, *Journal of Global Information Management*, 1(1).

Eldredge, N.: 1995, *Reinventing Darwin: The Great Evolutionary Debate*, Weidenfeld and Nicolson, London, UK.

Ellis, C. A., Gibbs, S. J. and Rein, G. L.: 1991, Groupware: some issues and experiences, *Communications of the ACM*, 34, 1, 39-58.

eMarketer: 1998, *The 1998 eOverview Report*, www.emarketer.com.

Engler, N.: 1996, Under construction, *LAN Times*, 1 April, pp. 75-79.

Evans, P. B. and Wurster, T. S.: 1997, Strategy and the new economics of information, *Harvard Business Review*, September-October, 71-82.

Eysenck, M. and Keane, M.: 1995, *Cognitive Psychology: A Student's Handbook*, 3rd edn, Psychology Press, UK.

Fabian, A. C.: 1998, Introduction, *Evolution: Society, Science and the Universe*, Cambridge University Press, Cambridge, UK.

Fayyad, U. M.: 1997, Editorial, *Data Mining and Knowledge Discovery*, 1(1), 5-10.

Fayyad, U. M. and Uthurasamy, R.:1996, Data mining and knowledge discovery in databases, *Communications of the ACM*, 39(11), 24-26.

Fellegi, I. P.: 1972, On the question of statistical confidentiality, *Journal of American Statistical Association*, March.

Fink, K., Griese, J., Roithmayr, F. and Sieber, P.: 1997, Business on the Internet: Some (r)evolutionary perspectives, *in* D. Vogel et al. (eds), *Proceedings of the 10th International Bled Electronic Commerce Conference*, Slovenia, Vol. 2, pp. 536-555.

Finnegan, P., Galliers, B. and Powell, P.: 1998;. Systems planning in an electronic commerce environment in Europe: Rethinking current approaches, *Electronic Markets*, 8(2), 35-38.

Finnie, G. R. and Wittig, G. E.: 1998, Intelligent support for Internet marketing with case based reasoning, *Proceedings of the 2nd Annual CollECTeR Conference on Electronic Commerce*, Sydney, Australia, September, pp. 6-14.

Flores, F. et al.: 1988, Design of systems for organizational communication, *ACM Transactions on Office Information Systems*, 6(2).

Ford W. and Baum, M. S.: 1997, *Secure Electronic Commerce*, Prentice Hall, New York.

Friedman A. D. and Hoffman, L. J.: 1980, Towards a fail-safe approach to secure databases, *Proceedings of the IEEE Symposium on Security and Privacy*.

FTC: 1998, *Privacy Online: A Report to Congress*, Federal Trade Commission, June.

FTC: 1998, *Responses to Questions Regarding Electronic Commerce*, Federal Trade Commission, US House Committee on Commerce, April.

Fuller W. A.: 1993, Masking procedures for microdata disclosure limitation, *Journal of Official Statistics*, 9(2), 383-406.

Furse, D. H., Punj, G. N. and Stewart, D. W.: 1984, A typology of individual search strategies among purchasers of new automobiles, *Journal of Consumer Research*, 10(4), 417-431.

Gandy, O. H.: 1993, *The Panoptic Sort: A Political Economy of Personal Information*, Westview Press, Boulder, CO.

Ganley, O. H. and Ganley, G. D.: 1989, *To Inform or to Control? The New Communications Networks*, Ablex, Norwood, NJ.

Garzotto, F., Mainetti, L. and Paolini, P.: 1993, HDM – A model based approach to hypermedia application design, *ACM Transactions on Information Systems*, 11(1), 1-26.

Gates, B.: 1996, Get on-line to get ahead, *The Banker*, January, 12-13.

Gidari, A. and Morgan, J.: 1997, *Survey of Electronic and Digital Signature Legislative Initiatives in the United States*, prepared for the Internet Law and Policy Forum, September, www.ilpf.org/digsig/digrep.htm.

Gilovich, T. and Medvec, V. H.: 1995, The experience of regret: What, when, and why, *Psychological Review*, 102, 379-395.

Glasson, B. C.: 1989, A model of system evolution, *Journal of Information and Software Technology*, 31(7), 351-356.

Gleason, K. and Heimann, D.: 1998, Channel integration, *in* C. Romm and F. Sudweeks (eds), *Doing Business Electronically: A Global Perspective of Electronic Commerce*, Springer, London, UK, pp. 175-188.

Goldman, S. L., Nagel, R. N. and Preiss, K.: 1995, *Agile Competitors and Virtual Organisations: Strategies for Enriching the Customer*, Van Nostrand Reinhold, New York.

Grabowski, M. and Roberts, K. H.: 1996, Human and organisational error in large scale systems, *IEEE Transactions on Systems, Man and Cybernetics*, 26(1), 2-16.

Gray, P. and Igbaria, M.: 1996, The virtual society, *ORMS Today*, December, pp. 44-48.

Green, P.E. and Srinivasan, V.: 1990, Conjoint analysis in marketing research: New developments and directions, *Journal of Marketing*, 54, 3-19.

Greiner, R. and Metes, G.: 1996, *Going Virtual: Moving our Organisation into the 21st Century*, Prentice Hall, Englewood Cliffs, NJ.

Grudin, J.: 1988, Why CSCW applications fail, *Proceedings of the ACM Conference* (CSCW'88), August.

Guay, D. and Ettwein, J.: 1998, Internet commerce basics, *International Journal of Electronic Markets*, 8(1), 12-15.

Gudykunst, W. B. and Ting-Toomey, S.: 1988, *Culture and Interpersonal Communication*, Sage, Newbury Park, CA.

Guengerich, S. L., Graham, D., Miller, M., and Skipper, M.: 1996, *Building the Corporate Intranet*, Wiley, New York.

Gupta, S.: 1995, HERMES: A research project on the commercial uses of the world wide web, www.umich.edu/~sgupta/hermes/.

Gurstein, M.: 1996, Managing technology for community economic development in a non-metropolitan environment, *International Conference on Technology Management: University/Industry/Government Collaboration (UNIG: UNESCO)*, Istanbul, Turkey, 24-26 June.

Gurstein, M.: 1998, Information and communications technologies and local economic development, *in* G. MacIntyre (ed.), *A Roundtable on Community Economic Development*, University College of Cape Breton Press, Sydney, NS.

Gurstein, M.: 1999, *Flexible Networking, Information and Communications Technology and Local Economic Development*, firstmonday.dk/issues/issue4_2/index.html (1 February).

Gurstein, M. and Andrews, K.: 1996, *Wire Nova Scotia (WiNS): Final Report*, Centre for Community and Enterprise Networking, University College of Cape Breton, Sydney, NS, 31 October.

Gurstein, M. and Dienes, B.: 1998, Community enterprise networks: Partnerships for local economic development, paper presented at the *Libraries as Leaders in Community Economic Development Conference*, Victoria, BC, available at ccen.uccb.ns

Gurstein, M., Lerner, S. and MacKay, M.: 1996, *The Initial WiNS Round: Added Value and Lessons Learned* (15 November), Centre for Community and Enterprise Networking, University College of Cape Breton, Sydney, NS.

Gustavson, J.: 1997, Netiquette and DM, *Marketing*, 10 November, 102(42).

Hagel, J. and Armstrong, A. G.: 1997, *Net Gain: Expanding Markets Through Virtual Communities*, Harvard Business School Press, Boston, MA.

Hall, E. T. and Hall, M. R.: 1990, *Understanding Cultural Differences: Germans, French, and Americans*, Intercultural Press, Yarmouth, Maine.

Hansen, G.: 1998, Smaller may be better for web marketing, *Marketing News*, 32(2).

Hansen, H. R.: 1995, Conceptual framework and guidelines for the implementation of mass information systems, *Information and Management*, 2, 125-142.

Hauser, J. R. and Wernerfelt, B.: 1990, An evaluation cost model of evoked sets, *Journal of Consumer Research*, 16, 393-408.

Hein, K.: 1997, Improve your online marketing, *Incentive*, New York, November.

Henderson, J. C. and Venkatraman, N.: 1994, Strategic alignment: A model for organizational transformation via information technology, *in* T. J. Allen, M. S. Scott-Morton (eds), *Information Technology and the Corporation of the 1990s: Research Studies*, Oxford University Press, NY, pp. 202-221.

Henning, P.: 1997, Wie sicher ist "Sicher", in: bank und markt, December.

Hill, D. J., King, M. F. and Cohen, E.: 1996, The perceived utility of information presented via electronic decision aids: A consumer perspective, *Journal of Consumer Policy*, 19(2), 137-166.

Hill, R. and Walden, I. 1999, *The Draft UNCITRAL Model Law for Electronic Commerce: Issues and Solutions*, www.batnet.com

Hills, J.: 1991, The restructuring of the telecommunications market, *The Democracy Gap: The Politics of Information and Communication Technologies in the United States and Europe*, Greenwood Press, USA.

Hills, M.: 1997, *Intranet Business Strategies*, Wiley, New York.

Hoffman, D. L. and Novak, T. P.: 1996a, Marketing in hypermedia computer-mediated environments: Conceptual foundations, *Journal of Marketing*, 60(Winter), 50-68.

Hoffman, D. L. and Novak, T. P.: 1996b, The future of interactive marketing, *Harvard Business Review*, 6, 151-162.

Hoffman, D. L., Novak, T. P. and Chatterjee, P.: 1995, Commercial scenarios for the web: Opportunities and challenges, *Journal of Computer-Mediated Communication*, jcmc.huji.il/vol1/issue3/vol1no3.html

Hofmann, D. L. and Novak, T. P.: 1996, A new marketing paradigm for electronic commerce, *The Information Society*, 13(1), 45-54.

Hofstede, G.: 1983, National cultures in four dimensions, *International Studies of Management and Organisation*, 13, 46-74.

Hofstede, G.: 1980, *Cultures Consequences: International Differences in Work Related Values*, Sage, Beverly Hills, CA.

Hofstede, G.: 1991, *Culture and Organizations*, McGraw-Hill, London.

Hofstede, G.: 1996, The windmills of our minds: A workshop on culture clash in CSCW, *in* B. Glasson et al. (eds), *Information Systems and Technology in the International Office of the Future*, Chapman and Hall, London, pp. 145-159.

Hollander, J.: 1999, Selling on the Internet: How to Get Started and How Much Does it Cost?, www.ecommercetimes.com

Howard, J. A.: 1977, *Consumer Behaviour: Application of Theory*, McGraw-Hill, New York.

Howard, J. A. and Sheth, J. N.: 1969, *The Theory of Buyer Behaviour*, Wiley, New York.

IDC (International Data Corporation): 1995, Small office/home computing in the USA, Japan and Western Europe, *Special Report from IDC's 1995 Global IT Survey*.

Igbaria, M. and Zviran, M.: 1996, Comparison of end-user computing characteristics US, Israel and Taiwan, *Information and Management*, 30, 1-13.

Internet Advertising Bureau: 1998, *Report on Online Advertising Revenue*, April.

Isakowitz, T.: 1996, Structured design and construction of hypermedia applications, *Proceedings of the 17th International Conference on Information Systems (ICIS)*, Cleveland, USA, pp. 525-527.

Isakowitz, T., Stohr, E.A. and Balasubramian, P.: 1995, RMM: A methodology for structured hypermedia design, *Communications of the ACM*, 38(8), 34-44.

Ishii, H., Kobayashi, M. and Arita, K.: 1995, Iterative design of seamless collaboration media, *Communications of the ACM*, 37, 83-97.

Jarvenpaa, S. L.: 1989, The effect of task and graphical format congruence on information processing strategies and decision-making performance, *Management Science*, 35, 285-303.

Jarvenpaa, S. L.: 1990, Graphical displays in decision making: The visual salience effect, *Journal of Behavioural Decision Making*, 3, 247-262.

Jeong, K H. and King, J.: 1996, National information infrastructure initiatives in Korea: Vision and policy issues, *Information Infrastructure and Policy*, 5(2).

Jin, J.: 1995, Policy options and development strategies of the Chinese telecommunication industry, Paper delivered to *Telecommunications Research Project Conference on Information Services and Technology in China and Hong Kong*, 24 May.

Johansen, R. and Swigart, R.: 1994, *Upsizing the Individual in the Downsized Organization: Managing in the Wake of Reengineering, Globalization, and Overwhelming Technological Change*, Addison Wesley, Reading, MA.

Johnson, E. J. and Russo, E.: 1981, Product familiarity and learning new information, *in* K. B. Monroe (ed.), *Advances in Consumer Research*, Vol.8, Association for Consumer Research, Ann Arbor, MI, pp. 151-160.

Jonsonn, S.: 1991, Action research, *in* H. Nissen, H. K. Klein and R. Hirschheim (eds), *Information Systems Research: Contemporary Approaches and Emergent Traditions*, North-Holland, New York.

Jupiter Communications: 1998, Web ad revenues, *Press Release*, 6 April.

Jupiter Communications: 1999, Europeans Do Not Understand the Net, www.nua.ie/surveys/, 1 February.

Kalakota, R. and Whinston, A.:1996, *Frontiers of Electronic Commerce*, Addison Wesley, Reading, MA.

Kardes, F. R., Kalyanaraman, G., Chandrashekaran, M. and Dornoff, R. J.: 1993, Brand retrieval, consideration set composition, consumer choice, and the pioneering advantage, *Journal of Consumer Research*, 20(June), 62-75.

Katzy, B. R.: 1998, Design and implementation of virtual organisations, *Proceedings of HICSS*, Vol. 4, pp. 142-152.

Keil, G. C. and Layton, R. A.: 1981, Dimensions of consumer information seeking, *Journal of Consumer Research*, 8(May), 233-239.

King, M. F. and Hill, D. J.: 1994, Electronic decision aids: Integration of a consumer perspective, *Journal of Consumer Policy*, 17, 181-206.

Kleinmuntz, D. N. and Schkade, D. A.: 1993, Information displays and decision processes, *Psychological Science*, 4(4), 221-227.

Kock, N. F. Jr.: 1997, *The Effects of Asynchronous Groupware on Business Process Improvement*, PhD Thesis, University of Waikato, New Zealand.

Kotteman, J. E. and Davis, F. D.: 1991, Decisional conflict and user acceptance of multi-criteria decision making aids, *Decision Sciences*, 22(4), 918-926.

KPMG: 1998, e-Christmas achievements and learning, KPMG Home Page, www.kpmg.co.uk.

KPMG: 1999, Home shopping: Retailers urged to experiment whilst matching customer needs, KPMG Home Page, www.kpmg.co.uk.

Kraemer, K., Dedrick, J., Jeong, K H., Thierry, V., West, J. and Wong, P. K.: 1996, National information infrastructure: A cross-country comparison, *Information Infrastructure and Policy*, 5(2).

Kraynak, M.: 1998, Electronic commerce, *SC Info Security Magazine*, August.

Lambert, A., Spencer, E. and Mohindra, N.: 1987, Automaticity and the capture of attention by a peripheral display change, *Current Psychological Research and Reviews*, 6, 136-147.

Lambert, D.: 1993, Measures of disclosure risk and harm, *Journal of Official Statistics*, 9(2), 313-331.

Landau, D and Zviran, M.: 1997, The Internet as an organisational competitive tool, *Status*, 78(December), 52-57 (in Hebrew).

Landry, J.: 1997, *Negotiating the Forum of Electronic Public Space: The Battle Among Community Computer Networks Constituency Groups*, Unpublished Master Thesis, Concordia University, Montreal.

Lavie, N.: 1995, Perceptual load as a necessary condition for selective attention, *Journal of Experimental Psychology: Human Perception and Performance*, 21(3), 451-468.

Lavie, N. and Tsal, Y.: 1994, Perceptual load as a major determinant of the locus of selection in visual attention, *Perception and Psychophysics*, 56, 183-197.

Lederer, A. L., Mirchandani, D. A. and Sims, K.: 1996, Electronic commerce: A strategic application? *in* M. Igbaria (ed.), *Proceedings of the 1996 SIGCPR/SIGMIS Conference*, Denver, Colorado, USA, pp. 277-287.

Lederer, A. L., Mirchandani, D. A. and Sims, K.: 1997, The link between information strategy and electronic commerce, *Journal of Organisational Computing and Electronic Commerce*, 7(1), 17-34.

Lefons D., Silvestri, A., and Tangorra, F.: 1983, An analytic approach to statistical databases, *Proceedings of the 6th Conference on Very Large Databases*.

Leung, K-Y.: 1999, China Internet user base has grown rapidly while subscription fees are dropping, *Hong Kong Economic Times*, Hong Kong, 26 January.

Levin, I. P. and Jasper, J. D.: 1995, Phased narrowing: A new process tracing method for decision making, *Organizational Behaviour and Human Decision Processes*, 64(1), 1-8.

Lewin, K.: 1946, Action research and minority problems: Resolving social conflicts, *in* G. W. Lewin (ed.), Harper and Row, New York.

Li, X., Wu J. and Liang, Y.: 1995, Connecting China education community to the global Internet – The China Education and Research Network Project, Paper delivered to *Telecommunications Research Project Conference on Information Services and Technology in China and Hong Kong*, 23 May.

Liew, C. K., Choi, W. J. and Liew, C. J.: 1985, Data distortion by probability distribution, *ACM Transactions on Database Systems*, 10(3).

Limb, P. R. and Meggs, G. J.: 1995, Data mining - tools and techniques, *British Telecom Technology Journal*, 12(4), 32-41.

Lovelock, P., Clark, T. E. and Petrazzini, B. A.: 1995, The 'Golden Projects': China's national networking initiative, *HKUST Working Paper*, Hong Kong University of Science and Technology, pp. 1-28

Lu, J., Zhao, C. and Glasson, B. C.: 1997, The methods and models of connecting the Web and databases, *Proceedings of the 1997 International Conference on Management Science and Engineering*, Nanjing, PR China, 3-6 November, pp. 26-34.

Lymer, A., Johnson, R. and Baldwin-Morgan, A.: 1997, The Internet and small businesses: A study of impacts, *Proceedings of the 5th European Conference on Information Systems*, Cork, Ireland, pp. 145-162.

Lynch, J. G. Jr and Ariely, D.: 1998, Interactive home shopping: Effects of search cost for price and quantity information on consumer price sensitivity, satisfaction with merchandise, and retention, *Working Paper*, Duke University.

Machlis, S.: 1998, New ads: 'rich concepts, not rich media', *Computerworld*, 32(35).

MacInnes, D.: 1998, Based on the MacFadyen Trust Lecture by Dr Dan MacInnes (St Francis Xavier University), given at Stirling Castle in April. (From *Celtic Heritage Magazine*, February/March 1999, fox.nstn.ca/~celtic/feature.htm).

Mackay, J. M., Barr, S. H, and Kletke, M. G.: 1992, An empirical investigation of the effects of decision aids on problem solving processes, *Decision Sciences*, 23(3), 648-672.

Maddox, K.: 1998, IAB: Ad revenue online projected to hit $2 bil in '98, *Advertising Age Interactive*, adage.com/interactive/articles/199811.02/article1.html.

Mahler, A. and Göbel, G.: 1996, Internetbanking: Das Leistungsspektrum, *Die Bank*, August, 488-492.

Malone, T. W. and Smith, S. A.: 1984, *Tradeoffs in Designing Organizations; Implications for New Forms of Human Organizations and Computer Systems*, Center for Information Systems Research, Sloan School of Management, Massachusetts Institute of Technology, Cambridge, MA.

Malone, T. W., Yates J. and Benjamin R. I.: 1994, Electronic markets and electronic hierarchies, *in* T. J. Allen and M. S. Scott Morton (eds), *Information Technology and the Corporation of the 1990s*, Oxford University Press, Oxford.

Malone, T. W.: 1987, *Formal Model of Organisational Structure and its use in Predicting Effect of Information Technology*, Center for Information Systems Research, Sloan School of Management, Massachusetts Institute of Technology, Cambridge, MA.

Marchionini, G.: 1995, *Information Seeking in Electronic Environments*, Cambridge University Press, Cambridge.

Markoff, J.: 1998, Internet is expanding arms race with junk e-mail, *New York Times*, 17 March, 147(51099).

Marshall, L.: 1997, Facilitating knowledge management and knowledge sharing: new opportunities for information professionals, *Online*, 21(5), 92-98.

Martin, J.: 1996, *Cybercorp: The New Business Revolution*, Amacom, New York.

Martin, J.: 1998, You've got junk mail, *PC World*, 16(4).

Massachusetts: 1997, Commonwealth of Massachusetts: Massachusetts Electronic Records and Signatures Act, *Draft Docment*, November 4 (www.magnet.state.ma.us/itd/ legal/.

Matloff, N. E.: 1986, Another look at the use of noise addition for database security, *Proceedings of the 9th Conference on Very Large Databases*.

Mayor, J. and Gonzalez-Marques, J.: 1994, Facilitation and interference effects in word and picture processing, *in* S. Ballesteros (ed.), *Cognitive Approaches to Human Perception*, Lawrence Erlbaum, pp. 155-198.

McCandlish, S.: 1999, *Electronic Frontier Foundation*, www.eff.org.

McGalliard, K.: 1998, Animate your Web site: Gif graphics, *Editor and Publishers*, NY, May.

Meyer, R. J.: 1981, A model of multi-attribute judgements under attribute uncertainty and information constraint, *Journal of Marketing Research*, 18, 428-441.

Miles, R. E. and Snow, C. C.: 1986, Organisations: New concepts for new forms, *California Management Review*, 28(3), 62-73.

Miller, D. B., Clemons, E .K. and Row, M. C.: 1993, Information technology and the global virtual corporation, *in* S. P. Bradley, J. A. Hausman, and R. L. Nolan, *Globalization, Technology and Competition*, HBS Press, pp. 283-307.

Miller, J. O.: 1991, The Flanker Compatibility Effect as a function of visual angle, attentional focus, visual transients, and perceptual load: A search for boundary conditions, *Perception and Psychophysics*, 49, 270-288.

Miller, M, Roehr, A. J., and Bernard, B.: 1998, *Managing the Corporate Intranet*, Wiley, New York.

Milosavljevic, M.: 1998, Electronic commerce via personalised virtual catalogues, *Proceedings of the 2nd Annual CollECTeR Conference on Electronic Commerce*, Sydney, Australia, September, pp. 26-37.

Moore, J. F.: 1993, Predators and prey: A new ecology of competition, *Harvard Business Review*, 71(3), 75-85.

Moore, J. F.: 1997, *The Death of Competition – Leadership and Strategy in the Age of Business Ecosystems*, Harper Collins, New York.

Mosley, J.: 1998, Deck us all in on-line shopping, *Marketing News*, 19 January, 32(2).

Nambisan, S. and Wang, Y.: 1999, Roadblocks to Web technology adoption? *Communications of the ACM* 42(1), 98-101.

Nedungadi, P.: 1990, Recall and consumer consideration sets: Influencing choice without altering brand evaluations, *Journal of Consumer Research*, 17(December), 263-276.

Needle, D.: 1994, *Business in Context*, 2nd edn, Thompson Business Press, London

Newman, J. W.: 1977, Consumer external search: Amount and determinants, *in* A. G. Woodside, J. N. Sheth, and P. D. Bennett (eds), *Consumer and Industrial Buying Behaviour*, North-Holland, Amsterdam, pp. 79-94.

Nielsen, J.: 1999, *Alertbox*, www.useit.com/alertbox.

Niemira, M.: 1996, Are nonstore sales a threat to traditional store business?, *Chain Store Age*, 26 September.

Nonaka, I. and Takeuchi, H.: 1995, *The Knowledge Creating Company*, Oxford University Press, New York.

Nouwens, J., and Bouwman, H.: 1995, Living apart together in electronic commerce: The use of information and communication technology to create network organizations, *Journal of Computer Mediated Communication*, 1(3), available at www.ascusc.org/jcmc/vol1/issue3/nouwens.html.

O'Hara-Devereaux, M. and Johansen, R.: 1994, *Globalwork: Bridging Distance, Culture and Time*, Jossey-Bass, San Francisco

O'Keefe, B. and O'Connor, G. C.: 1997, Viewing the Web as a marketplace: The case of small companies, *Decision Support Systems*, 21(3), 171-183.

Oliver, R. L. and Swan, J. E.: 1989a, Consumer perceptions of interpersonal equity and satisfaction in transactions: A field survey approach, *Journal of Marketing*, 53(April), 21-35.

Oliver, R. L. and Swan, J. E.: 1989b, Equity and disconfirmation perceptions as influences on merchant and product satisfaction, *Journal of Consumer Research*, 16(December), 372-383.

Olle, W., Hagelstein, J., McDonald, I., Rolland, C., Sol, H., Van Assche, F., Verrijn-Stuart, A.: 1991, *Information Systems Methodologies: A Framework for Understanding*, 2nd edn, Addison Wesley, Wokingham, UK.

Olson, D. L., Moshkovich, H. M., Schellenberger, R. and Mechitov, A. I.: 1995, Consistency and accuracy in decision aids, *Decision Sciences*, 26(6), 723-748.

Open Financial Exchange: 1998, OFX Specification 1.5, 29 June, www.ofx.net/ofx/ noreg.asp (01/99).

Ordinance: 1997, Verordnung zur digitalen Signatur, in der Fassung des Beschlusses der Bundesregierung, October.

Orenda Healing International: 1998, *YouthSpace Project*, available at www.nccn.net/ ~orenda/ (20 May).

Österle, H.: 1995, Business Engineering: Prozeß- und Systementwicklung, Band 1: Entwurfstechniken, Springer, Berlin, Germany.

Paese, P. W. and Sniezek, J.: 1991, Influences on the appropriateness of confidence in judgment: Practice, effort, information, and decision making, *Organizational Behaviour and Human Decision Processes*, 48(1), 100-130.

Palmer J. W. and Speier, C.: 1998, Teams: Virtualness and media choice, *Proceedings of HICSS*, Vol. 4, pp. 131-141.

Palmer, J. W.: 1997, Retailing on the WWW: The use of electronic product catalogs, *International Journal of Electronic Markets*, 7(3), 6-9.

Palva, S.: 1998, *AIS'98 Mini-Track on Global Information Technology and Global Electronic Commerce*, www.isworld.org/ais.ac.98.

Pashler, H.: 1998, *The Psychology of Attention*, MIT Press, Cambridge, MA.

Payne, J. W., Bettman, J. R. and Johnson, E. J.: 1993, *The Adaptive Decision Maker*, Cambridge University Press, Cambridge, UK.

Payne, J. W.: 1982, Contingent decision behaviour, *Psychological Bulletin*, 92, 382-402.

Pedersen, P. B. and Ivey, A.: 1993, *Culture-centered Counseling and Interviewing Skills*, Praeger, Westport.

Perin, C.: 1988, The moral fabric of the office: Organization habits vs high-tech options for work schedules flexibilities, *Working Paper 88-051*, MIT, June.

Peter J. P. and Olson, J. C.: 1990, *Consumer Behaviour and Marketing Strategy*, Irwin, Homewood, IL.

Peter, J. P. and Churchill, G. A.: 1986, Relationships among research design choices and psychometric properties of rating scales: A meta-analysis, *Journal of Marketing Research*, 23, 1-10.

Peters, M. and Robinson, V.: 1984, The origins and status of action research, *Journal of Applied Behavioral Science*, 20(2).

Petrazzini, B. A.: 1995, *The Political Economy of Telecommunications Reform in Developing Countries*, Praeger, Westport.

Petrazzini, B. A. and Clark, T. E.: 1996, Costs and benefits of telecommunications liberalization in developing countries, Paper presented at *Institute for International Economics Conference on Liberalizing Telecommunications Services*, 29 January, Washington, DC.

Petrazzini, B. A. and Lovelock, P.: 1996, The 'Asian-ness' of telecom reform, *InterMedia*, 24(3), 122-128

Pfeffer , J.: 1978, *Organizational Design*, Harlan Davidson, Arlington Heights.

Phillips, L. W.: 1981, Assessing measurement error in key informant reports: A methodological note on organizational analysis in marketing, *Journal of Marketing Research*, 18(November), 395-415.

Picot, A., Bortenlaenger, C. and Roehrl, H.: 1998, The automation of capital markets, *Journal of Computer Mediated Communication*, 1(3), available at www.usc.edu/dept/ annenberg/vol1/issue3/picot.html

Pigg, K.: 1998, *Missouri Express: Program Implementation Assessment*, University of Missouri, 15 May.

Piore, M. and Sable, C.: 1984, *The Second Industrial Divide: Possibilities for Prosperity*, Basic Books, New York.

Pomerantz, J., Carson, C. and Feldman, E.: 1994, Interference effects in perceptual organization, *in* S. Ballesteros (ed.), *Cognitive Approaches to Human Perception*, Lawrence Erlbaum, pp. 123-152.

Poon, S.: 1998, *Small Business Internet Commerce: A study of the Australian experience*, PhD (Information Systems) Thesis, School of Information Management and Systems, Monash University, Melbourne, Australia.

Poon, S.: 1999, The nature of goods and Internet commerce benefit: A preliminary study, *Proceedings of the 32nd Hawai'ian International Conference in Systems Sciences*, Maui, Hawaii, USA (to appear).

Poon, S. and Jevons, C.: 1997, Internet-enabled international marketing: A small business perspective, *Journal of Marketing Management*, 13(1-4), 29-41.

Poon, S. and Swatman, P. M. C.: 1997, Internet-based small business communication, *International Journal of Electronic Markets*, 7(2), 15-21.

Poon, S. and Swatman, P. M. C.: 1998, Small business Internet commerce: A longitudinal study, *Proceedings of the 11th International Bled Electronic Commerce Conference*, Slovenia, pp. 295-309.

Poon, S. and Swatman, P. M. C.: 1999, An exploratory study of small business Internet commerce issues, *Information and Management* 35(1), 9-18.

Porter, M. E.: 1990, *Competitive Advantage of Nations*, The Free Press, New York.

Powell, W. W.: 1990, Neither market nor hierarchy: Network forms of organisation, *Research in Organisational Behaviour*, 12, 295-336.

Power, D. J., Meyaraan, S. L. and Aldag, R. J.: 1994, Impacts of problem structure and computerised decision aids on decision attitudes and behaviours, *Information Management*, 26(5), 281-294.

Prahalad, C.K. and Hamel, G.: 1990, The core competence of the corporation, *Harvard Business Review*, May/June, 79–91.

Preiss, K., Goldman, S. L. and Nagel, R. N.: 1996, *Cooperate to Compete*, Van Nostrand Reinhold, New York.

Proctor, R. and Van Zandt, T.: 1994, *Human Factors in Simple and Complex Systems*, Allyn and Bacon.

Ptak, R. L.: 1998, Designing a business-justified intranet project, *Information Systems Management*, 15(2), 13-19

Punj, G. N. and Staelin, R.: 1983, A model of consumer information search behaviour for new automobiles, *Journal of Consumer Research*, 9(March), 366-380.

Punj, G. N. and Stewart, D.W.: 1983, An interaction framework of consumer decision making, *Journal of Consumer Research*, 10(September), 181-196.

Putterman, L.: 1995, Markets, hierachies, and information: on a paradox in the economics of organization, *Journal of Economic Behaviour and Organization*, 26(3), 373-390.

Quelch, J. A. and Klein, L. R.: 1996, The Internet and international marketing, *Sloan Management Review*, 37(3), 60-75.

Ragowsky, A.: 1986, *The Computerization in the Israeli Industry*, PhD Dissertation, Tel-Aviv University.

Ramakrishnan, R.: 1997, *Database Management Systems*, WCB/McGraw-Hill.

Raman, D.: 1996, EDI: The backbone for business on the Net, *Electronic Commerce and Communications*, 4, 18-21.

Ratchford, B. T.: 1980, The value of information for selected appliances, *Journal of Marketing Research*, 17(February), 14-25.

Ratneshwar, S. and Shocker, A. D.: 1991, The role of usage context in product category structures, *Journal of Marketing Research*, 28, 3.

Rayport, J. F. and Sviokla, J. J.: 1994, Managing in the marketspace, *Harvard Business Review*, 72(6).

Rayport, J. F. and Sviokla, J. J.: 1995, Exploiting the virtual value chain, *Harvard Business Review*, 73(6), 75-85.

RegTP (ed.): 1998, Massnahmenkatalog fuer digitale Signaturen, www.regtp.de/Fachinfo/ Digitalsign/start.htm.

Reinhard, W., Schweitzer, J. and Volsen, G.: 1994, CSCW tools: Concepts and architectures, *Communications of the ACM*, 27(5), 28-36.

Reiss, J. P.: 1980, Practical data-swapping: The first steps, *Proceedings of the IEEE Symposium on Security and Privacy*.

Rheingold, H.: 1993, *Virtual Community: Homesteading on the Electronic Frontier*, Addison Wesley, Reading, MA.

Rivest, R. L.: 1992, The MD5 message digest alogrithm, *RFC 1321*.

Roberts, J. H.: 1989, A grounded model of consideration set size and composition, *Advances in Consumer Research*, 16, 749-757.

Roberts, J. H. and Lattin, J. M.: 1991, Development and testing of a model of consideration set composition, *Journal of Marketing Research*, 28 (November), 429-440.

Rogers, D. M.: 1996, The challenge of fifth generation R&D, *Research Technology Management*, 39(4), 33-41.

Runge, A.: 1998, The need for supporting electronic commerce transactions with electronic contracting systems, *International Journal of Electronic Markets*, 8(1), 16-19.

Rusbridger, I.: 1999, How I fell in love with the Net, *The Guardian*, 11 January, G2, pp. 2-3.

Russo, J. E.: 1987, Toward intelligent product information systems for consumers, *Journal of Consumer Policy*, 10, 109-138.

Russo, J. E. and Leclerc, F.: 1991, Characteristics of successful product information systems, *Journal of Social Issues*, 47(1), 73-92.

Saad, G. and Russo, J. E.: 1996, Stopping criteria in sequential choice, *Organizational Behaviour and Human Decision Processes*, 67(3), 258-270.

Scanlon, T.: 1998, Seductive design for web sites, *Eye for Design*, July/August.

Scharl, A.: 1997, *Referenzmodellierung kommerzieller Masseninformationssysteme – Idealtypische Gestaltung von Informationsangeboten im World Wide Web am Beispiel der Branche Informationstechnik*, Peter Lang, Frankfurt, Germany.

Scharl, A.: 1998, Reference Modeling of Commercial Web Information Systems Using the extended World Wide Web Design Technique (eW3DT), *Proceedings of the 31st Hawaii International Conference on System Sciences (HICSS-31)*, Hawaii, USA, 6-9 January.

Scharl, A. and Brandtweiner, R.: 1998, A conceptual research framework for analyzing the evolution of electronic markets, *International Journal of Electronic Markets*, 8(2), 39-42.

Schein, E.: 1990, Organisational culture, *American Psychologist*, 45(2), 109-119.

Schkade, D. A. and Kleinmuntz, D. N.: 1994, Information displays and choice processes: Differential effects of organization form and sequence, *Organization Behaviour and Human Decision Processes*, 57(3), 319-337.

Schlorer, J.: 1983, Information loss in partitioned statistical databases, *Computing Journal*, 26(3), 218-223.

Schmid, B. and Lindemann, M.: 1998, Elements of a reference model for electronic markets, *Proceedings of the 31st Hawai'ian International Conference on System Sciences (HICSS-31)*, Los Alamitos.

Schofield, J.: 1997, The new seekers, *The Guardian Online*, 6 November, pp. 1-3.

Schroeder, E.: 1998, Chalk up another defeat for online privacy, *PC Week Online*, 18 August.

Schuler, D.: 1996, *New Community Networks: Wired for Change*, Addison Wesley, Reading, MA.

Schwabe, D. and Rossi, G.: 1995, The object-oriented hypermedia design model, *Communications of the ACM*, 38(8), 45-46.

Scott, M., Diamond, A. and Smith, B.: 1997, *Opportunities for Communities: Public Access to Networked IT*, Department of Social Security, Canberra, Australia.

Seeman, P.: 1997, A prescription for knowledge management: What Hoffmann-LaRoches case can teach others, *Perspectives on Business Innovation*, 1(1), 26-33.

Seemann, P.: 1996, Real-world knowledge management: What is working for Hoffmann-LaRoche, *Research Note CBI310*, Ernst & Young Center for Business Innovation.

Shafe, L.: 1996, *Building Intranet Applications: A Manager's Guide to Intranet Computing*, Intelligent Environments, NY.

Shankar, V. and Rangaswamy, A.: 1998, The impact of internet marketing on price sensitivity and price competition, *Working Paper*.

Shapiro, D. H. Jr, Schwarz, C. E. and Astin, J. A.: 1996, Controlling ourselves, controlling our world: Psychology's role in understanding positive and negative consequences of seeking and gaining control, *American Psychologist*, 51(2), 1213

Shocker, A. D., Ben-Akiva, M., Boccara, B. and Nedungadi, P.: 1991, Consideration set influences on consumer decision making and choice: Issues, models, and suggestions, *Marketing Letters*, 2, 181-197.

Shugan, S. M.: 1980, The cost of thinking, *Journal of Consumer Research*, 7, 99-111.

Sieber, P.: 1996, Virtuality as a strategic approach for small and medium sized IT companies to stay competitive in a global market, *in* J. I. DeGross, S. Jarvenpaa, A. Srinivasan (eds), *Proceedings of the 17th International Conference on Information Systems*, Cleveland, USA, S.468.

Simon, H. A.: 1978, Rationality as a process and product of thought, *American Economic Review*, 68, 1-16.

Simonson, I., Huber, J. and Payne, J.: 1988, The relationship between prior brand knowledge and information acquisition order, *Journal of Consumer Research*, 14, 566-578.

Smith, L.: 1999, *Big Brother Browsing*, www.zdnet.com.

Snow, M. S.: 1988, Telecommunications literature: A critical review of the economic, technological and public policy issues, *Telecommunications Policy*, June.

Srinivasan, N. and Ratchford, B.T.: 1991, An empirical test of a model of external search for automobiles, *Journal of Consumer Research*, 18(September), 233-242.

Srivastava, R. K., Alpert, M. I. and Shocker, A. D.: 1984, A consumer-oriented approach for determining market structures, *Journal of Marketing*, 48, 32-45.

Srivastava, R. K., Leone, R. P. and Shocker, A. D.: 1981, Market structure analysis: Hierarchical clustering for products based on simulation in use, *Journal of Marketing*, 45(Summer), 38-48.

Steinfield, C., Kraut, R., and Plummer, A.: 1995, The impact of electronic commerce on buyer-seller relationships, *Journal of Computer Mediated Communication*, 1(3), available at www.ascusc.org/jcmc/vol1/issue3/steinfld.html

Stigler, G.: 1961, The economics of information, *Journal of Political Economy*, 69(January/February), 213-225.

Stone, D. N. and Schkade, D. A.: 1991, Numeric and linguistic representation in multi-attribute choice, *Organizational Behaviour and Human Decision Processes*, 49(1), 42-59.

Strangelove, M.: 1995, The walls come down, *Internet World*, May, 40-44.

Strom, J., Preece, C., Miller, A. and Eccles, D.: 1998, Infocities: Experience with electronic commerce for city SMEs, *Proceedings of the 11th International Conference on Electronic Commerce*, Bled, Slovenia.

Susman, G. I. and Evered, R. D.: 1978, An assessment of the scientific merits of action research, *Administrative Science Quarterly*, 23.

Swatman, P. M. C. and Swatman, P. A.: 1992, EDI System integration: A definition and literature survey, *The Information Society*, 8, 165-205.

Taylor, M.: 1997, Intranets – a new technology changes all the rules, *Telecommunications*, 31(1), 39-41.

Tchong, M.: 1999, *The State of eCommerce*, www.emarketer.com, 22 February.

Telleen, S. L.: 1998, *Intranet Organization: Strategies for Managing Change*, www.intranetpartners.com/intranetorg/index.html.

Tendick, P. and Matloff, N.: 1994, A modified random perturbation method for database security, *ACM Transactions on Database Systems*, 19(1), 47-63.

Tenenbaum, J. M.: 1998, WISs and electronic commerce, *Communications of the ACM*, 41(7), 89-90.

Thoronton, E.: 1994, Revolution in Japanese retailing, *Fortune*, 144(February).

Timmers, P.: 1998, Business models for electronic markets, *Electronic Markets*, 8(2), 3-8.

Todd, P. and Benbasat, I.: 1992, The use of information in decision making: An experimental investigation of the impact of computer-based decision aids, *MIS Quarterly*, 16(3), 373-393.

Todd, P. and Benbasat, I.: 1994, The influence of decision aids on choice strategies: An experimental analysis of the role of cognitive effort, *Organization Behaviour and Human Decision Processes*, 60, 36-74.

Todd, P. and Benbasat, I.: 1996, The effects of decision support and task contingencies on model formulation: A cognitive perspective, *Decision Support Systems*, 17(4), 241-252.

Treisman, A.: 1991, Search, similarity, and integration of features between and within dimensions, *Journal of Experimental Psychology: Human Perception and Performance*, 17, 652-676.

Tushman, M. L. and O'Reilly, III, C. A.: 1996, Ambidextrous organisations: Managing evolutionary and revolutionary change, *California Management Review*, 38(4), 8-29.

Tversky, A., Sattath, S. and Slovic, P.: 1988, Contingent weighting in judgment and choice, *Psychological Review*, 95, 371-384.

Unisys, 1999: *The Unisys Finance Barometer*, www.internet-banking.com/barom.html (01/99).

Urbany, J. E., Dickson, P. R. and Wilkie, W. L.: 1989, Buyer uncertainty and information search, *Journal of Consumer Research*, 16(September), 208-215.

Ure, J.: 1994, Telecommunications, with Chinese characteristics, *Telecommunications Policy*, April, 182-194

Ure, J.: 1995, *Telecommunications in Asia: Policy, Planning, and Development*, Hong Kong University Press, Hong Kong.

USA Today: 1998, Internet advertisers learning as they go, 17 August.

Utah: 1995, *Utah Digital Signature Act*, www.commerce.state.ut.us/web/commerce/digsig/dsmain.htm.

van der Zeo, B.: 1999, @armchair.shopping, *The Guardian*, 14 January, p. 14.

Venkatraman, N. and Ramanajum, V.: 1987, Planning systems success: A conceptualization and an operational model, *Management Science*, 33(6), 687-705.

Venkatraman, N., Henderson, J. C. and Oldach, S.: 1993, Continuous strategic alignment: exploiting information technology capabilities for competitive success, *European Management Journal*, 11(2), 139-149.

Wang, H.: 1998, Consumer privacy concerns about Internet marketing, *Communications of the ACM*, 41(3).

Wang, N.: 1997, Researchers find banners boost product awareness, *Web Week*, 29 September.

Wanninger, A. L.: 1998, Profitable electronic commerce: Framework, examples, trends, *Proceedings of the 11th International Conference on Electronic Commerce*, Bled, Slovenia, June.

Webber, A. M.: 1993, What's so new about the new economy? *Harvard Business Review*, January-February, 23-34.

Webster's Dictionary: 1998, Warner Books.

Weston, R., and Nash, K.: 1996, Intranet Fever, *Computerworld*, 30(27), 1-15.

Whiteley, D.: 1998a, Would you buy an ice-cream cone over the Internet?, *Proceedings of the 11th International Conference on Electronic Commerce*, Bled, Slovenia.

Whiteley, D.: 1998b, EDI maturity: A business opportunity, *in* C. Romm and F. Sudweeks (eds), *Doing Business Electronically: A Global Perspective of Electronic Commerce*, Springer, London.

Whiteley, D.: 1999, *e-commerce Survey*, www.doc.mmu.ac.uk/STAFF/D.Whiteley/e-commerce.htm.

Whittemore, M.: 1994, Retailing looks to a new century, *Nations Business*, 82(December), 18-24.

Widing, R. E. and Talarzyk, W. W.: 1993, Electronic information systems for consumers: An evaluation of computer-assisted formats in multiple decision environments, *Journal of Marketing Research*, 30, 125-141.

Wigand, R.: 1997, Electronic commerce: Definition, theory and context, *The Information Society*, 13(1), 1-16.

Wigand, R. T. and Benjamin, R. I.: 1995, Electronic commerce: Effects on electronic markets, *Journal of Computer Mediated Communication*, 1(3), available at www.ascusc.org/jcmc/vol1/issue3/wigand.html.

Willett, S.: 1999, International e-commerce faces obstacles, *Computer Reseller News*, www.techweb.com/wire/story, 12 January.

Wilson, K.: 1997, From tags to riches, *The Guardian Online*, 4 December, p. 8.

Wood-Harper, A. T. and Fitzgerald, G.: 1982, A taxonomy of current approaches to systems analysis, *The Computer Journal*, 25(1), 12-16.

Workflow Management Coalition (WfMC): 1995, *Workflow Management Specification Glossary*.

Working Group 4: 1998, *Exploiting the Wired-up World: Best practice in managing virtual organisations (V.2.0)*, The Impact Program Ltd, available at www.achieve.ch/achieve_wg_4.html.

Yan, G. and Paradi, J.: 1998, Internet - The future delivery channel for banking services?, *Proceedings of the 31st Hawai'ian International Conference on System Sciences (HICSS-31)*, Los Alamitos

Yantis, S. and Jonides, J.: 1990, Abrupt visual onsets and selective attention: Voluntary versus automatic allocation, *Journal of Experimental Psychology: Human Perception and Performance*, 16, 121-134

Yin, R. K: 1989, *Case Study Research: Design and Methods*, Sage, New Bury Park.

Zeithaml, V.: 1996, *Services Marketing*, McGraw-Hill, NY.

Zettelmeyer, F.: 1997, The strategic use of consumer search cost, *Working Paper*, Massachussets Institute of Technology.

Zhang, P., von Dran, G., Small, R. and Barcellos, S.: 1999, Websites that satisfy users: A theoretical framework for Web user interface design and evaluation, *Proceedings of the 32nd Hawai'ian International Conference on System Sciences (HICSS-32)*, Hawaii, 5-8 January.

Zimmermann, H. D. and Kuhn, C.: 1995, Grundlegende Konzepte einer Electronic Mall, *in* B. Schmid (ed.), *Electronic Mall: Banking und Shopping in globalen Netzen*, Stuttgart, Germany.

Zuboff , S.: 1988, *In the Age of the Smart Machine: The Future of Work and Power*, Basic Books, New York.

Subject Index

About the Contributors

Monica Adya (adya@umbc.edu) is an Assistant Professor in Information Systems at the University of Maryland, Baltimore County. Her primary areas of interest relate to the design, validation, and use of intelligent decision support systems, the use of judgment and decision-making in the effective design of such systems, and the application of these systems for forecasting and health care tasks. She has published in *Information Systems Research* and the *Journal of Forecasting*.

Christian Bauer (bauerc@cbs.curtin.edu.au) received a Masters degree from the Vienna University of Economics and Business Administration. He was then employed by the Department of Information Systems as an assistant professor. After completion of his doctoral thesis, *Mass Information Systems for the Banking Industry: Reference Models Focusing on the World Wide Web (WWW)*, the Electronic Commerce Network of Curtin University, Perth, Australia, offered him a visiting position. In 1998, he was awarded a postdoctoral fellowship (three-year appointment). His research areas include Internet-based financial services and Web information systems.

Janice Burn (j.burn@cowan.edu.au), Foundation Professor and Head of School, Management Information Systems, Edith Cowan University, has extensive experience of working with organisations to develop strategies for information systems and has published widely in this area, including her most recent book, *Information Technology and the Challenge for Hong Kong* (1997). She currently focuses more specifically on strategies for virtual organisations and leads a research team comprising five PhD students and four academic staff at ECU, investigating various aspects of this phenomenon. Her industrial experience includes the primary commodity sector, manufacturing and consultancy for multi-national concerns.

Ted Clark (tclark@uxmail.ust.hk) is an assistant professor in the Department of Information Systems and Management, Hong Kong University of Science and Technology. His areas of research and teaching include electronic commerce, telecommunications, and information technology planning and strategy. He received a Doctorate in Business Administration from Harvard Business School in 1994, where he had previously graduated as a Baker Scholar from the MBA program in 1985. Prior to returning to Harvard for doctoral studies, Dr Clark worked with McKinsey and Co for more than five years, serving telecommunications and information technology clients in the US, Europe, and Asia.

Subhasish Dasgupta (dasgupta@alpha.fdu.edu) is an Assistant Professor of Information Systems at the Samuel J. Silberman College of Business Administration,

Fairleigh Dickinson University, NJ, USA. He holds BS and MBA degrees from the University of Calcutta, India, and a PhD from Baruch College, City University of New York. His research interests include electronic commerce, information technology diffusion, effectiveness of information technology investment, and knowledge based systems in group decision-making, and Internet-based simulation and games. He has published on these topics in the *International Journal of Electronic Markets* and *Logistics Information Management Journal*.

Schahram Dustdar (dustdar@ufg.ac.at) is the head of the Center for Informatics at the University of Art in Linz, and teaches at various other universities in Austria. His current research interests are multimedia information systems and organisational change. He has co-authored a book entitled *Multimedia Information Systems* and co-edited a book on *Telecooperation in Organizations*. He is on the editorial board of the *Journal of Multimedia Tools and Applications* and the *Journal of Computing and Information Technology*. He was a visiting research fellow in the Department of Information Systems at the London School of Economics during 1993-94 and a visiting research scientist at the NTT Multimedia Communications Laboratories, Palo Alto, in 1998. He is co-founder and director of technology strategy of Caramba Labs, a software company developing Java-based groupware and workflow systems.

Aryya Gangopadhyay (gangopad@umbc.edu) is an Assistant Professor of Information Systems at the University of Maryland, Baltimore County, USA. His research interests include electronic commerce, multimedia databases, data warehousing and mining, and geographic information systems. He has authored and co-authored two books, numerous papers in journals such as *IEEE Computer*, *IEEE Transactions on Knowledge and Data Engineering*, the *Journal of Management Information Systems*, and the *ACM Journal on Multimedia Systems*, and has presented papers at many national and international conferences.

Bernard Glasson (glassonb@cbs.curtin.edu.au) currently holds a professorial position at the Curtin Business School and has also been appointed Director of the Electronic Commerce Network, a joint venture between Curtin University and the Bank of Western Australia (BankWest). He began his career in the industry working with National Australia and managing information systems development projects. He authored a textbook on systems development, *EDP System Development Guidelines*. He completed his doctorate at the University of York in 1986 and currently chairs the International Federation of Information Processing (IFIP), Technical Committee 8, Information Systems. He has served on the organising committees of several leading international information systems conferences and is co-chairing the International Conference of Information Systems 2000 (ICIS) in Brisbane. His current research interest is Internet-enabled electronic commerce.

Michael Gurstein (mgurst2@ccen.uccb.ns.ca) completed a BA at the University of Saskatchewan and a PhD in Sociology at the University of Cambridge. He was a senior public servant in the Provinces of British Columbia and Saskatchewan. For a number of years, he was President of the consulting firm Socioscope Inc. in Ottawa,

Canada which specialized in the human aspects of advanced technologies. From 1992-95 he was a management advisor with the United Nations Secretariat in New York. Since 1995, Dr Gurstein has been the ECBC/NSERC/SSHRC Associate Chair of Management of Technological Change at the University College of Cape Breton and, since 1996, the Founder Director of the Centre for Community and Enterprise Networking (C\CEN). Dr Gurstein has published widely in both scholarly and more popular journals and has contracted with the Idea Group Publishers for a volume *Community Informatics: Enabling Communities Through Information and Communication Technologies*. His book *Burying Coal: Research and Development in a Marginal Community* awaiting publication later in 1999 by Collective Press, and *The Net Working Locally: Information and Communications Technology in Support of Local Economic Development* has been accepted for publication by a leading academic publisher.

Magid Igbaria (magid.igbaria@cgu.edu) is Professor of Information Science at Claremont Graduate University and at the Leon Racanati Graduate School of Business Administration, Tel Aviv University. He has a BA in Statistics and an MA in Information Systems and Operations Research from Hebrew University, and a PhD in Computers and Information Systems from Tel Aviv University. Professor Igbaria has published numerous articles in leading information systems journals including *Communications of the ACM, Computers and Operations Research, Decision Sciences, Decision Support Systems, Information and Management, The Information Society, Information Systems Research, Information Technology and People, International Journal of Information Management, International Journal of Operations and Production Management, Journal of End-User Computing, Journal of Engineering and Technology Management, Journal of MIS, Omega, Journal of Strategic Information Systems, MIS Quarterly*, and others. His current research interests focus on the virtual workplace, virtual society, information and computer economics, computer technology acceptance, quantitative research methods, and information systems issues such as management and personnel.

Wolfgang Koenig (koenig@wiwi.uni-frankfurt.de) has Diplomas in Business Administration and Business Pedagogics. In 1985, he was awarded a PhD at Frankfurt University and was appointed Professor of Information Systems at the Koblenz School of Corporate Management. He also served as Dean from 1986 to 1988. In 1991, he became Professor of Information Systems in the Faculty of Economics and Business Administration, Frankfurt University. He has spent more than two years at the IBM Research Laboratories in San Jose and Yorktown Heights, as well as at the Kellogg Graduate School of Management, Northwestern University, Evanston, and at the University of California, Berkeley. He is Editor-in-Chief of the leading German information systems journal *Wirtschaftsinformatik*. His research interests are in standardisation, networking, and group decision support systems.

Ook Lee (leeo@hansung.ac.kr) is a professor in the Department of Business Administration at Hansung University, Seoul, Korea. He has a PhD in Management

Information Systems from Claremont Graduate University, Claremont, USA, an MS in Computer Science from Northwestern University, Evanston, USA and a BS in Computer Science and Statistics from Seoul National University, Seoul, Korea. He was a senior researcher in the Information Research Center in Korea and a project director for Information Resources, Inc. in Chicago, USA. His articles have appeared in journals such as the *Journal of Software Maintenance, Systems Development Management, International Journal of Electronic Markets*, and *Annals of Cases on Information Technology Applications and Management in Organization*.

Peter Marshall (p.marshall@cowan.edu.au), Associate Professor in Management Information Systems, Edith Cowan University, has been involved in information systems research for the past 20 years. He has extensive experience of working with organisations on strategic IS planning, particularly in the public sector. Of late this has included work on formulating and evaluating strategies for electronic commerce, including the on-line provision of services. He is currently supervising a number of PhD and Masters students in this area.

Satish Nambisan (satish@comp.nus.edu.sg) is an assistant professor in the School of Computing, National University of Singapore, and a research affiliate at the Center for Telemedia Strategy, NUS. Later, in 1999, he will be joining the faculty at Lally School of Management and Technology, Rensselaer Polytechnic Institute, New York. Dr Nambisan received his PhD in Information Systems from Syracuse University, New York, in 1997. His primary research interests include electronic commerce, technology innovation and adoption, and technology strategy and entrepreneurship. His research has been published in various top international journals including *MIS Quarterly, Communications of the ACM*, and *IEEE Transactions in Engineering Management*. He has also presented papers at numerous international conferences including the International Conference on Information Systems (ICIS), the Annual Meeting of the Academy of Management, and the International Conference on Management of Technology.

Rex Eugene Pereira (Rex.E.Pereira.6@nd.edu) is an Assistant Professor of Business Administration in the Department of Management, College of Business Administration, University of Notre Dame, Indiana. His research interests include electronic commerce, consumer behaviour, and decision support systems.

Simpson Poon (spoon@murdoch.edu.au) is an Associate Professor in Information Systems at Murdoch University, Western Australia, Australia. He received his PhD from Monash University, Australia. His research interests include electronic commerce, small business and Internet marketing. His publications appear in the *International Journal of Electronic Commerce, Information and Management, International Marketing Review* and *Journal of Marketing Management*.

Thomas F. Rebel (rebel@isg.de) is a consultant in the Electronic Commerce Systems Group of Innovative Software GmbH. His work includes such areas as security in electronic commerce, pricing of information goods, and network economics. Currently he is working in a yield management project for high performance stock exchange information systems. Before joining Innovative Software GmbH, he was a PhD student at Frankfurt University, Germany. He has a diploma in Business Administration and Business Information Systems.

Celia Romm (c.romm@cqu.edu.au) is a Foundation Professor of Information Technology, Faculty of Informatics and Communication, Central Queensland University, Australia. She received her PhD from the University of Toronto, Canada in 1979. She has been a lecturer, consultant, and visiting scholar in Israel, Japan, Germany, Canada, USA and Australia. Her research interests lie in the area of the impact of information systems on organisations, with particular emphasis on human resources, culture, power, and electronic commerce issues. Dr Romm has completed two books *Electronic Commerce: A Global Perspective* (Springer, 1998) and *Virtual Politicking* (to be published by Hampton Press in 1999). She has also published more than sixty papers in refereed journals and chapters in collective volumes and presented her work in more than forty local and international conferences. Her research has been published in journals such as *Human Relations, Organisation Studies, Comparative Economic Studies, Studies in Popular Culture, Information and Management, The Journal of Information Systems Management, The Information Society, The Australian Journal of Information Systems, The Asia Pacific Journal of Human Resources, The European Journal of Education, Interchange, Journal of Professional Services Marketing, New Technology, Work, and Employment, The Journal of Management Development, Information Technology and People, International Journal of Information Systems, Communications of the ACM, Transactions on Information Systems,* and *The Harvard Business Review.*

Arno Scharl (scharl@wu-wien.ac.at) has a PhD and MBA from the Vienna University of Economics and Business Administration where he is employed as assistant professor at the MIS Department (electronic commerce research group). Additionally, he received a PhD and MSc from the Department of Sports Physiology, University of Vienna. Currently spending a semester as a visiting Research Fellow at Curtin University of Technology's Electronic Commerce Network in Perth, Western Australia, his research and teaching interests focus on the various aspects of Web information systems modelling, commercial electronic transactions, adaptive hypertext, and the customisation of electronic catalogues.

Avi Schechter (tikal@inter.net.il) is the Managing Director of a medium-sized service company as well as an e-commerce start-up. In 1991, he received his interdisciplinary BSc in Economics, Sociology and Political Science at Bar-Ilan University, Israel. He is currently completing his Masters degree in Information Systems at the Leon Recanati Graduate School of Business Administration, Tel-Aviv University.

Gerhard Steinke (gsteinke@spu.edu) is Professor of Management and Information Systems in the School of Business, Seattle Pacific University, and Chair of the Master of Science in Information Systems Management Degree program. He received a BS(Hons) in Computer Science from the University of Alberta, an MBA from Ball State University in Indiana and a PhD from the University of Passau, Germany. His research interests include security, electronic commerce, virtual organizations as well as privacy, legal and ethical implications of information systems and technology.

Fay Sudweeks (sudweeks@murdoch.edu.au) is a Senior Lecturer in Information Systems in the School of Information Technology, Murdoch University, Australia. She has a BA (psychology and sociology) and an MCogSc from the University of New South Wales and is completing her PhD in Business Systems at the University of Wollongong. She has given lectures in diverse countries such as Israel, Sweden, Germany, Bulgaria, Russia, and South Africa. She has published 5 books, including *Network and Netplay: Virtual Groups on the Internet* (MIT Press, 1998) and *Doing Business Electronically: A Global Perspective of Electronic Commerce* (Springer, 1998), 9 conference proceedings, and more than 30 papers in books, journals and conference proceedings. She has co-edited special issues of the *Journal of Computer Mediated Communication*, *Electronic Journal of Communication* and *AI and Society*. Her research interests are social and organisational informatics, social/cultural/economic aspects of computer mediated communication, and computer supported collaborative work.

Martyn Wild (m.wild@cowan.edu.au), Senior Research Fellow in Management Information Systems, Edith Cowan University, Australia, has been involved in Information Communications Technology (ICT) research for the last eight years at Edith Cowan and, prior to this, Exeter University in the UK. Dr Wild has published widely in the areas of ICT education, Web information systems, and electronic commerce, and attracted a range of competitive research funds, including ARC, DEETYA and DIST grants.

David Whiteley (d.whiteley@doc.mmu.ac.uk) is a senior lecturer at Manchester Metropolitan University. He teaches in Information Systems in the Department of Computing and Mathematics and his research interests are electronic trading in the Telematics Research and Application Centre (TRAC).

Ping Zhang (pzhang@syr.edu) is an assistant professor in the School of Information Studies, Syracuse University, New York. She has published papers in the areas of information visualisation, user interface studies, computer simulation, and technology-assisted education. She received an Excellence in Teaching award from the University of Texas at Austin and Best Paper award from the International Academy for Information Management. She has a PhD in Information Systems from the University of Texas, Austin, and an MSc and BSc in Computer Science from Peking University, Beijing, China.

Moshe Zviran (zviran@post.tau.ac.il) is a Senior Lecturer in Information Systems in the Leon Racanati Graduate School of Business Administration, Faculty of Management, Tel Aviv University. He has a BSc degree in Mathematics and

Computer Science, and MSc and PhD degrees in Information Systems from Tel Aviv University, Israel. His research interests include information systems planning, development and management of information systems, information systems security and information systems in health care and medicine. He is also a consultant in these areas for a number of leading organisations. His research has been published in numerous journals, including *MIS Quarterly, Communications of the ACM, Journal of Management Information Systems, IEEE Transactions on Engineering Management, Information and Management, Omega, The Computer Journal* and *Journal of Medical Systems*.